Simonetta Greggio

ONE HUNDRED & ONE
Beautiful SMALL TOWNS *in France*

RIZZOLI
NEW YORK

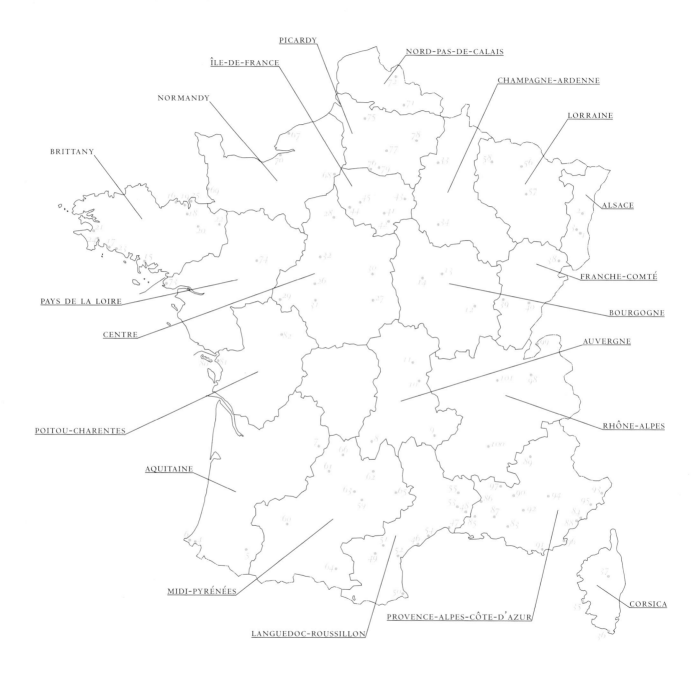

BRITTANY

NORMANDY

ÎLE-DE-FRANCE

PICARDY

NORD-PAS-DE-CALAIS

CHAMPAGNE-ARDENNE

LORRAINE

ALSACE

FRANCHE-COMTÉ

BOURGOGNE

AUVERGNE

RHÔNE-ALPES

PAYS DE LA LOIRE

CENTRE

POITOU-CHARENTES

AQUITAINE

MIDI-PYRÉNÉES

LANGUEDOC-ROUSSILLON

PROVENCE-ALPES-CÔTE-D'AZUR

CORSICA

REGIONAL CONTENTS

ALPHABETICAL CONTENTS

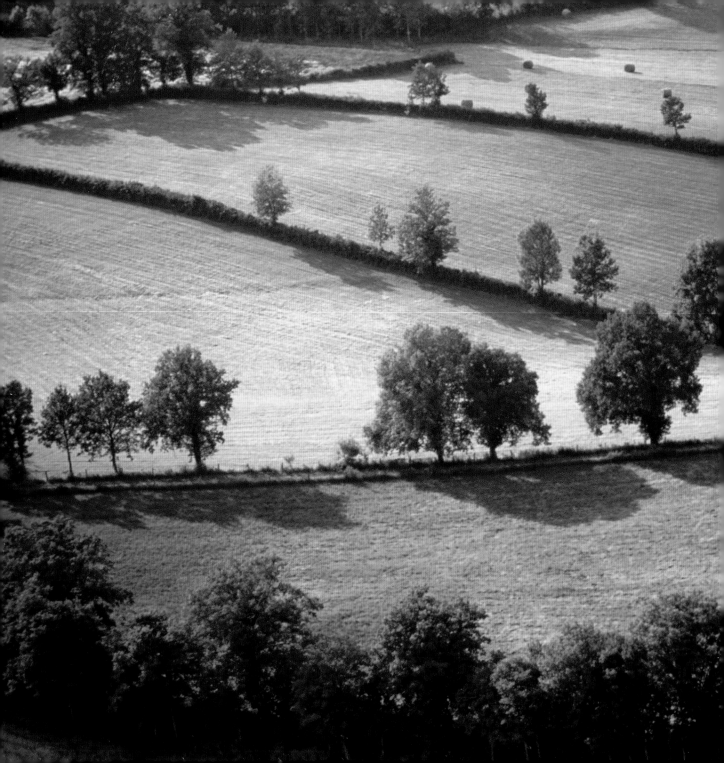

PREFACE

Touring all of France in only 101 towns is impossible. That said, when one wants to try, there is the exciting challenge of choosing, writing about, and capturing the most representative images of each one. What is it that makes one town more magnetic than another? What makes travelers leave one route for another—one that may be more difficult, but which suddenly reveals itself as the sole, most sought-after route?

Writing this book has been almost the same; it has required that I follow my intuition rather than a predefined order. It has been like pausing under an ancient olive tree for a lunch of bread and cheese just bought at the local market, and maybe even ignoring a three-star restaurant. This voyage has also brought the truest freedom—to ignore set programs and believe in the most unexpected possibilities, taking in a breath of lavender-scented air, traveling an unpaved road that suddenly opens up to a landscape gilded with sunflowers. Those who know how to travel also know that lightness and flexibility lead to pleasure and the great joy of making mistakes.

Hence I ask forgiveness if I have sometimes been more loquacious about some towns rather than others; if I have sometimes talked more about history than art, more about gastronomy than museums, or more about one painting than about an artist. We claim, as you will after your own visit, a surfeit of abundance, and a divine temptation to be reckless.

"*Bien cher ami, vous savez comment vont les choses . . . Lever, travail, repas, bavardages, travail, repas, coucher: les heures passent, les jours passent, on s'Habitue, on mène une vie exquise, mais où il n'y a plus de place pour rien d'autre que l'essentiel.*" "My dear friend, you know quite well how things go… You rise, work, have lunch, gossip, work, have dinner, then go to bed. The hours pass, the days go by, one gets used to it, life is wonderful, but there is no place for anything but the essential." Paraphrasing this part of a letter addressed to Gide, written in 1950 by his fellow writer Martin du Gard, who was living in the village of Cabris, one could say that during the journey there is the same useless heaviness, and the same serene clarity in the passing of time that is so well described by du Gard. Travel is, first of all, an encounter with oneself through what one discovers, feels, loves, and even what cannot be understood until later. It is even what repulses the hardiest explorer. This is why ink falling into a phrase from the pen of a writer, one day many years ago in the region of Grasse, not far from the enchanting village of Saint-Paul-de-Vence, can reveal to us a state of mind, a beauty, and serenity in so few words.

From perfect, secret, harmonious Menton, with its Italian climate and its gardens in a purely romantic setting; to the limpid, silvery Dinard; to the delectable Nice of the Cours Saleya flower market, with its succulent flowers and outdoor cafés, balconies and liquid-gold facades; to the austere, Breton, blue and red Concarneau; to the speckled mirrors of Versailles; to the ever-vital walls of Carcassonne; I have tried to give the reader an idea of what can be found in France. Now it is up to you to discover what is most pleasant. Choose your ideal itinerary from amid these riches—whether it is imaginary or real, I wish you *bon voyage*!

COLMAR
ALSATIAN ARTS

COLMAR IS A TREASURE TROVE OF ART AND BEAUTY. SET AMONG VINEYARDS and close to the mountains and valleys of the Vosges, Colmar is an ideal place from which to begin a visit to Alsace. In the Middle Ages the town was an important commercial center, and as a magnet for Rhenish art it has been able to preserve its beauty in spite of the upheaval of the Reformation, the devastation of the Thirty Years' War, the forced marriage with France under Louis XIV, the Prussian annexation in 1871, and that of Nazi Germany in 1940. Colmar well deserves its present peace. There is much to admire, from impressive buildings to unique museums. The town's legendary Christmas festivities last from the first Sunday of Advent until Epiphany, and feature such treats as spiced bread, wooden toys, and brightly lit houses that create an atmosphere of fable and excitement in the center of the town. Despite the damage of World Wars I and II, Colmar remains exceptionally romantic and is distinguished by charming Alsatian houses that surround a fifteenth-century customs house. Architectural details such as balconies, towers, bow windows, sculptures, antique signs, and frescoes testify to the productiveness of the Rhineland. La Petite Venise (Little Venice) is a delightful village on the banks of the Lauch River where visitors can wander around on foot or take in sights along the canals by boat. Colmar is still divided into small neighborhoods, each of which was home to a specific guild. In the quarter of the *Tanneurs* (leather workers), during the sixteenth, seventeenth, and eighteenth centuries, artisans washed their hides in the river and dried them in the attics of the character-istic half-timbered houses that still remain standing today. The town officials would gather in the customs house, which also served as a warehouse and market. By far the most picturesque corner of Colmar is found on the rue des Marchands, home to the old Guard House, with its splendid Renaissance loggia, and the Pfister House, where frescoes and medallions in the wooden gallery illustrate the traditional virtues of Christian life. On the same street is the Musée Bartholdi, birthplace of the local sculptor Frédéric Auguste Bartholdi, who is most famous for designing the Statue of Liberty. Other collections in Colmar include the Toy and Model Train Museum (Musée Animé du Jouet et des Petits Trains) and the Museum of Optical Instruments (Musée de l'Instrumentation Optique). One of the most frequented museums is the Musée d'Unterlinden, situated in a thirteenth-century Dominican convent and containing a collection of Rhenish art from the Middle Ages to the Renaissance. The most famous work on view is Matthias Grünewald's *Isenheim Altarpiece* (1512–16), and among the many treasures are also paintings by Claude Monet and Martin Schongauer.

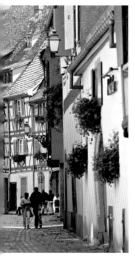

The lanes of the quartier des Tanneurs are paved in original cobblestone.

facing page Half-timbered houses in the quartier des Tanneurs.

Quite possibly the best restaurant in Colmar, Au Fer Rouge is located in a typical sixteenth-century Alsatian residence at the heart of Old Colmar in Little Venice. Chef Patrick Fulgraff's kitchen offers dishes of the highest quality: oysters with leeks; fried goose liver with smoked liver; croquette of coquilles Saint-Jacques; braised lobster and fennel; roasted fish with a caramelized sauce; and verbena ice cream, to cite just a few examples. For classic Colmar fare head to Chez Hansi, where the waiters don traditional dress and the menu offers such Alsatian delights as choucroute and pot-au-feu.

Although the Statue of Liberty, which at nearly 100 feet tall dominates the entrance to the port of New York, is the best-known work of Frédéric Auguste Bartholdi, the sculptor's Lion of Belfort is a close second. Sculpted in the same stone as the Citadel, the Lion of Belfort celebrates the heroic resistance during the siege of 1870. Reproductions of both statues are to be found in Paris, in the Place Denfert-Rochereau, and on the Île aux Cygnes (Isle of Swans), respectively. Bartholdi was born in Colmar in 1834 and was the most celebrated sculptor of the century both in Europe and North America. He was in high demand for patriotic sculpture commissions. His Schwendi Fountain (1897) stands in the Place dell'Ancienne Douane in Colmar, and pays homage to the baron who commanded the Imperial army that faced Suleiman the Magnificent in Hungary in the sixteenth century. Bartholdi died of tuberculosis in 1904 at the age of seventy.

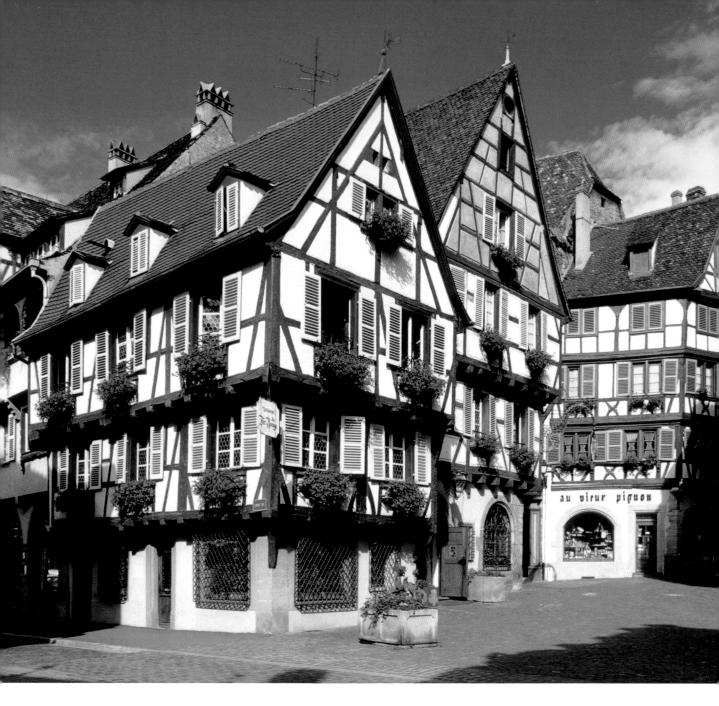

9

The Christmas market is lively both day and night.

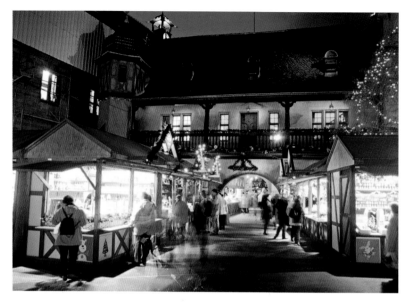

Alsace is particularly famous for its wines. Many diverse grape varieties flourish here, both white and red, strong and delicate, and dry and sweet types, making for regional wines that are perfect for an entire dinner, from aperitif to digestif. These great wines pair well with any kind of menu, including fish and seafood, chicken or red meat, game and cheese—there are enough varieties to suit every taste. They all have a recognizable character: The whites have a hint of flowers, sometimes with a scent of lychee or apple; the reds are fruity and full-bodied. A wine route has been created for the ever-increasing number of visitors interested in the noble art of winemaking. Paths lead from village to village, and like the wines, they are numerous and each is unique. The city of Colmar celebrates these nectars of the vineyard with a famous annual fair that takes place in the ten days before August 15. Contrary to other wine-growing regions, the wines of Alsace carry the name of the vine from which they come—Sylvaner, Pinot Blanc, Riesling, Muscat d'Alsace, Tocai, Pinot Gris, and Gewürztraminer. The Colmar fair is also a great occasion for free tastings of the excellent regional crustaceans, and visitors can discover the rich local cuisine and take part in the concerts and shows that attract a large public year after year.

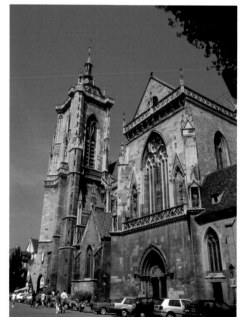

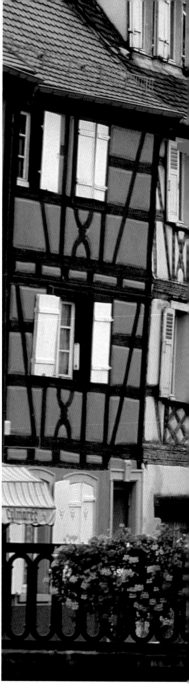

The facade and bell tower of the main cathedral.

far right
The colorful facades of houses along the quai de la Poissonerie.

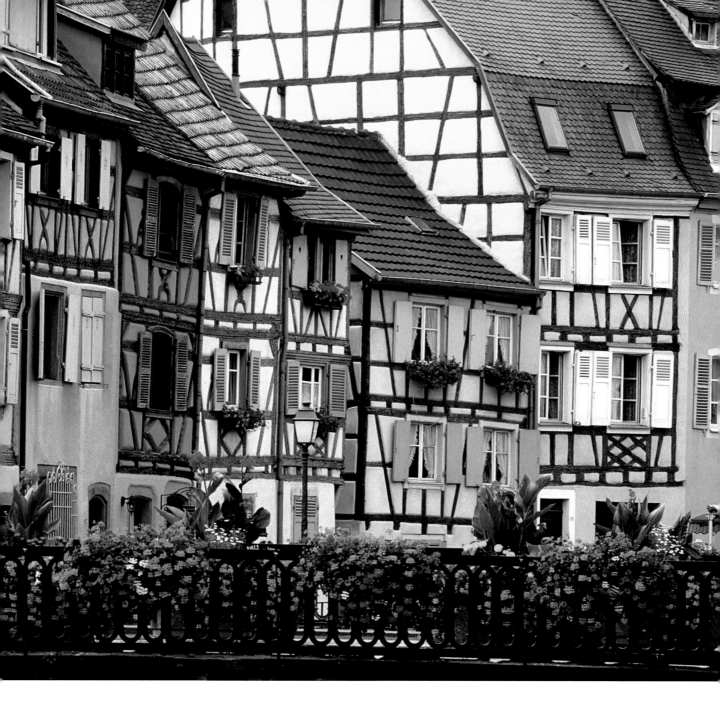

OBERNAI
PAINTED ROOFS AND PILGRIMS' PRAYERS

THIS DELIGHTFUL TOWN OF 12,000 INHABITANTS IS NESTLED IN A VALLEY of woods and orchards at the foot of Mont Sainte-Odile. The ruins of the ramparts and some ancient houses give Obernai its medieval stamp. The name of the town appears in archives for the first time around 1240, when the village was recognized as a town thanks to the support of the Hohenstaufen (a dynasty of German kings, many of whom were crowned Holy Roman Emperors). As a result the town was able to build fortifications, implement judicial and fiscal systems, and organize markets and fairs. Obernai's prosperity is due in large part to its artisanal traditions and its wine culture, and in 1354 it became a member of the Décapole, a powerful league of mutual assistance founded by the nine imperial cities of Alsace. Obernai reached its peak in the fifteenth and sixteenth centuries, after which in 1679 it was ceded to France, then annexed to Germany in 1871 (with all of Alsace), and became French again in 1918. Within the walls and in the historic center there is a beautiful group of Renaissance buildings, with a style that has influenced the line and architecture of many private houses and public buildings here, including the Municipality (1523 and 1610) and the grain market (1554). The grain market, with its gilded facade of bulls' heads, was originally a butcher shop as well as a salt deposit (salt was a city monopoly); it was also the customs house.

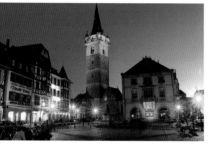

The illuminated Hotel de Ville and the chapel bell tower seen from the market square.

facing page
A hillside vineyard overlooking Obernai.

The clock tower chimes the opening and closing of the weekly market. The Kappelturm Beffroi (Chapel Tower Belfry) served as a lookout. It was the bell tower of an old chapel built during the difficult years at the end of the thirteenth century, enabling the inhabitants to attend mass while protected within the walls of the town; only the choir of the ancient chapel remains and serves today as the center for tourism. The first four floors of the bell tower were built circa 1280 from the pink sandstone of the Vosges. The fifth floor was added in 1597 and is surmounted by an octagonal tower. Another unusual and imposing monument is the Renaissance-style Well of Six Buckets. Its three Corinthian columns support a baldachin, upon which are inscribed passages from the New Testament regarding Christ's conversation with the Samaritan woman at Jacob's well and Christ's sermon on the "bread of life." The thirteenth-century double walls encircling the town still contain about thirty towers that are partly preserved and which in the past guaranteed the life and survival of Obernai. An enjoyable walk leads from the ramparts as far as a white cross on the hill behind the town. From here there is a splendid view of Obernai, particularly in the morning when, like a sort of wave, the pattern of the painted rooftops can be seen.

Mont Sainte-Odile is a place of pilgrimage, beauty, and light, even though these days it is difficult to find the peace necessary for spiritual meditation. In fact, the monastery of Sainte-Odile has become a tourist attraction, complete with restaurants, snack bars, souvenir shops, and a hotel. The view stretches to the tops of the Black Forest and as far as the Rhine. It is also a starting point for splendid walks among the rocks, springs, and age-old trees bathed in the characteristic light of the Vosges. Saint Odile is the patron saint of Alsace, and her relics are said to lie in the convent. Legend has it that this daughter of a noble family was born blind but recovered her sight on the day of her christening; in 680 she created the first abbey for women in Alsace.

The hotel À la cour d'Alsace, in the medieval center of Obernai, is the home as well as the wine cellar of the Barons of Gail, who have long lived in the region. The intimate and homey atmosphere of the castle welcomes guests in great, luminous rooms. The menu of the restaurant is prepared with love and experience and can satisfy the most demanding of palates. Another elegant hotel is Le Parc, which includes is a bar for smokers, a cocktail bar, swimming pools, a pleasant park, and a dining room where local Alsatian fare can be savored.

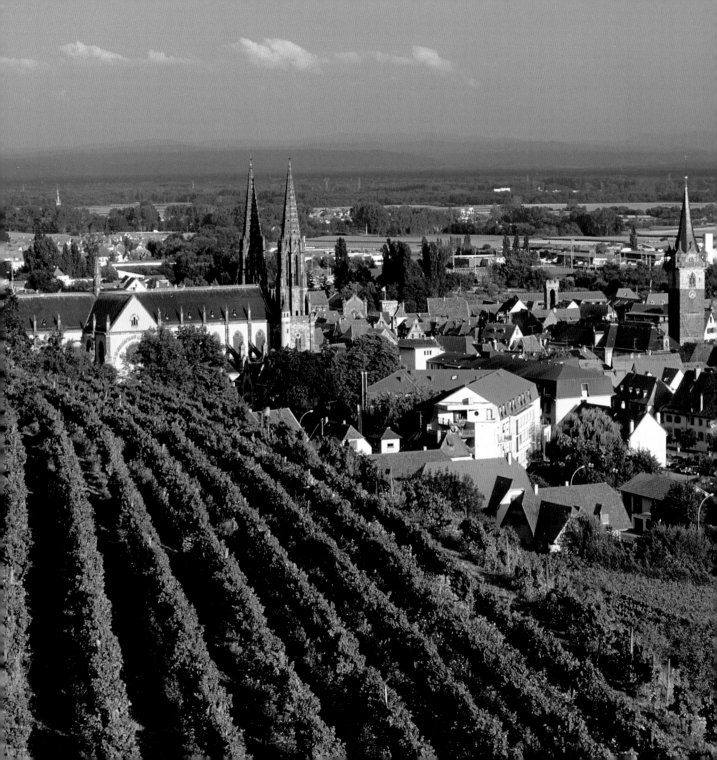

RIQUEWIHR
STORKS, CELLARS, AND SCENERY

RIQUEWIHR IS A FASCINATING ALSATIAN VILLAGE SURROUNDED BY VINEYARDS and ramparts, and studded with fountains and striped dovecote-like houses brimming with flowers. It is partly encircled by a thirteenth- to sixteenth-century double ring of walls in a rectangular pattern, and within its medieval labyrinth are some examples of the town's distinctive houses, the walls of which are made of a mixture of earth, clay, and shred-

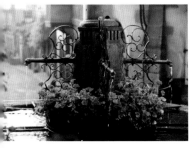

The Sinnbrunnen fountain.

facing page
Overflowing flower boxes add the final touch to an already colorful scene.

ded straw, and covered with a pink or green plaster. It is one of the best-known villages in the region and offers museums of excellent quality. The Hansi Museum, for example, contains the work of Jean-Jacques Waltz, known as Hansi, the famous illustrator and cartoonist from Alsace who ironically criticized the Prussian overlord at the beginning of the twentieth century. He also made oil and watercolor paintings of the villages and landscapes of the region. He was the curator of the Musée d'Unterlinden in Colmar, and his publicity posters are a precious source of documentation. The twelfth-century Dolder Tour Beffroi, a bell tower, is found along the ramparts of Riquewihr. It is the site of the small Dolder Museum, ded-icated to the town and its history. Various objects of local life are displayed, and there is a splendid collection of weapons from the fifteenth and sixteenth centuries. Along the ramparts the sentry patrol route passes by the Tour des Voleurs (Tower of Thieves). Inside, the Room of Torture and Secrets is not to be missed—a little-known museum that illustrates the punishments inflicted on the prisoners. In order to refuel and slake one's thirst, a visit to Gilbert Holl, representative of the artisan industry of beer-making, is a must. This distillery still produces beer the old-fashioned way, and Hollbier can be tasted on the spot or in some of the local bars. In the same vein, a visit to the Hugel family winery is necessary, as it pioneered the art of winemaking in Alsace. The cellar dates back to 1600, and the *foudre Catherine*, the oldest functioning barrel in the world, is on view. It was made in 1715, and the decorations on the oak are covered with a patina of three centuries of use and the history of wine. Riquewihr miraculously escaped destruction during World War II, and the many little alleys that radiate from the Grand Rue immerse us in the history of the town. The noble stables of the fourteenth-century house in the Musée de la Diligence possess a unique collection of stage- and post

The symbol of Alsace is the stork, which returns in spring and brings happiness. The great stilt builds enormous nests about six feet tall, weighing 1,100 pounds, and in the autumn migrates to Africa. The flights and stays of this migratory bird are often fatal; many storks die as a result of hunters, electric wires, pesticides, and the aridity of the Sahel region. In 1948 there were 173 pairs here; in 1983 there were only three. To protect the storks the people of Alsace have created repopulation centers, such as those at Hunawihr, near Riquewihr. For several years they have lived here in captivity and no longer migrate. In 2000 more than 200 pairs of storks nested in the villages of Alsace, Germany, and Switzerland.

coaches that traversed the roads in the eighteenth century. Another voyage in time can be made at the Postal Museum, in the Renaissance castle of the dukes of Württemberg, the ancient lords of Riquewihr. Here a collection illustrating 2,000 years of postal-service history is on display. The town is now classified among the most beautiful villages in France.

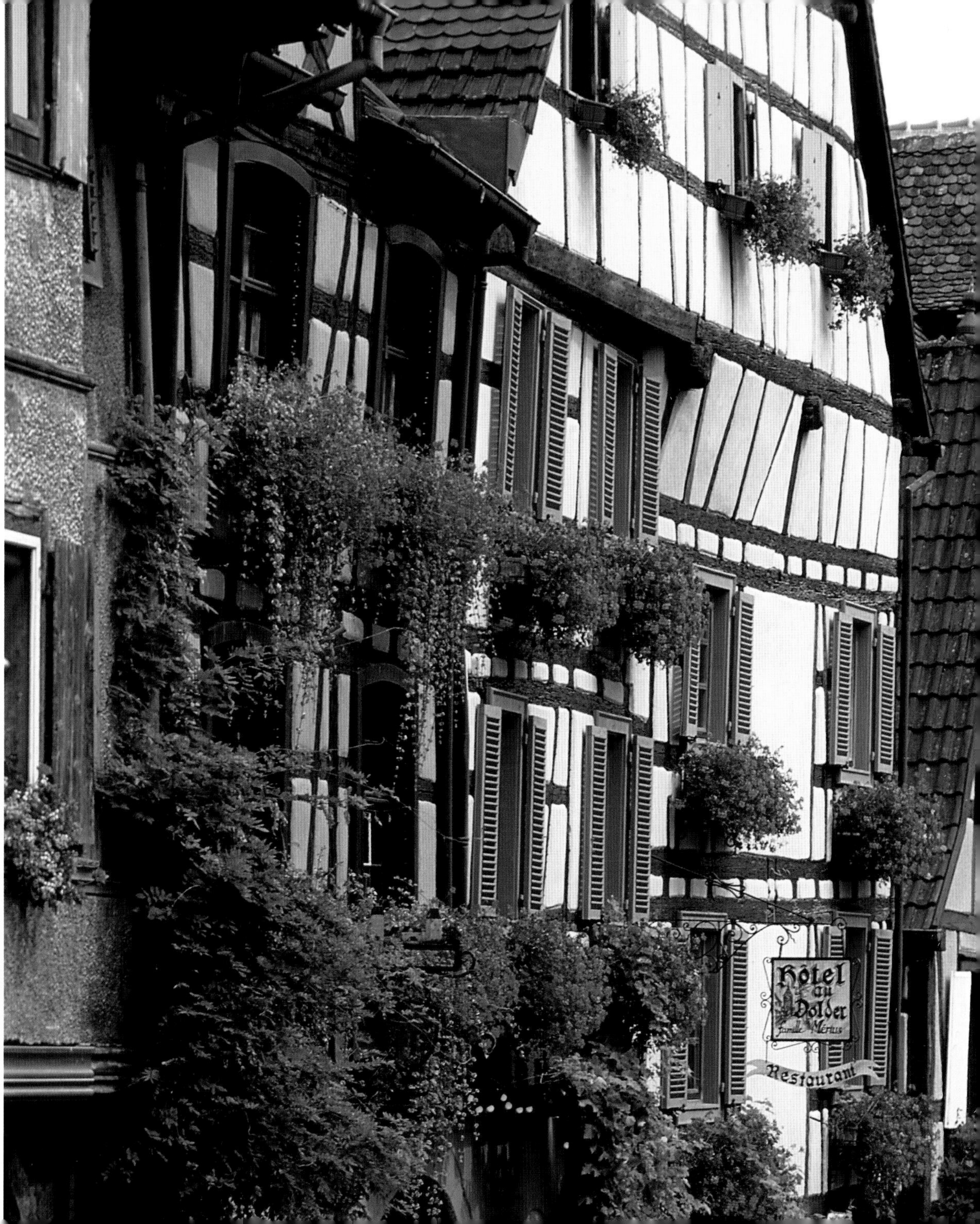

The wine route unfolds from north to south through Alsace, and its heart is in Ribeauvillé and Riquewihr; these two villages are connected by paths that contour beautiful hillside vineyards, with views of castle ruins and abandoned towers emerging from the countryside. The vineyards of Alsace offer vast, pleasant, and photogenic landscapes, punctuated by generous cellars and *winstubs*—the typical warm and welcoming Alsatian restaurants, where a mealtime stop is highly recommended.

Hôtel au Dolder
famille Mertius
Restaurant

BIARRITZ

ALL THE ARTS, FROM DECO TO NOUVEAU

FOR MORE THAN A CENTURY AND A HALF BIARRITZ HAS KEPT ITS BEAUTY FULLY INTACT. Once a simple fishing village, the path of Biarritz's history changed when, in 1854, Emperor Napoleon III and his wife, Eugénie, the Countess of Montijo, set up residence here. One thing is certain—the locals did not expect the emperor to enjoy swimming in the sea. Since 1609, in fact, the council of Lancre had thought this practice to be wholly uncivilized, describing it as "a raucous group of marriageable young women and young fishermen who are seen on the beach, naked under scant costumes, disporting themselves together in the waves." Residents would have to wait until the mid-seventeenth century before the therapeutic values of seawater were officially recognized. The locals, however, were indifferent to the opinions of others and continued to bathe in the sea, even when, in 1774, the city refused to build bathing cabanas.

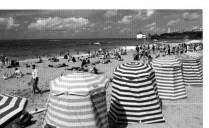

The main beach, dotted with traditional huts for a respite from the sun.

facing page
Villa Betiza overlooks the sea.

One of the first illustrious visitors to Biarritz was Victor Hugo, who arrived in 1843 and became enchanted by this "white village with red and green roofs, set down on a background of grass." He worried immediately that Biarritz would become a fashionable resort: "The day will soon come," he observed with foresight, and indeed, it came merely eleven years later. Eugénie de Montijo had stayed here in her childhood, and after her marriage to Napoleon III she resided here for two months with her entourage in great ostentation. The people greeted the imperial couple with enthusiasm, and they took up temporary residence at the castle of Gramont before Napoleon had the Villa Eugénie built for his wife. Biarritz became the favorite resort of the French and European aristocracy. The kings of Würtemberg, Belgium, and Portugal; the Russian, Polish, and Romanian princes; the grandees of Spain; and the aristocracy of England— all the aristocracy of Europe met in Biarritz. Villas sprang up and have left us with the best examples of the metamorphosis of architecture in the nineteenth and twentieth centuries: Art Nouveau and Art Deco mixed in with medieval and English styles. Like at Hossegor, the neo-regional Basque style appeared in the 1930s, with numerous roofs, curved balconies, and windows such as those at Villa Paz in avenue de l'Imperatrice, Maison Pasque in avenue Edouard-VII, or the municipality of Anglet. After 1945, thanks to the sumptuous parties given by the Marquis de Cuevas, Biarritz rediscovered the liveliness it had lost during the war. The little town continued to attract the rich and famous as well as kings, including Farouk of Egypt, Michael of Romania, and Pierre of Yugoslavia. Today Biarritz is more discreet, but the spa and beaches continue to draw a celebrity crowd and the so-called "beautiful people." It is, and will always be, an enchanting place.

The Basque pelota can travel at over 100 miles per hour, making it the fastest ball in the world. Pelota, a game similar to jai alai, is the passion of the region, and there are more than twenty varieties of it. The most popular, *pala* (paddle), is played on a *frontone*, and one can be found in every district of the town. The most challenging form of the game is *cesta punta*; even for the best player this type requires great strength. From July to September Biarritz holds meets and professional tournaments, but there are also some demonstrations for beginners, so everyone can try it. It is a spectacular sport with which one can easily fall deeply in love.

The Hôtel du Palais, Château du Clair de Lune, and Maison Garnier are the three best places to stay in Biarritz. The first has the style and atmosphere of the Belle Époque, where many royal couples danced legendary waltzes under its gilt decorations; the cuisine is also very famous. In the "Moonlight Castle," the boxwood-lined parks and lovely rooms still whisper the stories of centuries past. One can sleep in the castle or in the elegant hunting lodge—both are very romantic and ideal for lovers. Maison Garnier is a nineteenth-century gem with the purity and clear simplicity of some extraordinarily beautiful contemporary rooms.

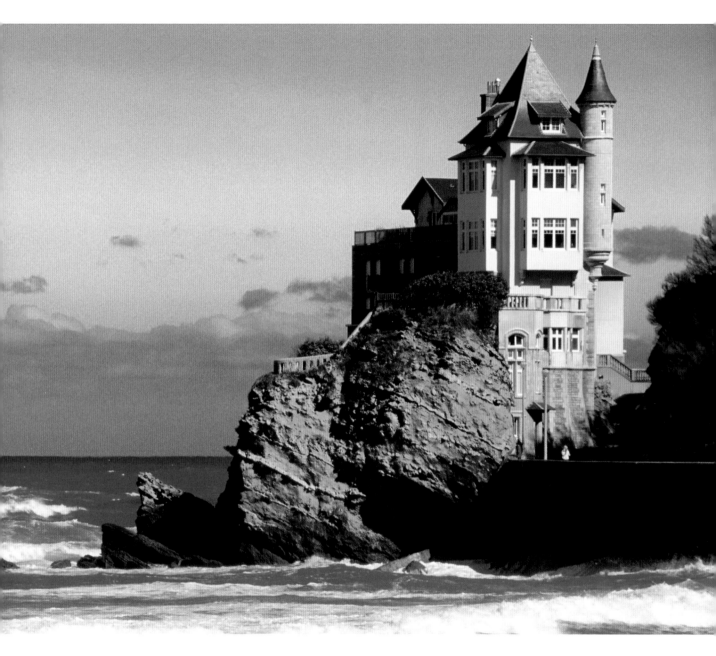

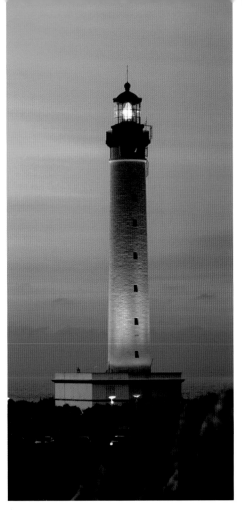
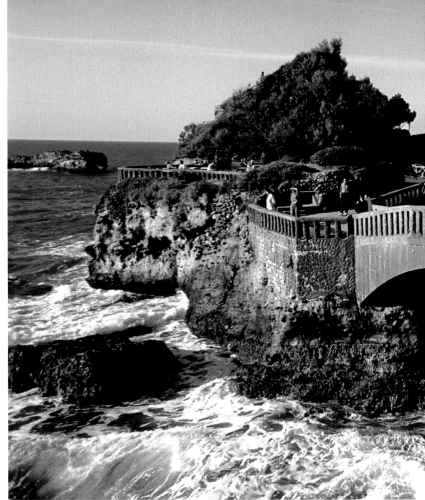
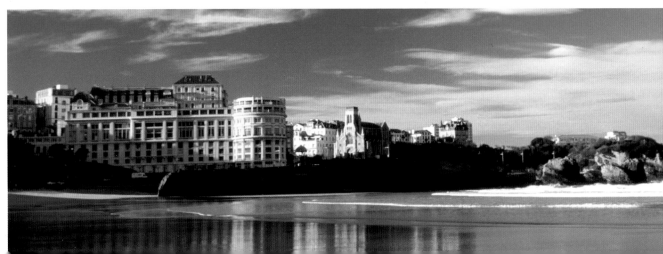

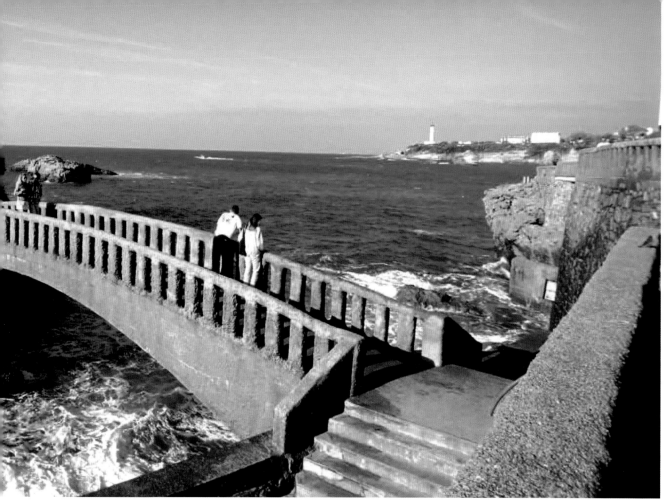

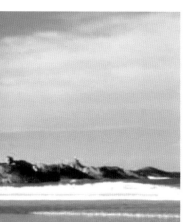

above, far left
The sunset provides a striking backdrop for the silhouetted lighthouse.

above, left
A sweeping view from a footbridge.

left
The most important town buildings overlook the gentle beach.

In 1957, during the shooting of the film *The Sun Also Rises*, Peter Viertel, the American screenwriter and husband of Deborah Kerr, would glide along the waves with the help of a curious board that had never before been seen in the Basque town. The first surf club of France was founded here two years later, and from that moment on this Hawaiian sport became the symbol of Biarritz. Today the "surf spirit" is present everywhere—shops, events, fashion . . . everything revolves around the surfboard. In summer and in winter the familiar presence of the surfers gliding over the waves is an integral part of the landscape. The Biarritz Surf Festival takes place each July, with demonstrations, films, concerts, and many other events with the sport's great champions, and each April the Biarritz Maïder Arosteguy brings the best French and European competitors to Biarritz after the winter respite.

P A U
PALISADES AND PARLIAMENT

IN THE BÉARN LANGUAGE, *PAU* MEANS "TENT PEG" OR "SUPPORT," and is recalls the twelfth century, when the town was just a modest village protected by a simple palisade. By the fifteenth century the local lords had developed it into the capital of the sovereign state of Navarre. Pau also gave France King Henry IV. The castle, built by Gaston Phébus in the fourteenth century, was the fortress of the viscounts of Béarn, and during the Renaissance was the royal residence of Marguerite d'Angoulême. There are at least nine centuries of history to explore here, and every stone, room, piece of furniture in the castle, and garden flowerbed is witness to a rich and lively past. Everybody knows that this was the birthplace of Henry, king of Navarre and, subsequently, France. The Renaissance gardens preserve the memory of Antoine de Bourbon, husband of Jeanne d'Albret, whose park was famous throughout Europe in the sixteenth century. On the second floor of the castle is the room that still houses the tortoise carapace that was the crib of the future king of France. The west wing was decorated by Louis-Philippe in a flamboyant style for Queen Marie-Amélie, his bride, but it was Eugénie de Montijo, wife of Napoleon III, who used it most during her travels between Biarritz and Béarn. These rooms came to be called the Apartments of the Empress thanks to her stays here. The castle of Pau has one of the most important collections of tapestries in France. It houses ninety-six pieces, most woven at the Gobelins workshop in Paris and selected in the nineteenth century by the architects of Louis-Philippe for the royal apartments and to decorate this magnificent castle. The castle's exterior is also incredible—the building appears as though suspended above the town of Pau, overlooking the dovecote houses that in turn overlook the Gave de Pau River, a fast-flowing tributary of the Adour, and the old Parliament of Navarre and place de la Monnaie. One of the local curiosities is the Peyré House, also known as "le Sully," a seventeenth-century hotel with a paved courtyard decorated with "peach pits," rounded stones taken from the Gave River. The Hédas neighborhood is evocative of the cabarets, inns, slaughterhouses, and tanneries that once abounded. The oldest area of Pau, this was once the profligate center of town. Today one can visit the bathhouse and fountain that, before the Revolution, were the townspeople's only sources of water. During the Napoleonic wars the English troops discovered Pau and the superior quality of its climate. The English majesty's subjects returned during the nineteenth century, marking the era of spas. The English built mansions here, some in the Trespoey area, others scattered in the neighborhoods near the center, and the beautiful gardens are witness to their connection with Pau.

The tree-lined avenue des Pyrénées.

facing page Entrance to the castle of Pau, which houses one of the most important tapestry collections in France.

In 1764 Jean-Baptiste Bernadotte was born in Pau. He was a simple soldier in 1780, a brigadier general with Napoleon, and later became marshal of the empire. He fought for France, but the Swedes appreciated him to such an extent that they offered him the throne in 1810. He was elected royal prince of Sweden, and succeeded King Charles XIII in 1818. He was also king of Norway and Eastern Pomerania, all of which explains how the descendants of a modest native of Pau still rule in Stockholm. The Bernadotte Museum is housed here in the building where he was born. It is a lovely building in the typical *bearnese* style, and recounts the fabulous epic life of that young officer, through portraits of the royal family, antique furniture, engravings, sculptures, weapons, and battle maps. Even the kitchen has been left precisely as it was two centuries ago.

"As an adolescent I met a glowing, imperious prince, a traitor like all the great seducers are—the Jurançon," wrote Colette, one of France's most legendary authors. This dry, smooth white wine, distinguished by the AOC label since 1936, is best tasted cold, and accompanied with foie gras, cheeses, and dessert. Jurançon is produced in Pau and the surrounding region, and is simply exquisite. Henry IV drank a drop of it at his christening, and later proclaimed it the ceremonial wine of the royal house. Another local grape that is widely appreciated and also labeled AOC is the Madiran, a powerful red that pairs well with candied fruit, sausages, and *magrets de canard.*

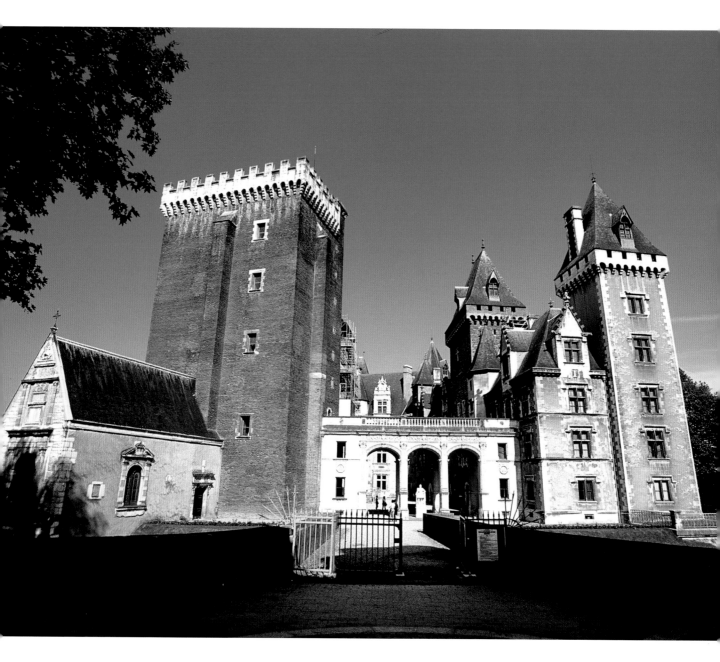

SAINT-JEAN DE-LUZ
FISHERMEN AND THE INFANTA

THE GULF OF SAINT-JEAN-DE-LUZ OPENS TO THE OCEAN ON BOTH SIDES, with the jutting headlands of the Pyrenees as a stunning backdrop. It is the only inlet on the coast between Arcachon and Spain, and has always been a sheltered place where fishermen protected their boats. The fame of Saint-Jean-de-Luz dates back to the seventeenth century, specifically to 1660, when the marriage of Louis XIV and the Infanta Marie-Thérèse of Austria was celebrated here in the church of Saint-Jean-Baptiste. During the Belle Époque the town became a resort where visitors were intoxicated by the pleasures of the sea and beach, which is situated in a bay closed in by breakwaters that have now become a favorite promenade. This place is the jewel of the marvelous Basque lands, between the ocean and the mountains, where France and Spain melt into each other.

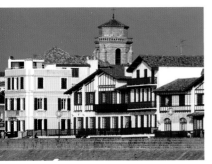

Seaside houses bask in full sun.

facing page
The intricate brickwork of the Infanta's historic home on the port is best taken in from afar.

The town's splendid buildings evoke its famous past. Place Saint-Louis XIV is the heart of the old center. Surrounded by the ship owners' grand homes, it bears testimony of a more prosperous age of fishing. Balls, *toros de fuego*, and concerts imbue the town with a festive atmosphere. The Infanta's residence is a brick-and-stone reminder of the architectural lines of the Italian palazzo, and La Pergola casino is a masterpiece of Art Deco by architect Mallet-Stevens. Nearby rue Gambetta, an old path connecting Bayonne to Spain, is the main pedestrian and commercial conduit of the town. Here you can admire the splendid mansions, including Maison Gorritienea, which belonged to Joachin, the famous corsair, and is a living reminder that Saint-Jean-de-Luz was a pirates' haven. Naval expeditions left from here to sail the Gulf of Gascony for whaling. Today this tradition is banned, but Saint-Jean-de-Luz remains one of the most important ports of France for sardine and tuna fishing—an activity that has been taking place, with highs and lows, since the 1950s. Two festivals not to be missed are the Feast of the Tuna in July and the Night of the Sardines in August. Another important event worth attending is the return of the fishing boats filled with sardines or tuna, depending on the season. The harbor is very picturesque with its brightly painted wooden boats, the constant crowds of people, and its

The traditional Basque home is a simple farmhouse that melts into the countryside with its white walls, an often asymmetrical, sloping roof that varies according to the region, and wooden doors and windows brightly painted in green, blue, or red. The famous Basque wine-colored red owes its characteristic hue to bull's blood, with which the farm workers painted the shutters of their houses. The Basque house is a symbol of the community spirit of a self-contained, rural society. Called *etxea*, it was a veritable family structure for ages. These houses were quite large, and inhabited by the owners, the oldest son or daughter with their respective spouses, and their children. The very youngest children, on the other hand, had to go and live elsewhere, putting themselves at the service of the oldest brother or marrying an heiress, whose name they would adopt. Some *etxeas* have been turned into charming hotels.

incomparable atmosphere of *douceur de vivre*. The Basque country between Spain and France has preserved its originality, its customs, and the vivacity of its language. The eco-museum of Basque traditions presents the characteristic trades of the region, from furniture to espadrilles, pelote, and embroidered linen, a long-time tradition and the true pride of the Basque people.

From Espelette to Hendaye, and on to Guéthary and Urcuit, the local delicacies are stuffed peppers, *chipirons* in parsley, grilled meat and fish—all dishes that create a lively, spicy symphony of flavors. Basque country provides a cuisine made from the simple produce of the land and matches the image of its people, who are still greatly attached to their ancestral culture and traditions. Cold meats, sausages, and ham are omnipresent, and the chili pepper of Esplette is the favorite spice. Any visit must absolutely include a taste of the *pettan mamia*, a delicious dessert of curdled ewe's milk served with black-cherry preserves.

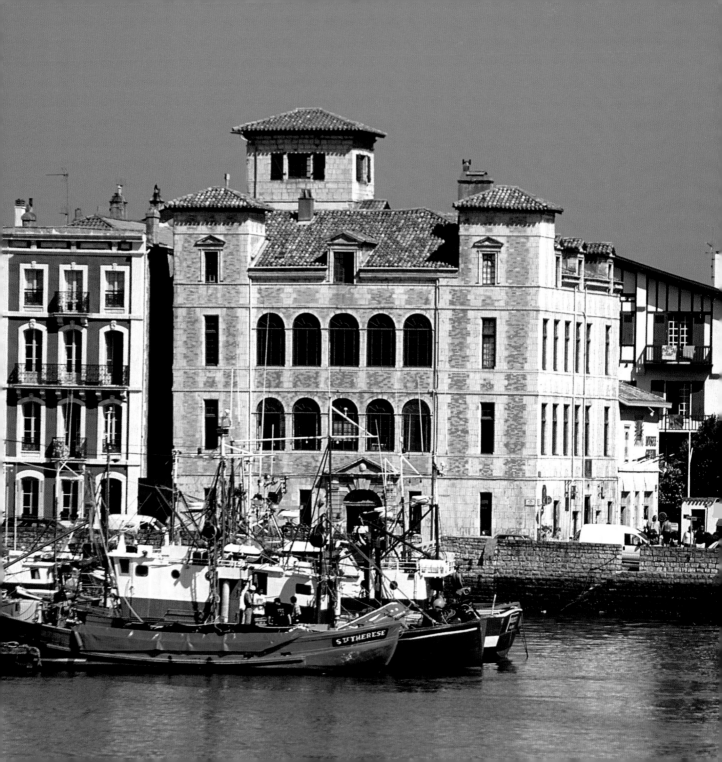

SARLAT
MUSE OF MONTAIGNE

SARLAT IS A MEDIEVAL TOWN THAT DEVELOPED AROUND ONE OF THE GREAT Benedictine abbeys and whose origins are lost in the history of the seventh century. We do know that the Vikings never touched it, and perhaps never even saw it, lost as it is in the Périgord Noir, the mythical area of France where towns, medieval villages, and prehistoric sites are scattered through an impenetrable landscape. Sarlat is one of the jewels of

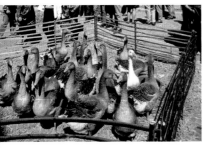

Even the geese show off during local fairs.

facing page
Both visitors and this sculpture get a glimpse of the town square.

the Périgord. Entering the town and walking along the ancient, narrow streets is like a trip to the sixteenth century. The enchantment of its ochre-colored walls is irresistible. In the Middle Ages it was a city of merchants, and later became a prosperous, fortified diocese. It was destroyed during the Hundred Years' War and ceded to the English with the Treaty of Brétigny in 1360, but nevertheless retained its uniqueness. It stood firm and returned to France, and King Charles VII even bestowed new privileges upon it. The town rediscovered its spirit and began building, beautifying, and increasing its wealth. The new houses of that period are characterized by thick stone walls, sharply sloped roofs shingled with volcanic stone, and wide interior courtyards. The medieval ground level is generally built upon with other floors in Renaissance style and completed with *pignons,* or gables, and decorated with classical motifs. Many buildings date back to the end of the fifteenth century and beginning of the sixteenth century, including the de la Boétie home and the Hôtel de Vienne. The town has attracted priests, merchants, and lawyers in particular. Among the other details of Sarlat is the curious architecture of the "lantern of death," also known as the Saint Bernard Tower, after the abbot of Clairvaux who stayed at Sarlat in 1147 during his investigations of reported heresy. A visit to the vault of the Pénitents is recommended, where the first abbey of Sarlat was built, and to the Présidial, the ex-tribunal founded by Henry II in 1552 as a symbol of royal justice. Many towns in France possess similar picturesque narrow alleyways and beautiful monuments, but if it is true that many treasures have been destroyed over the years, then Sarlat has been miraculously saved thanks to a law passed on August 4, 1962. The law concerns the restoration and protection of ancient centers, and was applied for the first time to Sarlat. The center of the little medieval town, with its sixty-five monuments and protected buildings, represented the pilot plan around which to organize the financing and criteria for the restoration. Many buildings have regained their authenticity—the Maleville, Plamon, and Grézel houses are key examples. Sarlat is memorable enough that many visitors return, and many English and American citizens have even moved to this picturesque town.

Étienne de la Boétie was born in Sarlat in 1530, and his house remains the centerpiece of the town. The relationship between Michel de Montaigne and de la Boétie is a famous example of perfect friendship. In *Essays* Montaigne writes, "On the one hand, what are usually called friends and friendships are only business relationships and familiarity connected by some occasion or usefulness from which our hearts take sustenance. In the friendship of which I speak, our souls join and melt together in such a universal world that they cancel each other out and can no longer find the original reason that first united them. If you ask me why I loved him, I feel that the only way to express it is to reply because he was he, and I was I." These words carry a tragic echo because this friendship, born when the two met at the Parliament of Bordeaux in 1557, was still young when de la Boétie, only thirty-three years old, died in 1563.

Food and culture of exceptional quality have always gone hand in hand; foie gras, truffles, nuts, and candied fruit on the one hand, famous festivals on the other. Every summer Sarlat sees an explosion of festivals, such as the national salon of photographic art, classical music concerts from Périgord Noir, and the famous theater festival. But Sarlat is only the heart of the Périgord, an entire region that offers thousands of treasures. Patience is required, and rewarded, when absorbing the local atmosphere, which Henry Miller described as "the paradise of the French."

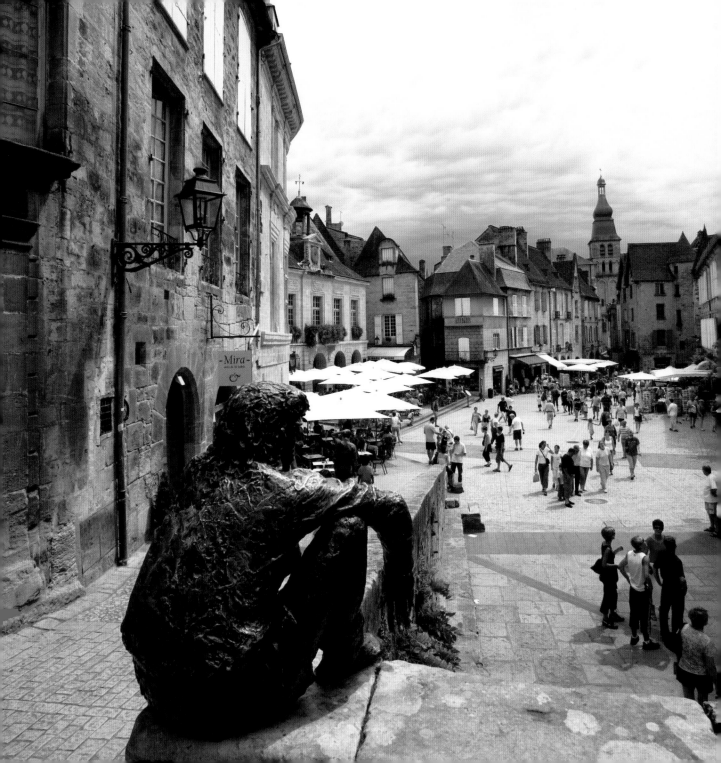

AURILLAC
AUTHENTICALLY AUVERGNE

THIS ANCIENT TOWN IS STILL PROUD OF ITS "POPE OF THE YEAR 1000," the local horse that Napoleon rode when he returned from Russia, the fact that about half of all French umbrellas are produced here, its many cheeses, the annual street-theater festival, and its magnificent panorama. The setting of the mountains of the Cantal that surround the city can be admired from the top of the thirteenth-century keep, within the castle of

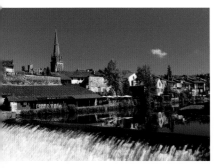

The town arises along the banks of the Jordane River.

facing page
Two crenellated towers of the castle that houses the Museum of Volcanoes.

Saint-Etienne. The castle is also the site of the excellent Museum of Volcanoes, where small-scale models are displayed; the eternal and exciting spectacle of the earth at work is depicted in documentaries, interactive devices, and games. Although the exhibition is enthralling, it is worth remembering that there is nothing to worry about, because the last eruption of the Massif Central occurred 6,000 years ago. At that time Aurillac did not exist; the city took shape only in the tenth century, when the abbey was founded. Traditional crafts such as tooled leather, lace embroidery, and cattle raising began to develop in the Middle Ages. The old city, a network of pathways, has preserved a lovely architectural unity. The facades of the houses, in gray granite, are richly detailed: Some preserve the original dovecotes and heavy doors sculpted in oak and basalt. Other buildings still have the large doors of the old shops or the small openings under the roofs indicating the building's former use as a grain loft. The Place du Square is a fascinating oasis in the heart of town, designed in the nineteenth century by Jean-Charles Alphand, who also designed the Parc Monceau in Paris. Those who like to idle come here to forget the big city, savor the scent of the flowers, and enjoy the view of the distant mountains. Arsène de Lacarrière-Latour, one of the founders of Baton Rouge, Louisiana, professor Henri Mondor, whose name was given to one of the greatest French hospitals, and Paul Doumer, a president of the French Republic, were all born in Aurillac. In rue du Consulat there is a well-preserved five-story watchtower that housed the mercenaries during the religious wars of the fifteenth century. This watchtower also witnessed the many

Huguenot sieges Aurillac survived. Have no fear and succumb to the natural temptation to push open the great doors; you will see the worn stone steps and feel a sense of intimacy, catching a glimpse of the town's true nature. The old town hides other architectural gems, particularly around the rue de la Coste, the ancient bourgeois fief of Aurillac. The original abbey was destroyed by the Protestants and was substituted by the church of Saint Géraud. Within the church there is an atmosphere of silence and meditation, and the Gothic nave is splendid.

Aurillac may preserve some traces of a Gallic-Roman past, but the real birth of the town dates to about 980, when local Count Géraud founded a monastery. The monks noticed a shepherd, Gerbert (938–1003), whose knowledge of the stars and vivacity was surprising. These qualities encouraged the monks to take great care of him and facilitate his studies. Gerbert attended the famous Arab universities in Spain, studying medicine, theology, and mathematics. He then became the abbot of the monastery of Bobbio in Italy, went on to become archbishop of Ravenna and Rheims, and worked as an astronomer, musician, and politician. He tutored the children of Emperor Otto I, supported Hugh Capet's accession to the throne of France, and became pope in 999, taking the name of Sylvester II, thereby becoming the first French pope, and so-called Pope of the Year 1000.

Authentic local artisan work can be bought at Aurillac. The robust, handmade umbrellas are famous, and the Piganiol company, which has been in business since 1884, is one of the oldest umbrella factories. Pewter jugs and platters made in the Haut Auvergne tradition are for sale, as are walnut and fruit brandies. The handmade knives of the Destannes family, whose cutlery business was founded in 1908, are also renowned, and can be personalized with an inscription on the blade.

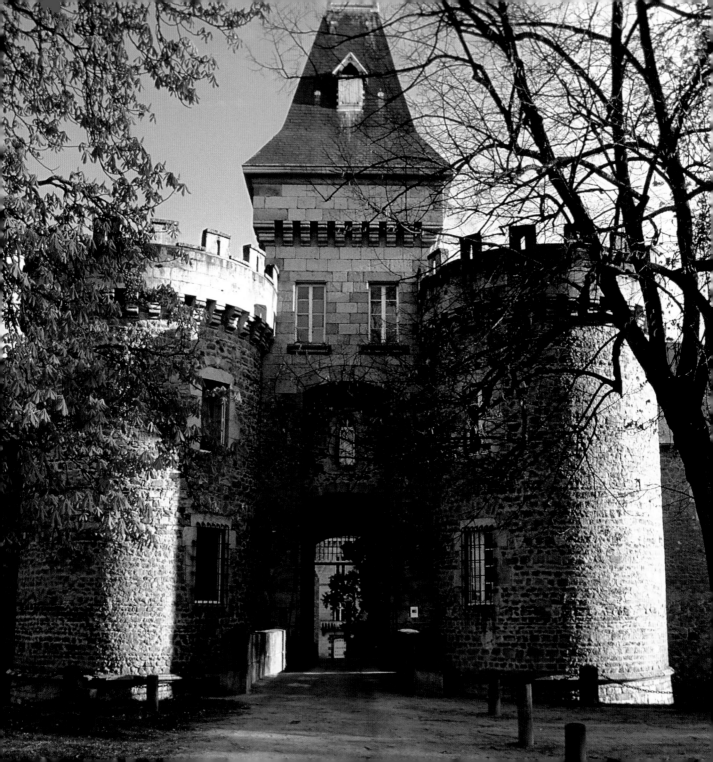

LE PUY
EN-VELAY
CITY OF THE VIRGIN

SITUATED BETWEEN TWO VOLCANIC HILLS, LE PUY-EN-VELAY OFFERS one of the most extraordinary natural landscapes in France and is one of the country's most popular pilgrimage destinations. Not-to-be-missed sights are the Saint-Michel fortress, the Romanesque cathedral of Notre-Dame-du-Puy with its oriental-styled bell tower, the Corneille fortress, and the colossal statue of Notre-Dame-de-France atop the Rocher Corneille. Le Puy-en-Velay has always been referred to as the City of the Virgin. Around the fifth century, apparitions, miraculous cures, and the presence of a dolmen table, called the Stone of Fevers, convinced the bishops to build a basilica and then, in the twelfth century, the present cathedral. The Romanesque-Byzantine statue of Notre-Dame-de-France has for centuries been an object of veneration by pilgrims on their way to Santiago de Compostela in Spain and San Galgano in Italy. In the Middle Ages, the pilgrimage to Le Puy-en-Velay became so important that the bishop of the city—and the only one in France—descended directly from the Vatican. Kings, princes, and popes visited the town to invoke the Virgin Mary. The prestige of the city grew with the arrival of the statue of the Black Madonna, which was brought by the Crusaders but burned in a fire during the French Revolution. Today a copy of the statue, dedicated in 1865, resides in its place. The cathedral of Notre-Dame-du-Puy, its exceptional treasure trove of religious art, and the cloister with its columns and capitals have been registered by UNESCO as a World Heritage site. The historian Émile Mâle described the building as "one of the most beautiful monuments of the Christian world, imbued with mystery. The singularity of its Arabic decorations and the oriental cupolas make it seem as though it has been transported to these mountains from a distant country." The tall houses with their red roofs and painted facades testify to ancient wealth: Grand homes of the fifteenth century, cantilevered facades, towers, and decorations of sculpted garlands all display the opulence that was once Le Puy-en-Velay. The Crozatier Museum tells the history of the town and displays objects of medieval art and an important collection of lace, the traditional craft that in the seventeenth century contributed to the town's economic development. Pilgrims and tourists visit throughout the year on their way to Santiago de Compostela in Spain. To best appreciate the town, climb up to the fortress of Saint Michel, a lake volcanic at an altitude of 224 feet, or scale the 268 steps of Corneille's rocky mountaintop to the monumental statue of Notre-Dame-de-France, where the view is simply divine.

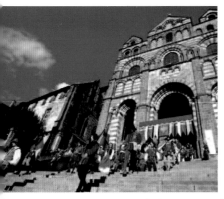

The procession during the Roi dell'Oiseau Renaissance festival.

During the famous Renaissance fair in September, the *haute ville* (upper town) undergoes its annual five-day metamorphosis. All the inhabitants take part in this picturesque celebration, with encampments of merchants or soldiers and scenes of daily life, street theater, troubadours, jugglers, pilgrims traveling to Santiago de Compostela, street peddlers, Renaissance concerts, and balls. The celebration is also called the Feast of the King of Birds in homage to a tradition that was instituted by Charles V in 1524, in which there is a competition to become the best archer in the town. In the sixteenth century the competition took place among the members of the brotherhood of archers of Puy. The winner of the pigeon-shooting competition was proclaimed King of the Birds for a year and benefited from important privileges: He had the right to carry a sword, command a company of harquebusiers, hold the keys to the town, and be exempted from taxes.

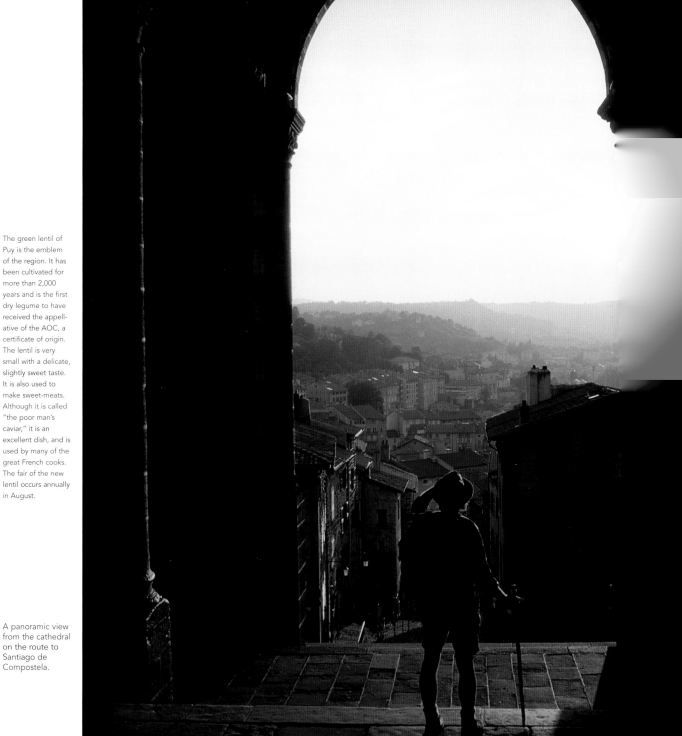

The green lentil of Puy is the emblem of the region. It has been cultivated for more than 2,000 years and is the first dry legume to have received the appell-ative of the AOC, a certificate of origin. The lentil is very small with a delicate, slightly sweet taste. It is also used to make sweet-meats. Although it is called "the poor man's caviar," it is an excellent dish, and is used by many of the great French cooks. The fair of the new lentil occurs annually in August.

A panoramic view from the cathedral on the route to Santiago de Compostela.

THIERS
CUTLERY AND CONTEMPORARY ART

THE UNIQUE AND SURREAL TOWN OF THIERS RISES IN A BEAUTIFUL PLACE, but unless you have the legs of an athlete it is difficult to reach. Like the steps of an amphitheater, clinging to the first outcrops of the Massif Central, Thiers is built along almost 2,300 feet of an uneven surface on the edges of a precipice where the Durolle River flows. The houses hang suspended on the slopes, and the floors are charmingly numbered backward, starting from the top floor down. Travelers will get the most out of their visit if they follow the natural inclines of the alleyways in the medieval town, take in the ancient half-timbered houses, and stroll under the *peddes*, covered passageways where old workshops rest below the dovecote buildings and the statues of fierce-looking characters. In the evenings, from the terrace of the ramparts, admire the sunset over the Auvergne, Limagne, and Dôme mountains. There is much to be explored in Thiers: The labyrinth of little streets that remind one of Near-Eastern medinas will certainly be a surprise to the tourist.

For more than five centuries Thiers has been France's foremost center for the production of knives. As a window on the past and the present, young artisans create luxury articles in the workshops of the Maison de la Coutellerie (Cutlery House), where you can discover the secrets of a guild that is still extremely active. The museum depicts the deafening world of the furnaces and demonstrates the more than 100 steps in the production of a knife. Along the banks of the Durolle generations of knife grinders' workshops have been replaced by prestigious knife factories. A pathway from the town gates leads to the heart of the Rouets Valley, where the atmosphere evokes the lives of the gentlemen knife-makers. Old abandoned workshops flank the banks of the river, their blackened facades and roofs tell of their story. Most of these old buildings have witnessed the mainstream establishment of the knife-making industry. The most renowned factory is at Pont de Seychal; built on the foundations of an old paper mill, the factory belonged to the Société Générale de Coutellerie et Orfèvrerie, whose main office was in Paris. Another well-known factory located in the gorges of the Durolle River, the Fabbrica du May, presents an example of refined industrial architecture and is listed in the *Inventaire supplémentaire des Monuments Historiques*. Next door is the Creux de l'Enfer (Mouth of Hell) factory, whose name comes from the spectacular waterfall nearby. Industry, local tradition, and contemporary creation here form a magical mix. The annual Festival du Couteau d'Art de Thiers (Knife Show) is an event that is eagerly awaited by collectors and lovers of original blades.

Thiers is home to the largest cutlery production center in France.

facing page
The Maison du Pirou with its typical half-timbered facade.

Since the fourteenth century, the waters of the Durolle have shared their power with so many workers and artisans that today, in the Center for Contemporary Art, opened in 1988, this energy seems to be sustained. Everything here is an homage to strength, art, and manual labor. The Creux de l'Enfer was born in an abandoned factory in the Vallé des Rouets and offers an artistic program where creativity and research combine with sculpture, painting, exhibitions, photography, video, and other arts. Artists work on a specific project, inspired by these undiscovered places. Guests of the Center for Contemporary Art have included Patrick Van Caeckenbergh, Pierrick Sorin, Luc Tuymans, and Erro. The Creux de l'Enfer aims to establish international recognition for its members.

When in Thiers, sample the foie gras, the sausage, and the *gaperon*, a strong cheese from Limagne prepared with garlic and pepper, now exported as far as Japan. Among the traditional dishes of Thiers are the *grattons*, small pieces of melted and roasted lard with which even croissants are made, tripe, and the famous *rapoutet*, which pairs well with leg of ham, cabbage, potatoes, and white beans from Soissons—the taste is decidedly strong and delicious.

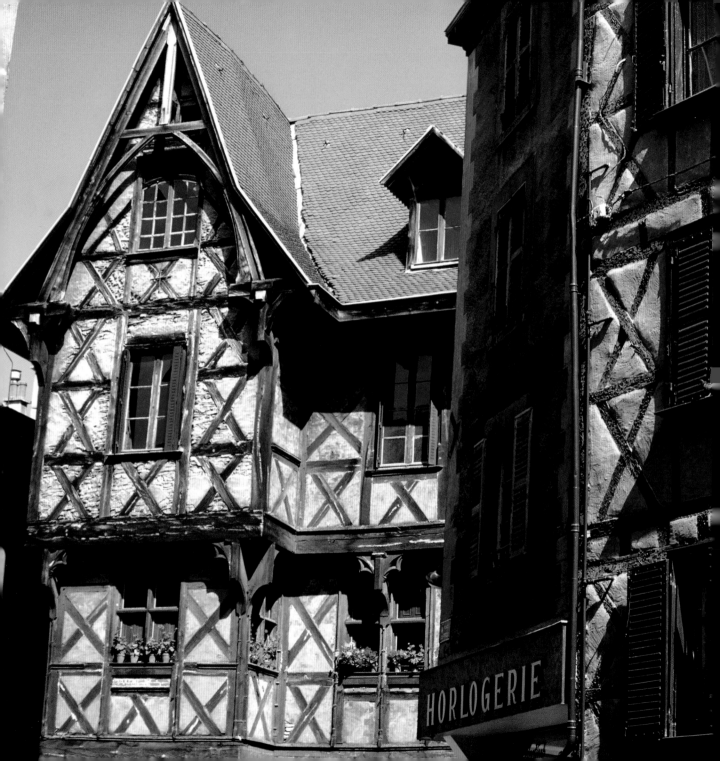

VICHY

THE SWEETEST SPRINGS

THE WATERS OF VICHY HAVE BEEN SYNONYMOUS WITH HEALTH SINCE THE TIMES of the ancient Romans. When the Bourbonnais region was annexed to the French throne in the sixteenth century, the waters became almost miraculously famous—even the royal family came for healing. Vichy became most important when Napoleon III began to spend long periods here, from 1861 to 1865. Here he wrote the *History of Julius Caesar*, causing the press to release an article with the headline "Veni, vidi, Vichy." The Empress Eugénie later joined him, as did his mistress, Marguerite Bellanger. The town was transformed and decorated with astonishingly fantastic architecture of the Belle Époque style for their welcome. There were Swiss chalets, Neoclassical, neo-medieval, and Moorish villas, not to mention the attractions of the casino, the opera, cloisters for concerts, and parks contributing to the charm of this spa town in the Auvergne. As a child the poet Valéry Larbaud wrote, "One would think one was abroad: the people in the streets speak unknown languages." Visits by the mother of Napoleon Bonaparte, Ivan Turgenev, Madame de Sévigné, and Coco Chanel all provided food for gossip in the local press.

During the Nazi occupation in 1940, given the city's proximity to the frontier, its more than 500 hotels, and the fact that it had the most efficient telephone system in Europe, Vichy was chosen by the Pétain government as the capital of the French state during the dark years that put an end to the Third Reich. Vichy was the administrative and political center of the collaborationist government, and after the Allied liberation the city managed to free itself of this unloved infamy. Years have since passed, and the waters of Vichy continue to cure thousands of people every year, just as its Belle Époque architecture continues to entrance. There is an exceptional concentration of monuments in the thermal area: The Parc des Sources is surrounded by a covered gallery built in the nineteenth century by the artist Émile Robert. The Grand Café, with a dance hall and terrace in the shade of chestnut trees, is a popular place for enjoyment and respite. The city's architecture is an eclectic mix of Art Nouveau, Art Deco, neo-Moorish, and neoclassical styles. The residential buildings have the sumptuous facades of early twentieth-century hotels. The Hall des Sources, where the six thermal springs of Vichy rise, is a splendid example of an Art Nouveau building in glass and metal, as are the Grand Casino and the Palais des Congrès Opéra, which was classified as a historical monument following restoration carried out between 1989 and 1995. The Centre Thermal des Dômes, with its beautiful blue and gold Byzantine cupolas, is another landmark. The art of wrought iron is ubiquitous in Vichy, particularly on buildings' facades, where ornate balconies can be admired.

The barometer crowns the pediment of the Casino.

facing page
The famous thermal baths of the Source des Célestines.

Since 1905 the Aletti Palace Hotel has welcomed kings and queens, princes and ambassadors, actors, and other famous figures to Vichy. This old and seductive palace still echoes with the legends and splendor of the Belle Époque. Its 133 rooms and one suite are refined and comfortable, as befits any palace. Elegant music comes from the piano at the Ascot Bar, and regional dishes can be tasted at the Véranda. The Aletti, however, is not overly expensive—a double room costs only 100 euros in the low season—making it the ideal home for any visitor.

The small town of Vichy is the home of three famous "inventions" of French culture: the design of the eponymous textile, a special candy, and carrots. The famous striped cotton printed with small pink and white squares had fallen into disuse until, at the end of the 1950s, Brigitte Bardot appeared at the market in Saint-Tropez wearing mini-shorts made with fabric printed in Vichy; it immediately became an international fashion. Some call the Vichy lozenge candy, others call it medicine; this unique octagonal sweet is aromatized with natural essences of mint, anise, or lemon, and was invented around 1825 by Monsieur Darcet by extracting mineral salts from the thermal water. Last but not least, the Vichy carrot, cooked in thermal spring water, mixed with a little sugar, a pat of butter, and parsley, is the base of the famous Vichyssoise soup.

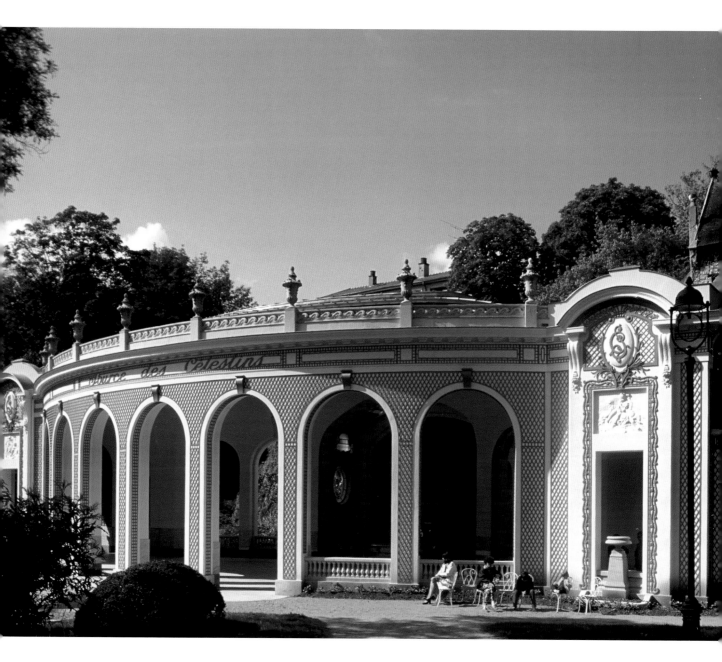

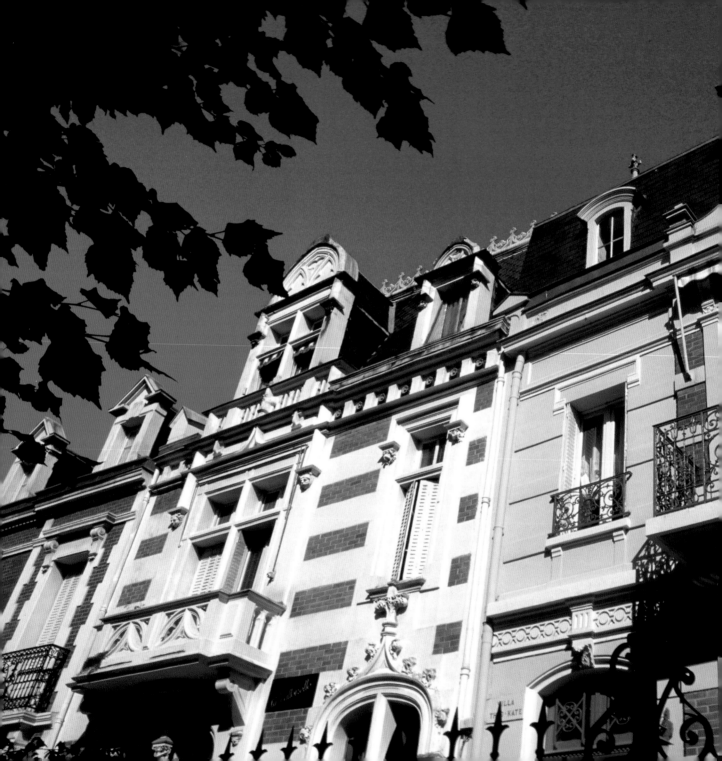

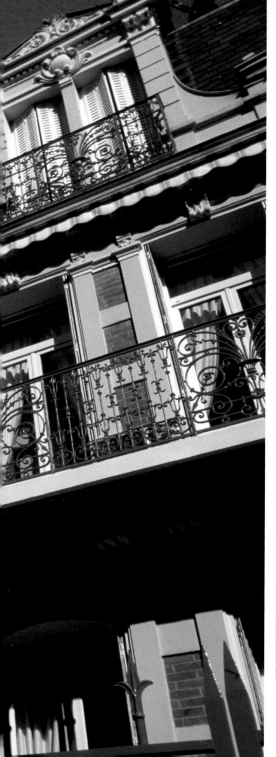

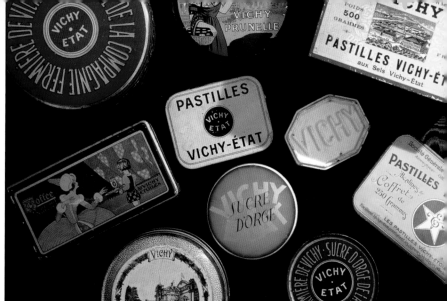

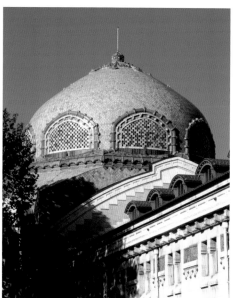

left
The elegant facades along rue Stucky.

above
An assortment of colorful tins for the invigorating Vichy pastilles, created in 1825.

below
A vibrantly tiled cupola of the Centre Thermal des Dômes.

In Vichy you can see and hear one of the most beautiful organs in all of France. This masterpiece, called the Aubertin, is in the church of Saint-Louis, and was inaugurated in January 1991. It stands in the middle of the nave upon a large platform, with three aligned and superimposed keyboards. The organ is suspended in the choir, with two sonorous towers mounted on the side railings, and is placed under the older grand organ. The church's sculptures represent local lore in friezes depicting salmon of the Allier River and Napoleon's eagles, and vegetable motifs decorate the doorways. The casework is made of oak, and the pipes are made of lead, tin, textiles, and pinewood. A precise and very light mechanism ensures that it can be played with great delicacy, and the range of sound is indescribably rich; for this reason the compositions of Buxtehude, Johann Sebastian Bach, Sweelinck, Cabezon, and Bruna sound as perfect as those of Mendelssohn and Brahms. This organ also elevates the sound of many contemporary compositions. Great organists have played and recorded on the Aubertin, including Marie-Claire Alain, Michel Chapuis, Gaston Litaize, François Henri Houbard, Olivier Latry, and Olivier Fernet.

BEAUNE
THE BEST OF BURGUNDY

BEAUNE IS IN THE HEART OF THE BURGUNDY REGION, NOT FAR FROM DIJON, and is a wine lovers' paradise. Along the cobblestones of tranquil streets, between historic buildings enlivened by multicolored roofs, centuries of history pass before the visitor's eyes. Beaune is famous for its excellent food, but also transports the traveler directly to the fifteenth century, when the basilica of Notre-Dame, a masterpiece of Gothic art,

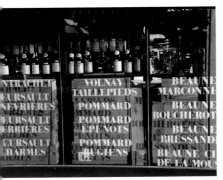

A wine shop in the heart of Burgundy.

and the famous hospices were built. Nicolas Rolin and his wife, Guigone de Salins, founded the hospices in 1443 to house the sick, poor, and aged populations. They wanted to support the recovery of Beaune after the traumatic Hundred Years' War. Rolin was named governor by King Philip the Good, and he administered the town for almost sixty years in the service to the Duchy of Burgundy. He was an excellent administrator and expert politician, and freed Burgundy from its alliance with the English. He was also a creator of the Treaty of Arras, which reconciled France and Burgundy and put an end to the Hundred Years' War. After the construction of Beaune's modern hospital in 1971, the Hôtel Dieu became a museum and testimony of the life and architecture of the High Middle Ages. Its flamboyant Gothic style and roofs covered in colored tiles make it the region's icon, an emblem of the golden age of the great duchies. It is also home to the *Last Judgement* polyptych by Rogier van der Weyden and the Salon des Povres. The hospices of Beaune are another city showpiece; visited every year by more than 400,000 people, they include about 140 acres of Grands Crus and Premiers Crus vineyards. The vineyards continue to be renowned for the high quality of their wines, and the growers are selected by the *Regisseur* (vineyard manager). The processing of the grapes follows the same rules required for controlled-denomination wines, and they are distinguished by the words *Hospices de Beaune* printed on the label together with the name of the buyer. The hospices owe a great part of their fame to the vineyards, and, according to a tradition dating back to 1859, the prestigious wines are sold every year at auction on the third Sunday of November. The best time to visit Beaune is during the harvest, but at that time the small producers are very busy. In October there is an atmosphere of celebration during the gathering of the grapes, from which the most famous and best-loved French crus—such as Meursault, Pinot Noir, and Chambertin—are made.

The Museum of Burgundy Wine, created by André Lagrange and Georges Henri Rivière in 1938, has been housed since 1946 in the ancient Palace of the Dukes of Burgundy, dating back to the fourteenth through eighteenth centuries. Here the history of the vineyards from ancient times up to the twentieth century is on display, chronicling the work of the vine dresser and the cask maker or cooper, as well as the rites and rituals of winemaking. On the ground floor the room of *les conditions naturelles* explains the geology and climate required for the wines of Burgundy. Another room is dedicated to the patron saints of the vineyard, while in the *tonnellerie* room a video offers a guided tour of all stages of wine-making. The museum visit ends with the Ambassadors' Room, which takes its name from a confraternity that, after the war, wanted to help promote the regional wine's image. The precious Lurçat tapestry displayed here was commissioned in 1947.

facing page
Over 140 acres of vineyards lie behind the decorative rooftops of the Hospices de Beaune.

Wine can be bought from the many small producers, but a visit to the hospices during the auctions is especially intriguing. After vinification, the hospices' management decides the amount of wine that will be put up for auction. The sale takes place in the market hall on the afternoon of the third Sunday of November. It is directed by an auctioneer, and is presided over by a different local figure each year. Bids start at 150 euros. The cuvées are presented in lots, and the names of the buyers—shopkeepers, restaurant owners, and private wine lovers from around the globe—are listed in a report of the result of the auction attached to the catalogue. The wine can only be sold in the traditionally shaped Burgundy bottles, with the label of the hospices, containing the denomination, name of the cuvée, and vintage year; the buyer can only add his name and address. The auction concludes with an important candlelight dinner in the medieval ambiance of the Hôtel Dieu.

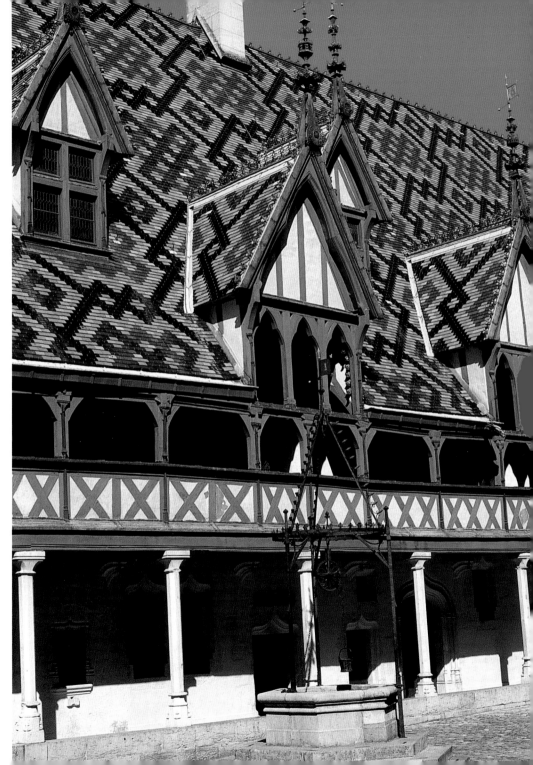

NOYERS
SUR-SEREIN
HUGUENOTS AND HALF-TIMBERED HOUSES

NOYERS IS AMONG THE MOST BEAUTIFUL MEDIEVAL CITIES IN FRANCE, famed for its dovecote houses, stone dwellings, columns with sculptured pinnacles, granite and limestone cobblestones, little streets and squares, and towers lapped by the waters of the meandering Serein River. Walking along the main street one can almost picture the horsemen, country folk, priests, or the bourgeois of long ago. Visitors understandably expect to meet a jovial Burgundian of yesteryear, or to hear a minstrel's song waft through the air from one of the sixteen towers surrounding the fortress, but the wandering singers of the past have been substituted by young foreign musicians playing Brahms, Schubert, and Chopin. Romanticism and the Middle Ages, naïve painting and traditional art all live in harmony at Noyers. The origin of the town is uncertain—it may have been founded by the Sequanes, a Gallic people, before the Roman conquest, or by Lucidormius, a contemporary of Julius Caesar who gave the city his name, Lucida. In the twelfth century the city was the fief of the Noyers, an important family that produced many illustrious figures in French history and, together with the Milles family, determined the fate of the city. Guy de Noyers, Bishop of Sens, crowned King Philippe Auguste in 1180. Miles X de Noyers was nominated Marshal of France by Philip the Fair in 1303 and commanded the best of the French cavalry, but it was nevertheless decimated by the English infantry during the last mission undertaken in the service of the king. At the end of the twelfth century Hugues de Noyers, Bishop of Auxerre, transformed the old castle into one of the most impregnable fortresses in France, which even resisted the siege of Blanche de Castille's army in 1217. In 1419, with the extinction of the Milles dynasty, the domain of Noyers passed to the Dukes of Burgundy. The Prince de Condé, who became Count de Noyers, transformed the fief into a center of Huguenot resistance and fled there in 1568 after the failure of the Amboise plot, but Catherine de Medici soon defeated the garrison and expelled him. It later became the refuge of Baron Vitteau, who was more bandit than gentleman, and the castle was demolished by King Henry IV, in 1559, after he had captured the baron. Following a long hibernation, the city was reborn under the protection of the Duke de Luynes, who in 1710 married the last descendant of the Condé family. The town is an agricultural center; commerce of wheat and wine has always flourished, and up until the twentieth century, local handicrafts boasted master craftsmen such as wheelwrights, saddlers, farriers, shoemakers, coopers, and smiths who made the iron bands for wine casks. Although their production has been reduced, farmers are still active, and Noyers has a country atmosphere even as it looks to the future.

The arches of the medieval town center.

facing page
A glimpse of Noyers-sur-Serein, one of the most tranquil villages in France.

Noyers' Musée Municipal d'Art Naïf (Museum of Naive Art) contains a collection of archaeological finds and relates the history of the de Bresse family, donated to the city by a descendant. The museum covers many disciplines, including national archaeology, modern and contemporary art, fine arts, photography, paleontology, and African and North African paintings. But above all, the most interesting is the exceptional collection of popular and folk art donated by the artist Jacques Yankel.

Burgundy's famous wines can be tasted with a selection of the delicious cheeses of Noyers: Saint Florentin, Soumaintrain, and Broughon pair exquisitely well with the red or rosé wine of Epineuil. Connoisseurs marry the strong Epoisses, a cheese washed with Burgundy marc during its aging process, with a glass of crisp, dry Chablis. The traditional aperitif in Noyers is *kir*, white wine flavored with a soupçon of crème de cassis (black currant-flavored liqueur), and often accompanied by a *duché*, a type of Chablis biscuit, or *gougères*, small puffballs of cheese pastry. The black currant is a popular ingredient in French dessert fare. In some recipes these small berries are pounded in a glass, or crushed, and eaten with a crunchy *buchette* or made into a Marguerite de Bourgogne, a favorite sweetmeat of pastry chefs.

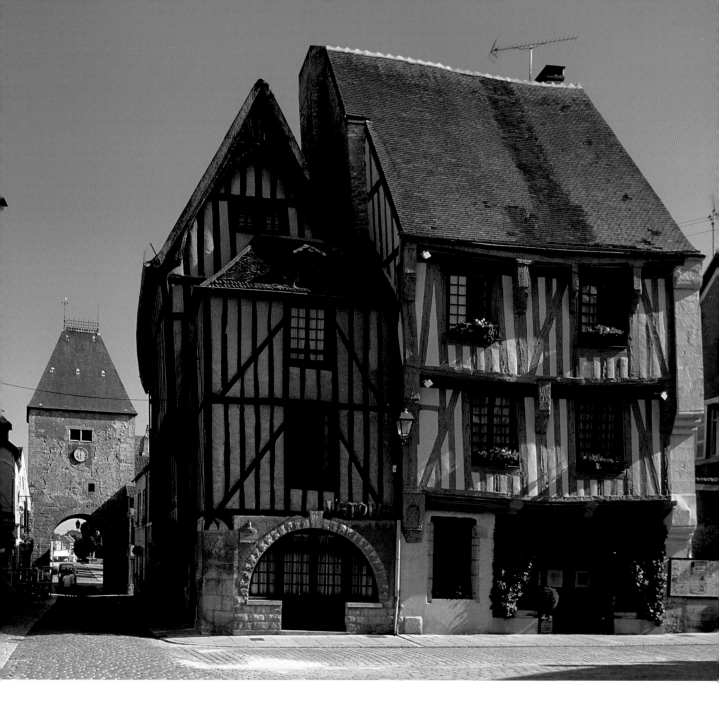

39

VÉZELAY
SAINT MAGDALENE'S CENTER

VÉZELAY HAS BEEN AN IMPORTANT PLACE OF PILGRIMAGE SINCE THE MIDDLE AGES, and today remains the place where Mary Magdalene's relics are preserved. It is also a meeting place on the road to Santiago de Compostela. The medieval village rests on a hillside and reveals its mysteries to the visitor who ventures among the old houses and walks along its narrow, twisted streets. Roman houses, including Centre Sainte Madeleine and the Maison des Ursulines, stand beside Renaissance buildings like the Maison Théodore de Bèze and seventeenth- and eighteenth-century buildings like the Hôtel de Ville and Maison du Pontot. When the climb becomes gentler and the view opens up, the basilica of Sainte-Madeleine, a masterpiece of Romanesque art saved from ruin and restored in the nineteenth century by the architect Viollet-le-Duc, comes into view.

Farther up the hill's ascent is the ancient Château des Abbés; from the terrace one can see the ancient walls surrounding the city, enjoy the great panorama of the "Valley of the Cure," and view the limestone hills to the north and as far as the Morvan forests to the south. In addition to the many pilgrims, Vézelay has seen a cortège of historic figures over the centuries. In 1146 Bernard de Clarvaux preached the Second Crusade here in the presence of Louis VII, Eleanor of Aquitaine, and the great vassals of the kingdom. It was here that Philippe Auguste and Richard the Lionheart met in 1190 to set off for the Third Crusade, and King Louis the Saint made many pilgrimages here. Thanks to all these events the fame and popularity of Vézelay increased, enabling the town to become incredibly rich. But this prosperity fed the jealousy of its powerful neighbors and attracted bands of brigands, forcing the city to defend itself with a double belt of walls built between the twelfth and fourteenth centuries. In the eleventh century the priory of Saint-Maximin declared that it possessed the relics of Saint Mary Magdalene, and from that moment the two villages declared a war of contradictory hagiographic information carried out by the monks of the opposing camps. The relics of the saint were officially discovered on September 9, 1279, at Saint-Maximin, and the decline of Vézelay began on that date. Vézelay kept its status of *Élection* (district) until 1790, but with the creation of the modern areas of jurisdiction this title was also taken away. The city was transformed into a simple provincial capital, and the population began to decline drastically. Between 1880 and 1900 phylloxera, a vine pest, destroyed what was left of the medieval vineyards, dealing another blow to the local economy, which suffered even further with the disappearance of local farming and traditional artisans. The fate of Vézelay began to improve after the basilica's restoration renewed tourists' interest in the town.

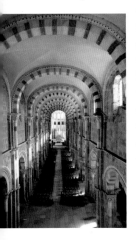

The interior of the Romanesque cathedral of Sainte-Madeleine.

facing page
Viollet-le-Duc restored Sainte-Madeleine in the nineteenth century.

Jules Roy, the novelist and man of letters who was born in Algeria in 1907, lived in a house close to the basilica of Saint Magdalene. He was an intellectual engaged in the struggles of his century, and published many works, including *La Guerre d'Algerie*, *La Vallée Heureuse* (Prix Renaudot, 1946), *Les Chevaux du Soleil*, *Memoires Barbares*, and *Lettre à Dieu*, which was published posthumously. He died in 2000 and is buried in the cemetery at Vézelay. His house, with its beautiful garden, is in rue des Écoles and is open to the public. The windows open onto the basilica of Vézelay, and his study is preserved just as he left it. Here the visitor can experience the atmosphere in which he worked and that inspired his last pieces.

The presence of vineyards in Vézelay and the surrounding villages dates back to the time of Roman Gaul. At the close of the ninth century the foundation of a Benedictine monastery by Girard de Roussillon gave a new impetus to vine cultivation. The wine that was produced began to be greatly appreciated in Paris, and in order to satisfy the capital's demand production was increased until it reached its apex in the eighteenth century, when the vineyards stretched over more than 1,200 acres. It was during this golden age that, in 1884, phylloxera destroyed everything. The vineyards were reborn in the 1970s, and in 1985 they obtained the protected denomination *Bourgogne* (Burgundy), and in 1997 that of AOC *Bourgogne Vézelay*.

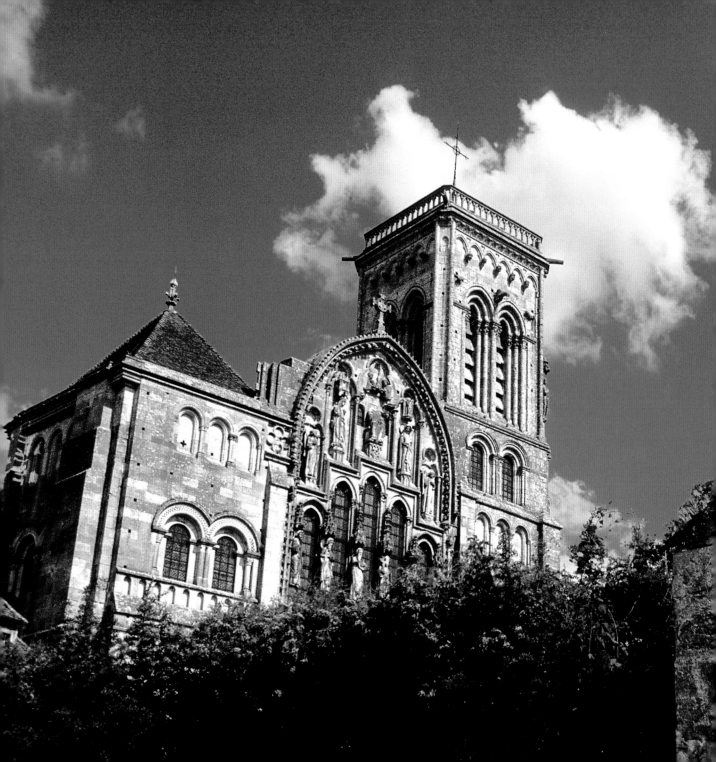

A U R A Y
DEVOTIONS AND INDULGENCES

THE ANCIENT, CAPTIVATING TOWN OF AURAY RESTS ALONG THE BANKS of the Loch River and is a treasure trove of art that has managed to keep its character and bustling daily life intact. Thanks to careful restoration, Auray has maintained its medieval character in appearance, the charm of its once busy port now used mainly for pleasure boats, and the ancient neighborhoods of the town. Some time is needed to discover Auray's

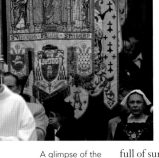

A glimpse of the procession held during the Ceremony of Indulgences in the church of Sainte-Anne-d'Auray.

inescapable charm, revealed in its characteristic dovecote houses, jewel-like churches, art markets, and the bustling Monday market, where tables overflow with fresh local produce and the fruits of the sea. Auray is worth exploring at all times of the year. Begin at the port of Saint-Goustan: Before the advent of the railroad, Saint-Goustan was one of the most important ports of Brittany as the point of departure for whaling, and later for cod fishing. Ships were built and sailed with cargoes of leather, timber, and salt from Guérande. Today, this characteristic area attracts and inspires painters. Among the notable figures who have stayed in Auray is Benjamin Franklin, who took refuge at the port on December 4, 1776, when he was impeded by a storm on his way to Versailles. Most important, Auray was the home of Georges Cadoudal, known as Chouan, the leader of the royal army in 1799 who was guillotined in 1804. His mausoleum was built at the end of a long avenue of centuries-old trees in the neighborhood of Kerléano, in the upper part of town. Auray is full of surprisingly beautiful places and delightful little buildings. In the eighteenth century specially assigned lookouts monitored the horizon, the sea, and the river from the tower of Loch, with its beautiful stone stairway rising among the horse chestnuts and linden trees. The alarm would be raised if an attack by pirates was feared. In 1800 the Chazelles fountain on the Quay Martin supplied drinking water for the citizens and the boats moored in the port. The bridge at Auray was once made of wood but has been subjected to much reconstruction—the last, in the sixteenth century, gave it its particular form; its buttress-shaped pylons are called breakwaters. The nearby villages of Ploemel, Crac'h, and Brec'h are must-sees. Follow the charming path of

The basilica of Sainte-Anne-d'Auray is the largest pilgrimage center in Brittany, and its fundamental role for Christianity was confirmed following the pastoral visit of Pope John Paul II. On September 20, 1996, the mass held by the pope was attended by tens of thousands of the faithful. The basilica is dedicated to Saint Anne, mother of the Virgin Mary, who appeared in 1623 to Yves Nicolazic, a farmhand. More than 800,000 believers visit every year. In the nearby nineteenth-century basilica, of Renaissance inspiration, the treasure room displays incredible ex-votos and numerous votive objects donated to the sanctuary. One could call it a museum of devotion. The first Ceremony of Indulgence of the year takes place on March 7, and the most important are held on July 25 and 26.

windmills in the Loch River valley, some of which are still active: Treuroux specializes in milling grains, and Estaign is an example of a windmill powered by water. Among the castles along the banks of the Loch is that of Plessis-Kaer, and there are villas hidden behind the woods: The Chapelle de Saint-Méen, the Chapelle de Locmaria, the Chapelle de Saint Cado and that of Saint-Laurent are all fascinating in their austerity. The menhir and dolmen at Mané Bogad are prehistoric monuments of great importance. Last but not least is the basilica of Sainte-Anne-d'Auray, the second-most important religious center in France.

According to the original recipe of Douarnenez, *kouign-amann* means a sweetmeat of butter. It is a leavened pastry to which, with a procedure that resembles that for short pastry, farm-made salted butter is added, together with flour and sugar. It has plenty of calories and is found in all the bakeries of Brittany that are worthy of the name. Salmon smoked over green beechwood and Guérande salt has a special taste and is prepared by hand in a small workshop. The smoked fish, which comes from Ireland and Scotland, is vacuum packed and will stay fresh for about one month. Wild salmon, called *rilettes*, is also available in the summer months, as is salmon butter.

facing page
The small port of the quartier Saint-Goustan is a lively corner of town.

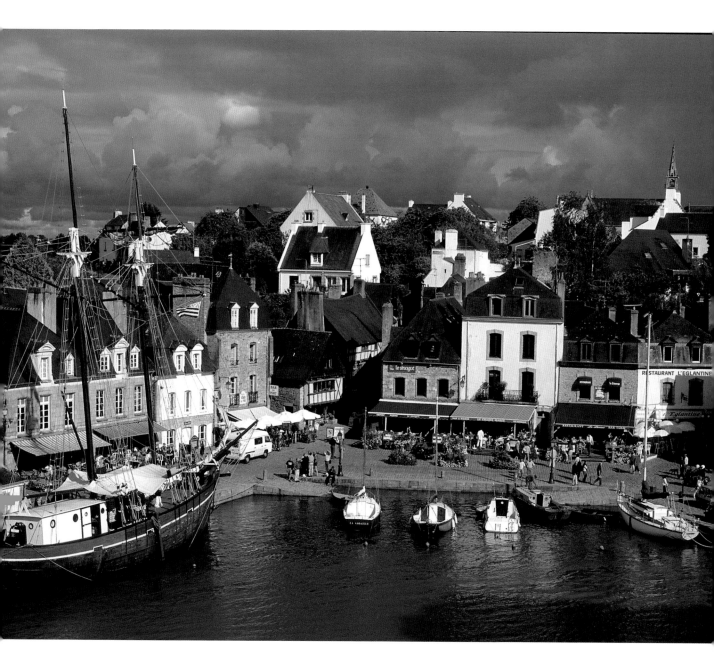

CANCALE
THE WORLD IS THINE OYSTER

VIEWED FROM THE SEA, CANCALE APPEARS AS A SMALL FISHING VILLAGE perched on a rock with a tiny port wedged between the shore and cliffs. For centuries the town's wealth has come from the sea—oysters, in particular. The once-flourishing port town had a flotilla of more than seventy ships for cod fishing and more than two hundred *bisquines* in the caravan that trawled the *bancs d'huîtres* (oyster beds), collecting the oysters once a year during low tide. Today, the port still has the oyster barges and about thirty boats for trawl net fishing. The oyster harvest has earned Cancale its nickname as the "Land of Taste." It is difficult—and unwise—to resist experiencing the nutty aftertaste of the flat oyster and the unique hint of iodine flavor in the *creuses* (deep-water oysters).

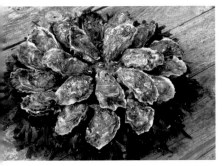

Local *creuses* oysters are a savory gift of the sea.

facing page
A view of the town and beach over the harbor.

The panoramic road overlooking the little port of La Houle is a special place where visitors can stroll among the oyster gatherers and seafood connoisseurs. Explore the many narrow pathways and climb the stairs leading up between two fishermen's houses in order to appreciate the enchantment of the narrow roofs, built one atop the other, facing the sea. Statues of the Virgin, protectress of the sea, line the town's walls, while the bell that announced a shipwreck still stands on the quay. Life revolves around the sea at Cancale, and La Houle is extremely active during the summer months. The eighteenth-century church of Saint-Méen houses a museum of arts and popular traditions that relates adventures of deep-sea fishing as well as events from the town's history. In September the Festival of the Song of the Sailor is not to be missed. In the off-season, when Breton weather can be particularly harsh, tours of the town are accompanied by a stop for hot chocolate. The many steps to reach the old town lead to the bell tower of the church of Mont-Saint-Michel, and the view from the promontory of Grouin is magnificent—when the weather is favorable, of course. The path of the Douanières along the Crolles headland follows the coast facing the Île des Rimains and leads to the bird sanctuary on the island of Landes. This corner of Brittany is characterized by the protected beaches of Port-Briac, Port-Pican, and Port-Mer, and the tall, jagged cliffs of Grouin soaring 150 feet above the sea. Toward Mont-Saint-Michel the coast's contour takes on a unique profile, as though it had been drawn with thick strokes of ink; the oyster farms create this optical effect and are characteristic of this region. Not only are the oysters flavorful at Cancale, but the fruit and vegetables are as well; potatoes, cauliflower, strawberries, black currants, and kiwi are all locally grown.

Cancale's name is writ large among the great seafaring traditions. The *bisquines* have sailed the waters of the bay for ages, and the deep-sea fishing boats have cast their nets as far abroad as the North American oceans. At the beginning of the nineteenth century, the *bisquines* were exceptional workboats. Thanks to their enormous sails they were extremely fast, but soon became victims of the changing times, with the end of the practice of dredging oysters and the arrival of the engine. Local sailors have not, however, forgotten their heritage. La Cancalaise, a replica of a *bisquine* (a nineteenth-century French fishing boat), has been moored at La Houle since 1987. This unique example of its glorious ancestors, with 1,050 square feet of sail, glides on the waters of the bay from April to October, the months during which the town's traditional festivals take place.

No visit to Cancale is complete without sampling the oysters. For an unforgettable experience, buy the flat ones and the *creuses* at the market and eat them at the foot of the lighthouse. Many restaurants along the port encourage tasting them, and this is another good way to enjoy them all year round and at any time of the day, eaten with shrimp or crab, or simply with a glass of white wine. Remember that only the flat oysters are available from May to August. The Oyster Museum is the only one of its kind in Europe and is well worth a visit.

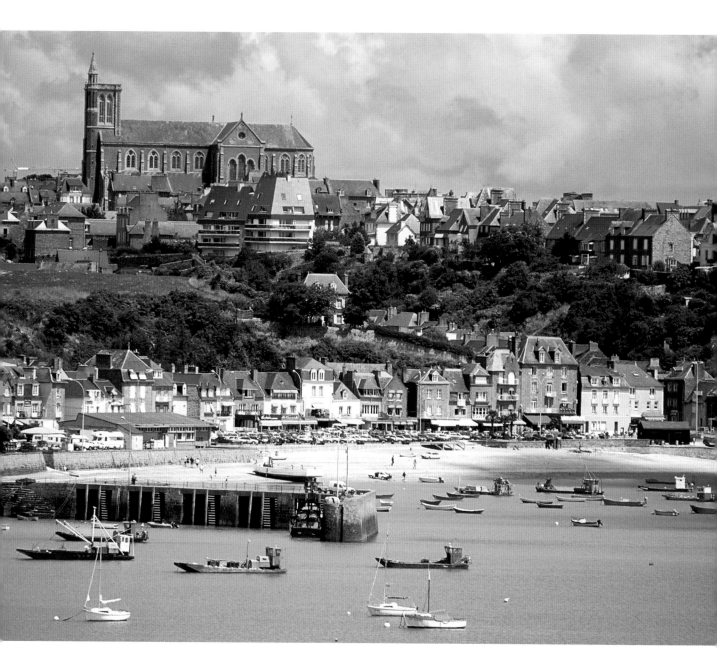

CONCARNEAU
BRITTANY'S MARINA

THE PORT, WITH ITS CALM WATERS, PROTECTS CONCARNEAU AND THE OLD TOWN. It is surrounded by the sea and ramparts, and rises on an irregular little island at the end of the bay. The town has grown up around Ville Close (walled town), the most frequented monument in Brittany. On land, the scenic road is lapped by the waves, follows fine sandy beaches, and borders the well-protected, hard-working fishing port. Concarneau is one of the most charming towns in south Brittany. It was fortified in the fourteenth century and became the fourth-most important fortress in Brittany. In 1373, after thirty years of English occupation, the Breton soldier Bertrand du Guesclin ceded the town to the duchy of Brittany. In 1491, thanks to the marriage of Anne of Brittany to Charles VIII, king of France, it became a royal center. The ramparts as they appear today underwent significant modifications in the eighteenth century. The Ville Close is a fortified islet in the center of town. Its narrow little streets retain their charm, and some of them have preserved their sixteenth-century origins. The ramparts, glimpses of the fishing port, the tourist port, the bay, Cabellou point, and the islands of the Glénan archipelago are all beautiful. Concarneau is the third-largest fishing port in France and the second in Europe for tuna fishing. The fishermen leave for long voyages off the coast of Africa, or toward the Indian Ocean. Who fishes what, where, and how are essential questions for anyone wishing to understand Brittany. The answers are all in the great fishing museum, which illustrates the history and techniques of fishing, shipbuilding, and the methods of fish conservation. The Marinarium invites visitors to discover the biodiversity of the oceans. Watch the auctions and experience the lively activity on the quays when the fishing boats return at the Criée fish market. The inland streets reveal other jewels: a sundial, the Hervo garrison, the chapel of the Trinité, place Saint Guénolé with its beautiful nineteenth-century fountain, and the Porte Aux Vins. A walk on the promontory leads to the Marinarium, continues along the protected and intimate beaches of Cornouaille and Sable-Blancs, and descends gently toward the calm waters of the sea. The Festival du Livre et Mer (Maritime Book Fair) in April, the Festival of Crime Fiction in July, and the Fête des Filets Bleus (Blue Nets Festival) in August, which lasts a week with shows and traditional dancing, are all worth a visit. The Glénan archipelago is an hour's sail away and is a magical, exotic world where the atmosphere lends itself to sunbathing on deserted beaches and diving into crystalline waters. It is said that this series of islands holds the same fascination as Moorea, in Polynesia, and is characterized by the same fine white sand.

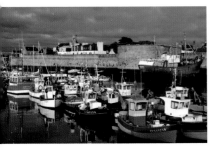

Fishing boats moored in the placid harbor.

facing page
One of the ramparts near an entrance into the walled city.

In the upper part of town the fifteenth-century Keriolet castle was given new life in 1860 when it was bought by Zénaïde Narischkine and Count Charles de Chaveau, *aide de camp* to Napoleon III. It was restructured by Joseph Bigot, an architect from Quimper, in an elegant but exasperatingly neo-Gothic, Mannerist style. Narischkine, the widow of Prince Youssoupoff, was in love with Brittany and, upon her death, left the castle to the regional government. But her legal heir, Prince Felix Youssoupoff, managed to get hold of the family's estate by winning a case brought to court in 1948. The castle was in danger of falling into ruins, but today, after patient restoration, it is again open to visitors.

The Confiserie des Remparts sells specialties based on salted butter caramel. Visit the Biscuiterie di Concarneau to taste the wafers, *palets*, madeleines, and the exceptional *kouign-amann* (Breton butter cake), whose secret is the extra smooth, freshly churned butter with no artificial coloring or preservatives from which it is prepared. The Conserverie Gonidec offers the high-quality *Mouettes d'Arvor*, specially hand-packed sardines, as well as tuna and mackerel marinated in olive oil and Muscadet, the white wine of the Loire Valley.

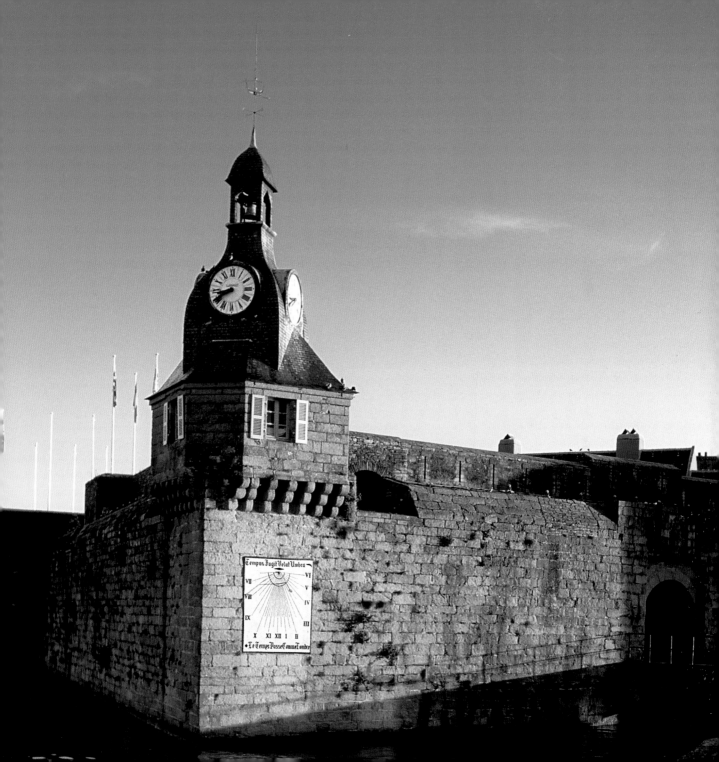

DINAN

BRETON BEAUTY AND THE BEAST

Neither time nor the English have been able to get the better of Dinan, the proud city of Bertrand du Guesclin, the popular fourteenth-century knight and warrior-hero of the Hundred Years' War. Dinan was the home of Leconte de l'Isle and Roger Vercel, praised by Theodore Botrel, and painted by Corot and Mathurin Méheut. Strolling along the beautifully preserved place des Merciers one has the impression of returning in time to the fifteenth century. Along rue du Jerzual tourists marvel at the many shops that are home to glass blowers, wood carvers, gilders, and weavers, and collectors exclaim with delight at finding rare pieces. The heart of Dinan lies in its wonderful succession of wooden houses, and those flanking rue de l'Apport are a mark of Dinan's great heritage. Built by naval carpenters in the seventeenth century, their great gabled windows resemble the sterns of merchant ships. Dinan possesses a unique strategic position; its stone walls served both to block the roads of the kingdoms of France and Normandy and to protect the city, which prospered as a ducal fief and military garrison from 1283. Later, under the influence of the Breton dukes Jean Roux and Jean II it became an important commercial center. The navigable Rance River was the fortune of Dinan, and encouraged a flourishing trade in textiles and leather goods. In the fourteenth century, under the protection of Duke Jean IV, Dinan became one of the principal fortified cities of Brittany. The fourteenth-century *donjon* (castle stronghold) was also his residence and is reminiscent of the Solidor tower at Saint-Malo. Today the fortress is a museum of local history beginning with the first lord of Dinan around the year 1000. A sentry path begins at the stronghold and encircles the ramparts with fourteen towers—the oldest in Brittany—for a distance of almost two miles. The colorful Ramparts Festival takes place in even years in July and recreates medieval France with street music, tournaments, crafts, and a parade. Dinan was a hub of intense commercial activity when boats from Saint-Malo delivered all kinds of goods— salt, cod, and tea, among other products—and departed restocked with leather goods, textiles, and timber for shipbuilding. Today it is a tourist port that has maintained the magic and liveliness typical of small ports. The summer is long and ideal for enjoying a glass of white wine on the square before setting off to discover the gems of the Rance Valley, the abbey of Saint-Magloire, and the ruins of the castle of Léhon.

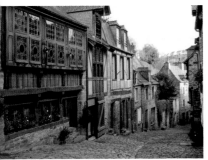

Traditional *pans de bois* houses in rue du Jerzual.

Bertrand du Guesclin was born near Dinan in 1320 and came under the service of King Jean the Good, during which he fought against the English, who ventured into the forest of Brocéliande in northern Brittany. During the Hundred Years' War du Guesclin became the terror of the occupiers, who called him the "black doge of Brocéliande." In 1364 he ended the siege of Dinan by winning a duel with Thomas of Canterbury. As a result, Charles V nominated the warrior-hero to supreme commander of the French militias. Du Guesclin strenuously fought against the bands of mercenaries that were sacking Normandy and Brittany. Although he was a particularly ugly fellow, he married the local beauty and member of Dinan's aristocracy, Tiphaine Raguenel, who was passionately interested in astrology. Du Guesclin lived at Mont Saint-Michel and his residence can still be seen today. Upon his death, in the siege of Châteauneuf-de-Randon in Auvergne in 1380, his body was sent back to Dinan to its final resting place. In a tender twist of fate, only the heart of this beloved knight reached its hometown; it is preserved in the basilica of Saint Sauveur.

Chef Jean-Pierre Crouzil, a lover of the fruits of both sea and land, has built a temple to Breton gastronomy at Plancoët, just outside of Dinan. Among the specialties on the menu are golden-fried coquilles Saint-Jacques, oysters glazed with carrot cream of Vouvray, lobster, and giant turbot stuffed with crab. After a grand meal, the height of the visit still awaits guests in one of the seven rooms of the Hôtel L'Ecrin, each named after a precious gemstone.

facing page
The medieval hamlet follows the curves of the Rance River.

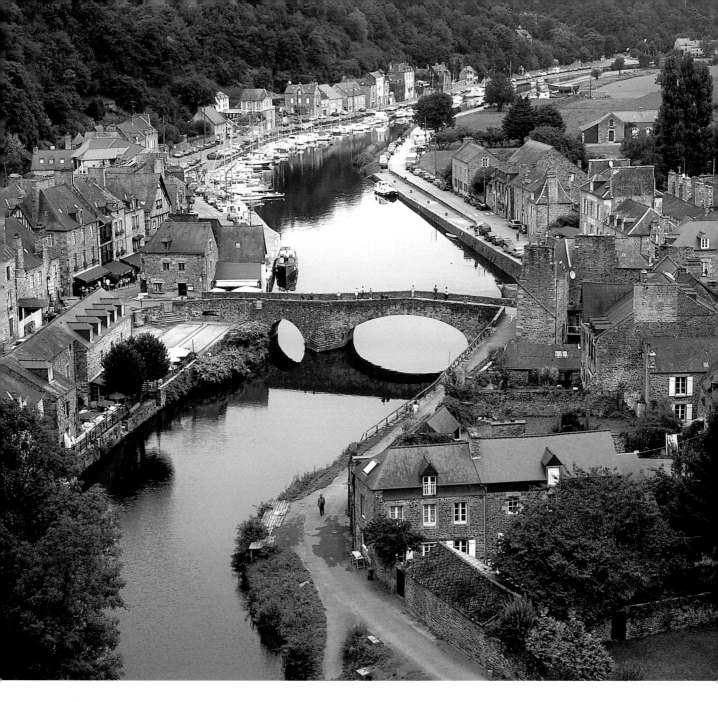

DINARD
THE MOST ELEGANT EPOCH

FROM THE PROMONTORY OF GROUIN TO THE CAPE OF ERQUY the coastline looks as though it has been ravaged by the rocks, cadenced by the little ports, and tamed by the soft beaches. Both land and sea reflect the rhythms of the tides, and the beautiful, greenish sea is as unchangeable as Dinard itself, the jewel of the Belle Époque, with its beaches dotted with blue-and-white striped cabanas. Since 1890 almost all the crowned heads of Europe have passed through, making it a famous and fashionable destination. In August 1891 Prince Mikhailovitch, son of Grand Duke Mikhail of Russia, uncle of the Tsar, spent a whole month here, occupying the entire first floor of the Hôtel des Terrasses overlooking the Ecluse beach. In August 1895 the Infanta of Spain, Eulalie, came, bringing the young Prince Alphonse and Prince Louis d'Orléans. She rented a whole wing of the same hotel, as it was the most renowned.

The most elegant and eccentric garden parties were organized for the illustrious vacationers in the splendid villas, English-style castles built alongside the castles in the style of Louis XIII, and the manors flanking the neo-Breton villas. Even after World War I, and until the stock crash of 1929, the elite continued to holiday in the luxury hotels. Dinard is best discovered on foot; boulevard Georges V traverses a residential area along the Rance River, where the oldest houses can be seen. Promenade de la Malouine reaches the beach of Saint-Enogat, an artificial barrier flanked by rocks built at the beginning of the twentieth century. This walk continues along a protected beach from which the Baroque villas can be seen. The scenery is the first attraction of the Promenade du Clair-de-Lune, and the curiously southern, Mediterranean vegetation enhances its charm. The Bric-à-Brac House holds the aquarium and is the first of the great bourgeois houses of this district. The best time to come here is on limpid days around eight o'clock in the evening, when the day is still light and the tide starts coming in. The evening reflections of the emerald sea seem to play with the colors of the palm, eucalyptus, and mimosa trees. Pointe de la Vicomté is more unusual, as it separates the beach of Prieuré from the mouth of the Rance. It is an oasis of peace and greenery, with myrtle and mulberry bushes growing among the spreading urbanization of the Rance dam area. The path is typical but also special, completely invisible from the sea, losing itself among the trees lining the rocks, which provide relief from the afternoon's high sun. The town's art galleries are a good conclusion to any trip, and in October Dinard returns to its origins and old loves with the British Film Festival.

The restaurant at the Pritania Hotel.

facing page
The most fanciful Baroque villas line the Promenade de la Malouine.

Sculptor Pierre Manoli (1927–2001) had his studio near Dinard. He worked with clay, majolica tile, and brass alike, without favoring one material but remaining forever faithful to fire. Flame was "nothing more than his hand at the right temperature," wrote David Rosenberg in a book, *Manoli, l'élan, la rencontre*, about the artist. Fire burned within Manoli; his human figures are slender, somber, and defy gravity. His animals—sheep, goats, cats, and panthers—seem to move in space. The monumental sculpture in front of the Jussieu building is his, as is the Grande Voile at the Montparnasse station in Paris, as well as the liturgical furnishings of the cathedral of Saint-Corentin at Quimper. Today visitors can see the place where the artist lived and worked for twenty-five years, and there are also spaces dedicated to other artistic, literary, and musical activities.

Each Tuesday, Thursday, and Saturday morning there is a wonderful market in the center of Dinard, with vendors of fruit, vegetables, fish, and oysters from the surrounding region. Seafood and fish are predominant, but there are also sausages, black puddings, cakes, and Breton wafers to be tasted right there at the market. Right next to this market are antiquarian dealers and vendors of secondhand clothing from the fashion houses at low prices, with many good deals to be had.

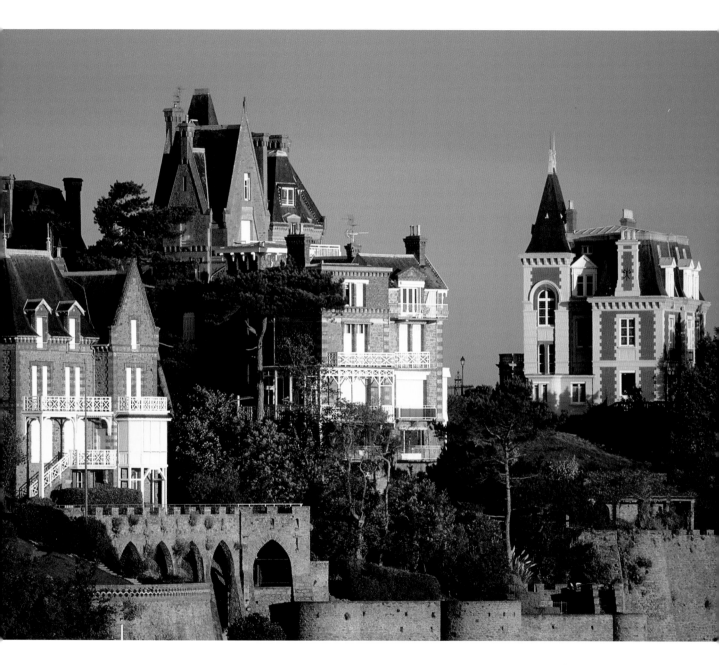

DOL-DE BRETAGNE
THE EBB AND FLOW OF TIME

WILLIAM THE CONQUEROR, KING JOHN, AND, BEFORE THEM, THE FRANKS AND NORMANS all tried to conquer Dol-de-Bretagne, often successfully. The French Revolution and following wars, with more than 15,000 casualties, marked the beginning of the town's decline. It was only in the nineteenth century, with the arrival of the railroad, that tourism came to this city of Saint Samson, one of the seven evangelists of

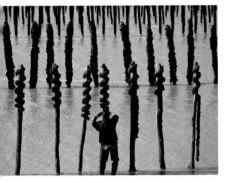

Beds for cultivating mussels follow the rhythm of the sea.

facing page
The cathedral of Dol is the archetype of Breton Gothic architecture.

Brittany. Dol is one of the most ancient Breton towns, and visitors can do little to resist being seduced by the medieval fascination that the picturesque streets and the timeless landscape exude. In the ninth century Breton King Nominoë turned this city into a flourishing religious capital. In the thirteenth century the cathedral's construction proclaimed the city's power and importance; it is an absolute masterpiece, and the pride of Gothic art in Brittany. The immense vaulted ceiling is more than twenty yards wide; the windows date to the end of the thirteenth century and are the oldest in the region; and the choir is extraordinary, with almost eighty fourteenth-century seats decorated with leaves and human figures, and a sixteenth-century throne. The heart of Dol-de-Bretagne is in the medieval part of town, which has inspired many painters and writers. According to Victor Hugo, "Dol is not a city . . . it is a street." This is indeed true, but what a street it is! The great rue des Stuarts, with its divided cobblestones, is lined with beautiful columned houses, and many dovecote homes. Further away, in the remarkable medieval quarter, one can admire the inn of the Croix Verte, the house of the Guillotiére, the Porche à Pain, and the sixteenth-century house of the Petits Palets. At the end of this road, the historical museum richly recounts Dol's past, and the Promenade des Douves offers a splendid view over the bay.

Every Saturday morning, and on Wednesday evenings in the summer, the road is enlivened by its traditional market where ducks, chickens, rabbits, shellfish, and regional produce can be found. Less than a mile away stands the granite mass of Dol Mountain. According to legend the giant Gargantua overturned his shoe in this area, and three stones fell out—Mont-Saint-Michel, Mont Dol, and Tombelaine. The view is unique, and the cliffs are a major attraction for tourists and rock climbers. The more curious travelers continue toward Carfantin to see the menhir of Champ Dolent, the most beautiful and tallest still standing in Brittany.

Dol-de-Bretagne opens onto the bay of the legendary Mont-Saint-Michel, famous for the most impressive tides in Europe. The phenomenon is influenced not only by the moon, but also by the particular configuration of the Brittany coast. The *marnage*—the difference between the levels of high and low tide—is exceptional all over Brittany. Almost twelve feet at Penmarch, and thirty-six in the bay of Saint-Malo, the *marnage* rises to more than forty-eight feet in the bay of Mont-Saint-Michel, which is quite notable considering that the world average is six feet. This natural phenomenon should not be missed during the equinoxes, when the sea surrounding Mont-Saint-Michel begins to lap at the beaches, and locals accurately claim that the waves rush up with the speed of a galloping horse.

In the bay of Mont-Saint-Michel the mussels, on their *bouchot*—tree trunks planted deep into the seabed— emerge from the water twice a day. They are the region's smallest mussels, and also the best, prepared in every imaginable style. Local seafood platters are also exquisite, with excellent flat and deep-water oysters from the bay.

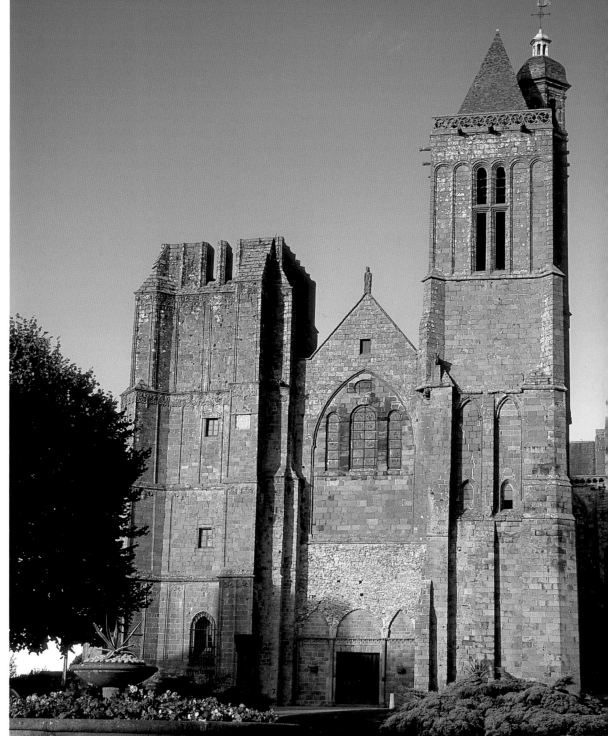

DOUARNENEZ
SARDINES AND SEAGULLS AT PLAY

IT APPEARS THAT A PACT WAS SIGNED BETWEEN DOUARNENEZ AND the local sardines; at one time there were about forty sardine canneries that enabled entire families to prosper, and now only three survive. From the beginning of the twentieth century through the 1970s more than 800 launches fished for this tender-skinned fish, and until a few years ago the port of Rosmeur was France's sixth largest. But even though there has been a decline in fishing, it is still possible to stroll along the port and taste these sardines, fried or roasted. Douarnenez has three ports—one for tourists, one for fishing, and a Port Musée, or Museum Port, where the ancient tradition of local lobster fishing is still preserved, exhibiting a method elsewhere abandoned long ago because the number of fishermen exceeded the catch, and also because protective laws were adopted by many countries, particularly in Africa. The museum celebrates the epic of the "lords of the warm seas," the *langoustiers* that returned from Mauritania and the rich ship owners of Nantes who built them. Thirty-three of these boats are on display in an old canning factory, and twenty-four are in the water at Port Rhu.

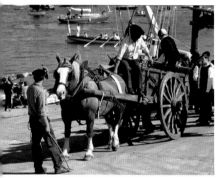

The Festival of the Sea is celebrated each July.

facing page
Old sailing ships anchored in the port.

Douarnenez is nestled on a rocky outcrop at the bottom of the eponymous bay. The town astonishes all visitors with its picturesque fishing houses and the beautiful nineteenth-century mansions rising along the tight alleyways that descend to the sea. A walk could end with a pleasant stop at a sailors' café, or continue through the old canning district, evoking the prosperous past. The Captain Cook factory is among the most famous, with a pink facade, and since its closing it has been transformed into a home. There is a path along the coast that leads to the little port of Tréboul and the delightful fishing village of Plomarch. Here there is a splendid view of Douarnenez and the Crozon peninsula. The inhabitants are proud of their reputation for being a brave and unruly people. They became pioneers by electing Sébastien Velly as the first Communist mayor in France in 1921, and once again in 1925, when Joséphine Pencalet broke the law and became the heroine of the *sardinières'* strike.

The magic spots all around Douarnenez, typical local dialect, sounds and colors, and festive spirit of the inhabitants attract sailors, researchers, painters, and poets. The town celebrates the seagull with a three-day holiday, and since 1978 has held an annual film festival dedicated to the world's minorities. During Carnival, in February, the whole of Brittany comes here to watch the Race of the Waiters and the Children's Ball.

Brittany's storytellers have a great repertory, and two famous legends take place in the bay of Douarnenez, reputed to be the world's most beautiful port. The first is about Tristan and Isolde and the drowned city. Tristan, a knight of the Round Table, is supposed to have given his name to the little island off the shores of Douarnenez. The island is 1,300 feet long, 750 feet wide, and accessible by land at low tide. It is on this miniscule bit of land that Tristan fell in love with the blonde Isolde, and it was here that the brigands hid their treasure. Travelers come to these places most certainly to dream, but also to discover an ancient, exotic garden, the remains of a convent, the rocky coastline, and the fertile orchards.

The *kouign-amann*, from the Breton *kouign* (sweet) and *amann* (butter) was invented in 1865 at Douarnenez. According to local lore, baker Yves-René Scordia did not want to throw away some dough that had not turned out right, so he added salted butter and sugar. The result is a tasty cake with a soft and slightly crispy surface and a surprising taste of caramelized sugar that precedes the taste of salted butter and fondant. Although recipes vary from village to village in Brittany, the staple ingredients remain the same: leavened dough, salted butter, and sugar. Today varieties exist with apples or algae, but purists prefer it simple and served warm.

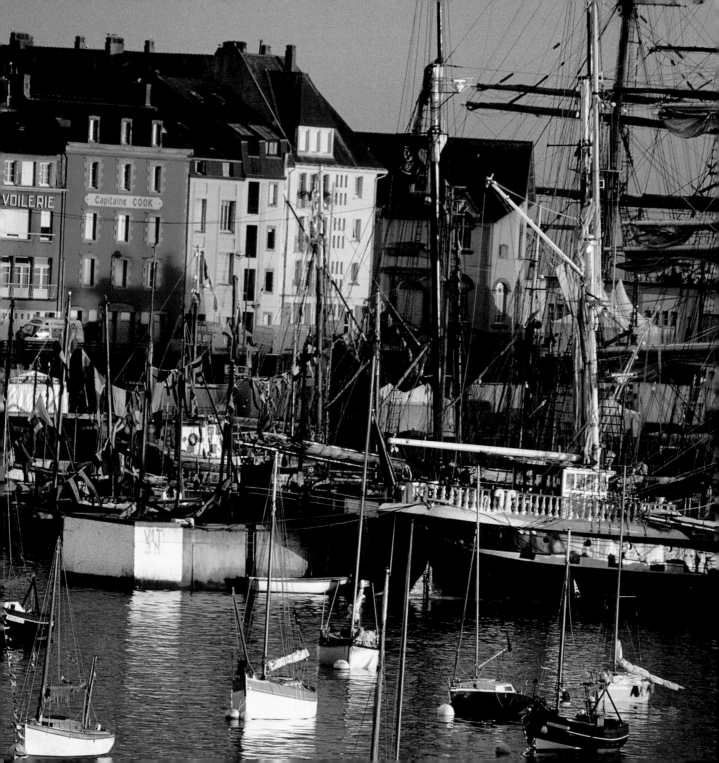

FOUGÈRES
A FORTRESS OF ARTISANS

RESTING ON A ROCKY PROMONTORY THAT DOMINATES THE VALLEY OF NANÇON, Fougères has preserved the majesty of a glorious past distinguished by important military exploits and the presence of famous writers. Victor Hugo wrote, "I am at Fougères, a town that should be visited with devotion by painters . . . . I have seen it in the sunshine, I have seen it at dusk, and by moonlight, and I have never wearied; it is admirable."

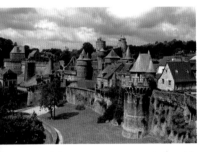

A long moat winds around the castle.

facing page
The fairy tale-like turrets of the fortified ramparts.

Balzac and Chateaubriand also spent time here. Founded in about the year 1000, the oldest part of town was built on a rocky island at the bottom of a valley, amid marshes and the Nançon River. It first became famous for its glassworks, footwear, and tapestry production. There is a long artisanal tradition that over time has grown into industry. The citadel has been fortified since Roman times, was the main defense of the duchy of Brittany, and has been called the "Carcassonne of the West." The ramparts, the many stairways of the old town, and the terraced gardens give it a decisive yet friendly character. The castle, in its powerful enclosure, appears suddenly on the horizon, defying both time and man. Its thirteen towers are linked by a massive curtainlike wall, which preserves the fort's integrity and attracts the visitor's attention. It is a masterpiece of military architecture and an interesting example of French medieval defense. It features a main structure; a lower courtyard where everyday life took place in peaceful times, and which became a refuge in time of war; and a more powerful third barrier dominating the whole fort and protecting the keep, from which the whole castle could be controlled. Fougères is still one of the largest and best-preserved strongholds in France. The church of Saint-Suplice and the Place du Marchix are in the upper town, bordered by wooden houses that seem to prolong this journey into the Middle Ages. The beautiful beams in the church's nave are shaped like an overturned hull, and the building was reconstructed in Gothic style. The choir is Rococo, the windows are Renaissance, and the altars are sculpted in granite.

The seventeenth-century convent of the Urbanistes nuns is also worth a visit. It has recently been restored

The Floral Park of Upper Brittany, with poetic and magical botanical gardens, is about six miles from Fougères. The Cité Antique, built in an old vegetable garden, has rows of junipers reminiscent of the portals delimiting the roads of a vanished old city. The Allées des Perles Blanches, with its subtle perfumes, allows us to travel across five continents of plant life. The Jardin Perse is inspired by the Moorish water gardens, and the City of Knossos is a leafy labyrinth with more than 300 varieties of camellias. Many other marvelous gardens await the visitor en route to the nursery, where some of the varieties of plants in the park are for sale. Purists will want to spend the night at the Foltière castle, in the heart of this immense park.

and is a classic monument. Below the high slate ceiling the splendor and richness of the granite is riveting for its pure, original style. The patio and cloister have a calm yet majestic atmosphere. Many shows are organized at Fougères during the year, such as the Voix du Pays, the choral festival of regional voices, held in July and a perfect occasion to discover music from all over the world, and in February there is the Flambée Musicales. The hamlets and villages of the region preserve their traditions, and the heart of the countryside is rooted in the stones of ancient houses, local castles, pools, paths, and in the ancient memories of the forest of Fougères, which holds well-preserved megaliths and traces of Roman roads.

Fougères' gastronomic specialties are incredibly seductive. They can be tasted both at Les Voyageurs and at Le Haute Sève. More pragmatically, the outlet store of the JB Martin company is also interesting; it has bargain prices for luxury clothes from Clerget, JB Martin, Kenzo, and many others. This company is one of the latest ladies' footwear factories in France, and can be visited during the summer.

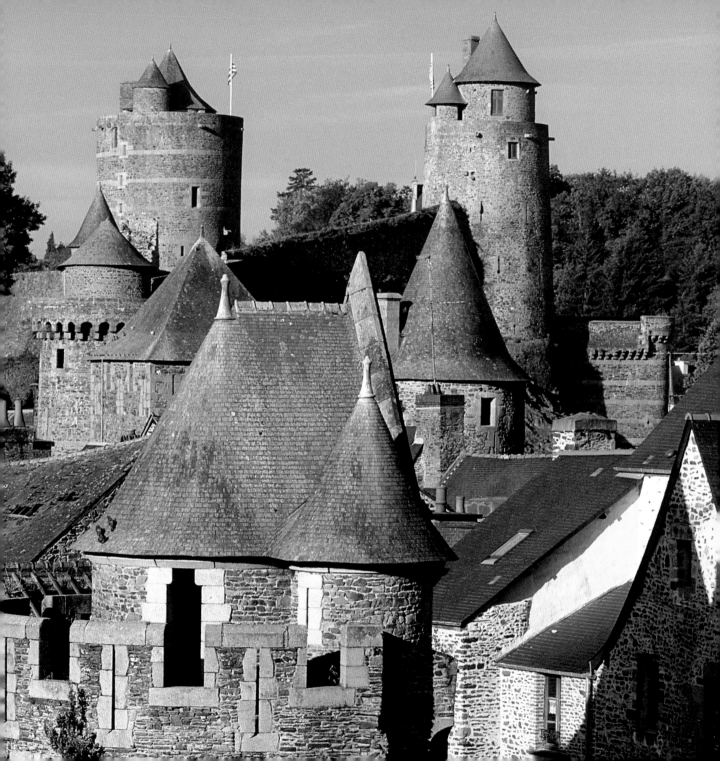

PONT-AVEN
PAINTERS AND BONS VIVANTS

PONT-AVEN IS KNOWN AS THE CITY OF FOURTEEN MILLS AND FIFTEEN HOUSES. Indeed, before the arrival of the artists that formed the Pont-Aven School, the village was known for its incredibly numerous mills. Situated at the bottom of an estuary between Lorient and Quimper, the Aven is a fast-flowing river that passes through the village. It descends from the black mountains, slows down, and is diverted over enormous blocks of granite that

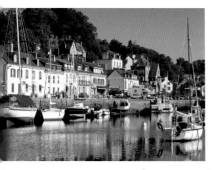

A charming harbor on the Aven.

facing page
One of the town's characteristic mills.

form a sort of natural barrier. These conditions are perfect for building the mills both upstream and downstream of the main bridge, which have been in service since the beginning of the twentieth century. In addition to bread, there are various ways of using grain, such as for ship's biscuits, plain biscuits, and most recently, the wafers that are famous all over France as a crunchy treat. Artists discovered Brittany around 1865, and the most famous group arrived at Pont-Aven between 1886 and 1896. Most of them were poor, and they all lived in the inns, painting together outdoors and in the evening discussing art. At first the residents were surprised at their arrival, but later they were more welcoming. Gauguin, Bernard, Sérusier, Denis, Filiger, Verkade, de Haan, Maufra, Moret, Seguin, Jourdan, Delavallée, de Chamaillard, Slewinski, O'Conor, Balin, and the list continues. There were about twenty artists of various nationalities that revolved around Gauguin and created the Pont-Aven School. They earnestly desired to create a new form of artistic expression, and the synthesis of pictorial symbolism developed from the meeting between Gauguin and Émile Bernard. Today's inhabitants are proud of the town's past; thanks to Gauguin and his colleagues the name of Pont-Aven has traveled the world. The museum in the main square illustrates the history of these artists and their visits. Unfortunately, the permanent collection does not include works by Gauguin, but holds many canvases by Bernard, Émile Jourdan, Maurice Denis, Paul Sérusier, and Maxime Maufra. Gauguin's famous painting *The Yellow Christ* (1889) was begun in Pont-Aven. The wooden cross said to have been the visual source for the crucified Jesus hangs in a local chapel. It was at Bois d'Amour that Sérusier painted *The Talisman* (1888), the future emblem of the Nabis group. Along the banks of the Aven, the Bois d'Amour is a sacred place in the history of painting.

Pont-Aven is also where one can find the most beautiful *coiffes* in all Brittany. These are the famous long and charming caps of starched lace and linen. Once again, thanks to the paintings of Gauguin and his friends, these extraordinary headdresses are known all over the world.

Paul Gauguin was often at Pont-Aven between 1886 and 1894, and here he found his long-sought artistic model. When Gauguin arrived for the first time, as a student and friend of Camille Pissarro, he was still "only an impressionist." Gauguin came to painting late, after he had been a sailor and stockbroker, and he turned thirty-eight before he decided to devote his life to art. He renounced a comfortable existence, rebelled against his father, and completely changed his life. Economic difficulties brought him to Pont-Aven, a "small, inexpensive place," as the painter Jobbé-Duval described it, where Breton life in 1886 was simpler than it was in the big city. Gauguin became the emblematic figure of Pont-Aven, and later traveled to Tahiti and the Marquesas Islands, where he died in 1903.

In 1890 Isidore Penven inherited his trade from his father and created the famous wafer, which he called the "delight of Pont-Aven." Today the same family continues the tradition, and tens of thousands of little wafers are produced every day and shipped by Penven to bakeries across France and as far as Japan, Switzerland, Germany, and Ireland. They are very worth a taste in Penven's shop at the tourist port.

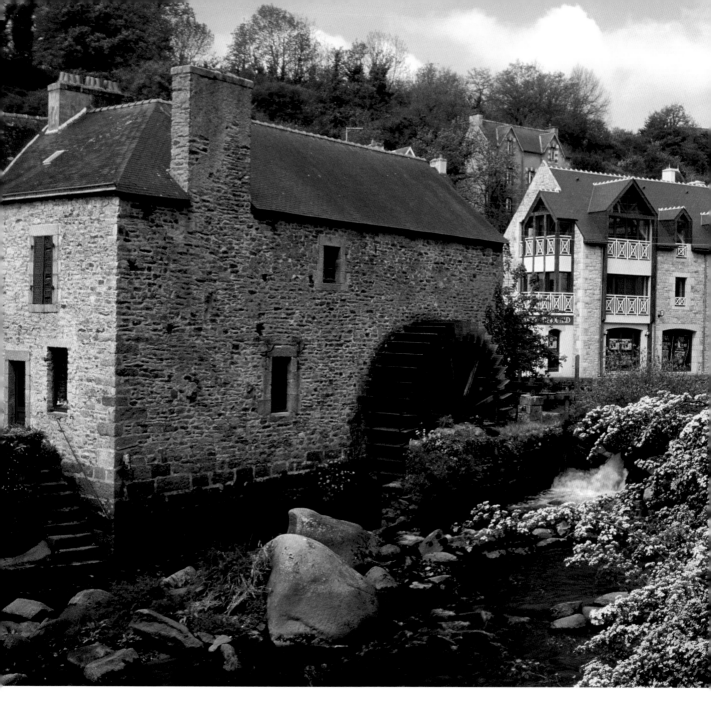

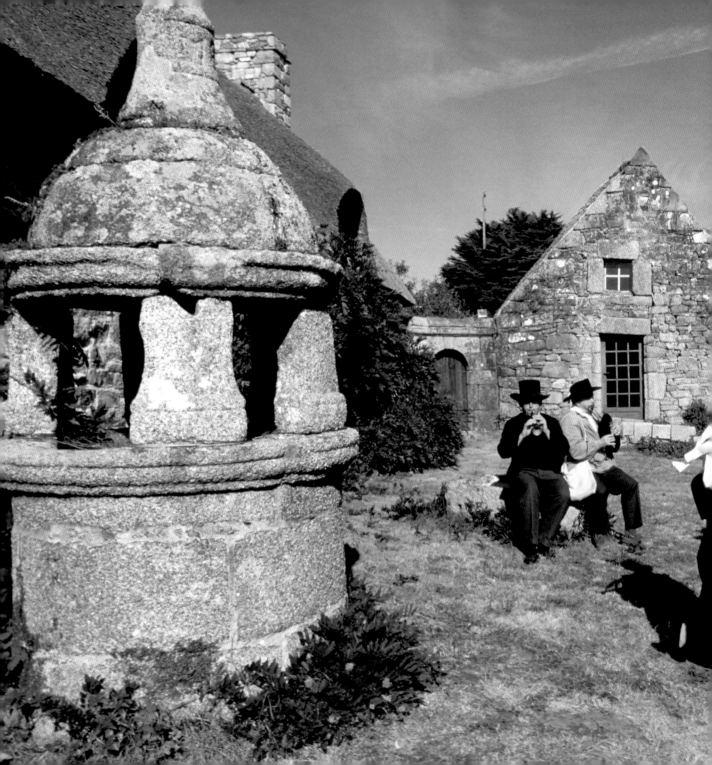

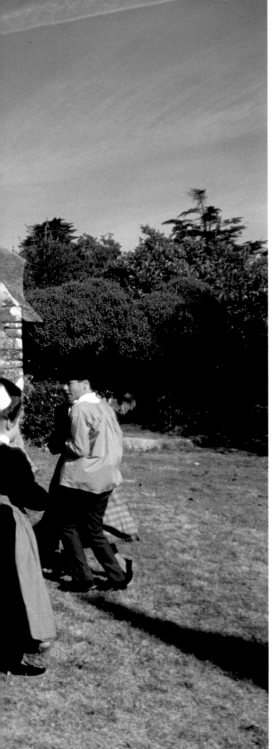

The great Fêtes de Cornouaille developed thanks to the tenacity of the old Breton culture. Traditional music prevails, and for this reason the number of fairs increases every year, from Pont-Aven to Quimper and nearby Lorient. One of the most important music festivals of Brittany takes place at Quimper in June, together with the Interceltique de Lorient Festival. To the sound of the *biniou*, an instrument similar to bagpipes, and the *bombardes*, an instrument in the oboe family, 4,500 musicians and dancers representing 175 *bagadou*—musical groups who sing in the Breton dialect—parade through the towns. Visitors are spellbound by the Celtic music and traditions, and an increasing number of Bretons themselves are redis-covering their ancient customs and the sounds of the past. Each group of performers represents a unique village or area, each set of costumes is different, and the instruments also vary slightly, making for a very expressive event. Courses of music and dance are also organized for an ever-growing number of enthusiasts.

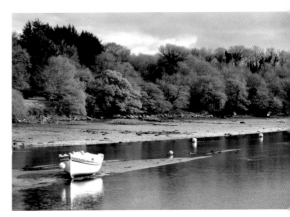

left
A folk group takes part in a traditional Celtic dance.

A boat beached at low tide.

The facade of an old inn is graced with a traditional sign.

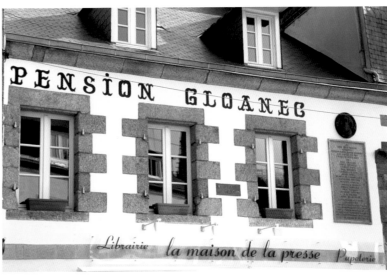

QUIMPER
A CONFLUENCE OF CULTURES

MAX JACOB'S OBSERVATION THAT QUIMPER IS "MORE BRETON than any other Breton town" remains true to this day. A writer, painter, and friend of Paul Éluard and Jean Cocteau, Jacob died in Drancy after the Nazi deportation, but his hometown infused all his creative work. The name Quimper comes from the Breton word *kemper*, meaning "confluence," and the town stands at the convergence of the Steir and Odet rivers, whose lively banks have flower-decorated footbridges crossing the water, imparting a singular, graceful air. The protruding facades of the houses in rue Kéréon and rue des Boucheries are lined with slate, and historic trades have left their mark. Construction of the cathedral of Saint-Corentin began in 1239, making it one of the oldest in Brittany, and its elegant, lacelike towers have a unique beauty. Secret passages can be found along the narrow streets of the old city and lead to picturesque wooden houses. Quimper is the historical and economic capital of the Cornouaille, a historic region in Brittany, and is particularly famous for its medieval heritage and ceramics. A regional museum of Brittany is housed in the sixteenth-century bishop's palace and boasts important collections of popular arts, embroidery, traditional Breton costumes and furniture, as well as some very beautiful pieces in ceramic and *grès*, the local stoneware. The Musée des Beaux-Arts holds works by French painters of the Pont-Aven School, many Italian, Dutch, and Flemish painters, and a room dedicated to Jacob.

The ceramics of Quimper are known all over the world, and have been closely linked to the town and its fortune for more than three centuries. In 1699 Jean-Baptiste Bousquet, a ceramist from Provence, moved to Quimper and created the first Breton ceramics. The craft's true success, however, arrived in the twentieth century, when a group of artists began to revitalize the decorative repertory of ceramic objects by combining modern styles with the Breton tradition. Among the more distinguished personalities are Alfred Beau, photographer, painter, and illustrator; François Bazin, sculptor; and the ceramic painters Paul Fouillen and Mathurin Méheut. One of Méheut's dish sets sold at auction for 80,000 euros recently. The most beautiful ceramics are produced at HB Henriot, a company that has handed down the famous tradition of the "brush stroke," referring to a freestyle decoration accompanied by the artist's signature. In July the lively festival of Cornouaille takes place at Quimper and includes ten days of concerts, *fest-noz* (a night festival of traditional dances), and processions.

The sun shimmers upon Quimper's ancient cobblestones.

Max Jacob was born in Quimper on July 11, 1876. He lived here through his formative years, and later in life brought his Surrealist friends to the Café de l'Epée. The Musée des Beaux-Arts has dedicated a room to him where the visitor can find mementos, a portrait of Jean Cocteau, and photographs of Jacob with Picasso, whom he had befriended during his first show in Paris at the Vollard gallery in 1901. Jacob also knew André Salmon, Apollinaire, Braque, and Modigliani. At the Bateau Lavoir in Paris he rented the old studio belonging to André Salmon and Pierre Mac Orlan. Picasso illustrated his *Saint-Mathorel* text with Cubist etchings, and *Le cornet à dés* and *Ruffian toujours, truand jamais* were other pieces he published. According to Paul Éluard, "He is not a great poet: he is simply, and in the full meaning of the word, a true poet." Despite this, none of his great artist friends, some of whom were very influential, could save him from death during the 1944 Nazi occupation.

The Breton bowl—a round and colorful ceramic with two large earlike handles—is traditionally offered as a gift at birth or baptism. For seventy years it has decorated the tables of Brittany and the world, and although it is not one of the best pieces, it is most certainly one of the most recognizable and charming. The Faïencerie HB Henriot produces beautiful plates and large soup bowls that are always in fashion. It is impossible to resist the temptation to buy the typical red or blue striped fisherman's sweater from Armor-Lux, or the fresh produce, hand-processed meats, and other regional specialties at the town's *grande halle* on market days.

facing page
The Gothic cathedral rises among the half-timbered houses of rue Kéréon.

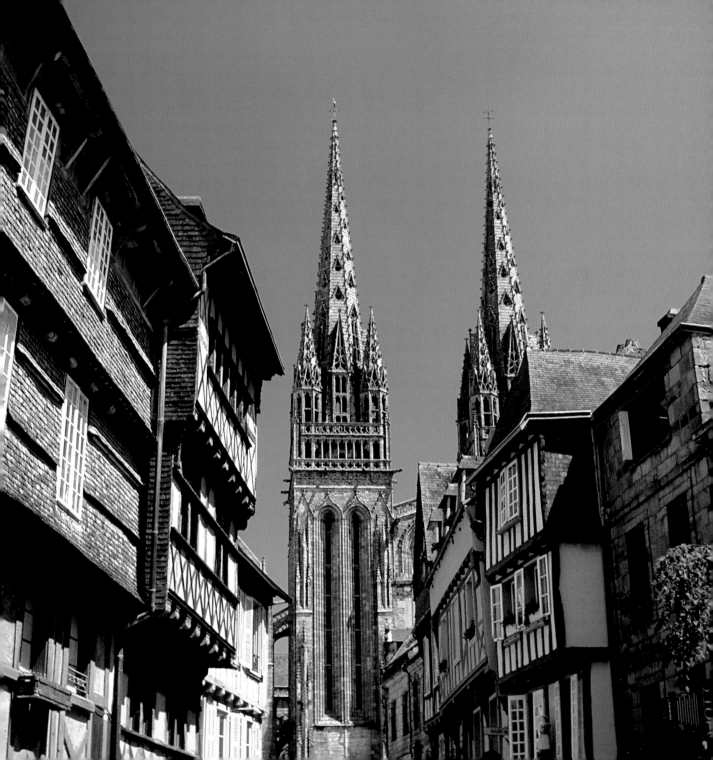

SAINT-MALO
ETERNAL RESISTANCE

THE SMOKE OF CANNONS, SWIFTLY LAUNCHED GRAPPLING HOOKS, a brandished sword, and a dagger between the teeth—this is the scene that comes to mind upon hearing the word "corsair." The history behind this word is still alive in Saint-Malo, and the city resounds with the enterprises of these adventurers. Business and commerce had encouraged the people of Saint-Malo to outfit their ships to trade all over the world. Their success

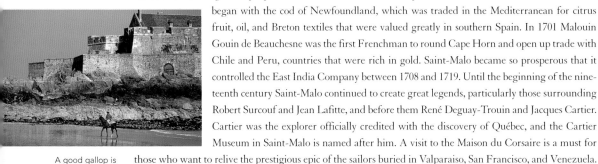

began with the cod of Newfoundland, which was traded in the Mediterranean for citrus fruit, oil, and Breton textiles that were valued greatly in southern Spain. In 1701 Malouin Gouin de Beauchesne was the first Frenchman to round Cape Horn and open up trade with Chile and Peru, countries that were rich in gold. Saint-Malo became so prosperous that it controlled the East India Company between 1708 and 1719. Until the beginning of the nineteenth century Saint-Malo continued to create great legends, particularly those surrounding Robert Surcouf and Jean Lafitte, and before them René Deguay-Trouin and Jacques Cartier. Cartier was the explorer officially credited with the discovery of Québec, and the Cartier Museum in Saint-Malo is named after him. A visit to the Maison du Corsaire is a must for those who want to relive the prestigious epic of the sailors buried in Valparaiso, San Francisco, and Venezuela.

A good gallop is the best way to discover the beaches of Saint-Malo.

facing page
A vertiginous view over the cathedral of Saint-Vincent.

This town of corsairs contains more than one legend. The curious story of 1590 quickly became history: Catholic Saint-Malo refused to recognize the Protestant Henry IV as king of France, and therefore proclaimed its independence; the republic lasted four years. Today Saint-Malo is a world closed unto itself, and its paved streets are walked by many tourists. There is a collection of lively cafés, small and large restaurants, and beautiful residences that attest to its glorious past. The bombardments of World War II destroyed Saint-Malo, but it has been rebuilt almost exactly as it was. The historical patrimony of the town is considerable, including the White Hotel, the house of Duchess Anne, the rue de Pie-qui-Boit, and the cathedral of Saint-Vincent. Visitors have the impression of being totally immersed in an unchanged past, especially when admiring the sunset from the ramparts, when crossing the walls to reach the plage du Mole, the most *malouine* (typical of Saint-Malo) of the beaches, or when gazing at the silhouette of the fortified city from the plage du Sillon. The quiet beaches to the

Seafood is important everywhere, but the Bar de l'Univers in place Chateaubriand is the best place for tasting the local delicacies. It boasts marine decorations in wood, and etchings, drawings, and photographs cover the walls and invoke the waves, salt, and rich history all around. It is a most eclectic meeting place where one can meet genuine Malouins, visiting intellectuals, and authors invited to the Festival des Étonnants Voyageurs, who share their love of the sea.

After the fall of Constantinople in 1453 the new Ottoman Empire imposed very high tariffs for crossing its borders to reach Asia, causing the Western powers to search out alternative routes. In 1492 Columbus discovered America for the Spanish crown, and in 1498 a Portuguese expedition commanded by Vasco da Gama reached India by circumnavigating Africa. The French King Francis I chose Jacques Cartier to travel toward the New World, and charged him with discovering new lands and a navigable passage to China. In 1534 Cartier discovered Canada, later returned twice, and died of the plague in 1557 near Saint-Malo.

south of the town and along the coast toward the northeast are splendid. Here the variations in the level of the sea are among the highest in the world; the water can rise up to nearly forty feet. The Fort du Petit Bé is where Chateaubriand is buried, and can be reached on foot at low tide. Saint-Malo is known for its cartoon festival, the Quai des Bulles, and for the literary festival, Étonnants Voyageurs. The regattas of the Route del Rhum and the transoceanic race from Québec to Saint-Malo are also a key part of life here.

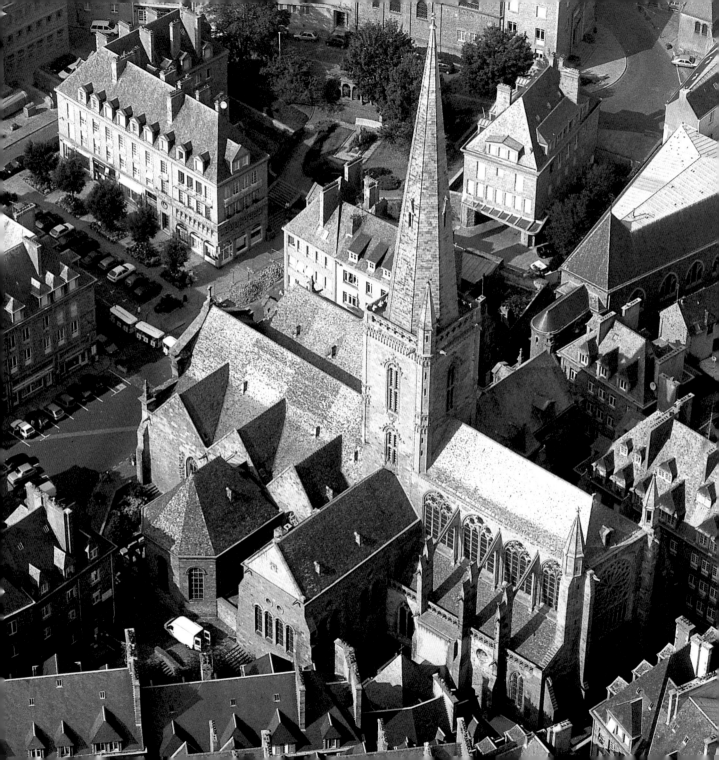

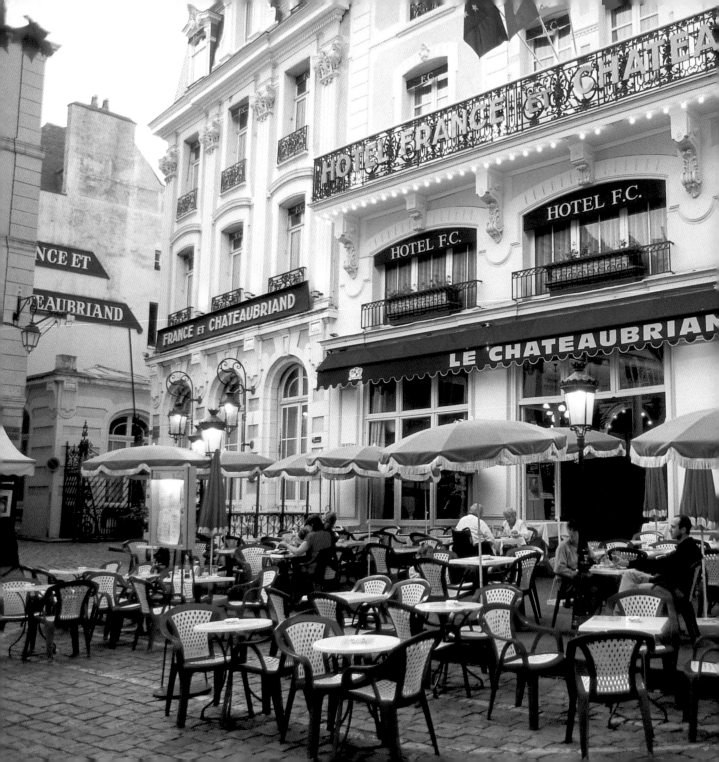

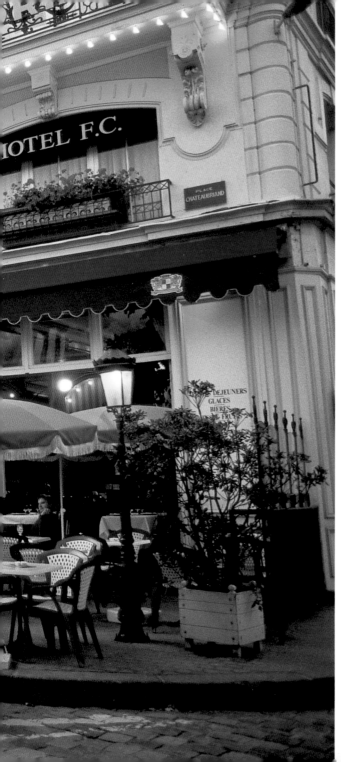

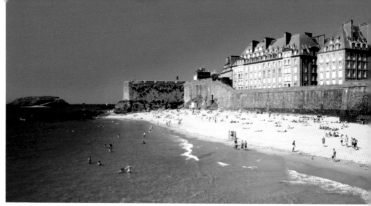

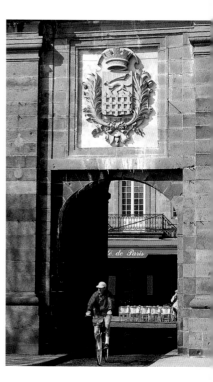

above
Du Mole beach is contoured by the historic town walls.

right
The Saint-Vincent gateway.

At the end of the seventeenth century, after they had made their fortunes with raids in the southern seas, the Malouin corsairs and ship owners wanted to have their social position recognized by living in a comfortable place at the gateway to the city. Here they built their splendid residences—great houses with thick, high walls, symmetrical architecture, and delightful interiors. There are more than a hundred of these houses; among them, the first and most easily recognized is Limoëlou, which belonged to Jacques Cartier. The Château de la Ville-Bague at Saint-Coulomb, built between the seventeenth and eighteenth centuries, is also well worth a visit. Additionally, the Chipaudière at Paramé, called the "house of pleasure," the Picaudais at Saint-Père-Marc-en-Poulet, and the Malouinière du Bos, along the Route de la Passagère at Quelmer, should be seen.

The best way to savor Saint-Malo's magic atmosphere is at an outdoor café in the center of town.

AMBOISE
VALIANTLY VALOIS

THE VIEW OVER THE LOIRE FROM THE HIGH BALCONY OF THE AMBOISE castle is stunning. It was one of the favorite places of the Valois kings—from Charles VIII to Louis XII and Francis I—who dreamt of conquering the Kingdom of Naples or the Dukedom of Milan. It was also a favorite of Henry II, who dreamt of art and beauty. Close ties between the Valois family and Italy's rulers influenced the castle's style, since Charlotte of Savoy was the mother of Charles VII, and Valentina Visconti, daughter of the Duke of Milan, was grandmother of Louis XII. Several sections of the building have been redesigned many times, and vary from a late Gothic style to a notable Renaissance style, hence Amboise is recognized as the cradle of the French Renaissance. Humanism was spread by Italian engineers and men of letters—among them, of course, Leonardo da Vinci—who also influenced the style of the castles of Blois, Chenonceau, Chambord, and Azay-le-Rideau.

Each king made his own changes to Amboise. Francis I altered it radically, while Henry II brought to it the Italian art of living. The castle's salons are decorated with paintings, sculpture, and tapestries with mythological themes. Trompe l'oeil paintings are ubiquitous, even outside, where the pleasure of perspective can be seen in the green arches on the banks of the Loire that perfectly highlight the view. The Mediterranean-style panoramic gardens are rich with flourishing vegetation and full of plants imported from Italy, including sage, rosemary, melons, artichokes, roses, violets, and carnations. The castle is furnished in an avant-garde taste, with sideboards, dressers, decorated columns, tables prepared in the Italian style with classic two-pronged forks, and enormous beds. During the summer evenings Renaissance festivals recall the magnificence of the past with prestigious theatrical events. Among the most interesting is the show about da Vinci, who lived the last three years of his life at the country house of Clos Luce. Nearby is a park of miniature castles, with reproductions of almost all the country's key castles—from the Loire to the Cher, from the Indre to the medieval city of Loche, from Montpoupon and Valençay to Chenonceau—represented to a scale of 1:25, including the gardens, creating a veritable Tour de France. Not far from Amboise is the ancient estate of the Duke of Choiseul, and visitors must not forget to visit the Pagoda of Chanteloup, a bizarre tower and an eighteenth-century *chinoiserie* remnant in the heart of a beautiful forest.

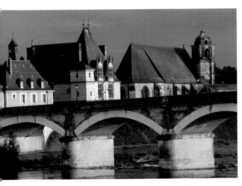

The bridge across the Loire and the Hôtel de Ville.

facing page
The castle reflected in the nighttime waters of the Loire.

The famous *tarte Tatin* was invented more than a hundred years ago when one of the Tatin sisters decided to add apples to her dough, and since 1913 the Bigot confectionery has passed the original recipe from mother to daughter. Their vodka truffles are exquisite, as are the *amboisinoises* (candied almonds created by Marc de Touraine), and the sorbets. Everything here is homemade with loving care, and is uniquely delicious.

Leonardo da Vinci came to Amboise in 1516, at the invitation of the king of France, and brought with him three paintings, the *Mona Lisa*, *St. Anne with the Madonna and Child*, and *St. John the Baptist*. He finished them in the country house at Clos Luce, which was a gift from Francis I so that he could feel free to "think, dream, and work." Da Vinci was a counselor to the king, a military engineer, and also organized many memorable feasts for his enlightened patron, who wanted to introduce as many innovative extravagances to his court as possible. It is very interesting to visit the country house that contains his works, texts, and scale models of inventions including sluice dams, tanks, and helicopters. Some of his inventions are reproduced to scale. Da Vinci died in 1519 and is buried in the chapel of Saint-Hubert in the castle of Amboise.

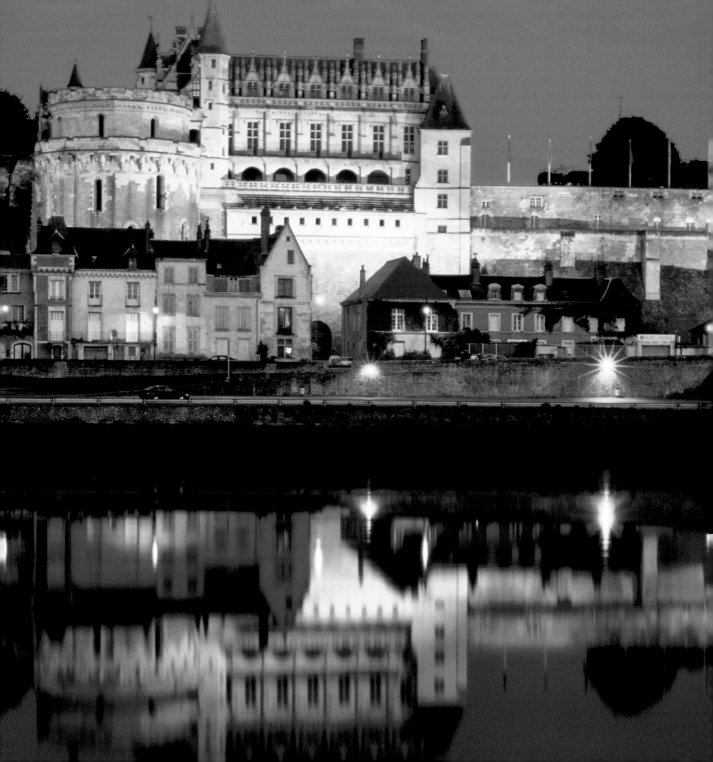

BOURGES
LIGHT NIGHTS

THE CATHEDRAL, JACQUES COEUR MANSION, AND EXCEPTIONALLY well-preserved wooden houses in the historic center are the jewels of Bourges. In 1100 the city was part of the Capet family's domain, but developed more rapidly in the fifteenth century under the arts patronage of the Duke of Berry and the auspices of King Charles VII and his sulfurous finance minister, Jacques Coeur. His former mansion, a marvelous Gothic building, was the model of modernity of that era. The Saint-Étienne cathedral, innovative in its use of buttresses and the exquisite counterforts that sustain the weight of the vault and the intersection of the arches, is among the most illustrious examples of the French Gothic style. Although its shape resembles that of a centipede, the majestic building, more than eight centuries old, is still noteworthy for its uniformity and liveliness. In the interior everything revolves around the number five: five naves, five beautiful chapels, a monumental portal with five doors, five floors, and stained-glass windows that reveal all the techniques spanning the five centuries from 1300 to 1800. These windows represent morality lessons, allegories, arts and letters, and the mystical spiritualism of the Holy Scriptures.

The old part of Bourges is a delightful labyrinth of typical narrow medieval streets. A walk along these lanes reveals the lovely facade of Hôtel Lallemant, which has become a museum for the decorative arts and contains many rare treasures, including clockwork mechanisms and a small private chapel with a vaulted ceiling and recessed panels decorated with winged cherubs. The whole museum is enjoyable, including the sculpted details in the internal courtyard. The Musée Maurice Estève is not far away. Estève was a local artist who worked during the second half of the twentieth century, inspired by Cubism and Fauvism, and influenced by Magritte and Bonnard. The nearby museum of the Rural School is picturesque and very small; here visitors breathe in a unique scholastic atmosphere—the smells of wax, ink, old books, the blackboard, and quill pens—and can even take a pen-and-ink calligraphy course. The marshes of Bourges are a surprising, unexpected stretch of 333 acres of private and vegetable gardens crossed by canals. The Prés Fichaux garden of the 1920s is also fascinating, and is listed as a historical monument.

Each year in April the Printemps de Bourges, a famous French music festival begun in 1977, takes place. Many new musical trends are discovered at the festival, from fusion to techno to rock. Between May and September the Nuits Lumière, magical processions, begin at dusk. Blue lights mark the route beginning at the ancient walls, continuing around the bishop's garden, winding around the cathedral, and culminating in a cloister where Monteverdi's Vespers echo in the air.

The cathedral of Noirlac is roughly eighty miles from Bourges, and is one of the most beautiful Cistercian monasteries in France for its coherence, equilibrium, and rigor. Standing in front of a procession of 200-year-old linden trees, the central nave appears in all its sparse medieval splendor; everything here is characterized by straight lines and moral rigor. The windows added in 1977 are nearly white, and are the work of Jean Pierre Raynaud, an artist known for his flower vases and white ceramics. Their style and pale colors are in complete keeping with the Cistercian style, and the natural light filtering through them evokes the light of God and interior clarity. The various convent buildings, cloister, chapter hall, refectory, and dormitory are spectacular. Concerts are often held within, and the experience is one of pure joy. The summer festival of Noirlac, dedicated to the vocal arts, has become very famous.

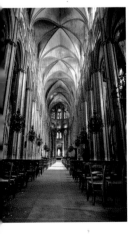

facing page
The superb facade of Saint-Étienne, a cathedral named a World Heritage site in 1992.

The interior of the cathedral is divided into five naves with light filtering through the soaring windows.

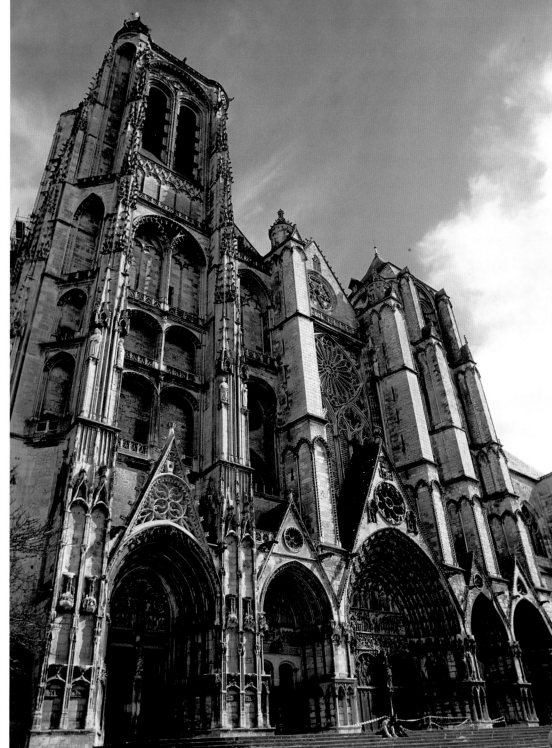

The *Forestine* is a
crunchy sweetmeat
filled with a praline
of almonds, peanuts,
and chocolate.
Invented in 1879, it
was the first soft-
centered candy, and
the responsible
party for this
exquisitely sinful
sweet was Georges
Forest, who came to
Bourges in 1884.
The Maison des
Forestines offers the
master confec-
tioner's specialties,
and can be admired
for its inlaid paneled
ceiling in the
nineteenth-century
turquoise ceramic of
Gien. Everything is
made on the
premises, and
connoisseurs can
taste Monin syrups
and *sable* (short-
bread) biscuits from
the marshes of
Bourges.

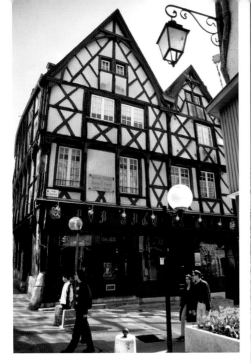

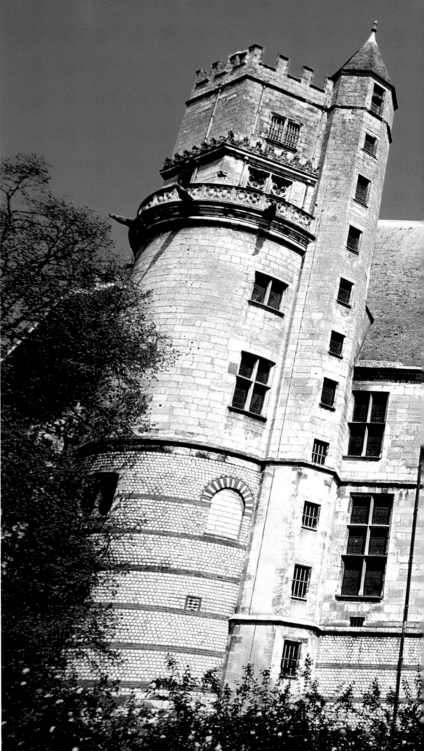

After three decades the Printemps de Bourges (Springtime in Bourges) has become one of the largest music festivals in France. Enthusiasts of contemporary song gather together in April for a week of all kinds of music, including world music, fusion, electronica, hip-hop, and rock. Unknown artists arrive from around the world, and both music critics and the public come to discover the young talent of tomorrow. Every year about 150 artists take part in concerts throughout the city. Shows begin every day around noon, and continue until dawn. There is something for everyone—for enthusiasts of light music or classical music, as well as for young people on the lookout for new sounds. Singer-songwriters and pop musicians perform, and the local trends in gypsy guitar music can be heard. The public's enthusiasm is so great that they look forward to the date with great anticipation. There are also some very original concerts in the surrounding countryside, with brunch and wine tastings for the many organized groups that make a special excursion by bus. The Printemps de Bourges is a truly special occasion.

above
The birthplace of Jacques Coeur, minister of finance under Charles VII.

right
Jacques Coeur's palace is a marvelous example of local Gothic architecture.

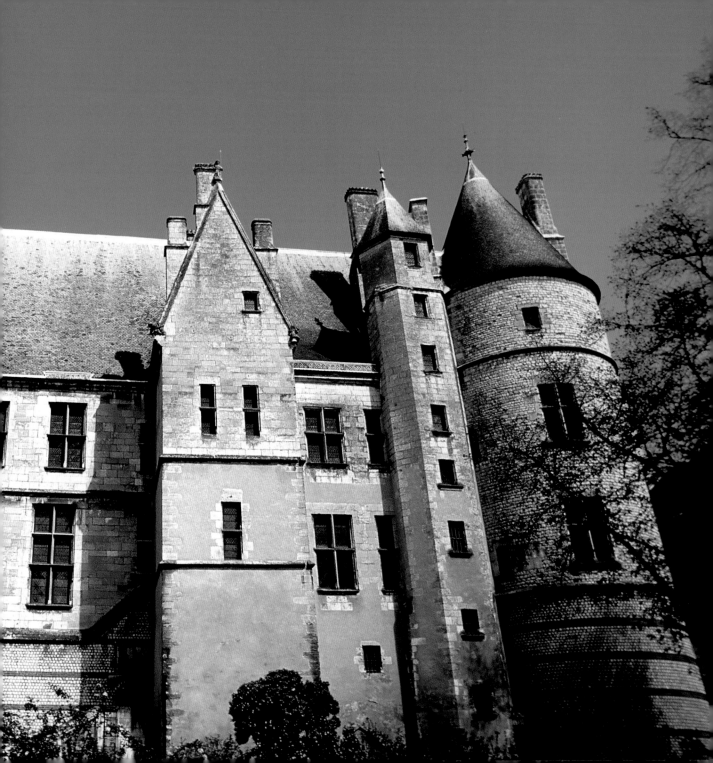

CHARTRES
STORIES IN STAINED GLASS

FROM ALMOST TEN MILES AWAY THE TWO TOWERS OF NOTRE DAME DE CHARTRES begin to appear above the flat, fertile, grain-cultivating land of Beauce. They rise up to the sky like arrows, one Romanesque, the other a flamboyant Gothic. The cathedral itself was built on the place where a Druidic temple once stood, dating back to 800 AD. The cathedral of Notre-Dame was built by the Cistercian monks, and is one of the major masterpieces of Gothic architecture, finely wrought in every detail. The towers have survived the Middle Ages and several fires, and are today a symbol of stylistic perfection. The crypt is the largest in France, and the thirteenth-century stained-glass windows are the finest, most complete, and unparalleled testaments to the life and faith of the Middle Ages. The brilliance and artistic value of the master glassmakers of Chartres have led to the creation, over the course of centuries, of the famous Centre international du vitrail located in Enclow de Loëns, which contains a vast collection of ancient and modern stained glass. Local workshops offer the creations of master glassmakers who keep this centuries-old art alive.

A stroll around Chartres will enable you to get lost in the winding streets, and to come across some real architectural treasures, such as the Queen Berthe tower with its stairway and columns, the fourteenth-century Boujou bridge, where the remains of an ancient watering trough can still be seen, and the multicolored nave of the church of Saint-Aignan, rebuilt at the beginning of the Belle Époque. Taking the narrow steps down to the medieval washbasins on the banks of the Eure River is a balancing act between the lower part of Chartres and the upper town, perched on the foundations of the historic town. The steps used to be called "the slippery ground of prostitutes," and they are still very steep and rather dangerous. One of the paths leads from the Saint-André college to the gardens of the bishop's palace, which is also the home of the Musée des Beaux-Arts, where an important collection of paintings by Maurice Vlaminck and Chaïm Soutine are held. The museum gardens overlook the valley, and to the south one can see glimmering fragments of the porcelain, glass, and ceramics of Maison Picassiette, the strange house of an artist. It was decorated entirely with colorful mosaics in 1938, and is a jewel of Art Brut, reminiscent of Gaudì. The towers of the cathedral of Notre-Dame carefully protect the blaze of the stained-glass windows and watch over the omnipresent light and the miracle of its colors. Chartres shows its best self in the summer, when the high medieval walls are laden with the history of France in images and photographs, and nightly walks by torchlight are organized, and in September when the Festival of Light is celebrated.

The cathedral of Notre-Dame.

facing page
Detail of one of the elaborate cathedral windows.

The stained-glass windows of the cathedral of Chartres are unique and unequalled in beauty and perfection. The 3,889 images are distributed over 197 windows, two-thirds of which date back to the construction of the building around 1220. The majority of the windows are donations from various kings of France and their families—the northern rose window was donated by Blanche of Castille—but the great lords also contributed, as did the confraternities of leather merchants, shoemakers, and stonemasons. The images represent scenes from the Bible or historic episodes, such as the scenes of Charlemagne at Aix La Chapelle, and his battles against the Saracens. Through these images a visit to Chartres can provide an account of the daily life of the people, and one can read the great history of France and that of the patron saints of the local guilds, a truly unique marvel.

One could kill for a good pâté—particularly for this one. It seems that the origin of the pâté of Chartres dates back to the reign of Louis XIV, and since then all the great chefs have had to prove themselves with this challenging recipe. Under a thick crust, a gelatin, and a very liquid savory jam lies a pâté of goose, duck, veal, or very spicy pork with a heart of foie gras, and sometimes covered with a sprinkling of truffle. It is the best local delicacy, and some restaurants in Chartres offer it on their menu. The Grand Monarque is one such restaurant, and is famous for its rich, traditional cuisine served in an ancient eighteenth-century *relais de Poste*. Here the chef carries on the tradition of dishes that are a monument to the French palate, fortunately not following the modern fad for light fare.

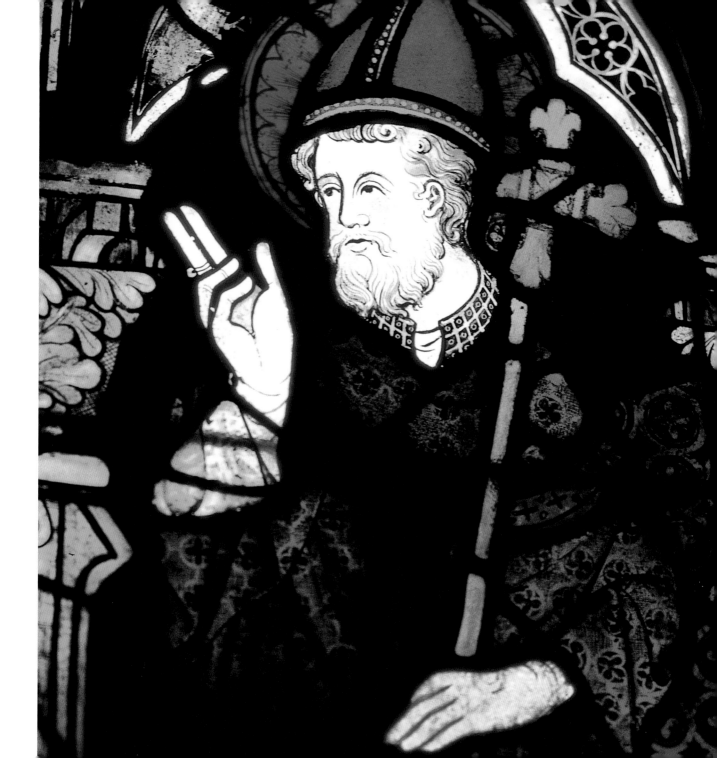

CHINON
RABELAIS AND RED WINE

CHINON AND ITS MEDIEVAL FORTRESS JEALOUSLY PROTECT THEIR MYTHIC HISTORY and their ambrosia wine. The vineyards of Cabernet Franc smell of wild strawberries and violet, and adding to the town's draw is the great history made by Rabelais, Cesare Borgia, and John Lackland (King John), the enigmatic brother of Richard the Lionheart. Only a romantic ruin of the fortress remains, clinging to its old golden promontory and lit by the rays of the setting sun over the nearby Vienne River.

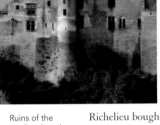

Ruins of the medieval castle still seem to rise in defense of the city.

facing page
Chinon wine aging in barrels.

The Plantagenet king of England, Henry II, died at Chinon in 1189. His son, John Lackland, seized the scepter and reignited the perennial wars between France and England, capturing Isabelle d'Angoulême and marrying her here. In 1427 Charles VII transferred his court to Chinon and continued to fight the English. One day he met a young country girl in his castle; her name was Joan of Arc, and she promised him the crown of France. In 1498 Louis XII was seeking an alliance with the pope, Cesare Borgia, the cruel and clever character who would later inspire Machiavelli to write *The Prince*. Borgia authorized the king to proceed with a second marriage (his first wife was dismissed as lame and unattractive) to Anne of Brittany, and he then acceded to the throne of France. When Cardinal Richelieu bought back the castle, in the seventeenth century, the fortress was dismantled. The violent winds and blood feuds of history have blown within and all around these thick walls, which remain most impressive, with 1,600 feet of facade, three autonomously fortified buildings once separated by a moat, the fortress of Saint Georges, the Milieu (Middle) castle, and the keep of Coudray, whose foundations date back to the twelfth century. The old Marie-Javelle bell has rung in the hours since 1399. The dull and powerful sound slips down to the old part of Chinon, which is characterized by the familiar labyrinth of pointed roofs, winding narrow streets, and sloping neighborhoods. There are still many fascinating dovecote houses, silent and timeless as though they have been lost in a medieval magic. The most beautiful of them are along rue Voltaire and around the Grand Carroi. The Governor Hôtel is interesting, as is the Hôtel des Etats Généreaux and the fourteenth-century Red House, with its sinuously curved two floors and protruding balconies. The blood of the earth, that blood of life, that divine land that saw the birth of Rabelais, son and God of Chinon, also remains to this day. His hero was pleasure-loving Gargantua, who was thirsty for knowledge and wine. This wine, protagonist of the Rabelaisian festivals of Chinon, still turns the heads of many a drinker.

Chinon is a red wine that, depending on its vintage, must be kept in the cellar for a long time, and is drunk starting at Easter. The rosés are delicate and very fruity, while the whites, on the other hand, have a more floral fragrance. Many vineyards offer tastings and bottles for sale, and the local wine fair takes place each April.

François Rabelais, son of a Chinon lawyer, was born around 1494 at La Devinière. He spent his childhood at Chinon and then entered the monastery of Fontenay le Comte and became a monk around 1520. There he was passionate about Greek, and was a great humanist who met with the great minds of the era. He became a Benedictine, took the habit of a secular priest in order to enter the university, became a doctor, and then, in Lyon, had two children. He published *Pantagruel* in 1532 under the anagrammed pseudonym of Alcofribas Nasier, and published *Gargantua* in 1534. The enthronement of the confraternity of the Rabelaisian Bon Entonneurs (Good Drinkers) takes place at the Caves Painctes of Chinon, where Pantagruel drank his fill. Four great dinners are organized every year following Rabelais's *art de vivre*; these are so popular that participation is by reservation only.

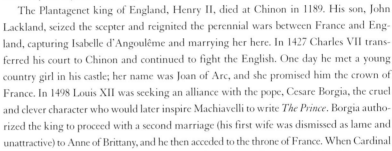

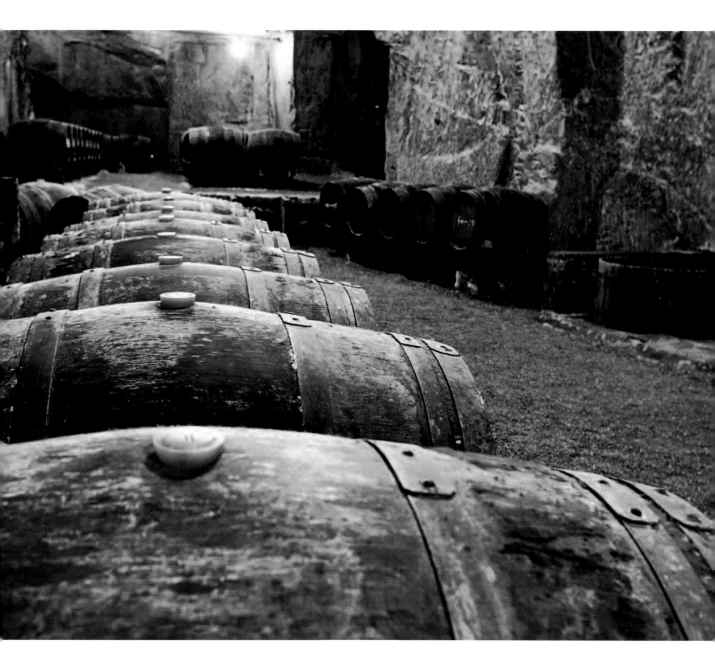

GIEN
FAMOUS FAÏENCE

ENTRENCHED BETWEEN THE RICH HUNTING COUNTRY OF THE SOLOGNE and the beautiful Orléans forest, Gien could not have been better situated for the prestigious Musée Internationale de la Chasse (Hunting Museum). The collection is enormous, with more than 3,000 objects and works of art that illustrate the evolution of techniques, hunting customs, and the very interesting history of royal falconry. There are weapons

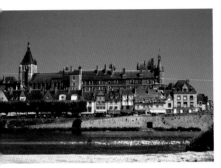

The castle houses the Hunting Museum within its beautiful brick walls.

facing page
The ancient bridge over the Loire.

with precious inscriptions, thousands of hunting horns, and the personal trophies of the great hunter Hettier de Boislambert. The magnificently restored attics contain a great collection of the painter Alexandre-François Desportes, the official portrait painter of the Polish court. The jewel box that houses this precious collection is in the castle of Gien, a stronghold made of bricks, covered with roofs of slate, and decorated with a few turrets. In the thirteenth century it was the property of the crown, and during the course of history its role has placed it among the great French monuments. It was Saint Louis who built the first stone bridge of Gien, which Joan of Arc passed through and stayed at before she went to Reims for the coronation of Charles VII. Anne de Beaujeu, daughter of Louis XI and the countess of Gien, assumed the regency upon the death of her father, and in 1484 built the castle. It was here that Francis I signed the act conferring the regency on Louise de Savoie (1523) during his Italian expedition. Henry II, Catherine de Medici, and Charles IX sought refuge here during the wars of religion, and later so did Anne of Austria, Mazarin, and Louis XIV. However, Gien has not only been the scene of tormented historical events. The small, harmonious town, at the edge of the circle of the Loire castles, is universally known for its ceramics. The Musée de la Faïencerie is dedicated to the art of faïence. The area is rich with clay, sand, wood, and water. Englishman Thomas Hall founded the Faïencerie of Gien in 1821, and introduced the English tradition to France. Today the Faïencerie of Gien exports to more than thirty countries and is part of the prestigious Colbert committee that includes the most representative French luxury companies. Inside the museum there are pieces made for the Universal Exposition of 1900, such as the clock-candelabra that can be seen from the entrance. The

Alexandre-François Desportes (1661–1743) was a pupil of the Flemish painter Nacasius Bernaerts, from whom he learned the art of painting animals. At the age of thirty-four he became the official portraitist at the Polish court, and when King Louis XIV called him home, the artist began to specialize in animal painting. The international Hunting Museum of Gien has housed his largest collection since 1952, thanks to the donation of the National Factories of Sèvres. In 1699 he was admitted to the French Royal Academy of Painting, and this bequest is composed essentially of studies from the artist's studio.

miniatures are an attraction for children as well as adults; among them is a splendid reproduction of a nineteenth-century dining room that can be held in the palm of a hand. The old ceramic bricks of the French métro come from Gien. The old city was reconstructed and well restored after World War II, and looks over a cliff onto the ever-flowing River of Kings at the foot of the lozenge-shaped bricks. *Sic transit Gloria mundi.*

The fame of the Faïencerie of Gien is due to masterly ability added to the combined talents of artisanry and industrial production, thereby mixing tradition and creation. After a visit to the museum at Gien there is nothing left but to go into one of the many shops and give yourself a present—a classical set of dishes or plates inspired by the Delftware and Rouen–style decorations, a decorative object, or a reproduction of an antique model, or maybe a piece from the numbered collection. Do not forget that you can also find very interesting and rare pieces in the secondhand department.

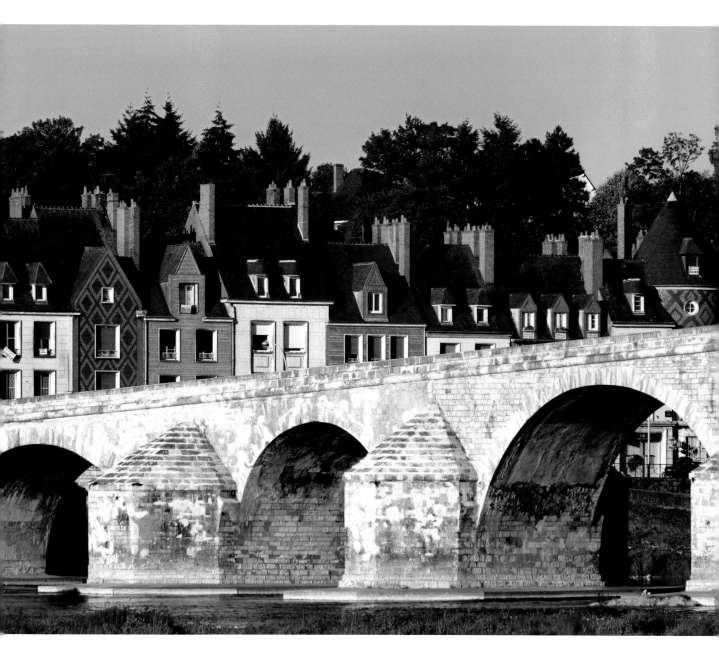

LOCHES

THE LADIES OF THE LOGIS ROYAL

THIS LITTLE MEDIEVAL TOWN, TUCKED AROUND THE REMAINS of its twelfth-century ramparts, dominates the fascinating Indre River valley. The town revives its great past in the gaiety of its summer evenings and bustling market days featuring local produce during the "Nocturnal Phantasmagories" and "Moonlight Markets," two local traditions very worth a visit.

Loches was a powerful military fortress adapted to become a royal residence, and is protected by three rows of reinforced walls. The portal of Cordeliers, which protects the eastern approach to the city with two drawbridges; some splendid mansions; the ancient bell tower of Saint-Antoine; and the houses of tufa stone, a material traditionally used in the Touraine area to build castles, are all well preserved. The 130-foot feudal fortress is particularly impressive, and within it the medieval town, the keep, the church of Saint-Oure, with three tenth-century chapels in the apse, and the thirteenth- to fourteenth-century castle of Charles VII, also known as the Logis Royal, await the visitor's discovery. Three illustrious women—Joan of Arc, Anne of Brittany, wife of Charles VII, and Agnès Sorel, the king's favorite known as the Lady of Beauty—have marked the Logis Royal's history. Several treasures are witness to their influence: the splendid Gothic style of the queen's private chapel, the sepulchral statue of Agnès Sorel sculpted in luminous alabaster in the magnificent triptych by the school of Jean Fouquet, and the room that housed the young Maid of Orléans. When the English occupied France at the beginning of the fifteenth century, and before their surrender, the king was known as the dauphin, or "King of Bourges." In 1429 Loches was the meeting place between Joan of Arc and the future King Charles VII, and it was here that she heard the famous voices and received encouragement to proceed to Reims for the coronation. The town is also proud of the presence of Agnès Sorel, a lady who wore trains twenty-six feet long and invented the *décolleté* dress, a low-cut style that scandalized many and seduced many more. The king officially accepted her at court in 1445, when she nominated her friend Jacques Coeur her counselor (it was this "friend" who was later responsible for her death by poisoning) and encouraged Charles VII to continue the war against the English.

Many underground passages and cells under the ramparts remain intact. Louis XI and Louis XII both made use of them to lock up enemies and traitors, including Cardinal Jean Balue and Ludovico Sforza, Duke of Milan. Sforza quite understandably scratched the words "he who is not content" on the walls of his cell, but today's visitors to Loches will carry away some very different and happier memories thanks to the town's gentle beauty.

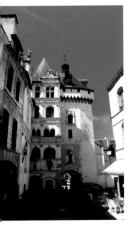

facing page
An aerial view of the Logis Royal, castle of Charles VII.

The Hôtel de Ville and Porte Pigois.

Joan of Arc (1412–1431) is the ultimate French heroine. According to legend she heard voices at the age of thirteen ordering her to free France from the English. On February 23, 1429, she went to Charles VII in Chinon and convinced him to put her at the head of an army. She tore Orléans away from the English on May 8, 1429, and continued her conquests. After the coronation of Charles VII at Reims she was showered with noble titles at Mehun-sur-Yèvre, but she was defeated at the gates of Paris and imprisoned by Burgundian officers who delivered her to the English. The ungrateful Charles VII abandoned her, and she died at the stake in Rouen. She was rehabilitated in 1456 and canonized in 1920.

The history of the castle of d'Artigny in Montbazon is worth telling. This imposing building escaped ruin in the Hundred Years' War, and in 1912 was bought by French perfumer François Coty. He demolished and completely rebuilt it in pure eighteenth-century style. After his death, in 1934, the castle was confiscated at the request of his many creditors, occupied by French naval staff, and taken by German troops until 1942, when it became a hospital. Today it is a luxury hotel that has hosted important figures including the Queen Mother of England and the Negus of Ethiopia. In 1973 the ministers of finance of the five world powers and members of the International Monetary Fund met here. The atmosphere is unconventional, the cuisine is very refined, and the wine cellar holds almost 20,000 bottles for wine lovers of all types.

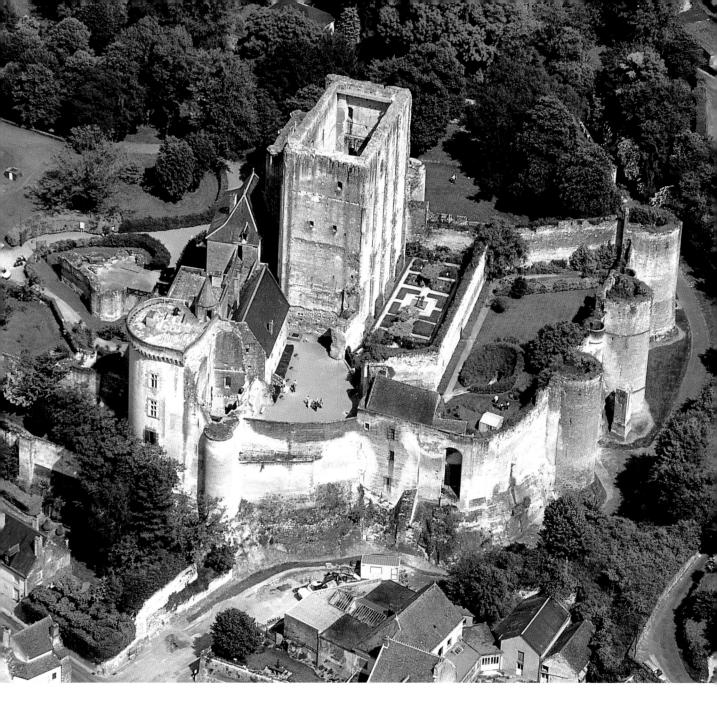

VENDÔME
BALZAC'S STUDY

VENDÔME COULD EASILY BE VIEWED AS A SORT OF SMALL VENICE, with its Porte d'Eau (water gate), bridges, round moss-covered stones, poplars in the wind, abandoned washhouses, and trembling willows on the banks of the Loire. The city owes its name to César de Vendôme, son of Henry IV and Gabrielle d'Estrées, to whom it was given by the king. During the Renaissance it was the center of the confraternity of glovemakers, who were famous all over Europe, and home to tanners, cobblers, and potters. Now film lovers come at the end of each year to the Film Festival of Vendôme. This is an important preview of many European theatrical films, documentaries, and new digital technologies.

The *petits jardins* of Vendôme can be admired during romantic boat rides between the Porte d'Eau and the Tour de l'Islette landmark tower. Old vegetable gardens have been transformed into flowering mosaics, and the apse of the abbey of Trinidad is immersed in a scented garden of damask roses, perfumed geraniums, mint, artemisia, and exotic plants such as licorice and vetiver. Inside the abbey, the Romanesque bell tower is noteworthy, as is the nave, with its fourteenth-century windows, grinning animal masks on the column capitals, and the twelfth-century frescoes in the chapter hall. The Sainte Larme is a precious relic brought from Constantinople by Geoffroy Martel, a knight and Count of Anjou. This relic transformed the abbey into a center of pilgrimage until the French Revolution. Among the collections in the museum of Vendôme, which range from ancient archaeology to contemporary art, Marie Antoinette's harp is an important piece. Higher up, the castle's ramparts are dotted with towers and *machicoulis*—openings through which molten lead and other objects could be dropped on assailants below. The ramparts also enclose the ruins of the collegiate church of Saint-Georges and a park containing a 200-year-old cedar of Lebanon. Many *Vendômois*, citizens either by birth or adoption, have written histories of literature and war, including Marshal Rochambeau, who fought in the American Revolution, and Honoré de Balzac, the famous and troubled student of the college of the Oratoriens.

Today this campus is the municipal building, whose surrounding Ronsard park is a constant reminder of the prior and poet born here in 1524. Nearby stands the chapel of Saint-Jacques, which since the twelfth century has been a stopping place for pilgrims on their way to Santiago de Compostela, and now exhibits temporary shows. The ideal way to enjoy a peaceful visit is to travel by boat.

The Porte d'Eau.

facing page
Ronsard park surrounds the ancient college of the Oratoriens, which now houses the municipal building.

The colorful Poncé-sur-le-Loir is a few miles from Vendôme. Most important is the garden of its sixteenth-century castle, which is a maze of pergolas and symmetrical boxwood hedges. There is also the magic and transparent world of artistic glassmaker Gérard Torcheux, who has his studio here. With great respect for this centuries-old art, he creates unique pieces, lamps, and decorative objects in a rainbow of colors.

Honoré de Balzac (1799–1859) was a young student in Vendôme in 1807. He made himself hated, and got locked up as punishment, so that he could read and write in peace. There are some interesting anecdotes in his personal history, such as the fact that he could not ride a bicycle. Balzac could not stand the pranks of his fellow students, and his health began to suffer. In despair, his grandmother exclaimed, "This is how the college treats the children we entrust to them!" In his later writings Balzac recounts many whippings and obligatory confessions made here.

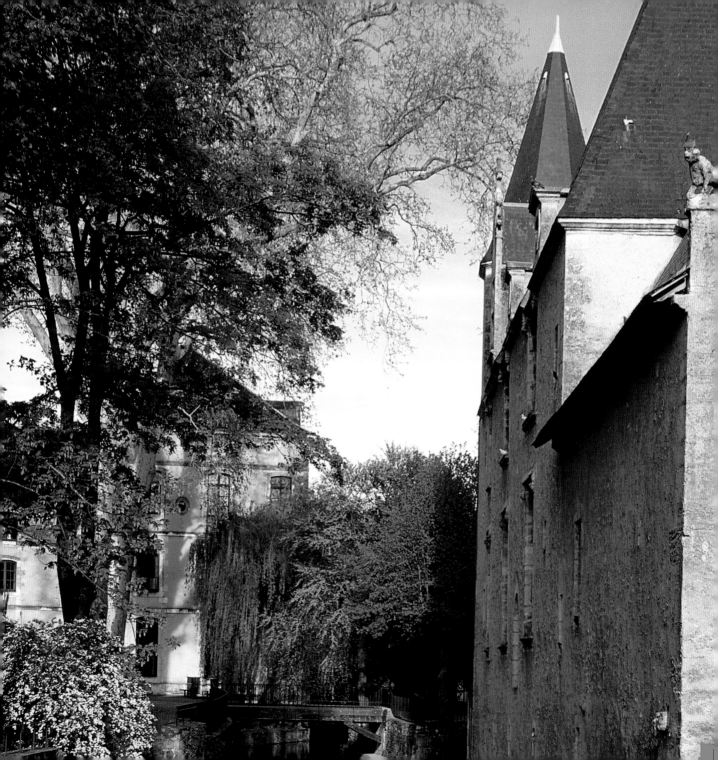

R E I M S
CHAMPAGNE'S SPARKLING HEART

IN THE SEVENTEENTH CENTURY MONK DOM PÈRIGNON STUDIED FERMENTATION and measured the dosage of wine necessary to create what was to become Champagne, Gold of the Marne. Beginning in 1728 the companies of Ruinart, Clicquot, and Heidsieck established this region's fame throughout Europe. The city of Reims, at the heart of Champagne, is so famous that the visitor does not even need to look for it on the map. All the kings of France were crowned here, in the cathedral of Notre-Dame, including Charles VII, who was accompanied by Joan of Arc. Reims is a city of flowers and many splendid monuments, most notably the elegant, perfectly proportioned, thirteenth-century cathedral. Aside from the original windows, a visit must be made to the newer windows of the apse, designed by Marc Chagall. The most enthusiastic visitors climb the 249 steps up the tower, where an extraordinary view awaits them. The Tau building contains the fabulous cathedral treasury, the golden chalice used for the Communion of Kings, the remains of the holy ampoule used for the baptism of Clovis in 496, and the splendid talisman of Charlemagne. The basilica and royal abbey of Saint-Remì are two World Heritage jewels. The basilica is a Romanesque construction, and the choir contains the tomb of Saint-Remì, the city's bishop and founder. The old abbey consists of two sumptuous buildings, built in the seventeenth and eighteenth centuries respectively, and contains a wonderful collection of Renaissance tapestries. The Musée des Beaux-Arts is another jewel, and the collection of the eighteenth-century Saint-Denis museum-abbey includes the main trends of French art from the Renaissance to the beginning of the twentieth century. Among its rarities are a collection of twenty-five pieces of fifteenth- and sixteenth-century fabric painted with tempera, and thirteen watercolor designs by both Lucas Cranach the Elder and the Younger, depicting prominent German figures. The rest speaks for itself: Philippe de Champaigne, Le Nain, Nicolas Poussin, Jean-Honoré Fragonard, Simon Vouet, François Boucher, and many others, a considerable range of works by nineteenth-century painters, including twenty-six landscapes by Jean-Baptiste-Camille Corot, and paintings by Gustave Courbet, Eugène Delacroix, Claude Monet, Pierre-Auguste Renoir, and Paul Gauguin. Nordic painters of the sixteenth and seventeenth centuries are also represented, and there is also an impressive ceramics collection. Contemporary art is also present in Reims at the Cartonnerie, a new center for modern culture, at the fairytale-like Manège, and in the cellars of the Champagne Pommery company, which regularly organizes exhibitions. It is quite an evocative place, ninety feet underground, to taste and discover the secrets of Champagne.

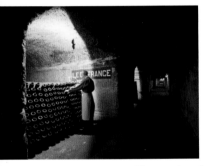

Champagne is lovingly looked after in the cellars of local producers.

facing page
All the kings of France have been crowned in the cathedral of Notre-Dame.

French destiny has been decided at least twice in Reims, first in 496, when the clairvoyant Clovis converted to Catholicism and was baptized. Thus, the first king of the Franks consolidated his authority, because the Catholic Church was the only institution to survive the fall of the Holy Roman Empire. The second time was in 1429, when the ambitious Charles VII was crowned in the cathedral after the triumphant re-conquest of his kingdom thanks to Joan of Arc. Since 816 all French kings, with the exception of Henry IV, Louis XVIII, and Louis Philippe, have been crowned here. Historians report that the heavy crown "pricked" Henry II and gave Louis XVI a headache.

Madame de Pompadour used to say of Champagne that it was the only drink that did not ruin the beauty of a woman's skin. Another legend claims that the Champagne glass, invented by Marie Antoinette, was originally modeled after the queen's breasts. Edward VII of England used to drink it out of the slippers of the dancers at Covent Garden, and Marilyn Monroe used over 350 bottles for her baths. Any visit should include the cellars of Piper Heidsieck, Pommery, and Ruinart, as they are the most impressive. Pink Fossier biscuits, the crunchy pastry of Reims made since 1756 according to an inimitable recipe, are worth a taste dipped in Champagne.

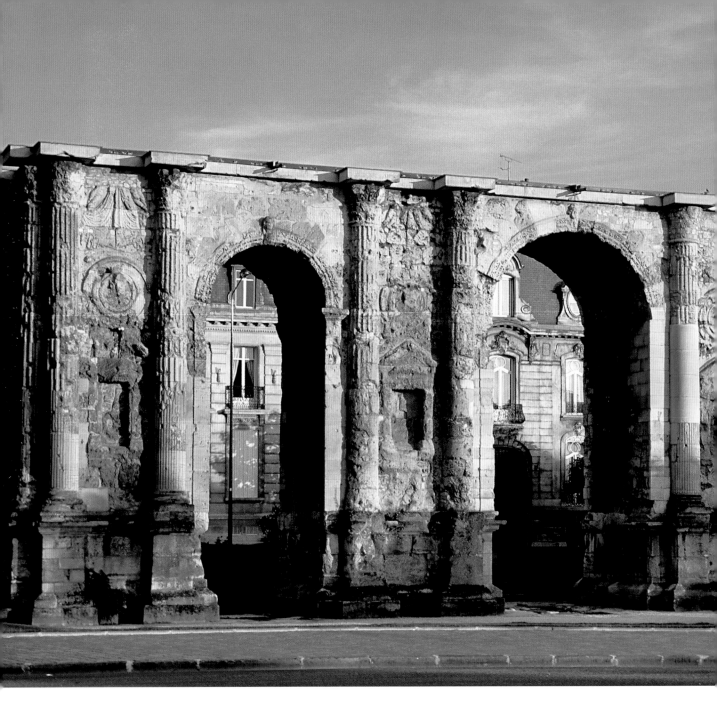

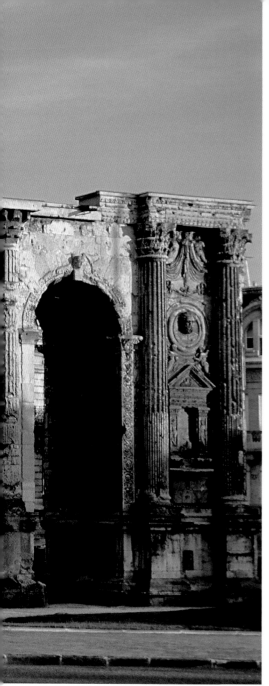

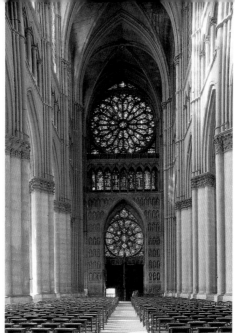

Le Voyage à Reims, titled the *Voyage to Reims* or the *Inn of the Golden Lily* in English, is a musical comedy in one act with a marvelous libretto by Luigi Bollochi. This scenic cantata was created in June 1825 and presented in Paris at the Théâtre-Italien on the occasion of the coronation of Charles X, with Rossini as conductor. The work was later lost and then rediscovered during the Festival of Pesaro in 1984. The story goes as follows: Some European personalities, on their way to the coronation of Charles X, come to the Inn of the Golden Lily. While they are waiting for their transportation, they decide to organize a banquet during which, one at a time, each member of the group will glorify his own nation. With this masterpiece Rossini once again proved his melodic virtuosity and creative sense of parody, producing a most imaginative opera. Rossini held the position of first composer to the king of France until the Revolution of 1830, putting an end to the period of the Restoration.

left
The Porte Mars, a Roman triumphal arch with three passageways.

above
The Notre-Dame cathedral interior.

The Hôtel le Vergeur, built in the fifteenth century, now houses the Musée de la Société des Amis du Vieux Reims.

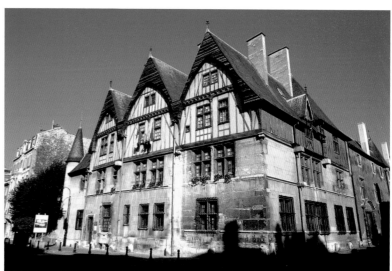

TROYES
THE FLEMISH AND THE FLORENTINES

THE WOOD PANELS IN THE HOUSES OF TROYES HAVE LONG BEEN HIDDEN under layers of plaster, but now they offer us the true character of a city that was in full flower during the Middle Ages and the Renaissance. The old city contains a unique architecture especially evident in the buildings that flank rue Champeaux leading to the town municipality. The street is lined with wonderful sixteenth-century half-timbered houses.

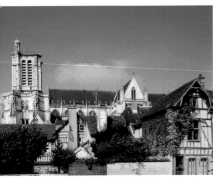

The cathedral of Saint-Pierre and Saint-Paul.

facing page Typical half-timbered houses along a pedestrian route.

The caryatids of the Orfevre tower and the facade of Hôtel Juvenal des Ursins should not be missed. There are other Renaissance architectural marvels along the cobbled and flower-decorated streets, such as the Vauluisant Palace, a typically *champenoise* checkerboard-patterned residence. Bricks and limestone enable the walls to preserve heat and absorb damp at the same time. Other, less noble *champenoise* houses are supported by oak beams and built of corncobs mixed with straw and earth. Some of these old houses' roofs are covered with tiles made of chestnut wood, and the roofing tiles of others are painted in bright colors. A walk along the rue des Chats reveals the fact that it is so narrow cats can jump from one roof to another. Characteristic low stones, called *chasse-roues*, mark the streets and the entrances and serve to protect the walls and the borders that are wider than the axles of carts and carriages. The old pharmacy of the Hôtel-Dieu-le-Comte is still intact, with its surprising collection of bronze mortars and ceramic vases exhibited like treasures. The other gem that should not be missed is the choir dais in the church of Sainte-Madeleine, with exquisite decorations like stone lace that turn into a sort of enchanted embroidery when lit by the changing light of the colored curtains.

The Musée des Beaux-Arts contains a collection of works by Stael and Courbet, Fauve works by Braque and Vlaminck, and a collection of pieces by glass artist Maurice Marinot, who fashioned in glass many sculptures, Art Deco glasses, and some pieces inspired by African and Oceanian art. Tapestries by Rubens, Van Dyke, Watteau, and Fragonard are displayed at the Musée d'Art et d'Histoire, an archaeological museum that also has a beautiful gallery of medieval sculpture. The knitwork museum is more specialized, but not less interesting, and is a key to understanding Troyes' rich history, as it was an activity that contributed to the city's prosperity in the eighteenth century. The Musée de l'Outil et de la Pensée Ouvrière—the museum of workers' utensils and ideas—contains more than 7,000 pieces of curious equipment and 25,000 objects.

During the reign of François I Troyes was a primary commercial city and the fifth most important in France, with a population of almost 30,000. Affluence is generally accompanied by a period of artistic growth, and among the artistic booms was a sculptural style that led to a local school with a marked Flemish influence, since Troyes had close commercial relations with Antwerp. The sculptures in the church of Villemaur-sur-Vanne, near Troyes, are drawn from details in Albrecht Dürer's paintings. The church of Saint-Jean-Baptiste in Caource also contains one of the most beautiful pieces of this school. Italian military campaigns brought many great artists here, and the city welcomed Florentine artist Dominique Le Florentin, whose work can still be found in the churches. The region possesses one of the most important collections of stained glass in France and in Europe.

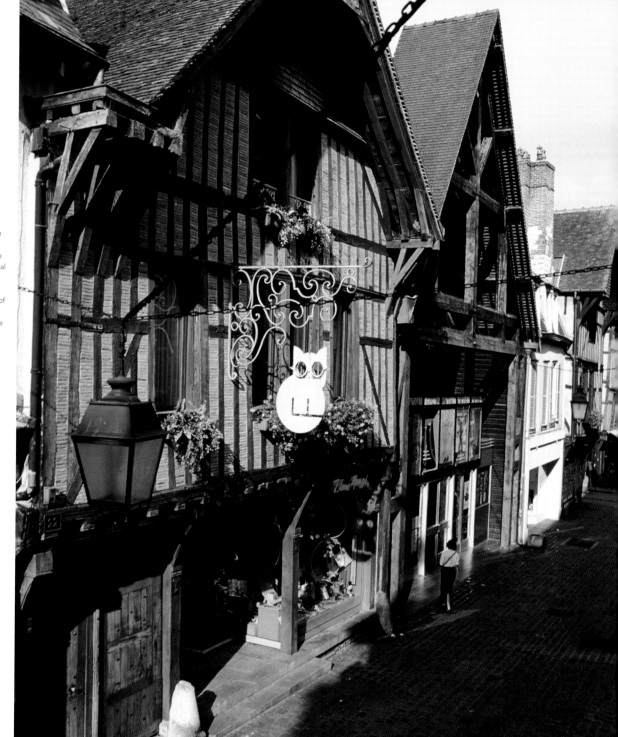

Many fabric warehouses appeared in Troyes during the 1960s to sell off the remnants of the local industries. At first they were reserved for the employees of the factories, and then the doors were opened to the public. Today they are so famous that nearly 3 million people come each year to take advantage of the excellent discounts ranging from thirty to seventy percent, and great international brands are also available at unbeatable prices.

AJACCIO
BONAPARTE'S BIRTHPLACE

THE OLD PORT ALONG AJACCIO'S BEAUTIFULLY CURVED GULF creates a picturesque scene when the fishermen hang out their brightly colored nets. The cafés are shaded by pergolas and look out onto the Promenade Napoleon, named after the emperor, who was born here. The view is enchanting, and daily life here is full of vitality. Monuments, avenues, squares, streets, museums, and the hills of the Casone are all reminders of Napoleon. It could well be said that his native city is a monument to the great Corsican, with a few houses around it. Yet Ajaccio is undeniably attractive and easygoing, and it is much more than just Napoleon's birthplace.

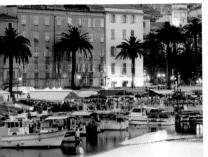

The old port illuminates each evening.

facing page
Napoleon's memory is alive and well in his hometown.

An ideal visit starts at the long and winding rue Cardinal Fesch, a busy main street that drops its anchor in the calm waters of the sea at the foot of the imposing citadel. Where the narrow little streets are more charming, shadows play on burnt-sienna facades, and market stalls sell products that are much more traditional than in the shops of the town center. This is where artisans still make ceramics, leather goods, and wooden objects. A stroll along the citadel grounds and the rue du Roi-de-Rome is most enjoyable. From the height of the citadel's ramparts, built by the French before Corsica was ceded to the city-state of Genoa, it is still possible to admire the coastline's unspoiled purity. The sixteenth-century cathedral of Notre-Dame de la Miséricorde is a classic of Baroque architecture of Venetian inspiration, and is attributed to Giacomo Della Porta, architect to Pope Gregory XIII. The church also has a painting by Eugène Delacroix. Near the pier of the Capuchins is the Fesch Museum, the magnificent nineteenth-century property of Cardinal Fesch, uncle of Napoleon and patron of the arts. The museum now houses more than 200 masterpieces by Veronese, Botticelli, Raphael, Bellini, and Antonello da Messina, making it an important collection of Italian painting second only to that in the Louvre. Another local reminder of Napoleon is the imperial chapel, built in the Renaissance style and inaugurated by Napoleon III; the crypt holds the remains of nine members of the Bonaparte family. Napoleon's nearby birthplace contains

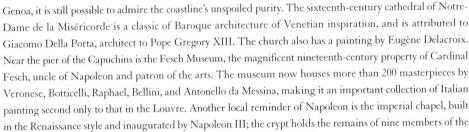

It couldn't have been easy to be the emperor's uncle. Joseph Fesch was born in Ajaccio in 1763 and was archdeacon of the town when the French Revolution took place. He saved himself by giving up his job and took part in the Italian campaign with his nephew as an army commissioner, a position that allowed him to deal with the objects that he most loved—works of art. In 1802 he returned to his ecclesiastical duties, Bonaparte nominated him first Archbishop of Lyon, and he later became cardinal. Fesch took part in the treaties that ensured the presence of the pope in Paris for the 1805 coronation of the emperor. Like all members of the Bonaparte family Fesch was banished from France after the abdication of Napoleon, and was exiled to Rome, where he lived out his life in piety, taking care of his art collection. He occasionally sent a chaplain to his nephew in St. Helena, and he died in Rome in 1839.

sumptuous ceilings painted in the Italian style. One can see the waving masts of the sailing ships moored in the port, take a walk along the cornice that winds up toward the Pointe de la Parata to admire the sunset behind the Sanguinaires Islands, or go to the beaches of the Capo di Feno—all recommended experiences. The following morning should be saved for exploring the local market, right on the water's edge, which is certainly the most beautiful in all of Corsica.

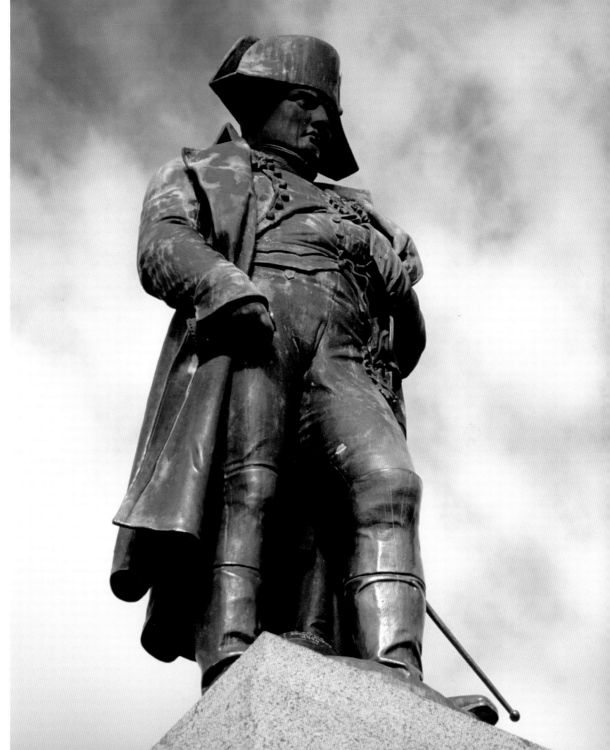

Ajaccio's artisans are still practicing their crafts in the old town. At the A Grotta gallery Pierre Poidvin creates original sculptures. Along the same delightful rue du Roi-de-Rome, at the Escarbouche, Nicole sews Corsican leather under the eyes of the watching visitors. U Ghjuvan Chris is a good address from which to take home olivewood souvenirs of the island. The Grand café Napoleon, located in front of the palm trees of the Palace of the Prefecture, is not to be missed, as it is the oldest and most beautiful café, not to mention the best place to see and be seen. Fresh shrimp and cold dishes, the so-called *chaud-froid*, of chicken and game are served in chestnut gelatin in the beautiful Second Empire room.

BONIFACIO
A CLIFF-TOP CITADEL

BONIFACIO IS A SURPRISING CITY PERCHED ON BRIGHT WHITE CLIFFS overhanging the azure Mediterranean. It seems to float on the blue sea between Corsica and Sardinia, slowly turning its gaze over the splendid Lavezzi Islands. The locals are understandably proud of their city, and no one can deny the marvel of the medieval village when a breathtaking landscape opens up along the patrol paths in the heart of the old military fortifications. Sunset is the best time to observe this spectacle from the ramparts that tower over the waves.

The citadel is the heart of Bonifacio, built in the twelfth century by the Genoese, and it encloses a large part of the peninsula. It must not be forgotten that the city was decimated during the great plague of 1528. The disease caused more than 3,000 deaths in a city that had a population of fewer than 4,000 people, and the walls were neither thick enough nor tall enough to protect it from the plague. It is said that the last victim went to die in the little Chapel San Roch, at the entrance to the town. There is no lack of architectural curiosities, beginning with the fourteenth-century drawbridge and the clock tower of the Romanesque church of Sainte-Marie-Majeure, a meeting place for the town's notables. There is a distinct Sardinian influence visible in Bonifacio's architecture. The residence of the local authority, or *Podestà*, stands facing the church and is one of the most elegant buildings in the city, with porticoes and a facade decorated with sculpted friezes. The Palazzo Publicu next door is the site of a small museum of sacred art where the treasures of the Corsican churches and relics of the confraternities are displayed. On rue des Deux Empereurs two historic residences can be admired—that of Charles V, built for his brief stay in 1541, and that of future emperor Bonaparte, where he lived for two months in 1793.

The fifteenth-century keep is particularly beautiful. At the end of rue de Pachas rises the stairway of the king of Aragon, which is the subject of more than one legend. It is said that its 177 steps were cut into the limestone in a single night. This stairway incised in the steep cliff, with an inclination spanning 195 feet, descends right to the sea, giving access to a grotto called the Well of Saint Barthélemy. The marina stands at the foot of the promontory, with fishing boats, yachts, restaurants, and market stalls. The most fascinating walk in Bonifacio is far from the crowds and should be enjoyed at twilight. It leads toward the cemetery, on the point of the peninsula, and continues around the unusual convent of Saint-François. The whole area deserves thorough exploration, and even if there are too many tourists in the summer, there is always a little hospitable village toward the interior where one can find a passionate vintner for a wine tasting and respite.

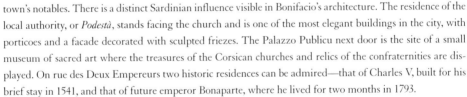

The terraces overlooking the port.

facing page Dramatic cliffs such as this one offer up breathtaking views of the cobalt blue sea.

Luxury hotels and the island's best restaurants await visitors on the southern point of Corsica. One is Marina di Cavu, perched over a cove, with rooms and houses for rent, a large swimming pool, and a spectacular view over the Lavezzi Islands. There is also the Stella d'Oro, which offers local dishes in pleasant rustic surroundings with wood-beam ceilings and an olive press. On the beach, Chez Marco offers *bouillabaisse*, lobster, and very popular fritters *à l'ancienne*. Visitors also come here because of the personality of the host, a charming bon vivant.

The Lavezzi Islands between Corsica and Sardinia are an archipelago of a dozen or so little islands emerging a few feet above sea level. This archipelago has been a nature reserve since 1982 and is a group of granite rocks with spectacular scenery. The best way to discover its riches is on foot or underwater. The private island of Cavallo is the best known, not by the tourists but by the paparazzi, since it is famed as the island of millionaires, and there are more than fifteen hidden villas, all unapproachable and under close video surveillance.

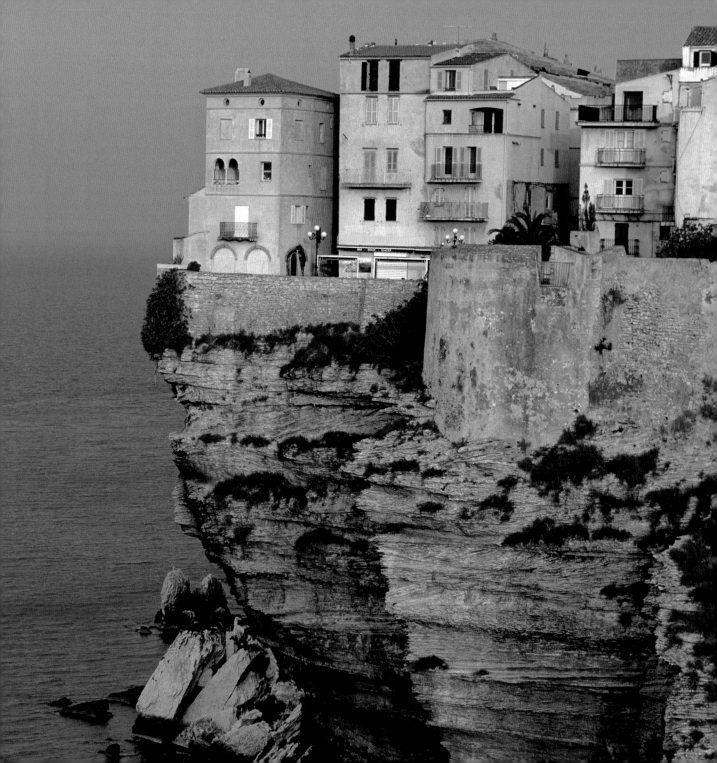

Plans for an international Corsican-Sardinian marine park include the nature reserves of the Straits of Bonifacio and the Tre Padule de Suartone, lands of the beach conservation authority, and the national park of the Archipelago of the Maddalena. It will afford hospitality, and refuge for the flora and fauna of the beaches, preserving the exceptional natural landscapes of Lavezzi, Cerbicali, Bruzzi, Monaci, the cliffs of Bonifacio, and the pools of Ventilegne. The islands and granite promontories are subject to erosion by water, wind, heat, and cold, and take on the strangest shapes, whose interpretation is left to the imagination of the beholder. The rocks' erosion also results in the characteristic shapes of the grottoes or *tafoni* (also called *lu tavòni*). Underwater marvels have become rare in the Mediterranean, but here you can see coral, giant limpets, *loup de mer* or grouper, and *posidonia* algae. Today the reserve is a precious sanctuary for cetaceans and birds, including the crested cormorant and Audoin seagull. Three rare species of lizard live among the granite rock formations. The local flora is luxuriant and characterized by Mediterranean plants mixed with many varieties of vegetation typically found in Africa.

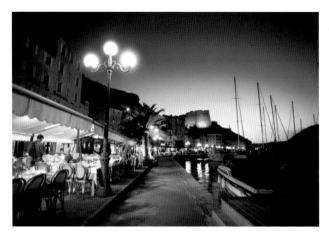

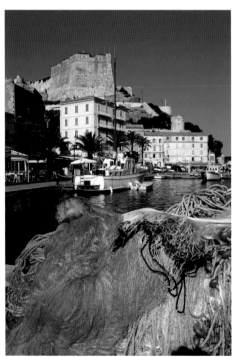

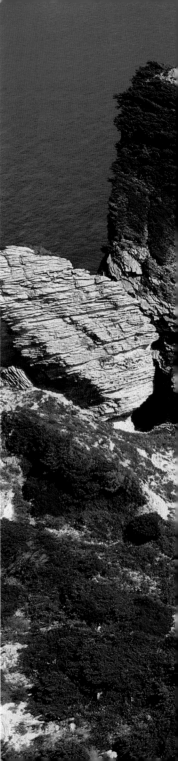

above
By night the port is a place for elegant dining and moonlit strolls.

left
Colorful fishing nets are spread in the sun.

right
The island's promontories and bays are also beautiful from above.

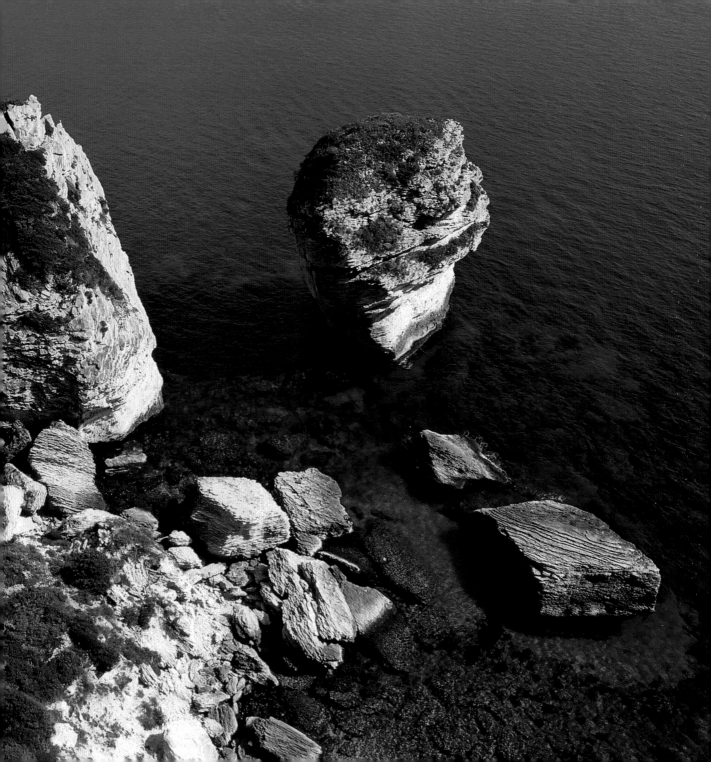

CORTE

CORSICA'S MOUNTAINOUS CORE

CORTE IS IN THE EXACT CENTER OF THE MOUNTAINOUS HEART OF CORSICA, in an area of plateaus, coves, and ancient glacial lakes, where Mount Cimo, the island's highest peak, rises to a height of 8,891 feet. The citadel of Corte is a powerful fortress that embodies the island's history, with a proud profile perched over the void that has withstood every siege.

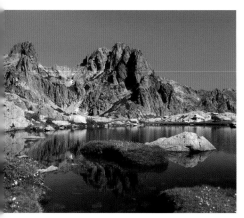

The crystal clear water of Lake Soglia.

facing page
The town lies in the mountainous heart of Corsica.

Vincentello of Istria, a Corsican gentleman, had this eagle's nest built in 1420, and only two towers of that period have survived. The fortress was later restored by the Genoese and rebuilt in 1769 for a garrison of 2,000 men. The army left its outpost here quite recently, in 1983. In Serrurier, one of the ancient barracks, there is a regional museum of anthropology. It is a majestic work by the architect Andrea Bruno, and interesting for the exhibitions on the religious confraternities' history, their famous polyphonic music, and many unique animals. It also contains the rich and diverse Doazan Collection, which is the heart of the museum's permanent collections, and testifies to the islanders' attachment to their culture and traditions. The setting is ancient and contemporary at the same time, and it is the symbol of a society that jealously guards its past while at the same time opens itself to the outside world and the future. There is a unique view from the fortress high above the city and the surrounding area. A little farther down, on a slope with narrow cobblestone streets, the town has preserved traces of the past, the scent of the mountains is in the air, and there is a feeling of austere charm. The biannual Festival of Dance takes place in June and always attracts passionate crowds with shows of traditional, contemporary, and classical dance, or with the ballet of the Opéra de Paris. The Restonica River originates nearby and traverses Corte. The area around its splendid gorges is protected, and the flora and fauna and the landscape are like no other. The seductive beauty of the crystalline water, the pools carved into the gorges, and the centennial pines that cover the valleys are seen in enchanting walks in the midst of a uniquely Mediterranean perfumed air. The mountain lakes of Melo, Niolo, and Capitello, at an altitude of almost 6,000 feet, are a joy for expert excursionists. One can also follow the ancient furrowed paths of the seasonal migration of men and animals through the Corsican mountains. The famous pecorino cheese of Niolo can be sampled throughout the countryside.

The *Cortenais* are well acquainted with the local Casanova confectionery. It stands on the corner of cours Paoli, is a necessary stopping place for those with a sweet tooth, and has been in the same family for more than a century. It offers traditional specialties prepared with extreme care. The most famous delicacy is the *falculelli*, dry biscuits of *brocciu* (the only DOP Corsican cheese) delicately scented with lemon and cooked on chestnut leaves. Sausages, cheeses, honey, wine, olive oil, and chestnut flour are other typical Corsican products.

Along with Bonaparte and Tino Rossi, another famous son of Ajaccio, Pasquale Paoli (1725–1807) is another important figure and father of Corsica's independence. Beginning in 1755 he organized the resistance against Genoan rule, promulgated a democratic constitution, developed agriculture, drained the marshes, minted a new currency, and administered justice. The local university was founded when Corte became the capital of the island. In 1768 after the treaty with Genoa, France defeated Paoli's troops at the Battle of Ponte Novi. In 1769 this "father of the nation" went into exile, and subsequently died in London. Twenty years later, in 1789, the French government annexed Corsica, creating a union that to this day is fiercely contested by Corsican separatists.

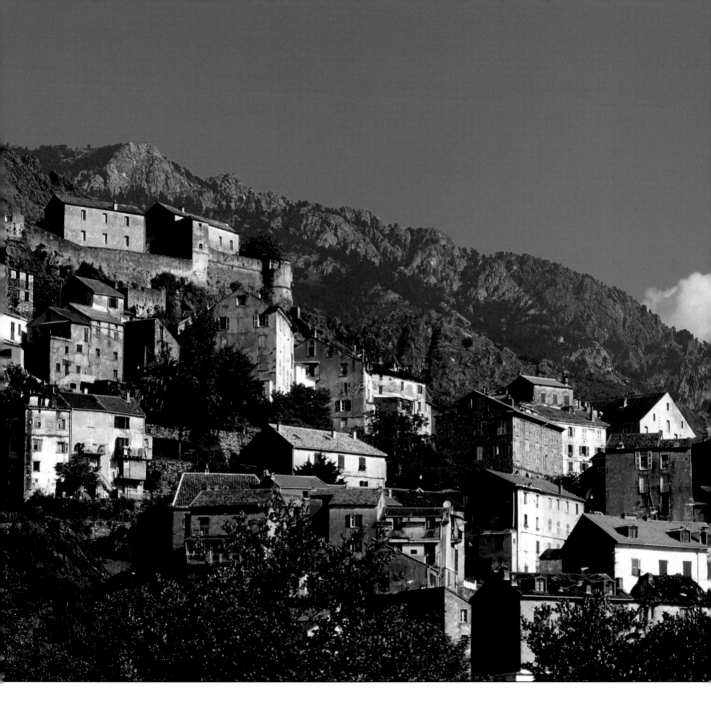

BELFORT
THE LION'S MANY SCULPTORS

THE GIGANTIC STONE LION OF BELFORT STANDS THIRTY-THREE FEET TALL, turns its back on the German border, and is backed onto the rocky promontory of the enormous citadel. It is the symbol of the town's wartime resistance. The territory surrounding Belfort, which is the smallest French region, was officially delineated in 1871. This was during the war against Prussia, when Belfort was invaded by the German army, and Napoleon III signed the armistice on January 28, 1871. Only southern Alsace, lead by Belfort and Colonel Pierre Denfert-Rochereau, decided to resist the invader. The town surrendered on February 18, 1871, after a heroic resistance of 103 days. In exchange, it won the privilege of remaining French, together with the area of Haut Rhin, of which it was the capital. The lion of Belfort statue was the work of Frédéric Auguste Bartholdi, the sculptor of the Statue of Liberty. It is made of the red sandstone of Vosges, and closely resembles a proud sphinx. At sunset its color strengthens, so it looks like a wounded animal that continues to roar. There is a smaller bronze version in Paris, at place Denfert-Rochereau.

The structure of Vauban's citadel is equally impressive. It was built at the end of the seventeenth century, and a refuge for both soldiers and animals can still be seen in its large underground chambers. The old sections of Belfort have been carefully restored, and the dominating colors are ochre, cadet blue, green, and faded rose. Visitors can admire many sights: the cathedral Saint-Christophe and its classical seventeenth-century facade, covered in a unique pink sandstone; the sixteenth-century grain market; the arsenal, with its vast roof in the Alsatian style of the eighteenth century; and the Brisach gateway, built by Vauban and decorated with the crest of King Louis XIV.

The Perello drugstore is even more original. It is the oldest in France, and on the mural painted by Ernest Pignon-Ernest, forty-seven stars of German and French culture are depicted, including Marlene Dietrich, Victor Hugo, Friedrich Nietzsche, Molière, Ludwig van Beethoven, and Pablo Picasso, among others. It is wonderful to stroll among the parks and gardens, starting at place Lechten, with its magnificently harmonious floral mosaics. Crossing the place du Souvenir, where an important cattle market was held in the early twentieth century, one comes to a monument in honor of World War I casualties. Place de la Roseraie offers the lovely scent of roses, and an ideal stroll is concluded at Parc de Loisire de la Douce, with its many lakes, or at Parc François Mitterand for a delightful picnic.

Forty-seven famous personalities of French and German culture populate Ernest Pignon-Ernest's painting.

facing page
The gigantic stone lion, symbol of the town's resistance.

The du Lion drugstore is a veritable kingdom of perfumes, colors, and specialties from all over the world. It carries thirty kinds of coffee and about 100 different types of tea. As a local institution, it is a protected historical monument and has preserved its antique furniture, dating back to 1825, and its Baroque and Rococo decorations. Michel Perello, the owner, has wonderfully preserved the tradition of displaying his wares in their original packaging—customers purchase bottles of wine in wooden cases, and buy flour in the original, historic white sacks.

The Route of Flowering Villages, at the foot of the Vosges, is without doubt one of the most beautiful walks in the area. It follows the path of one of the most ancient roads connecting Alsace to Paris, and is punctuated by a dozen or so charming villages that provide an excellent chance to explore the varied landscapes, take an excursion, or discover the little museums of local mining, iron, and steel manufacturing industries. These unique villages include Anjoutey, Etueffont, Rougegoutte, Giromagny, Auxelles-Haut—perched atop the mountain, at the end of the road—and Delle, with its colorful embankments.

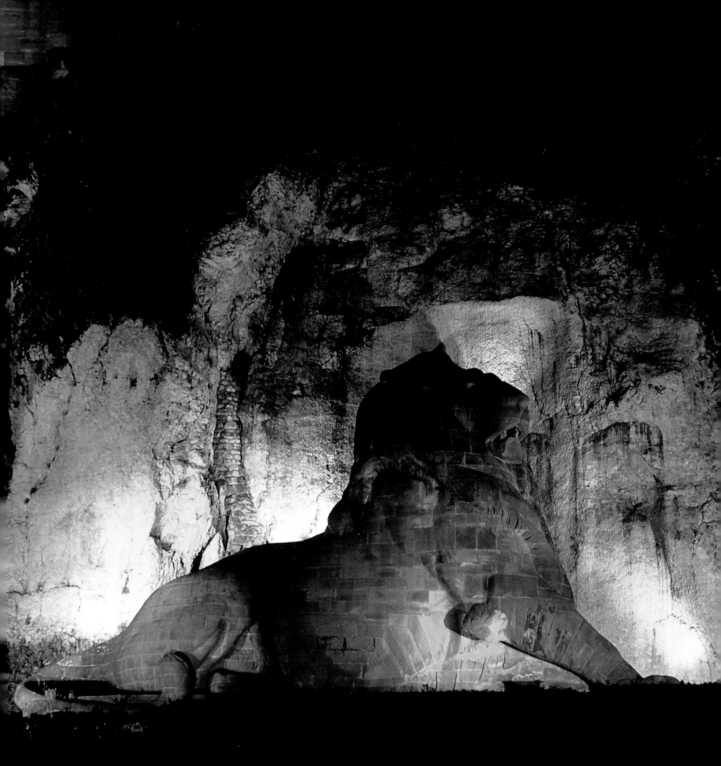

DOLE
PASTEUR'S BEGINNINGS

THE FAMOUS FRENCH NOVELIST MARCEL AYMÉE, AN ENTHUSIAST OF DOLE, wrote of how its "old houses tumble down like torrents toward the waters of the canal and the Doubs," and of its "secret gardens suspended above the imposing rampart-like walls . . . ." Although Dole is locally referred to as the "dethroned queen" and is now a fairly modest town, it has preserved the splendid architectural patrimony of an important past. In the fifteenth century the fame of its university and law school spread abroad, and its parliament was authorized to mint coinage. The many religious communities, numbering up to twelve convents in the seventeenth century, made the town a Reformation stronghold. Conquered by France, and with the signing of the peace treaty of Nimègue in 1658, the Franche-Comté was definitively annexed to the kingdom of France, and Dole lost its role as capital to Besançon. Louis XIV later ordered the destruction of the medieval ramparts, which led to a period of intense renovation, while the presence of the State Audit Office kept the wealthier families in Dole. The town huddles around the Gothic basilica of Notre-Dame, one of the most beautiful religious buildings in the region. The holy vestments and the organ, signed by the renowned organist Riepp, are exceptional.

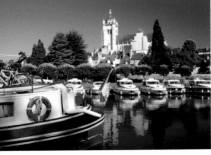

Boats at anchor in the port on the Rhône-Rhine canal.

facing page Houses overlooking the banks of the canal.

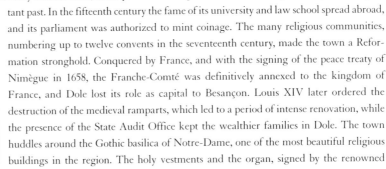

The old city leads visitors through steep, narrow streets overlooking the aristocratic Renaissance buildings that display decorations and coats of arms on their main doorways and corner towers. The splendid staircase of the Terrier mansion in Santans, the doorway of the convent of the Carmelites—a characteristic local work in colored marble—the College of the Arc where Aymée studied, or the imposing caryatid-supported balcony of the seventeenth-century Froissard mansion all carry away the viewer. Below, the river Doubs and its canals run softly, and to this day inspire many artists fascinated by its romantic flowered banks. The Dole Musée des Beaux-Arts is housed in an eighteenth-century military building. Many sections are dedicated to the sculpture of the Burgundy and Franche-Comté regions and to French painting of the seventeenth, eighteenth, and nineteenth centuries. The collection of contemporary art is also interesting, and art in Dole does not exclude science, as the most famous son of Dole is Louis Pasteur.

Franche-Comté is a region characterized by navigable streams and canals. It is possible to rent a boat in Dole, and following the Doubs River, one passes by Besançon, floating by delightful villages and landscapes.

Louis Pasteur (1822–1895) was born in Dole, where he went to elementary and secondary school. At the age of sixteen he moved to a pension in the Latin Quarter of Paris and prepared for the admission exams to the École Normale. Young Pasteur, however, was not fond of the capital, and returned home to take up his studies at the Royal College of Besançon. A few years later he discovered the bacteria responsible for the fermentation of milk and butter, the microbes responsible for the alterations in wine and beer, and he then perfected pasteurization, a method for more safely preserving fermentable liquids. He also invented the vaccine for rabies and became Secretary of the Academy of Life Sciences. Pasteur's discoveries have enabled medicine to take the greatest steps in its history. The celebrated Pasteur Institute, dedicated to research, was created in 1888. His birthplace, 43 rue Louis-Pasteur, is a museum where the personal objects and instruments of this scientist are on display.

In the little markets and traditional inns look for *Morteau* sausage and comté cheese, the gastronomic emblems of the region. When comté is aged it develops some divine aromas. Also worth a taste is *Montbéliard* sausage, with its crispy skin, *Luxeuil* ham, morbier, and emmenthal. The name cancoillotte probably derives from the Latin expression *concoctum lactem;* following tradition, this cheese is still cooked and served hot. Sausages and cheeses pair very well with wine, and the Jura wine will not be a disappointment. A savory bite of Roquefort accompanied by a glass of *griottine*, a wine obtained by the fermentation of cherry juice creating a local perfumed kirsch, is a key part of any visit.

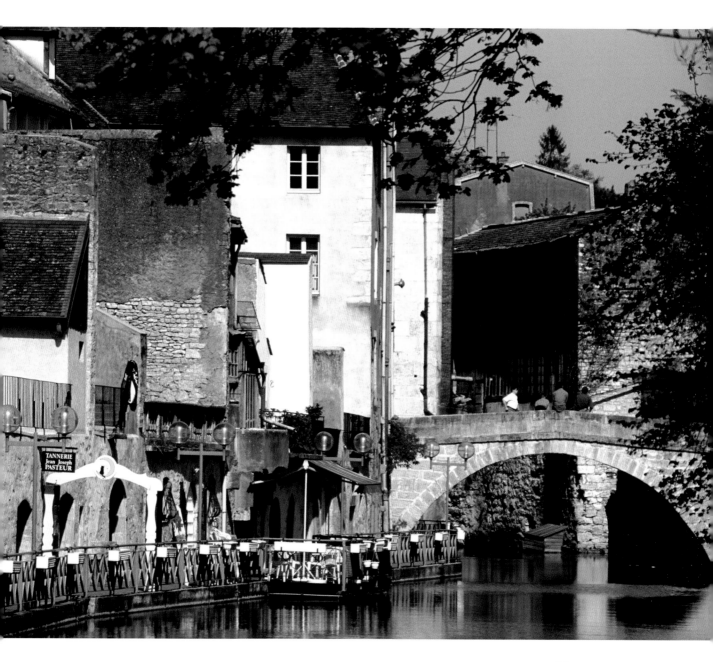

ORNANS

THE ORIGINS OF COURBET'S WORLD

THE AREA AROUND ORNANS LOOKS LIKE THE WORLD'S BEGINNING, with a circle of craggy rocks, valleys scored by pathways, and scattered stones in a landscape that has remained unchanged for centuries. It is crossed by the Loue River, a tributary of the Doubs, that is often very fast-flowing and sometimes completely silent. There is a hint of what were once the ancient sawmills and mills, and one can imagine the carts that

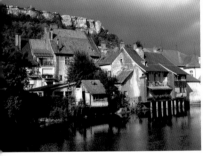

The Loue River frames the old town.

facing page
Ornans is colorfully resplendent nestled in the valley's light.

used to carry the grain and wood rattling by. Ghosts and legends still fire the imagination of the many excursionists and kayak enthusiasts as they travel along the paths of the lookout or are swallowed up by the deep gorges. The majestic Loue originates in Ornans and has excavated a canyon whose walls are almost 1,200 feet high. Upstream from Mouthier-Haute-Pierre and at the great waterfall at Syratu the view is magnificent. Some paths lead to the grottoes at Pontet or the Faux-Monnayeurs, which according to legend were a refuge for counterfeiters. It is not surprising that Gustave Courbet made so many paintings of his native land—no fewer than fourteen remarkable canvases.

In Ornans, the small capital of the valley, the Loue seems to find peace and enlarges its course to reflect the entire town. The scenery is ochre, the rocks are blond, the blue of the sky is a languid elegy, the pink of the nasturtiums is omnipresent, and washing is hung out to dry in the sun on the balconies jutting out over the river—all characteristic of Ornans. It reflects its great beauty on the surface of the river water and attracts countless artists and visitors each year. Three of the overhanging porticoes of the birthplace of Courbet rest on the river. This building now holds the museum dedicated to the artist with a collection of personal objects and paintings. Well before the birth of Courbet, Ornans boasted other architectural riches. In the fifteenth century the town was known as the "capital of leasehold," which meant that the legal representatives of the king or prince had to enforce the law throughout the whole territory. Ornans therefore had a militia to defend its immunity and privileges. The sumptuous buildings, some of which over-

Realist painter Gustave Courbet (1819–1877) was the son of a local noble family and was among the most hated artists of his time. He was a great drinker, never minced his words, and was vain and arrogant. Baudelaire detested him; nevertheless, he was recognized as an artist. His detractors described him as the "head of the brute school." His *Burial at Ornans* was painted in 1850, in very uncertain political times (the Second Empire was about to begin), and caused a great scandal. It was considered a shameful representation of the people, the death of the republic, the burial of Romanticism, and therefore aroused great indignation among the town's notables, many of whom were depicted in the painting. Another scandal was caused by his *Origin of the World*; painted in 1866 and now at the Louvre, this painting was a visually explicit homage to the most intimate region of a woman, without visual or metaphorical illusions. The artist was dedicated to the democratic movement during the bloody Paris Commune movement in 1871, which won him many dangerous political enemies.

hang the Loue, can hold their own with those of Besançon: the Grospain and Sanderet-de-Valonne mansions, the Gothic church of Saint Laurent, the eighteenth-century hospital of Saint Louis, the vault of the Monastery of the Visitation, and the curious fishing museum are all local points of interest. The best lunch is a freshly fished trout and, when in season, the famous timbales with stuffed *trombetta*, *spugnole*, *porcini*, and *gallinacci* mushrooms.

The castle of Germigney is known for its elegance and pastoral atmosphere, not to mention the ceiling decorations and noted restaurant. It offers a regional cuisine enriched with flavors from the Midi, the south of France. The rooms exude a characteristic perfume of lime and wax and are delicately decorated. The castle was built on the banks of the Loue and is surrounded by a splendid park of seven acres with rare herbs and centuries-old trees. Bowling and croquet are popular pastimes here.

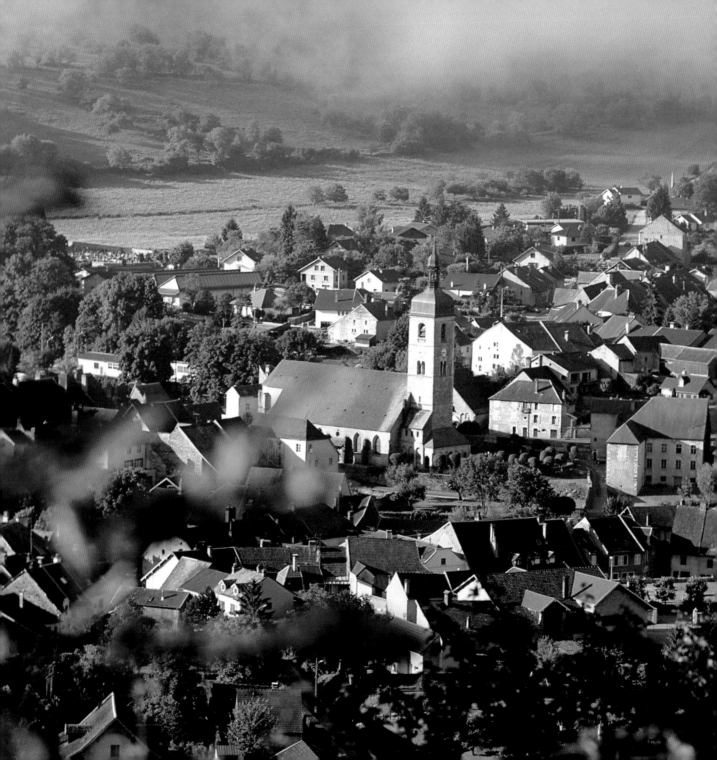

BARBIZON
MOTHER NATURE'S SCHOOL

BARBIZON STANDS AT THE EDGE OF THE FOREST OF FONTAINEBLEAU. In the eleventh century it was a land of farmers and charcoal makers, and later, between 1830 and 1875, it became a reference point for an entire generation of artists that opened the way for Impressionism. The artists of the Barbizon School, whose motto was *la nature chez elle* (nature as itself), were chiefly painters of landscapes and animals, and therefore rejected academic dogmas and were excluded from official exhibitions. Although the Italian tradition of travel for artistic formation was still important, instead of an international grand tour these artists went in search of the heart of France. Theirs was a return to nature, which had already begun in the early fourteenth century, as a reaction to the industrialization that had begun to empty the countryside.

Jean-Baptiste-Camille Corot and Gustave Courbet were among the first to come to the forest of Fontainebleau with their easels. Other artists came to Barbizon soon thereafter: In about 1850 there were approximately fifty *habitués,* and twenty years later there were 100 living in the area, in Moret or nearby Chailly. In 1864 Monet and Renoir were working near Fontainebleau, Cézanne was at Melun, and in 1865 Sisley took up residence at Verneux-les-Sablons and then at Melun. Seurat, Pissarro, Picabia, Picasso, Derain, Vlaminck, and Van Gogh all either passed through or stayed in Barbizon. The landscape artists painted from nature and placed importance on the emotions and sensations experienced in the open air. The invention in 1834 of the portable tube of colored paint also contributed to this freedom, liberating the artist from the indoor studio. Sensibilities changed and aesthetic motivations were different, but this independence united all of them. Jean-François Millet and Théodore Rousseau were the masters of the Barbizon School. The landscape may no longer resemble what it was then, but a certain charm remains. The Ganne Inn, where many artists stayed, opened circa 1824; it is still there, on the main road, and contains both the Maison-Atelier Rousseau and the museum of the Barbizon School. The studio of Millet is also worth a visit. It was here that some of his masterpieces were born, such as *L'Angélus* and *Les Glaneusses.* These two works were painted in the same period and are associated with the horizontal line typical of Millet and, above all, with the area's bucolic and gentle atmosphere. They emit a feeling of great serenity and beauty that can still be found in the summertime twilight on the plain of Brie. Barbizon is still the village of artists so dear to painters, and exhibitions are held throughout the year.

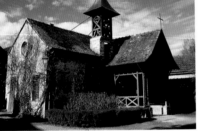

The little chapel of Barbizon.

facing page
The entrance of the Musée Ganne, in the ancient inn where many painters stayed.

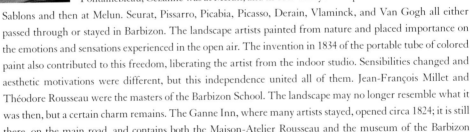

In the area surrounding Barbizon visitors can admire the scenery of the forest of Fontainebleau, Milly-la-Fôret, Provins, the mythical seventeenth-century castles of Fouquet in Vaux-le-Vicomte, and Courances, a splendid residence in the style of Louis XIII that was saved from ruin around 1870. There is also an exceptional collection of sixteenth- and seventeenth-century tapestries depicting monkeys and a magnificent garden with fountains and water basins. The medieval hamlet of Moret-sur-Loing is also beautiful; here Sisley spent the last twenty years of his life, and visitors can enjoy the "barley sugar of the sisters of Moret," a traditional local sweetmeat. The keep, the remains of the encircling walls, and the two fortified gateways testify to the town's military past. The *maison* of Georges Clemenceau is open to the public and displays many of the literary and theatrical works of the French politician, academic, and friend of Claude Monet.

Hôtellerie du Bas-Bréau, a local *relais* and chateaux, is laden with a rich history. It is a luxurious respite in the heart of Barbizon associated with the presence of Robert Louis Stevenson, who came here to cure his lungs and where he wrote *Forest Notes.* It is also famous for its excellent cuisine; game is the dish of choice when in season. Lobster is served roasted with a delicate white butter, and sea bass is served with oil and crushed tomatoes. Local wines to accompany each meal are chosen by Françoise Sagan, the notable chef, and Princess Grace of Monaco, Jacques Brel, and Marcello Mastroianni all used to come here to enjoy the magical rooms—decorated in the nineteenth-century style with antique furniture—the swimming pool in the park, and the tennis courts.

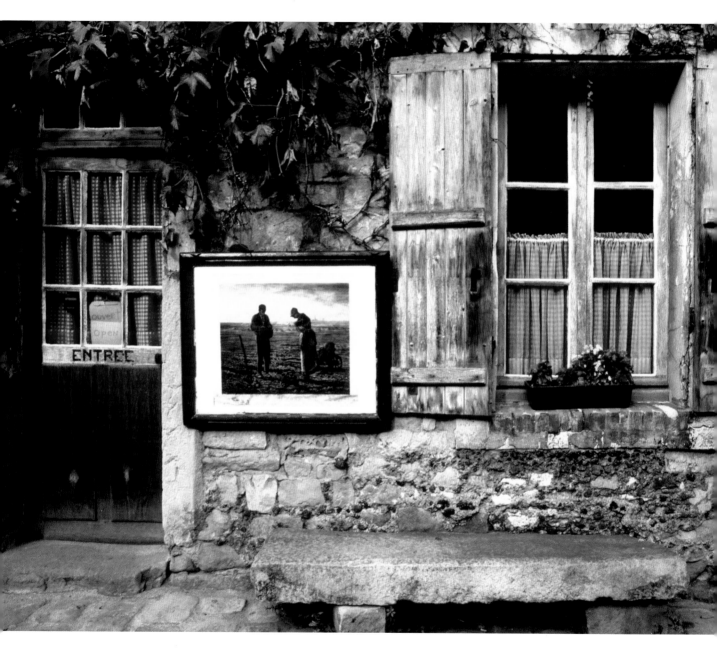

FONTAINEBLEAU
FRANCE'S MOST ROYAL HISTORY

THIS TOWN'S NAME IS FAMOUS WORLDWIDE, A MAGICAL NAME that evokes the forest for some and the castle for others. It is still a dazzling name because Fontainebleau remains the "capital of French history" and continues to deserve the description. There is no other royal castle that hosted thirty-four French sovereigns, from Louis VI (Louis the Fat) to Napoleon III. All came to Fontainebleau to live luxuriously and enjoy hunting, both traditional court activities. One could say that Fontainebleau was the sport's birthplace; from the twelfth century on the kings considered the forest an excellent terrain for hunting, a local tradition that continues today.

"This is the true residence of kings, home of the centuries," said Napoleon at Saint Helena in remembrance of this place he so greatly loved. Some sovereigns put a particular stamp on the history of the castle: Francis I, who loved to rest in the *delicieux deserts* of Fontainebleau, gave the palace its Renaissance style. Then came Henry IV, Louis XV, Louis-Philippe, and Napoleon. The guided tour of the castle leads visitors through the Renaissance rooms decorated by Italian artists, to the great apartments and the ballroom, which was a mirror of the life at court. Then one arrives at Napoleon's apartment, the Chinese museum of Empress Eugénie, and the museum dedicated to the emperor and his family. The gardens are the apotheosis of three centuries of the art of French gardening.

Today thousands of tourists from Paris and the surrounding areas, from amateur climbers to cyclists, horseback riders, and simple Sunday visitors, all come to the nearby forest of Fontainebleau, which extends over 50,000 acres. It has for some time been the object of special care, first on the part of the sovereigns, who set up special rules for the maintenance of the forest in order to jealously guard their hunting activities; later there were the *Grands Maîtres* of the water and forest, an equivalent of today's National Office for Forestry. Since the beginning of the nineteenth century artists have also been guardians of the landscape. Above all, the forest is a world of unique sensations; aesthetes stand breathless before such beauty, horsemen ride along the fine sandy *allées* among the aromas of resin and ferns; photographers, entomologists, and even woodsmen and hunters find their own worlds here. A visit should be paid to the Franchard gorges to admire the twelfth-century hermitage, the desert of Apremont with its mounds of stones, the birches, and the famous rocks that resemble animals.

A tree-lined avenue leads to the Cour du Cheval Blanc.

facing page
A peacock struts in the Garden of Diana.

King Francis I was a collector of stones, jewels, weapons, sculptures, and paintings, and he invited many Italian artists to court, including Rosso Fiorentino in 1530 and Primaticcio in 1532. This is where the first nineteenth-century School of Fontainebleau was formed, which later had a particular influence on the works of François Clouet and Antoine Caron. On the walls of Fontainebleau castle in the past one could admire Italian masterpieces such as Leonardo's *Mona Lisa* and Raphael's *Holy Family*, both of which are now in the Louvre. The school of this refined court art later developed into Mannerism. The second School of Fontainebleau, during the reign of Henry IV with the presence of Nicola dell'Abate, opens another sumptuous period that gained fame thanks to Flemish and French painters such as Ambroise Dubois, Martin Fréminet, and Toussaint Debreuil.

The Hôtel Napoleon is in the center of town and just 300 feet from the entrance to the castle of Fontainebleau. It is a very pleasant, ancient *relais* that has been enlarged and restored through the centuries, always maintaining its unique French atmosphere. The rooms are decorated in tasteful warm colors and overlook an interior courtyard. In the evening the chef of the Tables des Maréchaux offers a local menu based on fresh products in season, all of which allows visitors to live like kings during their stay.

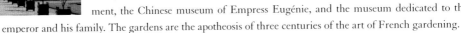

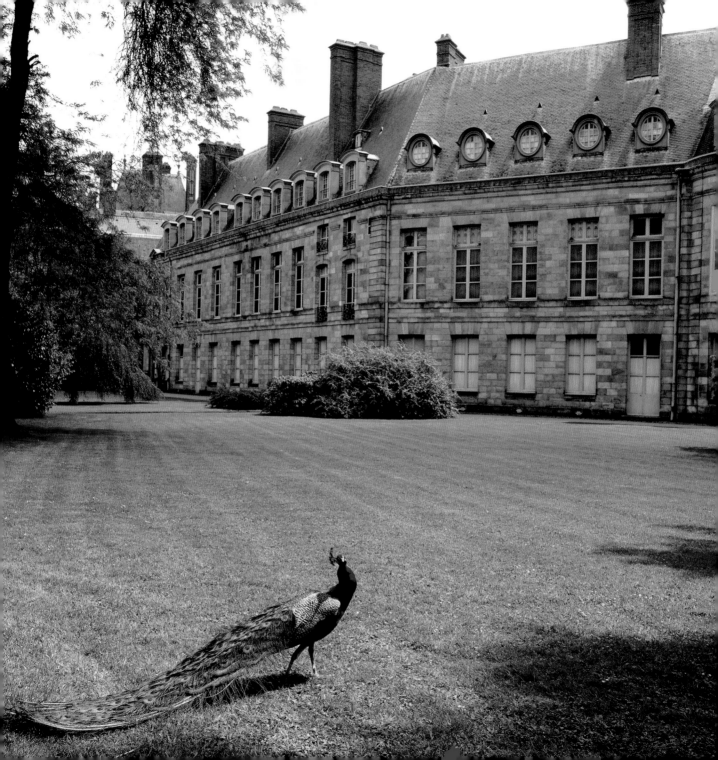

PROVINS
ROSES AND RAMPARTS

MANY WRITERS WHO HAVE PASSED THROUGH PROVINS HAVE COMMENTED on this town and its unique attraction, including Victor Hugo, Honoré de Balzac, Prosper Mérimée, Jules Verne, Marcel Proust, and even Umberto Eco. It is the capital of Champagne, built on a promontory in the heart of Brie. The wealth of its artistic patrimony is impressive; also known as the City of Roses, Provins already had a great reputation in the Middle Ages, when its fairs were famous throughout Europe. The city has preserved the structure of that period in its upper part, some of the lower part, and the encircling ramparts. The monuments, roads, and noble residences all attest to the prosperity of the twelfth and thirteenth centuries. Place de Châtel is at the heart of the city, surrounded by gabled houses. Nearby César Tower is flanked by four twelfth-century turrets and has served as both prison and mint. Today only the bare bones of the original edifice remain, but the wonderful view takes in a large part of the region. The eleventh-century Maison Romane is the oldest in Provins and contains the town museum, with traditional art objects and religious statues. The famous Grange aux Dimes—the "tax granary"—is an immense merchants' residence where people paid their tithes. It contains an exhibition dedicated to the life of Provins during the golden age of Champagne's great fairs. The ramparts, built in the middle of the thirteenth century by Count Thibaud IV de Champagne (known as the *Chansonnier*), are famous, and although only about half of the original three miles encircling the city remains, they are still worth seeing.

The urban plan of the lower town is medieval, and nothing has been changed. The houses are splendid, and in the Romanesque church of Saint-Ayoul visitors can admire a notable sixteenth-century *Pietà* in colored stone and a Virgin in marble with decorations in gold attributed to Germain Pilon. Among the local curiosities are the Souterrains, a network of medieval underground caves that are open to the public; these galleries were excavated to resemble civil and military roads, or for the extraction of clay, which was an essential material for Provins' tapestry industry. The Hôtel Dieu, which is said to have a mysterious network that still has not revealed all its secrets, begins in the splendid lower salon of the countesses' palace. Provins relives its great history during the medieval festivals. Visitors can take part in the show of birds of prey, harkening back to the hunting traditions of the noblemen of the Middle Ages, while in a medieval military camp built behind the fortifications, horsemen's tournaments can be watched. Provins greatly enjoys this ritual, which is a voyage into the heart of the Middle Ages and its history.

The fortified walls encircling the city.

facing page
The collegiate church of Saint-Quiriace is illuminated by a thousand lights each night.

In the twelfth and thirteenth centuries the region of Champagne, with the fairs of Provins, Troyes, and Lagny, was an important European commercial center. Flemish, German, Lombard, Provençal, and Catalan traders gathered for many weeks in May, June, and September. These fairs first attracted the merchants of Europe and then those from the East and Africa. Their success is due, in part, to the protection that the contract gave to the merchants and the tutelage offered by the *Champenois*. These meetings, fairs, and exchange of ideas ended in the sixteenth century. The *coup de grâce* to the fairs of Champagne was inflicted by the difficulty of crossing the Straits of Gibraltar and the Alps, religious wars, plague epidemics, and the abolition of the merchants' privileges.

The rose of Provins is one of the symbols of the city. According to legend, Thibaud of Champagne took the rose from the rose gardens of the Sultan of Damascus and brought it back from the crusades in 1240. Nothing is certain, but it seems that the *rosa gallica officinalis*, known for its medicinal properties, was offered to Catherine de Medici and Louis XIV when they passed through Provins. When it is candied or prepared as a syrup it aids digestion, its lotion cleanses and purifies the skin, and when it is made with the addition of barley sugar it cures a sore throat. The creativity here is infinite—candied rose, traditional candies, honey, chocolate, liqueur, and fruit purées all have locals and visitors alike saying *bon appétit*.

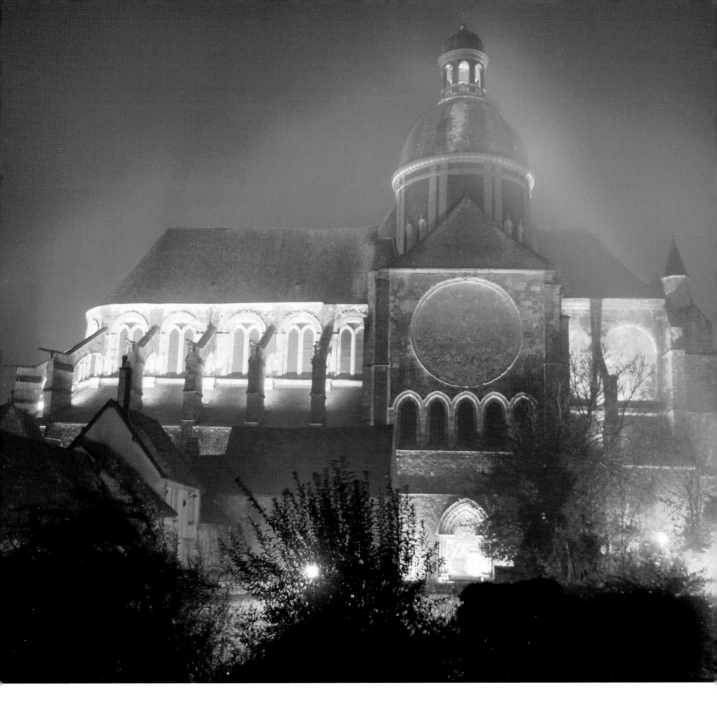

RAMBOUILLET
ROYAL FLORA, WILD FAUNA

RAMBOUILLET IS A SMALL RESIDENTIAL TOWN IMMERSED IN THE MAGICAL provinces outside Paris, and yet it is closely associated with France's national history. Its castle was the private residence of kings and emperors, and it belongs to the presidency of the French Republic. This fourteenth-century castle, surrounded by a French-style garden with many canals and islands, periodically hosts the world's heads of state. The interior decorations are very beautiful, such as those in the marble room, the eighteenth-century wood *boiserie*, or the neo-Pompeiian decorations of the First Empire. The *Laiterie de la Reine* and the *Chaumière aux coquillages* in the castle's English garden represent the ideal of a return to nature. The castle was built in 1779 and represents very precisely the style of the latter half of the eighteenth century. The *Chaumière aux coquillages* was conceived by the Duke of Penthièvre for the Princess of Lamballe between 1779 and 1780, and is one of the most beautiful mother-of-pearl and seashell decorations in the whole of Europe. The *Laiterie de la Reine* was built by Louis XVI for Marie Antoinette, and contains the sculpture *Almathée e Nymphe* by Pierre Julien. In its time it was a sort of royal hideaway, used for picnics and the queen's private dinner parties.

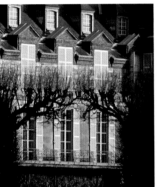

The facade of the castle is framed by impeccably trimmed trees.

Another interesting place at Rambouillet is the national Bergerie, the first experimental French farm founded in 1786. Louis XVI's wish was to build a place for exotic animals. Today visitors can tour a farm complete with stables, pigsties, barnyards, and sheep pens where more than 1,000 lambs are born each year, among which are the famous Mérino of Rambouillet. The palace of the King of Rome is also well worth a visit, with its themed exhibitions and romantic gardens. This government building was restructured and transformed by Napoleon I in 1812 for his son, the king of Rome. Another jewel of this palace is a wonderful museum of the "Goose" game, a relative of the "Snakes and Ladders" game, which contains 2,500 pieces of the Dietsch Collection displayed in chronological order from the seventeenth century to the present. The game has been used for every possible manner of entertainment, education, and propaganda. It offers an unmatched source of insight into social mores, customs, science, and industry. Another museum that is unique in France is the Rambolitrain, a collection of more than 4,000 miniature trains and 1,200 feet of track that combine to create a journey between childhood dreams and reality. Rambouillet is also a town surrounded by forest, from the regional park of the high valley of the Chevreuse to the Espace Rambouillet, where visitors' experiences vary with the seasons.

Rambouillet originally owed its history to the forest, surrounded as it was by an ancient royal hunting ground thick with oaks, pines, birch, scattered pools, and lookout places. Now it is greatly appreciated by excursionists and sportsmen. The Espace Rambouillet is in the heart of the large state-owned property, and allows people to approach wild animals, see deer in the distance, watch a roe or fallow deer leaping in the bushes, or discover wild boar tracks. The training of 120 birds of prey begins in April and can be watched as they are freed to fly. There is also a clinic, breeding area, and incubators behind great stretches of windows through which the chicks can be seen. In September, the natural breeding season, a forest guide takes visitors at nightfall to the place where the deer gather.

The Cheval Rouge offers traditional cuisine and is much appreciated for the courtesy of the staff, the simple, rustic surroundings, and the winter garden. There is nothing better than the chef's terrine with a compote of red onions, or calf's head in a *ravigote* sauce, a roasted lobster with green sauce, or a delicious home-cooked slice of beef. Save room for dessert, as their thin apple tart and *gratin* of raspberry with fruit purée are the perfect end to a great meal.

facing page
The castle's vast park contains a lake, six small islands, and many canals.

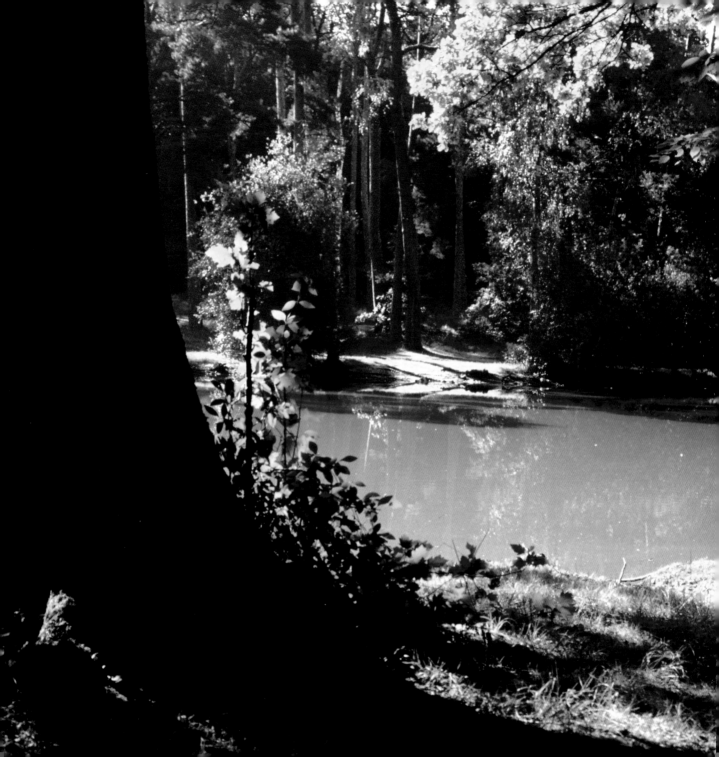

VERSAILLES
THE SUN KING'S MARBLE AND MIRRORS

TIME HAS NOT CHANGED THE SPLENDOR CREATED BY THE SUN KING. Travelers are still dazzled by the castle, the hall of mirrors, the sovereigns' apartments, the throne room, the gallery of battles, and the gardens, all created by the best artists of the age. Versailles was a royal hunting ground when the court still resided at Saint-Germain-en-Laye. It was particularly beloved of Louis XIII, the Melancholy King, who had a pavilion

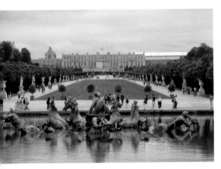

The fountain of Apollo.

facing page
The Orangerie was designed in 1684 by Jules-Hardouin Mansart.

built for concerts given in his honor. Orphaned at the age of five, Louis XIV inherited his father's love for Versailles. The transformation period was difficult, and Saint-Simon described Versailles as "the saddest of places, without a view, without forests, without water, and without land, because there is quicksand or marshland everywhere." But the young king had the last word. After a reception given in his honor by Fouquet, the superintendent of finance in his castle at Vaux-le-Vicomte, Louis XIV was overwhelmed by Versailles's beauty and magnificence. He ordered d'Artagnan to arrest Fouquet for embezzlement, and assembled the builders of his castle—the architect Le Vau (and Mansart upon the death of Le Vau), the gardener Le Notre, the painter Le Brun—and had the castle of Versailles built on an even more magnificent scale than that of Fouquet.

The remarkable building site was opened in 1661, and twenty-one years later, at the height of his glory, Louis XIV transferred his court to the palace. In 1703, Russian Tsar Peter the Great was inspired by this palace to build St. Petersburg and the Winter Palace on a vast area of mosquito-infested marshland.

Nothing remains of the preexisting village of Versailles. In 1671 a royal decree authorized the purchase of the land at advantageous financial conditions, upon the understanding that no building would be taller than the Marble Court. The city was developed, with the houses placed symmetrically in respect to the avenue de Paris (which was even wider than the Champs Elysées), forming on either side the quarters of Notre Dame and Saint-Louis, housing the ministries. Versailles was the political capital and the cradle of the French Revolution, but the government only left the castle definitively in 1879. Louis-Philippe transformed it into a museum dedicated to the glory of France, and the town has since preserved its monumental structure and the people's houses, remaining faithful to its image of respectability and traditional values. Many residents are part of high society and descendants of Louis XIV, such as Prince Carlo Emanuele of Borbone-Parma, who still lives in Versailles, in yet another palace.

"We must give ourselves to the public" was one of Louis XIV's mottos. In Versailles he organized a theatrical ceremony that was repeated unchanged for years, in the presence of the public, showing off the absolute king. Etiquette dictated exact rules, set out in the minutest detail, of gestures to make before the king, of who would help the king dress each day, who would take part in his toilette, who would make the collections in church, who would recite poetry to him, and who would hold the candelabra as he retired for the night. There are small and large vigils, audiences, and walks. There were 200 courtiers living in the castle, and all tried with every means possible to approach him; another thousand came to see him every day. The first way to earn the king's favor was to serve him well, in the army or in any other administrative capacity, but at Versailles the art of appearance was not enough, as the king also appreciated other qualities in his courtiers, such as beauty, intelligence, ability, and skill.

Louis XIV was fond of figs, melons, and strawberries, even in the winter. To this end a vegetable garden was built on the marshes of the Puant, a less-than-pleasant-smelling pool. This was the famous King's Vegetable Garden, and it supplied his table with fresh vegetables and the first fruits of the season. One can still see and buy the blue Hungarian pumpkin, Siamese squash, kiwi, and black currants. Another curiosity is the Osmothèque, where, among 1,400 perfumes, both the eau de toilette used by the Sun King and Napoleon's cologne are still preserved.

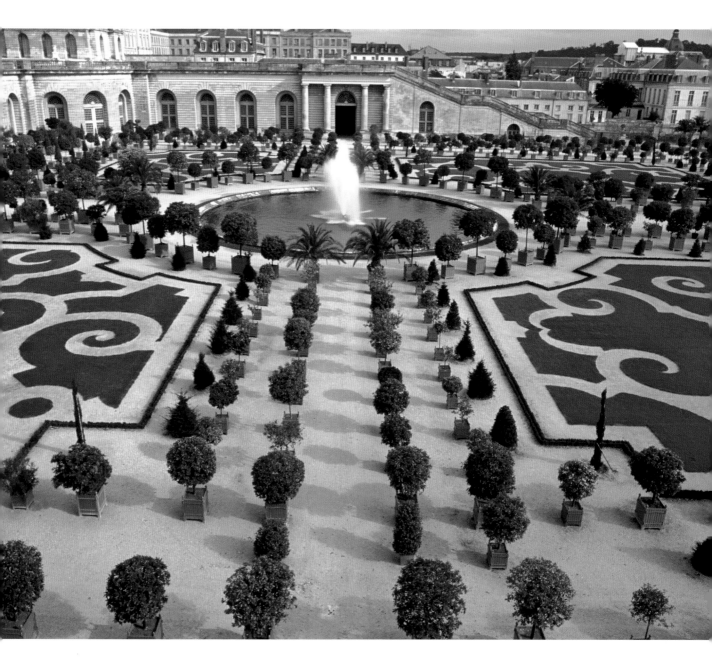

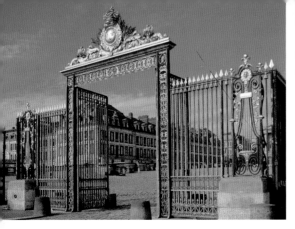

À Versailles, le Roi danse. Imported from Italy in the sixteenth century—particularly with the arrival of Catherine de Medici, wife of Henry II and Queen of France—court ballet reached its apotheosis during the reign of Louis XIV. The Sun King was not only a great enthusiast of this art, which he also used for political motives to subdue his courtiers, but he was also an excellent dancer. He appeared in several ballets, about thirty according to historic records, often playing the role of Jupiter or Apollo. Pierre de Beauchamp, his dance master, was ordered to codify the choreography, steps, and the positions. Now we can see his dances in the classical sequences, including the five positions, the positions of the arms, the various leaps, and pirouettes. He founded the Académie royale de Danse in 1661 and ordered his favorite artists, Jean-Baptiste Lully, who was also a dancer, and Jean-Baptiste Poquelin, known as Molière, to produce many comédies-ballets. Among them was the famous Bourgeois Gentilhomme. The recent rediscovery of Baroque arts has enabled excellent revivals of these ballets, because the choreography can be clearly read, as can the detailed descriptions of the dancing king's many sumptuous costumes.

above
One of the magnificent castle entrances.

right
Fountains, reflecting pools, and sculptures make Versailles a masterpiece of both architecture and hydraulic engineering.

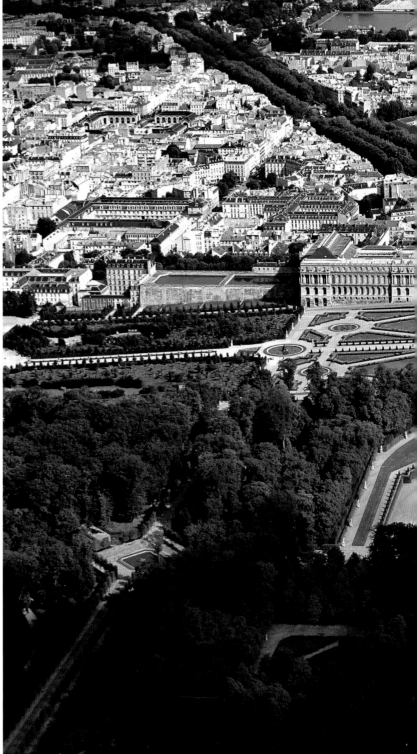

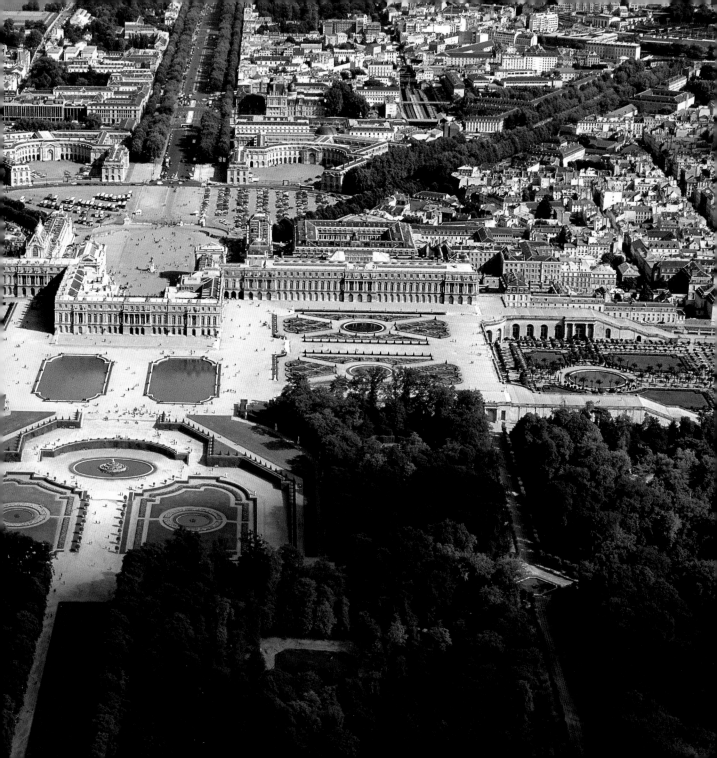

A G D E
AUSPICIOUS VINEYARDS

A bicycle ride is the best way to get to know the streets in the heart of the old town.

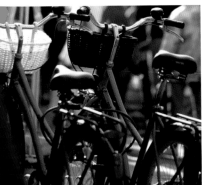

IN THE FIFTH CENTURY BC THE INHABITANTS OF THE PHOCIDE REGION OF GREECE set sail in search of new commercial centers in the Mediterranean. They reached the coast beyond Massalia (present-day Marseilles) and were attracted by the area's harmonious beauty and fertile land. Between the volcano and the sea they founded Agathé Tyché (meaning "good luck") and planted vast vineyards. Since then Agde has been the capital of an ideal area for the cultivation of vines, but the sea is also of importance, and local commerce includes fishing and naval construction. The town was destroyed and reconquered many times up through the sixteenth century. The fortified cathedral has stood since the beginning of the twelfth century and is the emblematic monument of the town's eventful past. The port was created in the fifth century BC and reached the height of its importance in the seventeenth century. Agde's fleet increased rapidly along the Hérault River's navigable waters. There were twenty-seven ships in 1664, growing to 130 in 1743, and the river was used for commercial traffic, above all for the transport of wine, and for military service. During these years the shipyards built 116 fishing vessels for use in both river and sea, and they continued to expand. The construction of the ancient municipality was finished in 1652. Today this includes the Maison du Coeur, the Glacière, and the greater part of the houses and mansions of the old city. During the Second Republic, in 1848, the walls were demolished, and thirty years later, when the moderate Republicans were in power, work began on several important buildings, including the Mirabel garrison—the present municipal building—the covered market, and bringing electricity to the entire city. At the end of the nineteenth century Emmanuel Laurens built an unusual castle on his Belle Isle estate, on the other bank of the Hérault. Technically and artistically it was a daring architectural work, especially regarding the interiors, where floral decorations abounded, with characteristic stained-glass windows and a luxurious bathroom—a true Art Nouveau masterpiece. The houses and the cathedral in the old city are made of basalt, the black volcanic stone native to Agde and known as the black pearl of the Mediterranean. Walking in town one can admire the beautiful fountains, squares, and imposing ramparts that date back to the twelfth century and were built over the ruins of the ancient Greek walls of the fourth century BC. The inhabitants, known as *Aghatois*, have preserved many of their traditions, such as the Festival of New Wine, the Festival of the Sea, and the tournaments of the Languedoc, which are duels that take place at the foot of the Laurens castle.

facing page
Houses and terraces overlook the Hérault River, with the illuminated cathedral of Saint-Etienne in the background.

Claude Terrisse was born at Agde in 1598. He was an accomplished sailor, but above all he was a generous benefactor of the city. As a famous navigator and king's pirate during the reigns of Louis XIII and Louis XIV he had a very eventful life, traveling between naval battles and being a commercial escort for the Savoyard rulers. He was made captain of the French Royal Fleet, was charged with overseeing maritime traffic in the Gulf of Lyon, and also managed to intercept Spanish spies. He was consul more than once in his long career, and when he died in 1673 he left his immense fortune to the city's poor, for whom he created a charitable foundation. A bust of Terrisse sculpted by Auguste Baussan can be seen on the promenade.

A world of feminine beauty is visible everywhere in Agde, from the sculptures that have become emblematic of the city landscape (*la République, Belle Aghatoise, l'Amphitrite,* and *l'Allégorie de la Science*) to the name Agathé Tyché, the goddess whose statue rendered with traditional female dress can be seen at Olympia. Her garb includes an embroidered cap, called a *sarret*, a shawl of beautiful fabric decorated with the finest pearls, and the typical *coulane,* a chain of gold and pearls reaching down to the waist. The project Site des Métiers d'Art is also dedicated to feminine beauty, and many artists' studios are part of it, including the Maison d'Art and the Galerie de la Perle Noir where numerous exhibitions are organized.

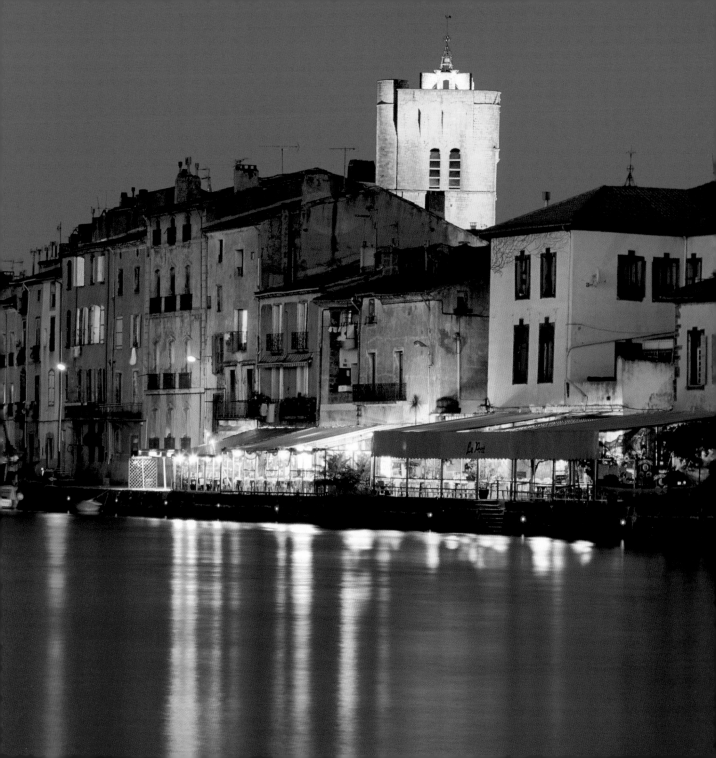

AIGUES-MORTES
BETWEEN DOG AND WOLF

WHEN SAINT LOUIS ORGANIZED HIS FIRST CRUSADE at the beginning of the thirteenth century, he was poor and completely unarmed. Montpellier belonged to the Counts of Toulouse, and Marseilles to the Roman Empire. Only the city of Aigues-Mortes could serve as his base. This was not decided by chance, but because the surrounding marshes were thought to be very unhealthy, fever-ridden and full of contagions. Even so, Saint Louis created a port and in 1246 issued a declaration of immunity granting the settlement royal protection and tax exemption to all new residents. The heart of the city grew around the church, while the city walls were built much later, during the reign of Saint Louis's son, Philip the Brave. The fortified city is completely enclosed in the irregular quadrangle of its perfectly preserved walls, with ten gateways and five towers. They were built in a single casting, which is why they have preserved all their harmony and uniformity to this day. Only two gateways open to the north, but five small gateways open to the south for access to the loading wharfs. They are the Organeau gate, the Moulins, the Galeons, the Marine, the tower of the Poudrière, and the Mèche (the fuse). Today the nearly 5,000-foot perimeter of the walls can be covered on foot and offers a dramatic view of the surrounding town and plains.

Aigues-Mortes is a beautifully melancholic town, suited to the colors of twilight—"between dog and wolf" as the French saying goes—a city of dead waters that shiver, majestic towers that rest on the moonlit salt flats, and walls that emerge from the bewitched pools and reflect in their waters. Every year in August, in remembrance of King Louis IX's visit in July 1248, the inhabitants relive the past. They dress up in period costumes and organize historical shows with ladies, jesters, tumblers, peasants, beggars, and gentlemen. The market comes alive again at the foot of the walls, the inn of the Reine Blanche reopens its doors, and farms proudly display their barnyard animals. Acrobats, jugglers, tightrope walkers, and fire-eaters perform masterfully, just as they did 700 years ago. Guests watch the entire show, from the donkey race to the archery competition and the dueling contest. The dueling is not a mere pretense; there are many schools here that instruct young lovers in this ancient art—young men who imagine themselves half in the role of Highlander, half as valiant cavaliers—and train them to faithfully re-create their art during the show. The exquisite medieval lines of Aigues-Mortes lend themselves to reenacting the past, preserving all its intense emotions. Aigues-Mortes is also the true port of the Camargue, still closely tied to the tradition of the *bouvine* celebrated in November each year.

The town is linked with the sea by the Grau-du-Roi canal.

facing page
The walls encircling the town's perimeter can be toured entirely on foot.

The Grau-du-Roi looks exactly like a postcard of a fishing port. Unlike other ports that have preserved their past only as a facade, here it really exists, with its scent of roasted sardines and its returning trawlers marking the passage of days and evenings. Originally Grau was just a group of fishermen's huts, and it was only toward the middle of the nineteenth century that the village detached itself from Aigues-Mortes. Now it is the second most important fishing port in the Mediterranean and boasts the largest tourist port in Europe, Port Camargue. The best walk imaginable begins at the Espiguette lighthouse and continues through virgin countryside, with nothing but mile after mile of beautiful dunes and sea.

Salt provided the wealth of this city, ideally separated from the Mediterranean by vast marshes and salt flats. Like water and air, salt—a product of these two elements—is essential for human life. The *Gabelle*, a royal tax, made salt the most important means of exchange. The French Revolution ended this tax, although it was later substituted with other taxes, and Aigues-Mortes soon became the supplier of soda for the soap factories of Marseilles. In 1856 the many owners of the salt flats united to found the *Salins du Midi*. The crystals, called "flowers of salt," solidified on the waves and were once reserved for the owners. Now it has become a luxury product, very much in fashion, reinvigorating the original market and turning the city into the home of the famous *La Balaine* and *Fleur de Sel de la Camargue* sea salt exported worldwide. Today Aigues-Mortes produces more than 500,000 tons of salt each year.

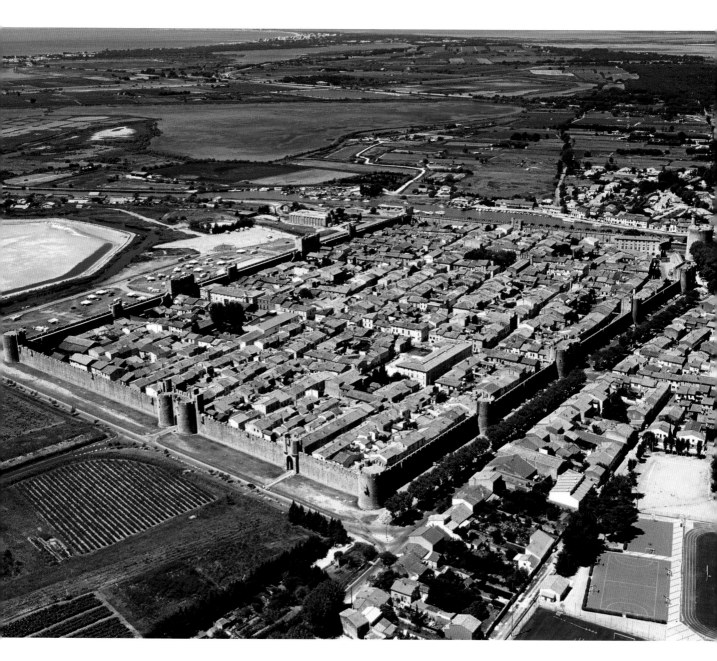

BEAUCAIRE
BEAUTIFUL STONE

BEAUCAIRE BEGAN AS A ROMAN CITY, WAS MARKED SUCCESSIVELY by the medieval and classical periods that are still visible when walking its streets, and has been the theater of many important historical events. Founded in the seventh century BC with the name of Ugernum, it was a stopping point on the Domitian way that connected Italy and Spain. Here the Roman road forked, leading to Arles, Nîmes, Remoulins, and Saint Gilles. The present name Beaucaire (meaning "beautiful stone") first appeared in 1067, when the Barbarian and Saracen invasions checked the development of the medieval cities. It was then that the first fortifications were built and the castle was enlarged; Beaucaire became one of the most important towns in the Midi, and entered into legend during the wars against the Albigensians. In 1216 Raymond VII, Count of Toulouse, and the Provençals besieged the fortress, overthrowing the crusaders led by Raymond de Montfort, and were in their turn also overcome. In 1632 Richelieu ordered the castle's demolition, and in 1845 a garden was created among the ruins. Important traces of the past remain on the castle grounds, including the great polygonal tower, a chapel, and the fourteenth-century walls.

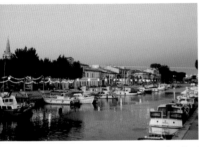

The little harbor on the Aven.

facing page
The towers of the majestic castle.

Despite the Hundred Years' War and following religious wars (from the fourteenth century through the sixteenth century), the splendor and elegance of Beaucaire's architecture increased with merchant prosperity. From the seventeenth century through the nineteenth century the city reached international fame for its Fair of the Madeleine—ten days of trading that produced a volume of business equal to the annual income of the port of Marseilles. Even the French Revolution did not halt commerce, and during this era the most beautiful noble residences and houses were built, such as the Hôtel Clausonette, the largest on the ancient rue Haute de la Drapierei (today the rue de la République), originally named for the fact that during the period of the fairs, the depositories on the ground floor were rented to silk and textile merchants.

In December 2001 the city was designated a *Ville d'art et d'historie*, a prestigious recognition for its cultural vivacity and safeguarding of its artistic and historical patrimony. The Musée August Jacquet de Beaucaire has a rich collection of archaeological objects and can take you on a voyage through the history of Europe, the Mediterranean, and above all the city, its builders, and its people. The prehistoric section displays sepulchral objects dating back to the Bronze Age. The museum's science library contains archaeological, geological, and historical treasures, and also has a complete collection of works on the *félibrige* (works by poet sages) in the local Provençal dialect.

Beaucaire is part of the Achipel des Métiers d'Art, a group supporting the presence of qualified craftsmen, particularly potters and cabinetmakers but also glassmakers, decorators, and framers. Not to be missed are the vineyards of the Terre d'Argence, where the soil is enriched by the floods of the Rhône and covered with shingle and sand. Three DOC wines are produced here: the Costière de Nimes, the Clairette de Bellegarde, and the Côtes du Rhône, but many others are worthy of interest as well, such as those of the Pays du Gard, the organically produced wines, and the Romains wines.

The image of the bull is omnipresent in the traditional culture of Beaucaire, and there are many statues honoring the famous local bullfighters, or *cocardiers*. Beaucaire is the home of bullfighting, the *camarguaises* contests, and similar events in the arenas and streets, all watched by a large crowd at the foot of the castle. The *razeteurs*, dressed in white, challenge the bulls in an attempt to remove the cockades and other ornaments hanging from the animal's horns and on its head. The *encierro* is the exhilarating spectacle of the freed bulls galloping through the streets. During the *abrivado*, however, while some horsemen try to control the animal, the most courageous attempt to immobilize it.

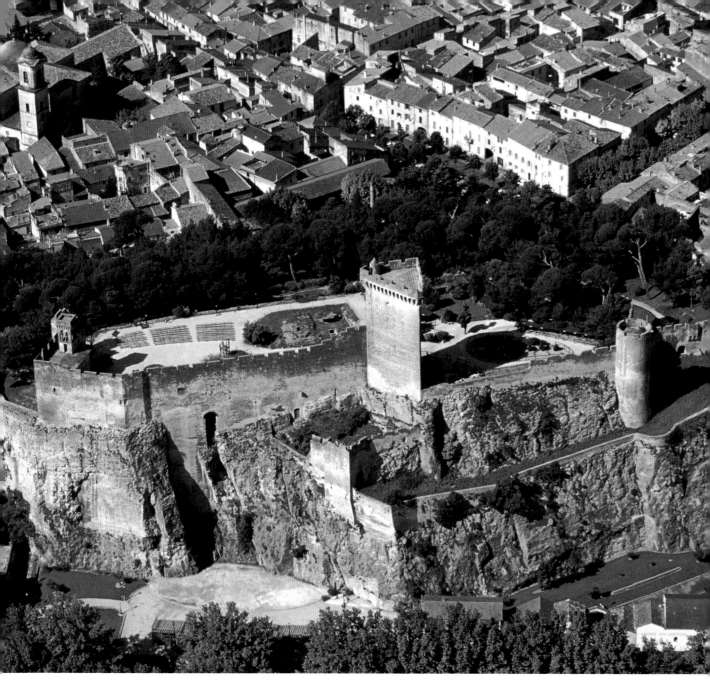

CARCASSONNE
A COLOSSAL FORTRESS

SITUATED IN THE HEART OF CATHAR COUNTRY, WHERE THE PEOPLE who opposed the crusades at the beginning of the thirteenth century were declared heretics and narrowly escaped massacre, Carcassonne seems to have come out of an old movie. It has been declared a World Heritage site, and is the largest medieval site in Europe. It was the most powerful fortress, strategically situated at the natural crossroads between the Corbières and the Montagne Noire. Although the restoration begun by Prosper Mer-imée and carried on by Eugène Viollet-le-Duc (1844–1870) may have included mistakes and approximations, today the city represents well what was, in the words of Viollet-le-Duc, "the probable ancient state of a fortified medieval city."

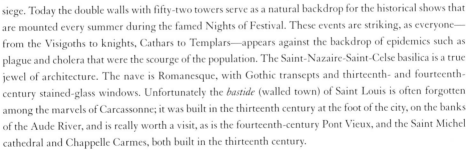

A view of the western ramparts, the count's castle, and the Porte d'Aude.

facing page
The bridge crossing the Aude River leads to the medieval town.

The ideal visit begins through the Narbonnaise gateway, flanked by two thirteenth-century towers and preceded by a drawbridge. The Lices is an immense patrol route between the double encircling walls. Then, from the steep rue Cros Mayreveielle—the cobblestones and ancient houses that flank this street are so picturesque that even the many souvenir shops cannot overshadow its beauty—one reaches the nobles' castle. Built in the twelfth century by the Trencavel family, the viscounts of Carcassonne, it was from this "fortress within the fortresses" that the city's nobles coordinated defense in case of siege. Today the double walls with fifty-two towers serve as a natural backdrop for the historical shows that are mounted every summer during the famed Nights of Festival. These events are striking, as everyone—from the Visigoths to knights, Cathars to Templars—appears against the backdrop of epidemics such as plague and cholera that were the scourge of the population. The Saint-Nazaire-Saint-Celse basilica is a true jewel of architecture. The nave is Romanesque, with Gothic transepts and thirteenth- and fourteenth-century stained-glass windows. Unfortunately the *bastide* (walled town) of Saint Louis is often forgotten among the marvels of Carcassonne; it was built in the thirteenth century at the foot of the city, on the banks of the Aude River, and is really worth a visit, as is the fourteenth-century Pont Vieux, and the Saint Michel cathedral and Chappelle Carmes, both built in the thirteenth century.

The Canal du Midi and surrounding area are the exceptional work of Pierre-Paul Riquet. It was built in the seventeenth century and declared a UNESCO World Heritage site in 1996. In order to understand and appreciate the greatness of this work carried out three centuries ago, one should see the work as a whole, including the village Les Cammazes, the San Ferréol dam, and the Fonséranes lock, among other sights. It is an excellent concentration of many arts, including hydrography, topography, geometry, and architecture. The present port at Carcassonne opened on May 31, 1810, and the present plan of the city also dates to that period.

The lower town was founded in the thirteenth century. It is crossed by the Canal du Midi and the Aude River, and has preserved the characteristics of the *bastides* both in its town planning as well as its way of life: the art of well-being, embroidered by the lazy languor of the South, mixed with a strange, almost Nordic precision and rigidity. It is a breathtaking city to fully appreciate with no inhibitions.

The culinary specialties of Carcassonne are a mixture of influences, including the Mediterranean's seafood and shellfish; the Massif Central's trout, game, and sausages; and Gascogne's foie gras and *confits.* Excellent *jambonneau* (a special ham), the famous *gésiers de volailles confits* (chicken gizzards), and the delectable goose and duck *confits* can be found throughout the city. One of the best dishes, however, is without doubt the *cassoulet,* with a white-bean base to which goose *confit,* garlic, sausage, pork rind, and sometimes partridge or mutton are added, depending on the recipe and local availability of the ingredients. It is cooked slowly, for at least two hours, in a terracotta container called a *cassole,* and is absolutely one of the richest, most savory French dishes.

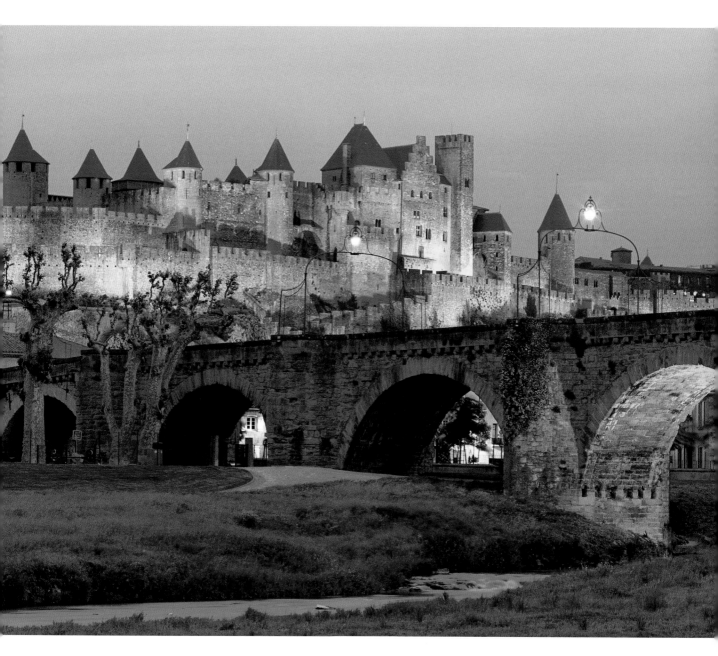

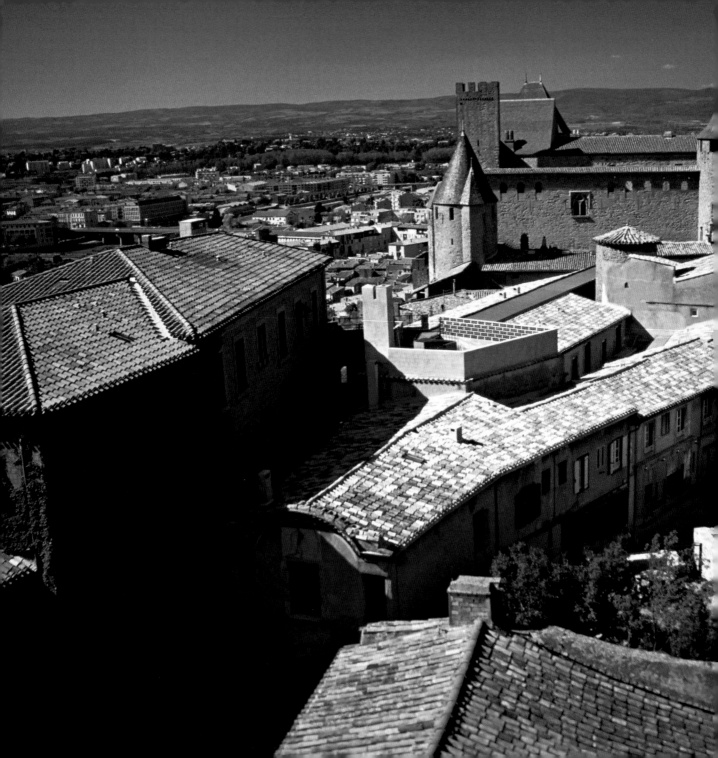

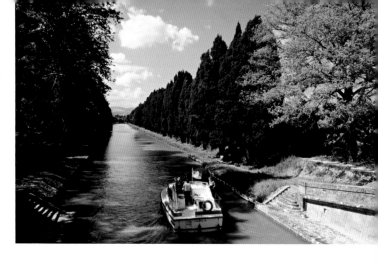

left
A striking view of the town's tiled rooftops.

right
A boat floats down the shaded Canal du Midi.

below
The basilica of Saint-Nazaire.

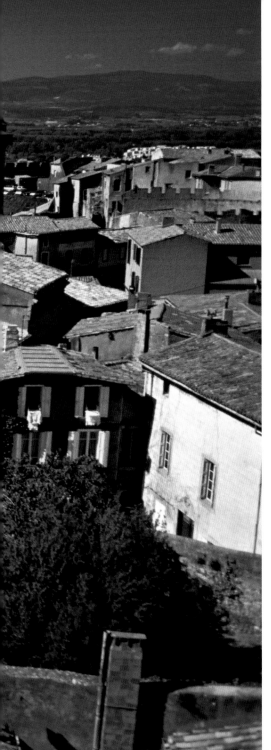

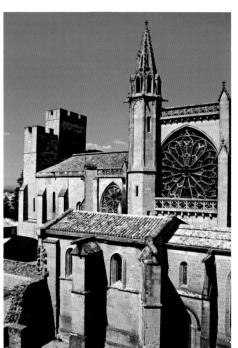

Carcassonne has an unparalleled medieval heritage, and for several decades the city has offered summer festivals for an increasing number of visitors eager to experience the ancient atmosphere in all its glory. Medieval tournaments take place in July and August, reconstructed in the finest detail, including duels and combats on horseback. The Festival of Carcassonne also takes place in July, and offers dance, opera, theater, and concerts in all the city's many different quarters. In August a great historical tableau is formed at the Grand Théâtre de la Cité Médiévale, with jousting, light shows, and incredible pyrotechnical effects—each year it becomes more elaborate. This show makes such an impression that neither adults nor children ever tire of the beauty and enchantment of the fireworks. On the evening of July 14, Bastille Day, there is a show called L'embarasement de Carcassonne. This is an impressive fireworks display, and it literally lights up all 1,800 feet of the city's defensive walls. The special effects culminate in a grand finale, making Carcassonne a decidedly flamboyant sight.

COLLIOURE
CATALONIAN CROSSROADS

The castle overlooks the picturesque harbor.

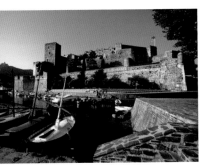

facing page
Beyond the seaside castle walls is the bell tower of the church of Notre-Dame, which also served as a lighthouse.

THIS DELIGHTFUL CATALAN PORT IN THE EXTREME SOUTH OF FRANCE is wedged into an inlet where the waters of the Mediterranean lap at the rocks of the Pyrenees. Beginning in 981 the counts of Roussillon and the king of Majorca began to plan the fortified structure of Collioure on an ancient Roman site. From 1276 to 1344 the castle was the summer residence of the kings of Aragon. The town was on the route of the crusaders during the thirteenth century, the Templars in 1207, the Cistercians in 1242, and the Dominicans in 1280. The discovery of America signaled the decline of the port and soon thereafter, during the reign of Louis XI, the French occupation began—and rapidly ended—in 1493. In 1642 the Catalan city freed itself from Spanish influence, but was occupied once again by the French. The present form of Collioure took shape during this period, when Vauban, commissioner of fortifications for Louis XIV, reinforced the royal castle and the hilltops dominating the city and demolished the external walls and bleachers. In 1659 the Treaty of the Pyrenees definitively tied the region of Roussillon to the crown of France. In 1922 the fortress was classified as a historical monument, and in that same period it was completely restored. It was occupied by the French army during World War II, and in 1951 was sold to the General Council of the Eastern Pyrenees.

The fort of Saint-Elme was built in 1552 by Charles V of Spain and for many years was the stronghold of the coastal defense system. Put up for auction, the fort passed into private hands on August 21, 1913. The Tour de Madeloc dates to the thirteenth century, and the view from the top dominates the plain and the coast of all Roussillon. The Tour de la Massane is an old lookout tower that served as strategic protection against attacks by land and sea. The church of Notre-Dame is a true historical jigsaw puzzle whose medieval bell tower doubled as a lighthouse for the port. After Vauban's demolition of the church of Sainte-Marie, in the old city, in 1672, another was built in 1684 abutting the bell tower. The Gothic style of the exterior is austere, and the interior is rich with architectural features. The main altarpiece was carved in wood and covered with gold leaf by Catalan sculptor Joseph Sunyer. The most definitive aspect of the church dates to 1810, when the cupola was added to the top of the bell tower. The cloister of the Dominican convent was built in the fourteenth century beside the old church belonging to the same order, which no longer exists. The cloister structure itself was the victim of an illicit trade in works of art, and architectural elements were rediscovered in Anglet in 1992. The town of Collioure then bought them, and in 1997 eleven of its original arches were installed in the garden of the Parc Pams.

Collioure has always been an inspiration for writers, poets, singers, and painters, all of whom have been enchanted by its magical atmosphere. Among others, Picasso, Matisse, Derain, Dufy, Chagall, and Marquet came here with their easels to immortalize the archetypal Catalan port. Others found refuge, such as Antonio Machado; this great Spanish poet and militant Republican, born in Seville on July 26, 1875, left Barcelona for exile at Collioure with his family and a few friends. Tired and quite ill, he died in the comfort of the Casa Quintana on February 22, 1939. He now lies in a modest tomb in the old village cemetery and is a symbol of so many poets' exiles. His memory grows in the silence of Collioure, while the Antonio Machado Foundation keeps his legacy alive by organizing an international poetry competition in February each year.

The anchovy is the centerpiece of a great local tradition. It is prepared in a typically Catalan way that was inherited from an ancient and natural method, and in 1994 this dish was awarded the honor of becoming a *marque site remarquable du goût*. This is a recognition conferred by the ministries of culture and agriculture. The preparation of the anchovy fillets is still carried out by hand, and the *anchoieuses* are remarkably clever at managing this little fish. Not a single phase of preparation—from salting to removal of the heads, cleaning, filleting, packaging, and preserving—can be done by machine. The anchovies of Collioure are an exquisite appetizer served either fresh, in vinegar, salted, or in oil.

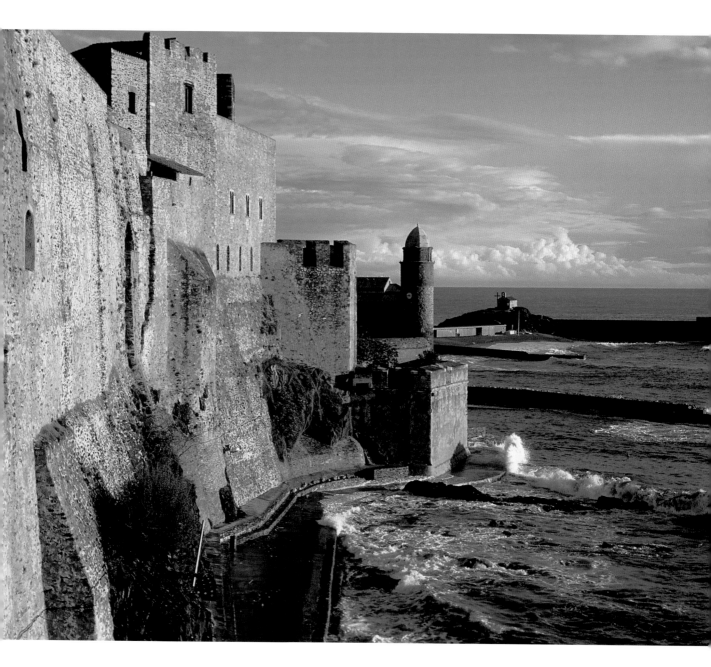

MINERVE
A HERETICAL HISTORY

MINERVE IS LOCATED TO THE WEST OF THE HÉRAULT REGION, NEAR THE AUDE RIVER, about twenty miles from Béziers. It is a small community whose settlement dates back to prehistoric times. It stands at the confluence of two rivers, the Brian and the Cesse, and overlooks a natural tunnel excavated by them. The tunnel is more than 600 feet long and 150 feet wide and is at points more than 690 feet deep.

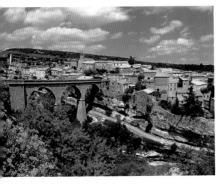

A natural bridge dominates the valley.

facing page
Another tower has been left as a testament to the town's medieval past.

The history of Minerve is closely linked to Catharism. At the beginning of the thirteenth century the local lord, Guillaume de Minerve, turned the city into a refuge for all the people who adhered to this religious doctrine. The result, in 1210, was that more than a hundred Cathars were living there. After the Grand Mazel (the massacre of Béziers on July 22, 1209) and the capture of Carcassonne during the crusade of the Albigensians, Simon de Montfort set up an inquisition against the Cathars. He moved on Minerve to root out this "nest of heretics." On June 15, 1210, there were about 1,000 Cathars and Minervoises in the city, and they watched Montfort's troops deployed on the facing slopes. Montfort positioned the giant catapult, known by the inhabitants of the town as the *Malvoisine* (the evil neighbor), and began to strike the walls with stone projectiles more than ten inches in diameter. Unbeknownst to the attackers, Minerve's provisions were abundant and the city was ready to withstand the siege, but the only well with drinking water for the whole village was outside the city walls. A fortified pathway led to the well, but it soon became a target of the *Malvoisine*. The Minervoises tried to destroy this instrument of death by organizing a sortie, but the operation failed. The following day, a better-aimed blow managed to destroy the fortified stairway that led to the well. Thirst soon claimed many victims, and after five weeks of siege the people were forced to capitulate. De Montfort agreed to spare the Christian population and the Cathars, provided they gave up their faith, but the Cathars of Minerve refused and threw themselves into the fire that had been lit in the dry beds of the Brian and Cesse rivers.

About three miles west of Minerve there is a surprising part of the road called L'Auriol (or Lauriole) where the traveler gets the impression of climbing and descending at the same time, and it would seem that a falling ball can rise up the slope just as a car without brakes also climbs. The local inhabitants call it *"la route qui monte et qui descend,"* the road that rises and falls. In reality, there is nothing magical or supernatural about it: It is all due to a difference in height of some five inches. It seems that the effect comes from an optical illusion caused by the surrounding land, so that the sense of falling—letting a cylindrical or spherical object roll downward, for example—corresponds in fact to the line set by a leveling instrument.

Today the Musée Hurepel stands on the rue des Martyrs, where scenes of the Cathars are depicted in terracotta miniatures. The Jean-Luc Séverac gallery is also interesting; he was the painter and sculptor of the famous dove on the monument to the Cathars. The castle and fortifications, the gateway of the Templars, and the eleventh-century church all remain from that bloody period.

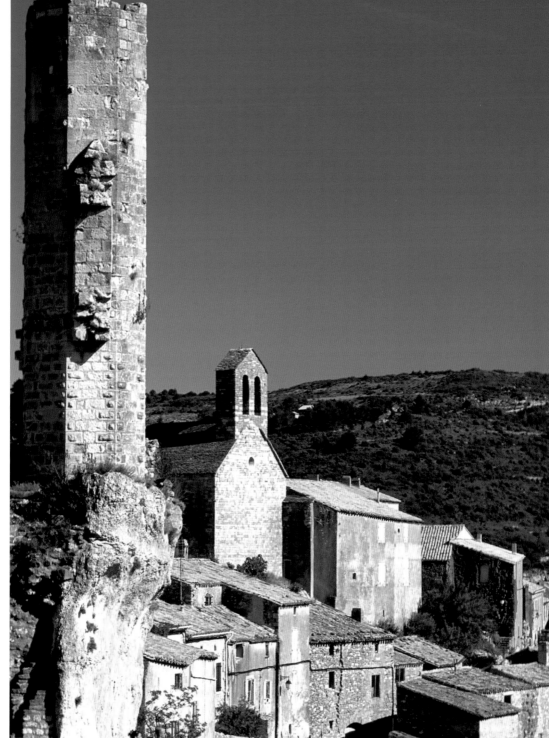

The Minervois area is recognized as one of the oldest vineyards of Europe, and produces very high-quality wines. The deep reds with their fine, balanced taste are suitable for ageing and have no equal. Since the 1950s, the winemakers have developed a system of production that has given good results, and the area received its DOC classification in 1985. Here, on more than 10,000 acres, 176 private cellars and 36 cooperatives produce red, rosé, white, and dessert wines. The Cru Minervois syndicate has built its strategy with determination, bringing the production of the area to such a high level of quality that these wines are greatly appreciated both in France and around the globe.

NARBONNE
ROMAN COLONIES

ROMAN NARBO, THE ORIGIN OF NARBONNE, WAS THE OLDEST COLONY outside Italy. It was founded in 118 BC, and during the empire of Augustus (27 BC to 14 AD) the colony enjoyed exceptional prosperity and notable urban development, as testified to by the great monuments that were built in that period and still exist today. Narbonne gives its name to the Narbonensis province, of which it is the capital. Its geographical position on the commercial route toward Aquitaine was very favorable, with both a river and seaport. Narbonne has long been a rival city of Arles and Marseilles, and maritime commerce has always been fundamental to it. At the beginning of its history the trade connections were made mainly with Italy, but there soon followed a development of routes toward Spain and the eastern part of the Roman Empire. The port played a key role in the export of Gallic ceramics, but iron, wheat, and wine were also important. The economic dynamism of the city was also due to the use of local resources such as fishing, oyster cultivation, the fish-salting industry, mines, vineyards, and olive groves. The presence of natural water basins permitted a constant profit from fish, and the salt extracted from the nearby salina beds was very important for the economy.

Narbonne began to decline in the third century, when the commercial routes were deviated toward Arles. Furthermore, the city was exposed to Barbarian invasion, so walls were built during this period to defend the city. Following the fall of the Roman Empire the city preserved its religious and political role and continued to be an important center up until the invasions of the French and the Moors. Today almost nothing is left of the ancient city except for the Horreum, a series of underground galleries that were used for storing grain, oil, and water. The archaeological museum contains pieces found in the area of the ramparts, and a collection of frescoes found at the domus of Clos de la Lombarde; a Gallic military milestone found south of Narbonne is another important piece. A paved portion of the Domitian Way has recently been discovered in the center of the city. This Roman artery enters the city near what is today known as the rue de Lattre de Tassigny, skirts the Clos de la Lombarde area, crosses the forum (between place Bistan and the Victor Hugo College), and leaves Narbonne by crossing the Aude River (the ancient Atax River) over the des Marchands bridge. Although it is hard to see the Roman parts, the city is nevertheless unique in the south of France for its particular houses.

Boats can be rented in the summer to float down the Robine canal.

facing page
The Gothic cathedral of Saint-Just is lit at dusk.

The Robine de Narbonne is an old branch of the Aude River that was abandoned after ancient times. As a result of the importance of the Canal Royal, which became the Canal du Midi during the Revolution, work began in 1686 to connect Narbonne to the canal by modifying the bed of the Robine as far as Gailhousy. The link from here to the canal had been achieved by road until, in 1776, the Canal de Jonction was built. Today it connects the Aude with the Canal du Midi passing through the Sallèles d'Aude. The whole project is composed of nine locks—six on the connecting canal and three on the Robine—and the drainage area of Gailhousy, which was designed to fill the basin of Capestang with the silt from the Aude's floods.

Beekeepers in the Languedoc-Roussillon area produce many types of honey. The clear, almost white rosemary honey, with a strong scent, has been appreciated since Roman times for it properties as a cleanser and aid for the liver. Clear or dark chestnut honey, depending on the purity of the flower, has a strong bitter aroma and is used mostly for sweet and sour dishes. Forest honey is rather dark, reddish brown, and produced everywhere. Thyme honey is the color of cinnamon with rust-colored reflections and is Europe's oldest type. Here one also finds bright yellow sunflower honey. Production of this honey is the largest in France, and it is used to make *millefleurs* cakes. Lavender honey can be clear, white, or golden yellow, and is one of the most common on the market, while the color of heath honey is a light velvet brown and tastes of candy.

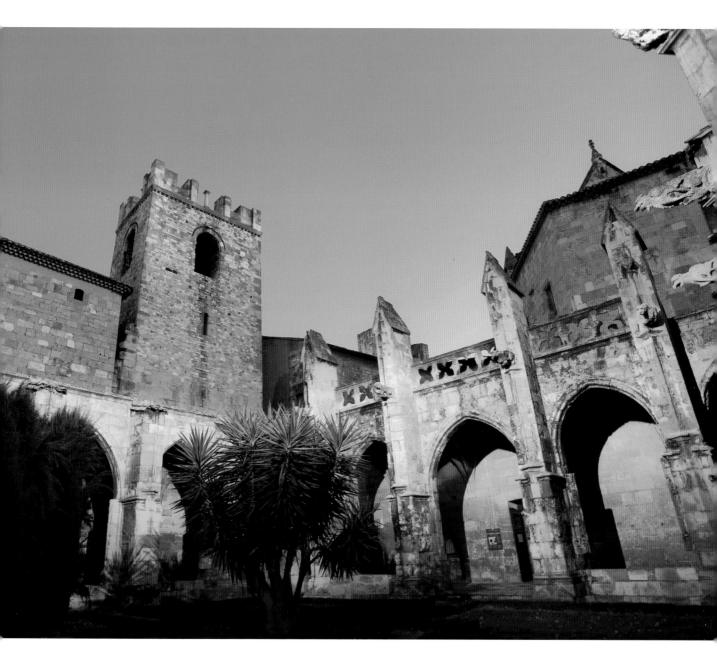

NÎMES
A CITY OF TWO CAESARS

NÎMES IS AS AMUSING AS IT IS BEAUTIFUL, SO SETTLED, COMPACT, AND WELL PLANTED between the plain and the shrub forests. It is an ancient town, with its Tour Magne, the temple of Diana, and eighteenth-century fountains, but it is also contemporary, as can be seen from the Carré d'Art with its surprising architecture. It has a schizophrenic aspect, given its Protestant heritage—one would expect to see austerity—and its festive enthusiasm, which brings about a party on the occasion of each festival. Regarding the Maison Carrée, this "Square House" is neither a house nor square in shape; it is, rather, a Roman temple of Greek influence measuring seventy-five by thirty-six feet in size. It was originally dedicated to Augustus and subsequently to Caius and Lucius Caesar. The latter two where thought of as princes, heroes of youth, and have become the symbols of Nîmes.

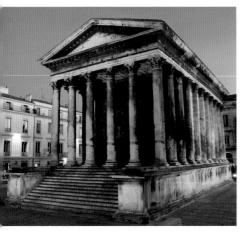

The Maison Carrée is a Roman temple originally dedicated to Augustus.

The temple was built at the beginning of the Christian era and has had various functions over the course of its history. It was a meeting place, a private residence, a stable, and even a church. Today the Maison Carrée has become a *carré d'art*—a place dedicated to art exhibitions. The gardens of the fountain are near the Tour Magne and, in 1750, were the first public gardens in France. There are many stone balconies, vases, statues of nymphs and fauns, terraces, and large fountains. Crossing the fountain gardens one comes to the octagonal Tour Magne, which has still not revealed all its secrets. It was probably a mausoleum and lookout tower, a place of cult worship, and even a lighthouse. Another mystery still exists in the temple of Diana, within the gardens. The cathedral of Notre-Dame-et-Saint-Castor, destroyed and rebuilt many times, is a splendid example of the early Romanesque style in the region. Behind it is the tomb of the famous Cardinal Bernis, the favorite of Madame de Pompadour, who died after falling into ruin during the French Revolution.

The arenas date to the first and second centuries AD and are well-preserved testimonies of the Roman presence. The Roman amphitheater, which was inspired by the architecture of the Coliseum, was mainly used for gladiatorial combat. About 2,000 years ago Roman legions and merchants began a drive westward toward Cadiz, and many traces of these massive movements remain along the Domitian Way at both Nîmes and Pont du Gard.

The Domitian Way was originally built for military purposes and then became an extraordinarily important artery of commerce and communications. It facilitated trade between Rome and the colonies, increasing communication between other cities and villages. Along its base of earth and gravel ran a deep carriageway. Runoff was achieved through lateral canals. Construction of the road was a long, meticulous, extremely complicated job. The Romans were experts in this kind of urban engineering and erected a network with more than 50,000 miles of public roads. Most roads took the name of the emperor or consul who had commissioned them, hence the Domitian Way was built in 118 BC and took its name from Domitius Ahenobarbus, proconsul of the province of Narbonne.

facing page Outside the arena a statue pays tribute to the bullfight, an event that still takes place today.

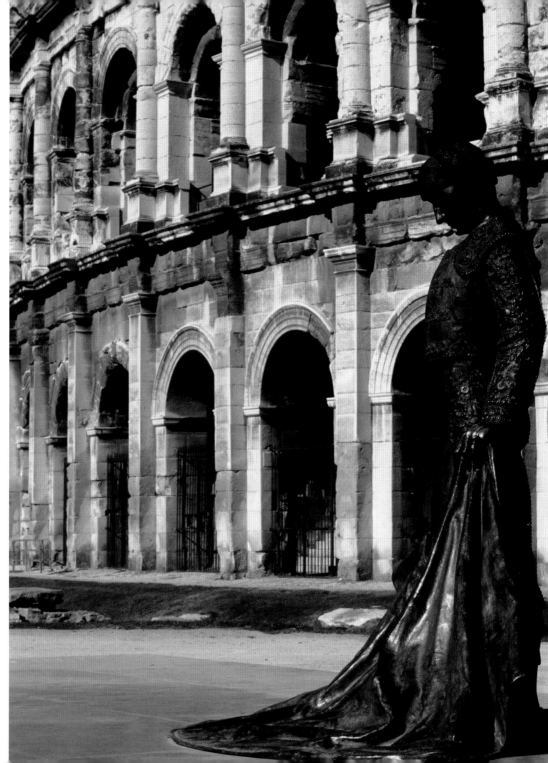

The *courses camarguaises*, also known as the race of the cockade, has long been a popular form of entertainment that takes place in many villages of the Gard and Hérault regions. The rules are very precise, and it can be dangerous. Men dressed in white must circle around a bull (the circle is called a *razet*) and try to snatch the cockade tied to the animal's horns. What counts is the style, agility, and courage of the contestants—and their panache. After the competition the bravest bullfighters are celebrated with statues in their honor.

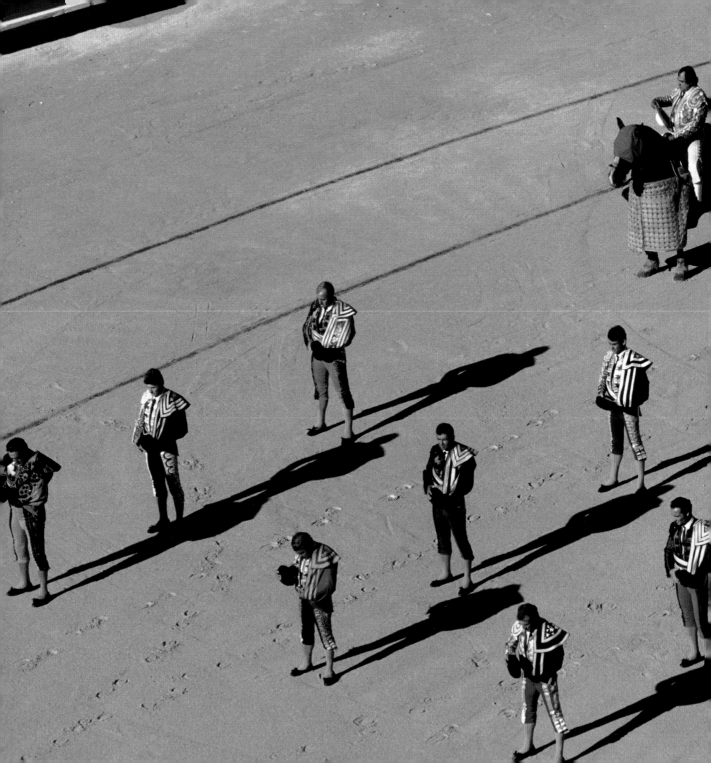

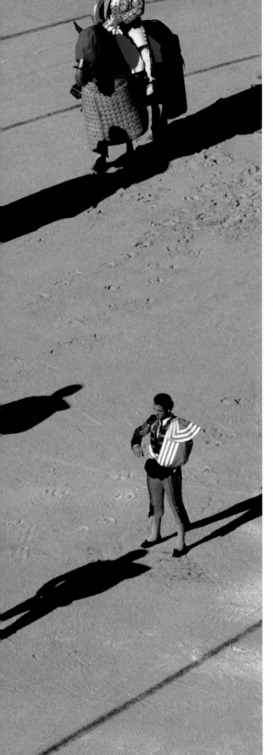

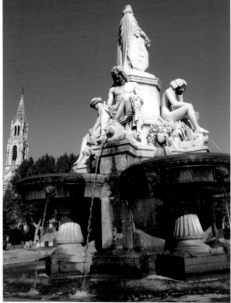

Toward the middle of the first century BC, during the reign of Claudius, the need to bring water to the ancient city lead to the construction of a great aqueduct. It is almost thirty miles long and collects water from a spring near Uzès, bringing it as far as Castellum, near Nîmes. Most of the aqueduct is underground, but there are several difficult geographical features that had to be overcome, inspiring one of the most beautiful works of civil engineering in the entire Roman Empire, the Pont du Gard. This monumental work was built entirely in stone without any mortar. It has three levels of arches that sustain a covered channel for a length of about 800 feet at a height of almost 150 feet. In the Middle Ages the secondary level of the bridge was used as a walkway, which endangered the original stability of the structure. In the eighteenth century an attempt was made to restore the bridge by moving the walkway to the lower level. This magnificent bridge is now one of UNESCO's World Heritage sites, and the nearby museum displays details of this great feat of engineering.

left
The *corridas* take place during the famous fairs of the harvest, spring, and Pentecost.

above
One of the town's many impressive fountains.

below
The Pont du Gard, with its three tiers of arches, is part of an ancient Roman aqueduct.

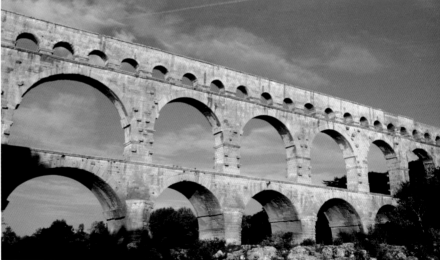

S È T E
LANGUEDOC'S NEWEST ARRIVAL

LYING BETWEEN THE THAU BASIN AND THE SEA, Sète is one of the main fishing, trade, and recreational sailing ports of the Mediterranean Sea. The town lives with the rhythm of its fishing boats, cargoes, and ferries. Suspended on top of Mont Saint-Clair, it provides a stunning view over the gulf, the Thau basin, and the sailors' cemetery. But where does its infinite seduction come from? Comparing Sète with its beautiful neighbors and ancient rivals, such as Agde, Aigues-Mortes, or Montpellier, it cannot boast of their prestigious long history nor the splendor of their exceptional monuments. In an area where nearly every citizen can claim a millennial past, this so-called Venice of the Languedoc, founded in 1666, is virtually considered a new town. Gallic-Roman remains have certainly been found on the site of the town, and other signs reveal evidence of a medieval town, but there is no trace of a real settlement. The true city rose thanks to the progressive silting of the Agde River and growth of Aigues-Mortes, Lattes—the *avant-port* of Montpellier—and Narbonne. It was also thanks to Colbert's desire to give France a powerful Mediterranean port, and also to Pierre-Paul Riquet, who proposed an outlet for the Canal du Midi. Sète most likely owes its existence to this last fact.

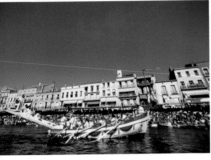

The famous nautical tournament of Saint-Louis takes place on August 25.

Its secret is that it is the final port city of the Languedoc and has all the color and freshness of youth. This is not a place to look for sublime churches or unapproachable historical monuments; the charm of Sète is in its perfumes of iodine and *garrigue*—the unique land of heath and heather between the hills and the sea—its special light, the festive atmosphere of its quays, the incredible grace of its natural environment, and the naval cemetery. Mont Saint-Clair rises dramatically behind, and Sète is divided between a lower city and upper city. The lower city is along the shoreline, with the canals and bridges that make it look like a lake. The Saint-Louis quay protects the port and recreational boats, and the quais de la Consigne and du Général-Durand, where the fishing boats are moored, are the most lively. Facing them, the quai Aspirant-Herber offers a beautiful view of the city. Between the city and the Thau basin, at the mouth of the canal, La Pointe Courte is an authentic fishermen's village. The upper town has spread its residential areas and its wide open spaces around Mont Saint-Clair, and both Paul Valéry and Georges Brassens were laid to rest on the hillside, facing the sea.

George Brassens, the famed singer-songwriter, was born in Sète in 1921. He died in 1981 and wished to be buried in the most beautiful and moving sailors' cemetery, where Paul Valéry was also buried. With Jacques Brel and Léo Ferré, Brassens was one of the most important figures of twentieth-century French music. His songs, many of which have been translated and performed in other languages, were often political, and many spoke of the sadness of lost love. Others were carefree, but they were always characterized by a great sweetness. One of his best-known songs was dedicated to passing encounters: "I dedicate this song / to every woman who is an object of love / in a moment of freedom / to the one you have just met / but there was no time nor was it worth losing more than a century / to the almost imagined woman / you saw her so fleetingly / passing on the balcony to a secret beyond / and you like to remember the smile that she didn't give you / and that you decided upon in a moment of emptiness . . . ."

The Mediterranean flavors of the cuisine of Sète are particularly famous. Local specialties include *rouille*, *macaronades*, and *tielle*. *Tielle* is a sort of squid pot pie, made with a simple pastry of flour, water, and yeast. The squid is cooked in a *court bouillon*, a broth scented with bay leaf, white wine, onions, and parsley. The *macaronade* is a vegetable soup cooked for a long time with beef, sausage, parmesan, and red wine. *Rouille* is the sauce with which *bouillabaisse*, the typical fish soup of this part of the Mediterranean, is dressed.

facing page
A typical oyster farm in the Thau lagoon.

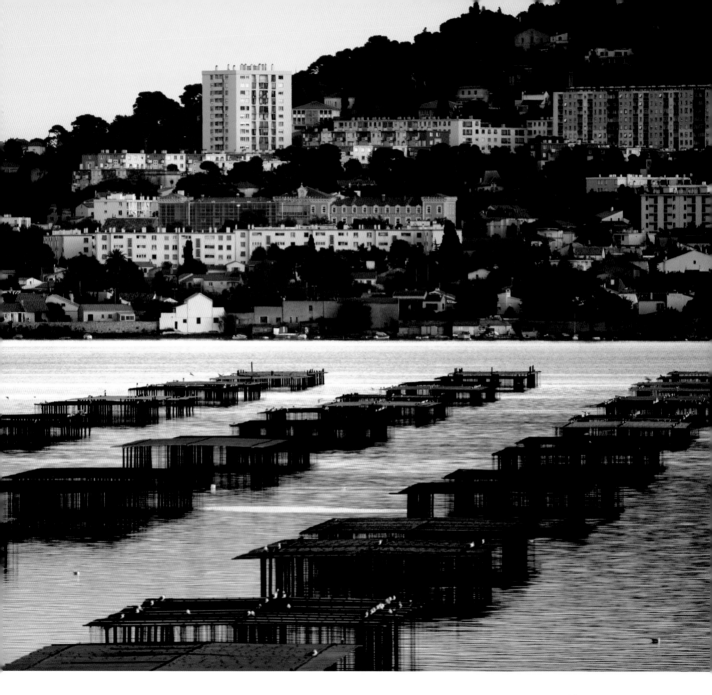

UZÈS
FRANCE'S FIRST DUCHY

THE ADORABLE, DISCERNING, ATTRACTIVE, AND DELIGHTFUL UZÈS was the first duchy in France. The city shows itself off almost flirtatiously, pointing out all the graces around its eleventh-century ducal castle, from the cathedral to the Italianate towers. It was at the height of splendor in the eighteenth century, the period during which the sumptuous *hôtels particuliers*—the mansions of the nobility—were built. They can be seen all over the city and are still admired today.

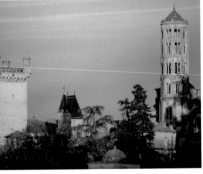

The elegant Finestrelle tower is among the many splendid buildings in the duchy.

Uzès was a bishopric and consular center as well as a duchy, and it is also famous because Jean Racine spent a long time here in 1661. Most important, it was set apart for protection by André Malraux, who included Uzès among the fifty French towns whose architecture and character it was essential to save. Looking from a distance at the towers silhouetted against the beautiful sky of the Gard region, it is obvious that Uzès is a town unlike any other. With merely 8,000 inhabitants, it is more like a large village than a town, but it has an incredible history and wealth. It was likely founded by the Greeks in about the sixth century BC and was next a Roman *castrum*, or garrison. In 417 it became a bishopric, and in 1565 it became a duchy. Thanks to the textile industry it had a period of prosperity between the sixteenth and eighteenth centuries, before it fell into decline and eventually into ruin. Its glory returned once again at the beginning of the 1970s, although it was very different from that of its past. Malraux's attention was the salvation of Uzès. After the town was restored and found its original grace and beauty again, Uzès became what it is today, one of the loveliest pearls of southern France.

The Duché, the jewel of Uzès, is a complex of the ducal castle with a Renaissance facade, fifteenth-century Gothic chapel, and the Bermonde tower, an eleventh-century keep. The exceptional tower remains the property of the Crussol d'Uzès family. Among other major monuments the Finestrelle tower is unique, with a round bell tower thought to be one of the purest masterpieces of Romanesque art. Its elegant silhouette rises impressively beside the eighteenth-century bishop's palace.

The medieval garden of Uzès is very worth a visit. Situated in the heart of the village, it is in the historic area at the foot of the eleventh-century Tours du Roi and the Eveque, and is a veritable herbarium. Lilies and roses, religious allegories of love, and historically important grains and legumes are to be found in the greenhouse. Some of the plants are not for use in the modern kitchen but for medicinal purposes, and some have symbolic value. Pamphlets give detailed explanations of the use of each plant and its history. There are also exhibitions of contemporary art that mingle well with the green shoots, luxuriant leaves, and colorful berries.

The best walk is around the romantic promenade des Marronniers, where Racine's former house can be visited. The market of Uzès is also wonderful, and to live in the area is everyone's dream. It is one of the most beautiful places in France, and there is a famous truffle market when these local treasures are in season.

facing page
A glimpse of the bold Tour de Vigie.

The Museum of the Bonbon, where one can enjoy more than a century of candy's history, welcomes both children and adults. Those who love *Tagada* strawberries and *Hari Croco* candies will appreciate the marvelous history of the Haribo delicacies, from their origins to the present day. Founder Hans Riegel was born in 1893 at Bonn-Friesdorf and began his company on December 13, 1920, the day of Saint Lucia. He called the company Haribo, an acronym for Hans Riegel Bon. His starting capital was a sack full of sugar and many good ideas, from which sprang his first success, the "dancing bear," a gummy treat still appreciated by children of all nations.

METZ
ARCHITECTURE, ACOUSTICS, AND ART

METZ IS A REGIONAL CAPITAL AND A PLEASANT TOWN CROSSED BY CANALS, blessed with splendid museums, and refined by many gardens and parks. Three thousand years of history are collected behind its walls. An ideal visit begins in the historic center, in the distinctly medieval place Saint Louis, with its arches, stone buttresses, and fourteenth-, fifteenth-, and sixteenth-century houses. In the Middle Ages this is where fairs, markets, feasts, and sumptuous ceremonies were held.

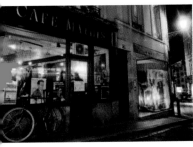

Café Mathis first opened in the fifteenth century as a wine shop.

facing page
The cathedral of Saint-Étienne illuminated at night.

Here one can visit the thirteenth- and fifteenth-century church of Saint Martin, with the beautiful stained-glass windows and grouped sculptures inside. The apse and bell tower of the twelfth-century church of Saint Maximin are Romanesque, the central and lateral naves are Gothic, the portal is Baroque, and the windows inside are the work of Jean Cocteau. The Portes des Allemands is a little castle with four towers that defended the bridge over the Seille River, and a romantic walk along the ruins of the ancient walls begins here. The theater, an eighteenth-century building and now the oldest active theater in France, stands on the place de la Comédie. The cathedral of Saint-Étienne is the most important building in Metz from a historical and artistic point of view and is one of the most beautiful and tallest Gothic buildings in France. The cathedral is also called "God's Beacon" because of its immense windows—6,500 square yards' worth—created between the twelfth and sixteenth centuries. Among the most recent windows are "Earthly Paradise" and "Original Sin" by Marc Chagall. The cathedral of Saint-Étienne is striking for its height and, at the same time, its harmony, with a truly notable stylistic unity. Here the Gothic style has managed to combine elevation, which in other equally interesting buildings seems out of balance, and the golden section of architectural elegance. The two towers were built in the thirteenth century, as were the bas-reliefs of the portal of Notre-Dame la Ronde. The nave is magnificently decorated with leaves and drapery and measures over 126 feet high, making it one of the tallest in France. Visit the Cour d'Or Museum in the old convent des Petits Carmes and study the details of religious art richly represented in thirty-four panels of sculpted wood. There are sculptures from the Middle Ages and European painting of many ages, with works by Delacroix, Corot, Picasso, Vuillard, and others. The museum includes a Roman wall, Merovingian sepulcher, Romanesque architrave, medieval ceiling, Gothic pointed arch, the facade of a Renaissance palace, and the extravagance of a Baroque staircase. Metz is full of places to discover, and its atmosphere is absolutely inebriating.

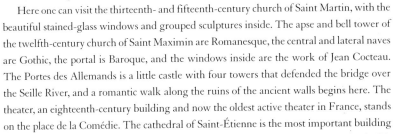

The Arsenal cultural center was founded in 1978, when the municipality of Metz decided to build a different kind of concert hall. In 1985 the project was given to Ricardo Bofil, and the architect transformed the military edifice built by Napoleon III into a daringly contemporary yet classical building. With the cooperation of the local architects of Metz, he managed to combine classicism with technical modernity, choosing not to build an all-purpose hall but rather to create an exceptional place for listening to exquisite music. Architecture, acoustics, and art were the Arsenal's three A's. After a concert on February 26, 1989, Rostropovitch said that "the acoustics are fantastic, the proportions are ideal for music, and I find the atmosphere exceptional. All the music of the world will find its right dimension here."

The *mirabelle* of Lorraine is a sweet, honey-colored plum. The name means "beautiful to look at," and the *mirabellier* is the most important fruit tree of the region. "This fruit could only come from the earth of Lorraine—elsewhere it would be hard and wild, but here you can make a liqueur from it that will save you from even the plague." These were the words of Saint Nicolas, quoted by the abbot Miot de Foug, author of a famous legend about *mirabelle*. No other fruit as perfect as this can exist outside this territory. In fact, the soil is clay-laden and heavy, the harsh climate is but a blessing for this delicious fruit that, since 1996, has been assigned the European IGP, denoting its *Indication Géographique Progégéè*.

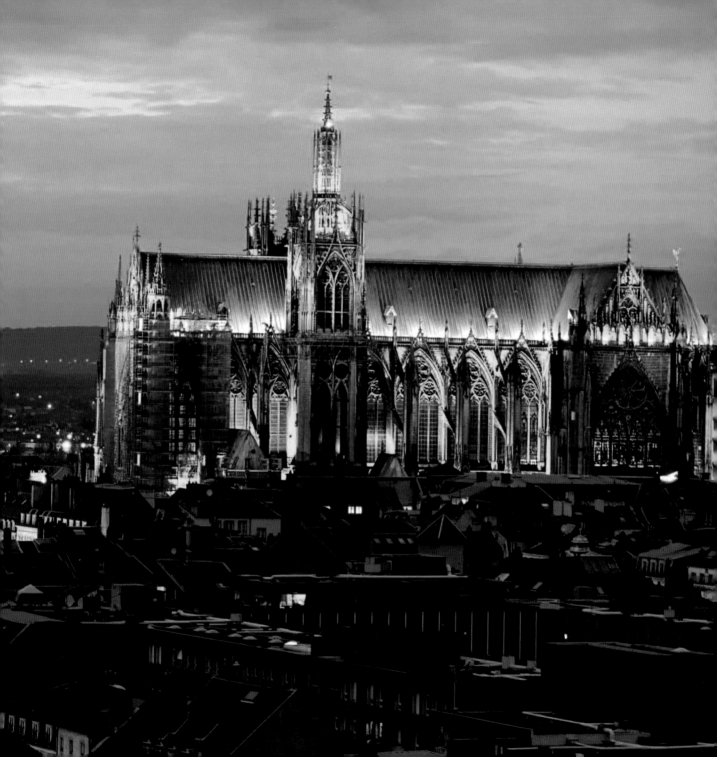

NANCY
ART NOUVEAU TREASURES

Nancy was beautified in the eighteenth century by Stanislas Leszczynski, the king of Poland and duke of Lorraine. This historic capital of the duchy has some very notable architecture and is a UNESCO World Heritage site. Stanislas Square is known as one of the most beautiful in Europe; it seduces its visitors and, for the residents, is the heart of the city. The gilded wrought-iron railings, designed by Jean Lamour, seem to connect the buildings to one another, and the celebrated fountains of Amphitrite and Neptune are the work of Barthélémy Guibal. It is among the first squares in France and made even more grandiose by the triumphant arch that is an homage to King Louis XV, son-in-law of King Stanislas. The Musée des Beaux-Arts is another jewel and contains a vast collection of European art from the fourteenth through the twentieth centuries, including paintings by Caravaggio, Rubens, Boucher, Delacroix, Manet, and Picasso, sculpture by Rodin and César, and engravings and lithographs by Callot and Grandville. There is also an exceptional collection of 300 pieces of Daum glass. The Musée Lorrain is in a Renaissance ducal palace and contains a vast amount of documentation on the history of the region and King Stanislas, with sculpture, ceramics, and paintings—including a few by Georges de La Tour, native of Vic-sur-Seille. Nearby stands the beautiful, monumental Porte de la Craffe,

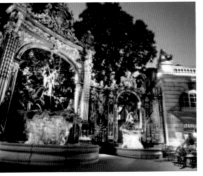

Place Stanislas, built for the glory of King Louis XV, was completed in 1755.

a last rare trace of the fortifications of the old city, together with two massive twin towers that were built in 1463 and have resisted every siege. Nancy is known as one of the great European capitals of Art Nouveau. The movement began in the early twentieth century and was characterized by architecture, furniture, glass, wrought iron, and ceramic masterpieces. Nature is everywhere in these splendid and colorful art forms. A walk in the city lets the visitor discover some splendid Art Nouveau buildings, such as the Brasserie Excelsior decorated by Majorelle, the building of the daily newspaper *L'est republicain*, and the Crédit Lyonnais bank with stained-glass windows by Gruber. The Museum of the Nancy School provides a fantastic panorama of this prolific design art, with furniture and objects by Émile Gallé, Louis Majorelle, Eugène Vallin, Jacques Gruber, and the Daum brothers. The religious patrimony of Nancy is also interesting and includes the cathedral, the church of the Cordeliers, and the stupendous funerary monument of the Duchess of Gueldres sculpted in limestone and painted by Ligier Richier. The Museum of Arts and Popular Traditions is also very interesting. A walk among the rose gardens of the Parc de la Pepinière, in the heart of the city, will give any visitor an appetite, and many good restaurants offer delicious local specialties for dinner.

One of the greatest periods in the history of Lorraine is without doubt the Art Nouveau era. The arrival of the railroad, the birth of the university, and the development of the steel and chemical industries further enlivened this artistic movement. By giving artistic value to objects, the Nancy School confirmed the alliance between art and industry that characterizes the modern world and re-established a relationship between the ordinary and the exceptional that had almost disappeared. Émile Gallé was a glassmaker and furniture designer, and from 1901 on he welcomed many artists to the Nancy School to learn about the contemporary art of floral decoration. After the success of Gallé, many local artists in Paris in 1884 and during the Universal Exposition of 1889 followed his example. Among them were Majorelle, Vallin, Daum, and Gruber.

facing page
The lit facade of one of the palaces overlooking Place Stanislas.

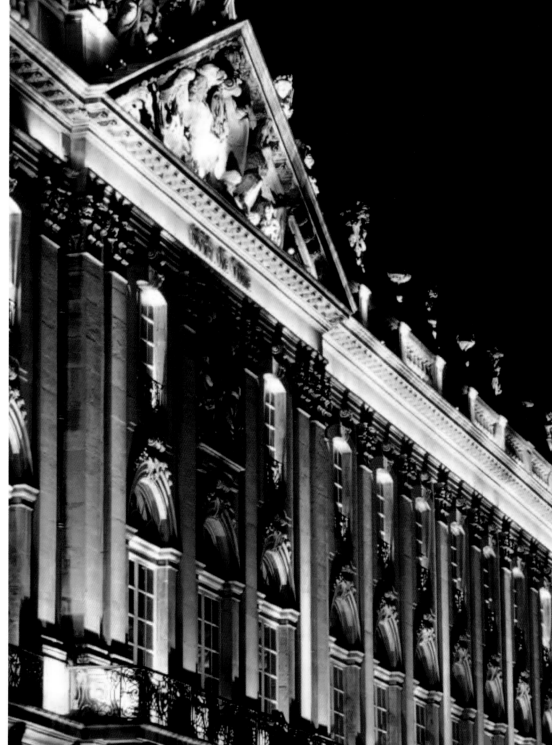

Nancy is a city of superb cuisine. One day King Stanislas Leszczynski found that the *kouglof* was a little too dry and asked for some Malaga wine to be poured over it—a small gesture that led to the birth of the *babà*, which was later moistened with rum. His daughter, Queen Marie Leszczynski, invented *vol-au-vent*, that delicious puff pastry filled with pieces of chicken, giblets, mushrooms, and many other kinds of wonderful fillings. The dessert specialties are *bergamotte*, a mixture of sugar and essential oil of bergamot, the transparent golden caramel, and the macaroon, invented in 1793 by two nuns who were subsequently called the *macaron* sisters.

VERDUN
VALIANT SURVIVOR

VERDUN IS UNIVERSALLY KNOWN FOR THE TERRIBLE BATTLE OF 1916. The *voie sacrée* is a moving memorial that was set up after World War I as a tribute to the role that Verdun played during that battle, upon which the destiny of France depended. More than 2 million *poilus* (the French soldiers of World War I) took part, 162,000 died on the field of honor, and 216,000 were wounded. It is surprising, however, to discover a town that is so far from the image created by the history books. Goethe described it as a town surrounded by lawns and gardens. The center of the city has been restored, and the tourist port gives Verdun the atmosphere of a seaside resort, with the beach of Pré l'Évêque and the avenues of the Parc Horticole.

Verdun's history began in the Stone Age, as can be seen in the Musée de la Princerie, a beautiful sixteenth-century noble mansion. Its facade is somber, characterized by cross-shaped windows with jutting iron grilles and a heavy main door surmounted by a statue of the Virgin. This leads to a cloister on two floors, decorated with columns. This museum of art and history contains arrowheads, flint tools, a beautiful collection of sacred objects, and many paintings of the Lorraine region. It could be said that the history of Verdun was at the crossroads of the history of Europe. Here, in 843, the traces of modern Europe were sketched when the treaty of Verdun, signed by the descendants of Charlemagne, divided the empire into three distinct states: France, Lotharingia, and Germany. Enthusiasts of ancient sites should stroll the narrow medieval streets, visit the cathedral, whose oldest sections date to the eleventh century, and pass through the Roman Porte Chatel, which was modified during the Renaissance. To get to Paris and Champagne merchants discovered the path of the sentries along the walls of the town and a tunnel almost four miles long that was a veritable underground city where troops had previously taken refuge. In the old town the fountains are a reminder of the presence of the river and canals. From the amphitheater at the tourist port the river and its navigating boats can be seen. A great square dominates the town and is enlivened by many cafés and restaurants—this is the area of Verdun where festivals and cultural events take place throughout the year. Places of remembrance include the battlefields where almost 800,000 men died between 1916 and 1917. The Centre de la Paix, in the old bishop's palace, serves as a reminder that in 1987 Verdun was the world capital of peace, liberty, and human rights.

Simple white crosses in front of the charnel house of Doualmont.

Verdun is etched deeply into the memory of the French people. In 1916 the war was bogged down on all fronts, and to discourage the Allied coalition and thwart the imminent Anglo-French attack on the Somme, the Germans were determined to unleash a decisive blow to the French army. They chose Verdun, hoping to attack the largest part of the French forces. The battle began at dawn on February 21, 1916, under a rain of fire and metal from 1,225 cannons. Offensives and counter-offensives continued along these few square yards until July, a period now called the Hell of Verdun. The soldiers in the trenches suffered the infernal attacks of gas, mud, fear, and cold. It was one of the bloodiest battles and was won by the French, but at a terrible price: 360,000 French and 330,000 Germans were killed or reported missing.

Local delicacies include honey, *quiche lorraine*, wines of the Mosa, the Mirabelle honey tart, the winter hotpot of pork and cabbage, the madeleines of Commercy to be dipped in a cup of tea, and finally the famed *dragée* of Verdun, the sugared-almond stars of the city. According to legend, sugared almonds were invented in 1220 by a local pharmacist. He was looking for a way of preserving and transporting almonds, so he covered them with a hard coat of sugar and honey. Good for fresh breath and digestion, they are thought to be, above all, a defense against sterility, and for this reason they are always present at wedding and baptismal banquets.

facing page
The twin towers of the Porte Chaussée reflected in the Meuse.

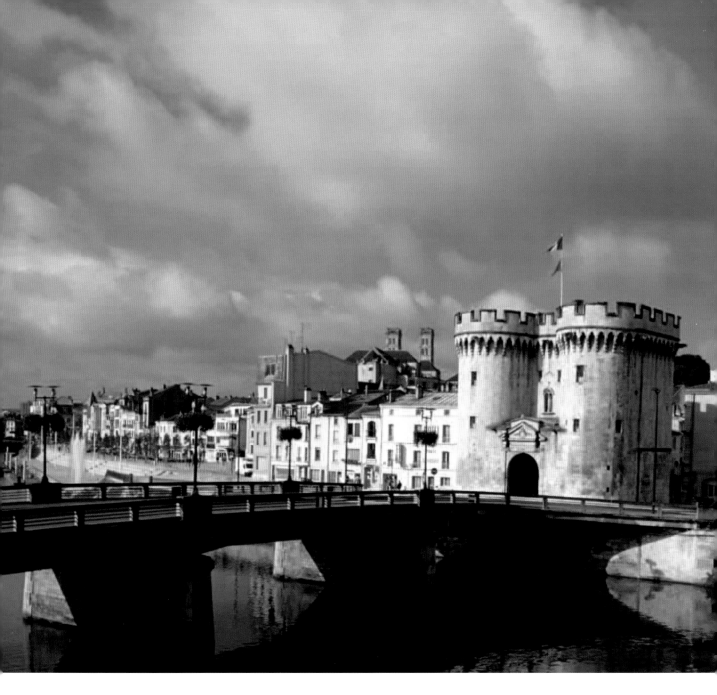

A L B I
A PURE RED PRINCESS

ALBI, ILLUMINATED BY THE SUN AND THE WATERS OF THE TARN RIVER, has a unique charm. The town is dressed in red tiles and bricks, with a cathedral and imposing nave characterized by the magnificent contrast between its rigorous exterior and the sumptuous richness of the interior—a living testimony to the power of the Christian faith before the Cathar heresy. It was the hometown of a famous navigator named Lapérouse, and a unique artist, the Count of Toulouse-Lautrec. The site of so-called Red Albi was inhabited well before the Roman colonization in the second century BC. From the fifth through seventh centuries the Vandals, Visigoths, and Moors all asserted their power here. Later on Albi was reunited to the kingdom of France, but relations grew complicated in the tenth century, when the Cathar heresy erupted. The pope and the king became close allies until the movement was completely annihilated. In 1209 the first crusade against the Albigensians took place, but the Cathar fortress of Monségur was not vanquished until 1244. Albi was never deemed a heretical city, even though the population certainly had some sympathy for the Cathar doctrine. In order to restore the authority of the church, the clergy decided to build the splendid cathedral of Sainte-Cécile, an imposing structure of red brick consecrated in 1480. The single nave is nearly 300 feet long, and the vault rises to a soaring 90 feet. The interior walls are completely painted over, and a magnificent, richly sculpted portico-baldachin leads to the vault. The extraordinary *jubé*—the stone or wooden dais that separated the liturgical choir from the nave—looks like a surprising embroidery in stone in a flamboyant Gothic style. A painting of the Last Judgment, a masterpiece of the fifteenth century, fills the western wall. Above it stands a beautiful eighteenth-century organ, and many Gothic fifteenth- and sixteenth-century statues and frescoes complete the rich decoration of the interior. The ancient bishop's palace of Berbie, near the cathedral of Sainte-Cécile, contains the Toulouse-Lautrec Museum. This great artist was a habitué of the cafés-concerts of Paris, and his early works are witness to a ferocious talent full of compassion for travelers of the night such as Aristide Bruant, La Goulue, and Yvette Guilbert, who lived in Montmartre. The streets at the ancient heart of Albi offer more beautiful buildings for the visitor, such as the medieval and Renaissance houses and the seventeenth- and eighteenth-century *hôtels particuliers*. There is a beautiful view of the town from the Pont Vieux, and an excursion on the crystalline waters of the Tarn in a *gabarre*, the traditional flat-bottomed boat, is highly recommended.

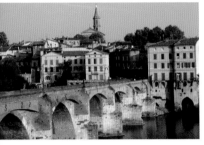

The old bridge on the Tarn River.

facing page
The Berbie palace's garden is decorated with graceful geometric forms.

The Cathar heresy (from the Greek *katharos*, meaning "pure") and the repression that followed have been etched deeply into the memory of southwestern France. This doctrine, of Eastern origin, invoked as a principle the struggle between Good and Evil. The first was destined for the eternal kingdom of the spirit created by God, while the second was corruptible materialism, which belonged to the realm of Satan. The Cathar way was, therefore, that of purification that transformed them into *Parfaits*. All this was, of course, seen as a rejection of Rome's authority. Very soon the counts of Foix and Béziers, and also the Viscount of Carcassonne, converted to the doctrine under the protection of the Count of Toulouse. Two crusades, in 1209 and 1226, and the inquisition created in 1223, were instituted in the struggle against the heretics. The famous Cathar fortress of Montségur fell in 1244, and the last one, Quéribus, fell in 1255. From that moment the lands of the *langue d'oïl* (the North) took the upper hand over those of the *langue d'oc* of Occitaine and Aquitaine.

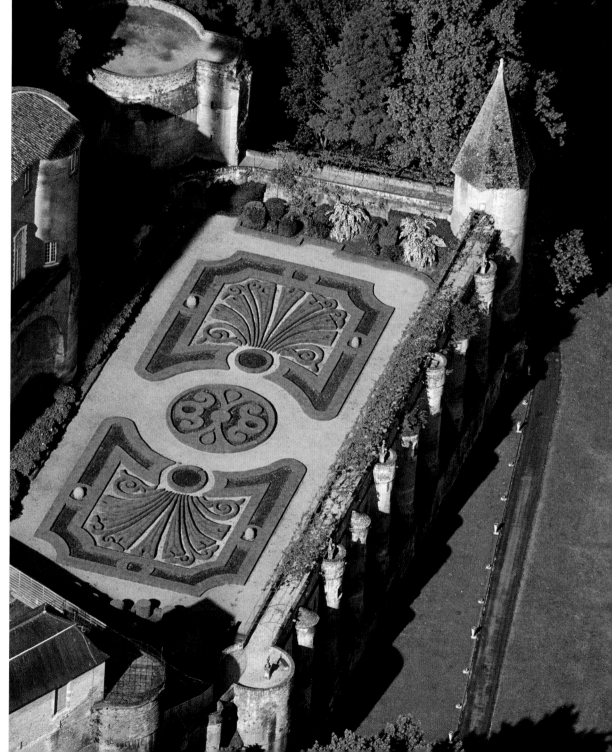

Pastel was the traditional plant of dyers, from which the many shades of blue were added to local textiles, and was also known since antiquity for its medicinal properties. It was cultivated in the Mediterranean basin, and beginning in the fourteenth century production at Albi, Toulouse, and Carcassonne became very important, and it was sold all over Europe. The leaves of *pastel* were reduced to a paste that was transformed, by means of a special treatment, into small balls, the precious *coques* or *cocagnes*. Cultivation stopped in the sixteenth century, after the religious wars and with the arrival of indigo, a dye imported from the Indies. Modern cosmetics are reevaluating this plant; as a result cultivation has begun again, and it is once again commonly found in local markets.

A U C H
G A S C O N Y ' S   H E A R T

AUCH IS A CHARMING CAPITAL UNDER SUNSHINE THAT LIGHTS UP ITS PALE STONES. Leaning up against a limestone hill, it spreads around the cathedral and the Tour d'Armagnac and then rests at the amphitheater on the banks of the Gers River. The old city is divided into upper and lower parts; between these two levels there is an intricate series of little stairways, called *pousterles*. These steps originated in the Middle Ages, bordered by the old houses, and make for a quiet and picturesque scene.

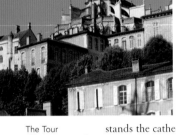

The Tour d'Armagnac and cathedral rise atop the old town.

facing page
A statue of D'Artagnan, the musketeer made famous by Dumas' pen.

Quite the opposite can be said of the monumental stairway of 370 steps built in 1673. At the top stands the statue of the city's most famous son, Charles de Batz, Count of Artagnan, officer of the musketeers of Louis XIV, and hero of Dumas' famous novel *The Three Musketeers*. This celebrated musketeer was born in 1610, died in 1673, and is better known as a literary character than a historical figure, but he is certainly the standard-bearer of Gascony, his native land. Elegant, generous, and sometimes reckless, he can only be described with one word—*panache*. This was D'Artagnan's famous motto, and it is best translated as some sort of combination of pride, risk-taking, and fearlessness. The more important houses are concentrated in the upper city. On the shaded place Salinis stands the cathedral of Sainte-Marie, one of the last built in France, between the fifteenth and seventeeth centuries, in a splendid Gothic style with Renaissance and classical touches. The Renaissance stained-glass windows are the work of the artist Pierre de Moles, and the 113 choir stalls are from the same period, but Gothic in style and magnificently decorated with 1,500 delicate sculptures. Beside the cathedral stands the Palais de l'Officialité, once the ecclesiastical court, and the fifteenth-century Tour d'Armagnac, the court prison, which rises to a height of more than 120 feet. To the left of Sainte-Marie is the old convent of the Jacobins, and beside it is the archbishopric, which was rebuilt in the eighteenth century, and is now the prefecture of the Gers region. Today the convent is a delightful museum displaying the local arts and traditions and has a beautiful collection of pre-Colombian art, sacred art from Latin America, and Egyptian art. Auch can also be proud of something that is not exactly visited but rather is tasted: It is the gastronomic capital of foie gras and armagnac, the two main ingredients in the region's fantastic traditional cuisine. Many other culinary specialties attest to the art of which the Gascons are so proud and which has earned them the reputation of being true bons vivants.

The *corrida*, or bullfight, was imported from nearby Spain in the nineteenth century, and the *course landaise* has taken place since the Middle Ages as a similar race without the death of the animal. Both are an integral part of Gascon culture. Thousands of enthusiasts pour into the arenas of the Gers each year. The Pentecostal feast in Vic-Fézensac, near Auch, is one of the most famous in the southwest, and takes place over three days and three nights. The *course landaise* begins with the parade of the teams that will face each other, and the object is to jump over a wild cow, with all the bobbing and weaving that this involves. The public forms a great crowd and passionately participates. The jury judges the elegance and precision of the jumper's movements, or the animal's loss of ground. The deafening music of the *bandas* and local fanfare add to the exuberant atmosphere.

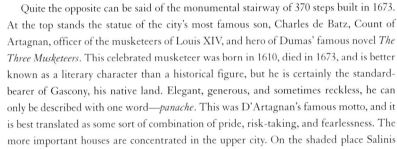

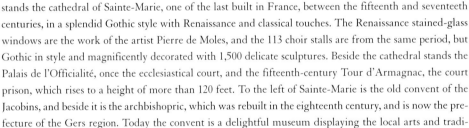

The Maison de Gascogne is inside the Halle aux Grains on place Jean David, not far from the cathedral. Every summer it becomes a showcase for local products. The shelves groan under the weight of various types of armagnac, foie gras (Gers is the most important region for the production of goose foie gras), and many different wines and sliced meats. The apple tarts and candied fruits are not to be missed, and enthusiasts can take part in tastings and observe the curious encounters between the local producers in this garden of delights.

D´ARTAGNAN

CAHORS
DIONYSUS' DARK ALLURE

CAHORS LIES IN THE HEART OF QUERCE, AN ANCIENT LAND crossed by the Lot River and beloved vineyard area famous since the dawn of time for its so-called black wine. This wine is the proud source of the town's wealth and is actually purple in color. Roman emperors, the English court, popes, kings of France, and even the tsar loved this wine. Cahors' name comes from the Gallic tribe of the Cadourques, which was later suppressed by the Romans. The village's historic prosperity is evident in the remains of the ancient thermal baths. The Visigoths destroyed Cahors in the sixth century, but it rose again around an early cathedral built under Bishop San Didier. The Moors and Normans both sacked the town, but it was restored in 1119 with the consecration of a new cathedral, and under the protection of an authoritative bishopric it became one of the most powerful cities in France. Its wealth came from the wine and from financial exchanges with Lombard bankers (the *Cahorsin*), whom Dante denounced in the *Divine Comedy* (*Inferno*, canto XI). Pope John XXII was born here, and in 1331 he founded the local university. During the Hundred Years' War the city passed to English rule, and during the religious wars it was sacked by Henry of Navarre, future King Henry IV of France, who withdrew many of its privileges because of its Catholicism, thereby slowing its growth.

Cahors preserves an impressive medieval and Renaissance patrimony, and the Soubirous and Bademes quarters are its ancient heart. The cathedral of Saint-Étienne is built in a particular Romanesque-Gothic style, with two wide cupolas straddling the nave; the main northern doorway is finely sculpted and reminds one of the famous abbey church of Moissac. Nearby is the Renaissance palace of the Archdeacon. The fifteenth-century Maison Roaldès borders the Lot River, as does the church of Sainte-Urcisse, built between the twelfth and the thirteenth centuries. On the opposite bank stands the fourteenth-century church of Notre-Dame, and farther north is the Barbacane, a fifteenth-century fortification with a "Tower of Hanged Men." The beautiful Valentré bridge is a rare example of fifteenth-century fortification, with two tall towers. Not far away is the des Chartreux fountain, praised by the Latin poet Ausonius, and a walk here is like going back in time to see the many mansions set into the tight maze of medieval and Renaissance streets.

Cahors offers an interesting variety of museums that display the works of classical and contemporary artists. The walls of the ancient library are lined with rare books, and a beautiful external staircase leads to the upper gallery where innumerable volumes are displayed—a marvelous sight for any bibliophile. The antiquities housed here include 40,000 documents that Jacques-Charles Brunet, who is famous for having written the *Manuel du Libraire*, spent years classifying.

The medieval Valentré bridge spans the Lot River.

facing page
Known to the Romans as "black wine," vin de Cahors is a rich tannic red.

The annual truffle feast takes place in Limogne and Lalbenque, near Cahors. This is a celebration of the finest, most delicate, powerful, and mysterious mushroom. In order to grow it needs a high-calcium soil, Mediterranean climate, and the presence of hazel and oak trees. Trained dogs and pigs manage to find the truffles hidden underground. More than an exceptionally fine produce, it is also called the black pearl or black diamond of Quercy. Because it cannot be cultivated it is very rare and a savory addition to the local cuisine.

Since ancient Roman times the wines of Cahors have been considered the best, and since 1225 have been quoted on the London market. It was the favorite wine of Peter the Great, so much so that he had vineyards planted in the Crimea. The local wine was also used for the Orthodox liturgy. Even though a plague of phylloxera nearly destroyed the vines in 1878, the cultivators managed to save it. It is considered *de garde* wine, meaning it lends itself well to ageing. Tannin-rich, it has a bright red color and full-bodied flavor. When young it pairs well with foie gras, sliced ham, salami, and meat. As it ages it acquires a delicate and complex bouquet and is very good with truffles, red meat, and game. You can find out all about Cahors at the Maison du vin, located in an ancient thirteenth-century building, at La Chantrerie, and at the many cellars that offer tastings.

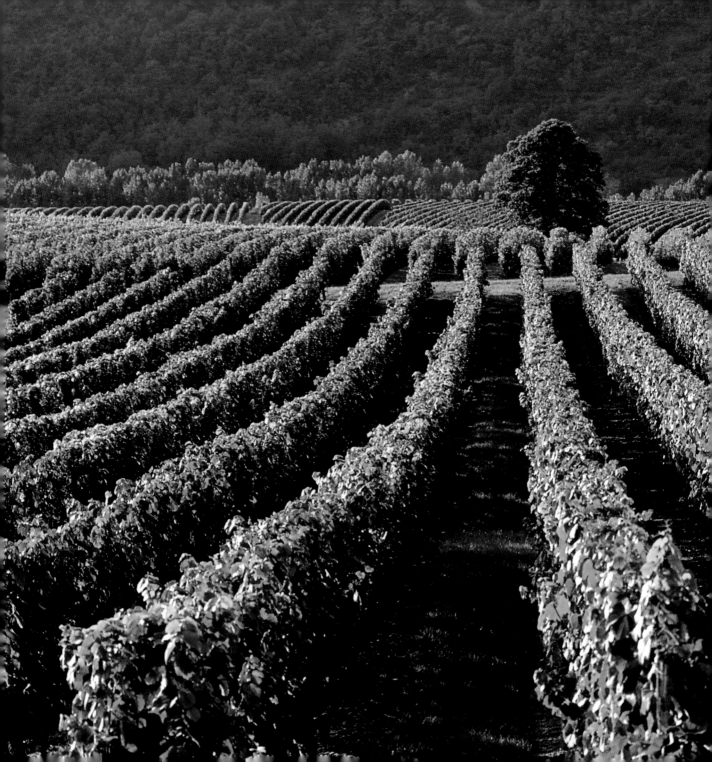

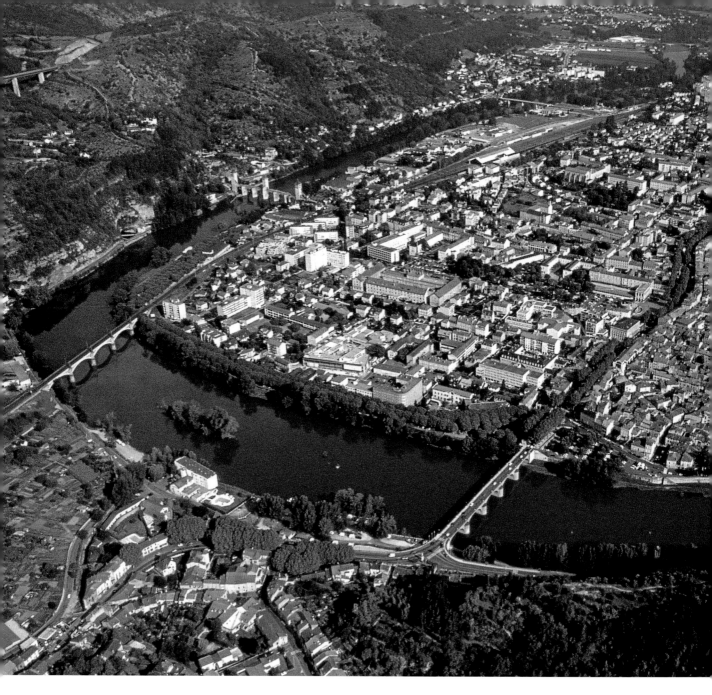

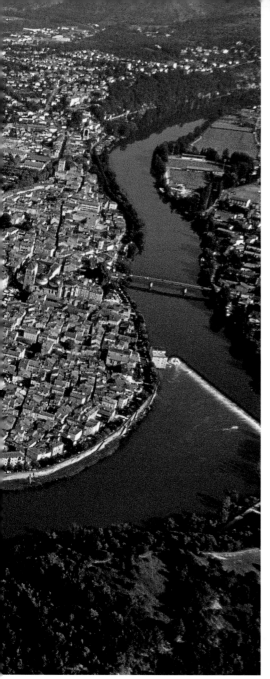

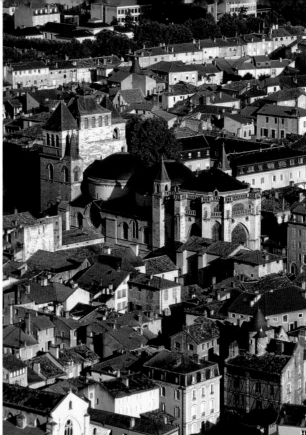

The Romanesque cathedral of Saint-Étienne rises among the rooftops.

The town is circled in an embrace by the Lot River.

About five miles west of Cahors, on the road to Figeac, there is an exceptional archaeological site that offers visitors an extraordinary journey through time. This is the grotto of Pech Merle, which, together with the more famous caves in Lascaux farther north, is among the great marvels of prehistoric art in the Western world. Just a few yards suffice to give the feeling of stepping back 30,000 years to rediscover a fabulous sanctuary of cave painting. The cave consists of two networks of tunnels, and only the lower parts are decorated. The site was discovered in 1922 and opened to the public in 1926. The paintings were done with many different techniques and represent primarily dappled horses but also goats, deer, and bison. Hand- and fingerprints can also be seen. An ossuary was discovered at the same time as the cave, containing the bones of bears, hyenas, horses, and even the footprints of an ancient child. The caves are open to the public from April to November, and it is best to make a reservation by telephone a couple of days before visiting.

CONQUES

A HERMETIC HAVEN

CONQUES IS AN EXCEPTIONAL PLACE IN THE WILD ROUERGUE, now in the Aveyron region, and is an isolated village marked with reddish flashes of cistus, an evergreen Mediterranean shrub, in a valley that widens into a gentle basin. Its abbey of Sainte-Foy holds the miraculous, serene power of a Romanesque masterpiece. It is said that in the eighth century a hermit in search of solitude stopped here for rest and was soon joined by other monks. The little community even enjoyed the favor of Charlemagne, but by the Middle Ages it had no relics, in a time when the presence of a relic was fundamental to the creation of a monastery or church. Suddenly the relics of Sainte-Foy (a fourth-century virgin martyr) appeared, and pilgrims began to flock to the site, making Conques a stop along the pilgrimage route to Santiago de Compostela, and in the eleventh century the abbey church was built.

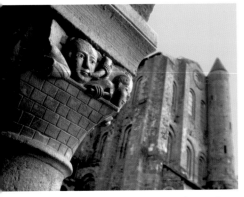

A fanciful capital in the cloister of the abbey of Sainte-Foy.

facing page
The illuminated abbey of Sainte-Foy.

The main door of the principal facade is a masterpiece with a magnificent Last Supper of the early twelfth century sculpted on the tympanum. The interior has a majestically serene, extremely somber architecture with solid, harmonious proportions. The altar dais, the lower parts of the nave, and the transept underscore the effect of rare beauty, and crowds of pilgrims walk around the choir admiring the precious relics protected by a twelfth-century wrought-iron gate. An octagonal cupola rises on the cross vault, and the 104 glass windows in a magnificent translucent white sensitive to the many variations of light were created by the painter Pierre Soulages. The abbey caught fire during the religious wars, was abandoned, and ran the risk of falling into ruin at the beginning of the nineteenth century, when the cloister was demolished. The layout was subsequently restored, and this jewel owes its salvation to the writer Prosper Mérime, who was inspector of historical monuments at the time.

Today the abbey is a UNESCO World Heritage site whose treasury includes a collection of many religious articles in gold and relics of the eleventh, twelfth, and sixteenth centuries. Among them is the tenth-century wooden statue of Sainte-Foy and sixteenth-century furnishings and tapestries. The statue was hidden during the French Revolution and thus saved from destruction. The village, with its unmistakable slate roofs, is within the abbey's boundaries and has steeply sloped, picturesque streets.

Every year thousands of pilgrims take the long road to Compostela on foot, by bicycle, and even on horseback. Very often the road to Santiago leaves the main route and follows little pathways. A Pilgrims' Organization issues a sort of passport (called Credential) that allows travelers to stay in the refuges and the monasteries along the road. Upon arrival they receive a certificate in Latin, the *Compostella*, that proves their participation. Since 1998 the pilgrimage routes to Santiago have been included on the list of UNESCO World Heritage sites. The *camino frances*, in Spain, represents the last part of the road from France, and has been recognized by UNESCO's World Heritage organization since 1993.

A stay in the Aveyron, at Conques or in the surrounding area, offers many opportunities to discover the regional cuisine. The local produce is exquisite, and the region boasts many specialties: sliced ham, sausage, pork cracknels, foie gras, tripe, *aligot* (a mixture of mashed potatoes and fresh tomato that takes a long time to prepare), kid with sorrel, stuffed cabbage, and *fouace*, a sweet flatbread dating back to the Middle Ages and Renaissance. The meat is excellent—especially the beef of Aubrac—and veal, lamb, and the wines of Marcillac, Entravgues, Fel, and d'Estaing are all worth a taste.

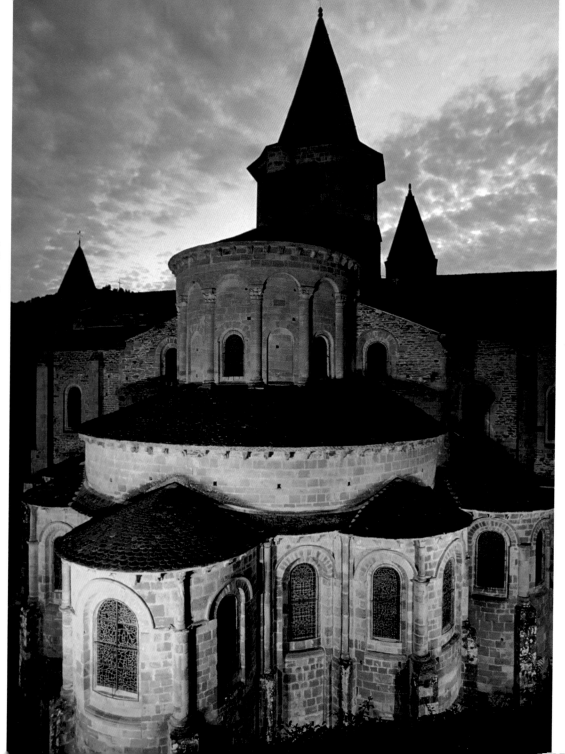

CORDES-SUR-CIEL
A FORTRESS IN THE CLOUDS

PERCHED ON A ROCK OVERLOOKING THE CÉROU VALLEY, Cordes-sur-Ciel is a magnificent fortress that was founded in 1222 by Raymond VII, Count of Toulouse. The original twelfth- and fourteenth-century fortifications have a very regular scheme that provides for a central *place à couverts*, surrounded by porticoes and a market. During the crusades against the Albigensians the fortress city quickly became the center that sheltered the heretical Cathars, who were being persecuted by an inquisition. After this period of religious turbulence, Cordes enjoyed a golden age thanks to its artisan tanners, dyers, and tapestry makers. But toward the end of the fifteenth century, due to the outbreak of new religious wars and the plague, the city declined. The Anglo-French wars produced bitter rivalry among local lords, who founded new cities endowed with privileges (land, houses, tax exemptions) to attract new inhabitants.

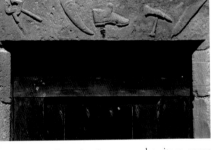

The sculpted architrave reminds visitors that a shoemaker once lived here.

facing page
Cordes dominates the Cérou Valley from high above.

With the exception of a brief period at the end of the nineteenth century, during which Cordes was dynamic and economically vital thanks to the development of mechanized embroidery, the city faded, enclosed within its walls. The inhabitants recovered from the deterioration of their stupendous Gothic patrimony when artists and writers, among them Camus, arrived to contribute to the town's rebirth, the walled city of a hundred pointed arches. It is protected by three fortified gateways and the encircling walls—including the lower city, there are five such walls—and along the paved roads, like the Grand Rue, are the old houses with magnificent facades of pink slate with gray tinges. They open out into the street with great porticoes and arched windows, and are decorated with sculptures of fantastic animals, hunting scenes, and important historical figures. The Prunet, Grand Ecuyer, Grand Fauconnier, and Grand Veneur mansions should not be missed. The impressive La Halle was once reserved for the trade of textiles, and is held up by twenty-four octagonal columns. The church of Saint-Michel has been restructured many times during the course of the centuries and has preserved the original thirteenth-century choir, transept curved over pointed crosses, a stunning fourteenth-century rose window, and a beautiful sixteenth-century altarpiece decorated with twisting columns. The Musée d'Art et d'Histoire Charles Portal, named after a great historian from Cordes, displays collections from the history of the town and its prehistoric remains. This delightful citadel is enlivened by many stalls of blacksmiths, enamel workers, engravers, weavers, sculptors, and painters set along the uneven, winding streets. A visit will remain unforgettable.

Six notable places can be discovered by following the Circuit of the City Fortress along a pleasant country road that circles the great forest of Grésigne. They were all built at the same time as Cordes, and all follow the same scheme: a marketplace surrounded by porticoes or a typical *halle*. Castelnau-de-Montmiral has splendid dovecote houses and the square *à couverts*; picturesque Puycelsi is perched on a cliff; Penne clings to the rock; the old towns of Larroque and Lisle-sur-Tarn have singular *pountes*, inhabited bridges between one house and another, and lovely river banks; and visitors are rewarded by the benefice of Vaour. A free guide to this delightful tour is available at the tourist office of Cordes.

The region of Cordes, stretching between the mountainside and left bank of the Tarn River, includes Gaillac, one of the oldest vineyards in France. Ever since the sixth century various types of this vine have been cultivated in this vast territory full of contrasts. The dry, white Gaillac is curiously fruity and nervy, the famous pearl white is elegant and subtle, the sweet Gaillac is aristocratic, the rosé is light, while the red Gaillac is dark and full-bodied. Although the white and rosé varieties are consumed when young, the reds, referred to as *de garde*, age very well. The pearl-white type pairs well with sliced ham or salami, the sweet type is good with foie gras or Roquefort cheese, and the reds go well with roasts and other cheeses. All types of this special wine merit a taste.

FOIX
ANDORRAN WINDS

LEANING UP AGAINST THE FIRST SPURS OF THE PYRENEES that separate it from nearby Catalonia and situated in one of the most sparsely populated regions of France, Foix is a paradise for enthusiasts of wild places. It is a little capital with a laid-back atmosphere, but the proud medieval castle that overlooks the town is a reminder that it has had complex relations with the kingdom of France. The history of the town is bound to that of an illustrious family with many famous personalities, such as Gaston Phébus, who was richer than the king, and it also is tied to the torment of the Cathars and the religious wars. Foix only became part of the French lands in 1607, when Henry of Navarre became king under the name of Henry IV, after he had twice abjured his Protestant faith. The city became a county in the eleventh century during the spread of the religion of the Cathars, who preached for a purified church. The local lords converted and faced the crusades launched by the popes and the king of France against the heretics. The powerful family of Foix, heirs of Navarre, was defeated in 1229 and took refuge in the nearby state of Béam, which they had recently inherited through succession. During the Reformation they supported Calvinism. The imposing castle of Foix, which was abandoned by the counts in favor of the castle of Béam, became a prison in the fifteenth century. It is surrounded by three magnificent towers and two rings of forbidding encircling walls: The narrow tower was built in the twelfth century, the central, square tower in the fourteenth century, and the round one in the fifteenth century. Inside the castle there are beautiful halls with vaulted ceilings that are now home to a display of medieval weaponry and armor and prehistoric treasures found in the caves of the Ariège Valley. There is a wonderful view of the landscape below and out over the city from the terrace of the castle, as well as from the top of the round tower. Below the castle stands the twelfth-century church of Saint-Volusien, which was destroyed during the religious wars and subsequently rebuilt in the sixteenth century. The old city is home to beautiful dovecote houses and *pontils,* covered passageways above the street, and the magnificent bronze Fontaine de l'Oie.

On Highway 20, which leads from Foix to Tarascon-sur-Ariège, there is a double-arched, twelfth-century bridge, called the Devil's Bridge. Legend has it that the devil made the bridge in one night, but in exchange he asked for the soul of the first being who crossed over it, so it was decided to make a cat cross the bridge. The devil was so angry that he fell from the bridge and was imprisoned by the parish priest with the help of a few drops of holy water. Even today crossing the bridge is a shiver-inducing experience.

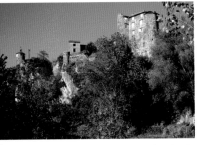

The Tour de Castella at Tarascon.

facing page
The imposing castle and towers.

The principality of Andorra has long enjoyed a special system of guardianship inherited from an ancient feudal privilege. It was ratified by treaty in 1278, creating a joint sovereignty of the Bishop of Urgel, in Spain, and the Counts of Foix. When Henry IV became king the French tutelage passed to the kingdom and then to the republic and its president. In 1993, through a referendum, the people of Andorra chose independence. The official language is Catalan, accompanied by French and Spanish. The magnificent mountain landscapes and the free port attract many travelers, and visitors can buy all kinds of things at prices that are by no means feudal, regardless of the charming ambience.

There are many paths leading to the mountainous massif in the area surrounding Foix, including the *Route Verte,* the *Route de la Crouzette,* and the *Port de Lers.* There is another special road in the park of the Pyrenees at Tarascon-sur-Ariège that will take you back in time to the prehistoric period and its art. Approximately 300 grottoes have been discovered in the region, of which sixty are being excavated. They date back to the Paleolithic Bronze Age, and the beautiful cave of Niaux is famous as the epitome of Magdalenian (circa 11,000 BC) cave art. The de la Vache cave (circa 13,000 BC) contains the remains of furniture, and the Bédeilhac grotto is resplendent with bas-reliefs and stone carvings. The Lombrives grotto is one of the largest in Europe without decorations, and is the tomb of Pyrène, the beloved princess of Hercules. Some of the grottoe that cannot be visited have been reconstructed in the park.

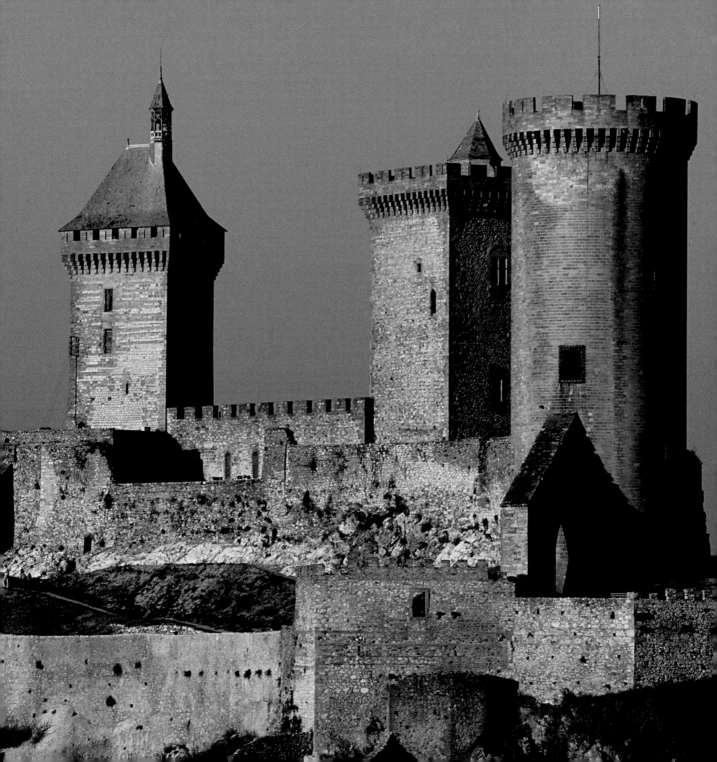

MILLAU
TERRACOTTA MOUNTAINS

AT THE EDGE OF THE CAUSSE NOIR, MILLAU STANDS AT THE ENTRANCE of the Causse du Larzac, which is part of the Grands Causses park and the vast limestone plates of the Massif Central. There is a strange atmosphere along the roads, as though Millau were an embassy of some Mediterranean country, and this has been the case for a long time. In the ancient times of Roman Gaul Millau was famous for the terracotta objects it exported to the most distant parts of the empire. Pieces have been found in England, Sudan, and even in India. The site has been inhabited since prehistoric times, as proved by the dolmen. In the Roman era the town was the center of a great terracotta production, but it was only during the Middle Ages that trade began to develop thanks to the strategic positioning of the town as a link between the north and south of France. Salt, spices, and fish passed through in great quantities, but the real wealth came from the working and trading of leather goods. There was a rapid development of leather tanning, and especially of glove making, for which the town soon became famous. Millau became prosperous and merchants began to build elegant houses here. The old quarters of the historic center have been restored in a less-than-successful attempt to combine the old with the new. The historic town is centered around place

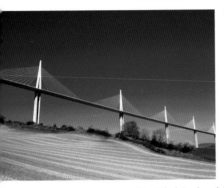

The breathtaking Millau Viaduct is the highest in the world.

facing page
Old mills on the banks of the Tarn River.

Maréchal Foch, which is surrounded by porticoes, and some of the columns date back to the twelfth century. The church of Notre-Dame de l'Espinasse stands in the square. Its original structure dates back to the twelfth century but was later remodeled. The vault, in particular, was rebuilt in the sixteenth and seventeenth centuries. The delightful bell tower is in the style of Toulouse architecture, and the main door is decorated with Baroque scrolls; the twelfth-century tower was once a prison. The intersection with rue de la Payrollerie brings a visitor to the lovely ancient houses, with narrow passages and quaint dead-end streets. Farther along the rue des Cuirs leads to the old commoners' quarter, with the charming rue del Voultre, where the tanners worked near the thirteenth-century fortified gateway. The old washing trough is a

The Millau Viaduct, the highest in the world, is a cable-stayed motorway bridge 7,290 feet long. The ninety-six-foot metal deck rests on seven cement columns and is supported by additional columns that are 267 feet tall and hold the cable stays. Including the deck, the highest column is 1,029 feet tall (60 feet higher than the Eiffel Tower), so that one crosses the Tarn at a height of more than 810 feet. Another characteristic is its slight curve, which was designed to overcome the sense of fear that one feels while crossing a void. The somber and audacious design is by the British architect Sir Norman Foster and was opened at the end of 2004 with great success. The bridge itself is beautiful, and the site, at the confluence of the Dourbie and Tarn valleys, is magnificent.

monumental work of the eighteenth century, and there is a fifteenth-century mill on the Tarn River, with the remains of a twelfth-century bridge. Crossing from one bridge to another one comes to the Millau Viaduct, opened in December 2004. It is the highest viaduct in the world, and at more than 800 feet it dominates the Tarn Valley. It is considered to be one of the most significant architectural projects of the twenty-first century.

Millau's tanners and glove makers have been famous for centuries. The city museum displays all phases of their work, from the perishable raw pieces to the soft and velvety finished products. The tanners have taken advantage both of their ancient traditions as well as modern technology, and one can admire the ability of the glove makers as they cut, sew, and embroider or decorate the gloves. Today the workshops of Millau supply the luxury industry and high-fashion world, and they export all over the globe. It is difficult to leave the museum without having your hand measured for a glove!

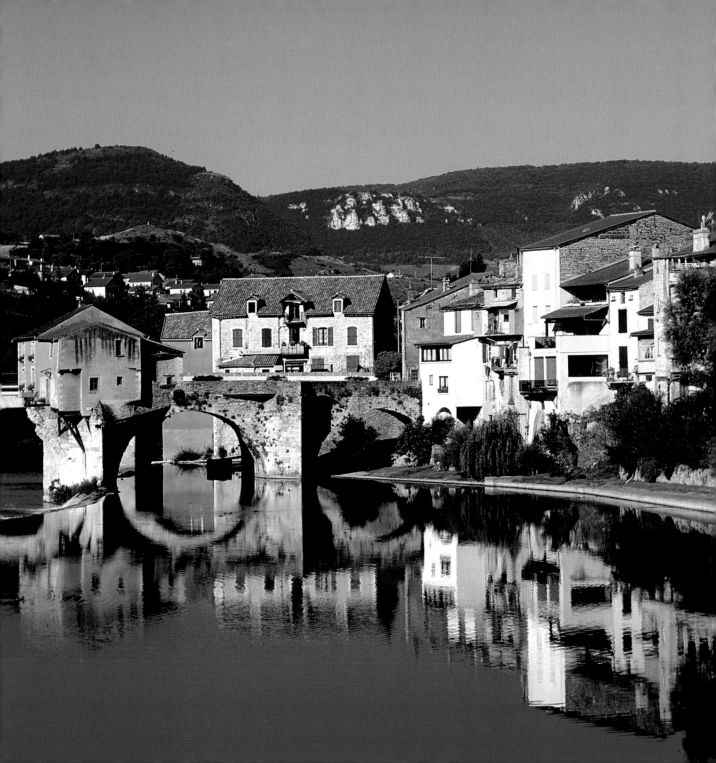

ROCAMADOUR
VERTIGINOUS BEAUTY

ROCAMADOUR IS A MOVING, SACRED CITY WITH A VERTIGINOUS, very spiritual view and extraordinarily beautiful geographical position. The surrounding Causses is a vast limestone plain that suddenly drops off, and its side turns into an immense gray precipice that propels itself into the spectacular Alzou gorges. This extraordinary site was a place of pilgrimage throughout the Middle Ages; even kings came here to pray, and they built votive chapels that were later turned into a sanctuary. The site was originally venerated by the cult of the Black Virgin, but its creation is attributed to the hermit Amadour, who withdrew to this cliff just after the death of the Virgin. In 1166 the discovery of the saint's remains led to the arrival of a great number of pilgrims and gave rise to the golden age of Rocamadour. But the religious wars that soon followed ruined the sanctuary, and it was only around 1850 that the church once again became a place of pilgrimage.

The fountain of Saint-Georges at the Gouffre de Padirac.

Clinging to the rocks, Rocamadour unfolds on several levels. The view out over the valley can be admired from the ancient hamlet of Hospitalet, while the village is further up, and still higher up is the religious sanctuary. Atop it all stands the castle. Every area of the city was enclosed by one of the eleven fortified gateways—of which only eight remain—that were used both to control the flow of pilgrims and as a means of defense. The Figuier gateway opens to the main road of Rocamadour, the Grand Rue that leads to the sanctuary, passing among the many medieval houses that still have their leaded windows and typical arches. Halfway up the ascent, having scaled the 216 steps of the great stairway on their knees, the pilgrims would reach the heart of the religious citadel with its seven churches (or chapels) that were built between the twelfth and the fifteenth centuries. The chapel of Notre-Dame contains the tomb of Saint Amadour and the twelfth-century statue of the Black Virgin. The consecrated courtyard was once covered by paintings, but only scenes of the Annunciation and Visitation are still intact. The Saint-Michel chapel, on the other hand, is resplendent with its original twelfth-century frescoes.

Local lore often speaks of the *Gouffre de Padirac* (Padirac Abyss); if at Rocamadour they talk about the Virgin, at Padirac they talk about the devil, who purportedly disappeared into hell through the precipice that he himself created while challenging Saint Martin. Le Gouffre ("deep hole" or "bottomless pit") is a gigantic underground cathedral, an exceptional geographical curiosity formed by an ancient sinkhole in the rock that opened a natural cavity nearly 225 feet deep and 100 feet in diameter. It is the starting point of an entire network of underground cavities, and among them is the Grand Dôme that, with its almost 280-foot vault, is one of the tallest in Europe. With a flat-bottomed boat, and at a depth of almost 300 feet, it is possible to navigate the underground river that is a quarter-mile long. The Grande Pendeloque, a stupendous 225-foot-long stalactite, can be seen at Lac de la Pluie and is a vertigo-inspiring sight.

Among the treasures now in the Museum of Sacred Art is the seventeenth-century reliquary of Saint Amadour in gilded wood, a thirteenth-century stained-glass panel depicting the Temptation of Saint Martin, and a poorly preserved sixteenth-century *Pietà* in polychrome wood.

Cabécou is the cheese of the famous city of the Black Virgin, where it has been produced since the fifteenth century with milk from the goats of the Causses, which gives this precious food its musty scent and inimitable taste. It is made entirely from pure goats' milk, and you can enjoy it either while fresh and creamy or aged and warmed, ideally with a salad or slice of bread. A red wine of Cahors with ruby tints is the best accompaniment. At Rocamadour the Cabécou is mixed with pepper and brandy, or served *flambé* with armagnac.

facing page
Rocamadour rises on a sheer cliff atop the limestone plateau of La Causse.

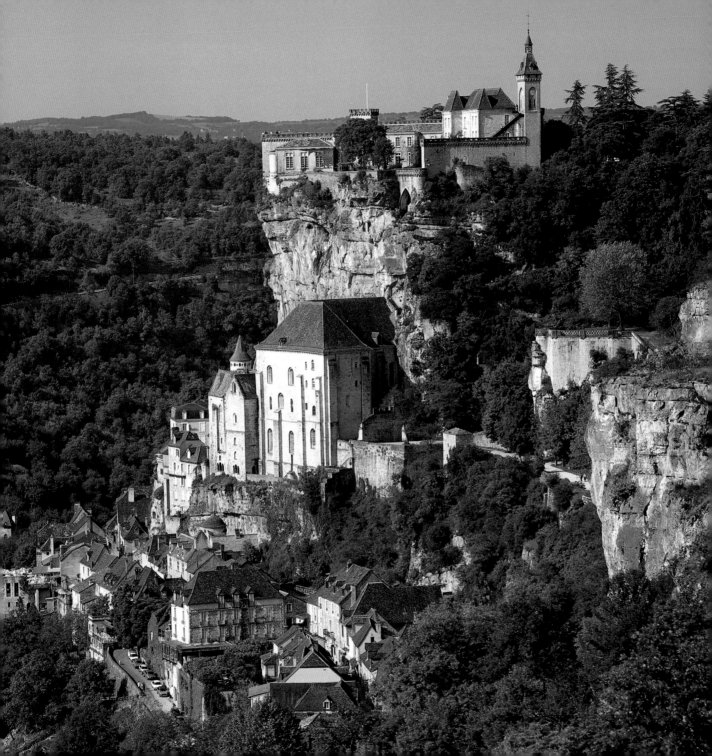

FÉCAMP
NEWFOUNDLAND'S FOREFATHERS

FÉCAMP IS NESTLED IN AN IMPRESSIVE VALLEY EXCAVATED AMONG ROCKS skirting the seaside. The city was founded before the Viking invasions, has a port that has been active since the eleventh century, and over the years has developed a strong fishing industry. Beginning in the sixteenth century the sailors of Fécamp crossed the Atlantic to fish for cod, reaching as far as Newfoundland and prompting shipbuilders, naval dockyards, and sailing shops to multiply. Fécamp soon became one of the most important French ports, and alongside these activities came the workshops and industries for processing deep-sea fish, adding to the town's prosperity. In the nineteenth century deep-sea fishing began to decline, and in the 1830s the great adventure of Newfoundland came to an end. Coastal fishing has remained, however, and Fécamp is still an important commercial port today.

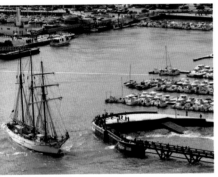

The city was once the most important French port for deep-sea fishing.

During the Middle Ages Fécamp was a monastic center of great interest, and the dukes who later became the English royal family chose it as their capital. Between the twelfth and thirteenth centuries they built the abbey church of Sainte-Trinité over the ruins of an ancient seventh-century chapel. Sainte-Trinité is primarily in the Gothic style, with some later additions, such as the facade, which was rebuilt in the eighteenth century. The building is of very large proportions; the nave is almost 380 feet long, and the *tiburium*, which covers the cupola, is nearly 195 feet high. The bell tower is a lovely example of the Norman Gothic style. There are many precious works of art inside, including a high altar with baldachin, choir stalls, chapels, tombs, and stained-glass windows, all made between the twelfth and eighteenth centuries. There is a beautiful chapel of the Virgin in the apse, designed in a splendidly pure fifteenth-century Gothic style. In front of the main door stand the ruins of the old castle of the dukes of Normandy, of which only the tower remains.

A walk along the port, beginning at the Guy de Maupassant pier, leads along the *sente des matelots* to the

The Musée de Terres-Nueves et de la Pêche faces the sea and relates the adventures of cod fishing and how the city has lived according to its natural rhythm for more than four centuries. Maritime traditions and various fishing techniques are displayed, from the first sailing ships to the steam fishing boats and modern boats with refrigeration on board. The sailor's life is also recounted, as is his complex relationship to the sea, always torn between attraction and fear. Expeditions lasted many months, and sailors faced particularly dangerous situations, such as violent storms, extreme cold, and the ever-present risk of hitting an iceberg and sinking. Many sailors never returned, and a visit here is a fascinating, but also deeply moving, experience.

hill to the north of the city. Here one can admire the eleventh-century Notre-Dame-du-Salut chapel, a place of pilgrimage for sailors, who came here to pray before boarding ship. There are many votive paintings, some done by sailors who had narrowly escaped drowning. There is a splendid view from here of the city below and the rocks of the southern coast. Maupassant lived here and set *Maison Tellier*, as well as some of the episodes in his short stories, at Fécamp.

facing page
The magnificent
Palais Bénédictine.

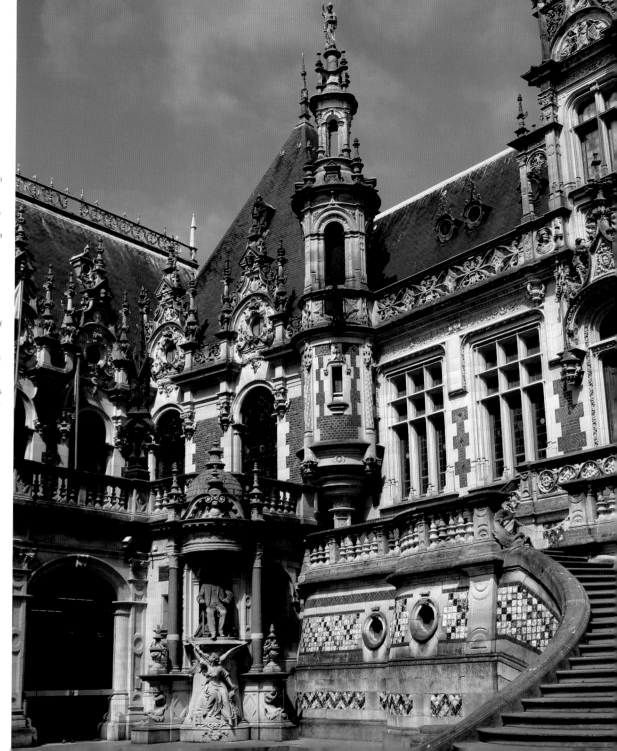

In 1863 Alexandre Le Grand, a Fécamp shopkeeper, rediscovered the magic formula of an elixir originally created in 1510 by a Benedictine monk, father Bernardo Vincelli. The elixir was distilled from local plants, including balsam, mint, angelica, and hyssop, for a total of twenty-seven plants and herbs. The liquor, with a unique bittersweet taste, was called *Bénédictine* and was sold as far as Russia. Le Grand later built a mansion where he displayed his extraordinary collection of sacred and profane objects dating from the fifteenth to the eighteenth centuries. He also created the Bénédictine Museum, where visitors can see the rooms with the plant ingredients and distilling apparatus; tours end, naturally, in the tasting room.

GIVERNY

MONET'S GARDEN

GIVERNY IS A CALM PLACE, PERCHED ON A HILL ALONG THE SEINE, about forty miles from Paris. One day in 1883 a curious man arrived to live in a big pink house with green shutters and did not leave until the day of his death on a December evening in 1926. It was here that Claude Monet, who revolutionized painting by defining light with such sensitivity, made his home and many of his masterpieces.

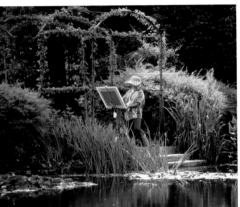

The Musée Claude Monet is an open-air studio.

The story of Giverny is that of a man and his garden, the unique adventure of an artist and his art. It all began in 1858 in a shop in Le Havre, when a painter from Honfleur, Eugène Boudin, met a young man drawing caricatures of the local notables. Boudin, who painted landscapes and seascapes, guided him toward painting. He knew that the fate of this art was to be determined outside the studio, as the artist looks for hidden colors in the subtle vibrations of light. Monet's numerous studies show how the problem of color is inseparable from that of light, and how light is connected to the passing of the hours. He shows time sliding by in the colors of the world, and this is the heart of Impressionism. A pure, live, luminous sensation must be drawn out of color. *Impression, soleil levant* is the title of an 1872 sunrise work by Monet, which gave a name to the movement of which he was to become the master.

At Giverny, Monet transformed the existing garden. He built greenhouses and planted the flowers that nourished him with color. He later enlarged the property by buying adjoining land, and after a thousand administrative difficulties, he managed to create his *jardin d'eau*, the water garden with its famous Japanese bridge, weeping willows, wisteria, azaleas, and water lily pond. It is a jewel box of water and sky, conceived to penetrate the depths of light's effects, and it brought out his fantastic universe of water lilies. It was at Giverny and its surroundings that Monet painted the celebrated series that made him famous. The many series he completed here include twenty-five *Meules,* four *Peupliers,* the *Cathédrales,* the *Matinée sur la Seine,* the *Pont japonais,* the *Glycines,* and the renowned *Nymphéas,* all of which are now at the Musée de l'Orangerie in Paris. Today the master's garden has been perfectly restored, and one can admire the famous *Tableau execute à meme la nature,* which his contemporaries considered to be one of his masterpieces.

The Musée d'Art Américain of Giverny is immersed in a garden. It was opened in 1992, and visiting hours are the same as the nearby garden of Monet. Founded by Daniel J. Terra, of the Terra Museum of American Art in Chicago, it underlines the important connection between American and French painting at the end of the nineteenth and beginning of the twentieth centuries. The fascinating landscape and the master of Impressionism did, in fact, attract many American and European artists. At the end of World War II an important colony of artists was drawn to Giverny by Monet's adventure in painting. Through its ambitious program of exhibitions the museum shows the history of American art and its many ties to French art, from 1750 to the present.

Monet's house and garden are managed by the Claude Monet Foundation and are open to visitors from April 1 to October 31 every day, except Monday, from 10 am to 6 pm. There are no original paintings in the house—only copies—but his vast collection of Japanese prints can be admired. The foundation shop is in the studio of the *Nymphéas.* Here, among other objects, there is a rich collection of more than 2,000 works on Monet and the Impressionists that is sure to delight any devotee.

facing page Vibrant flowers and climbing plants surround Monet's house.

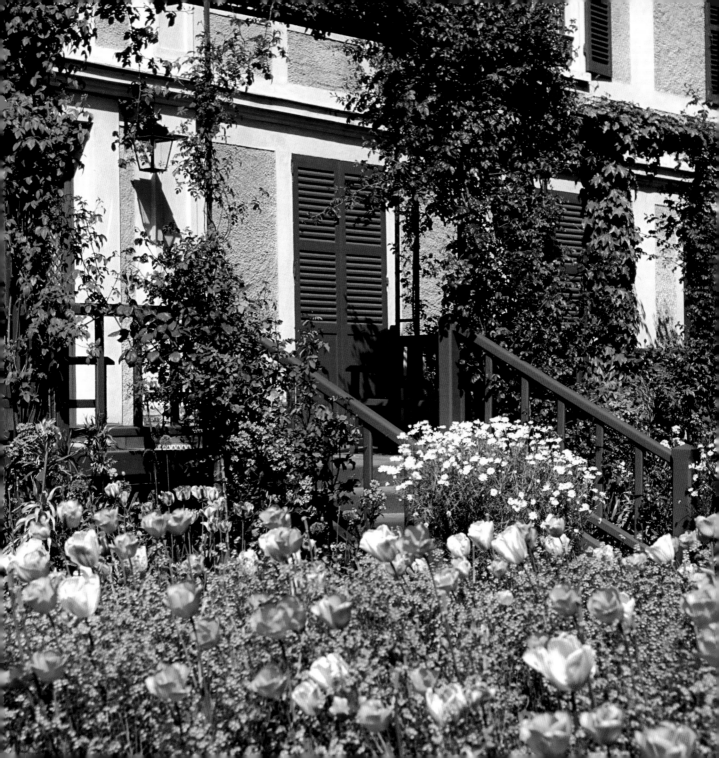

GRANVILLE
THE OLD WORLD'S NEW LOOK

GRANVILLE IS A FASCINATING SEASIDE RESORT ON THE ENGLISH CHANNEL famed for its seafood, lobsters, and Christian Dior. The birthplace of the designer is at the cliff's edge and overlooks the sea where the Chausey Islands rise in the distance. The house was bought by the city in 1938 and is now a museum containing the universe of this complete artist, who was so Proustian, a great aesthete, and creator of the New Look. This style of flowered fabrics, soft shoulders, and tight waists revolutionized women's fashion. The first anecdote about Dior, however, is neither perfumed nor sparkly; as their publicity slogan at the end of the nineteenth century boldly asserted, "Dior manure is gold." The family believed in the inventions that gave rise to the Belle Époque: Louis Dior, great-grandfather of Christian, was a farmer and town mayor who made his fortune with natural manure, both human and animal, and with guano imported from Peru. The children carried on the business with chemical fertilizers, bleach, and detergents, and also manufactured beer and lemonade. The fertilizer factory gained national importance, and Lucien Dior, Christian's uncle, became the minister of commerce. However, the family was ruined within days after the stock crash of 1929. Christian was a cultured dandy, in love with art, and after the death of his mother he began to travel and to make his first sketches, all of which mirrored the luxury and elegance of his own life. In 1947 he opened a boutique on boulevard Montaigne, and in only seven years his label made up half of all French haute couture exports.

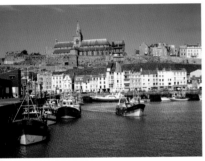

Ferries to the Chausey Islands leave from the town's harbor.

Today Granville preserves the fascination and elegance that it had during the life of this famous fashion designer. His garden is perfumed with fresh marine air and climbing roses. It overlooks the path des Douanniers that circles the upper city, skirting the ramparts and crossing the beach. This lovely walk among the granite rocks is known as the Walk of Empty Pockets, because one knows that the job of bandits, past and present, is to empty the pockets of passersby. It continues beyond the great port and drawbridge, both of which witnessed the bloody war against the Vandéens after the French Revolution. This city preserves the traces of Normandy's lively past of corsairs, admirals, and fishermen. The little church of Notre-Dame-de-Cap-Libou has been anchored on the edge of the pointe de Granville since the fifteenth century. It has sheltered the fishermen who entrust their lives to its benevolence, and the church will always protect them.

Departing from the south of Granville by car, the twenty-five-mile bay road leads to the legendary Mont-Saint-Michel. This rather narrow road provides a wonderful view of beaches, rocks, and dunes. To visit the Chausey Islands, a handful of land eight miles offshore, one must leave by boat in the morning. This island part of Granville is rich with minerals and is the largest archipelago in Europe. Roger Vercel aptly described Chausey as *un pot de fleurs français empourpré de geraniums et de fuchsias arborescents*—a vase of French flowers painted purple with geraniums and branching fuschias—a perfect description. The warm currents of the Channel provide a particularly mild microclimate and luxuriant vegetation. The most impressive high tides in the old world can be seen at Chausey. There is no pollution, and it is a paradise for fish, shells, birds, dolphins, penguins, and seals. In the summer some fishermen's families live in the casemates, the fortified chambers of the old fort, near the pointe du Tour, while in the winter only ten or twelve people live in this protected, wild, and wonderfully natural place.

There are some good restaurants along the sheltered fishermen's port, where the fish auctions are held. Among them are the famous Citadelle and Cabestan, which looks more like a bistro. They offer the best of Granville: the famous *bouquet de Chausey*; grilled, roasted, or stewed lobster; mussels; squid; a plate of limpets; Venus clams; and sea bass. Everything served depends on the day's catch, and the local fish soup is also excellent. On Wednesday and Saturday the markets teem with avid fans of the famous fishermen's sweaters.

facing page
The long seaside promenade.

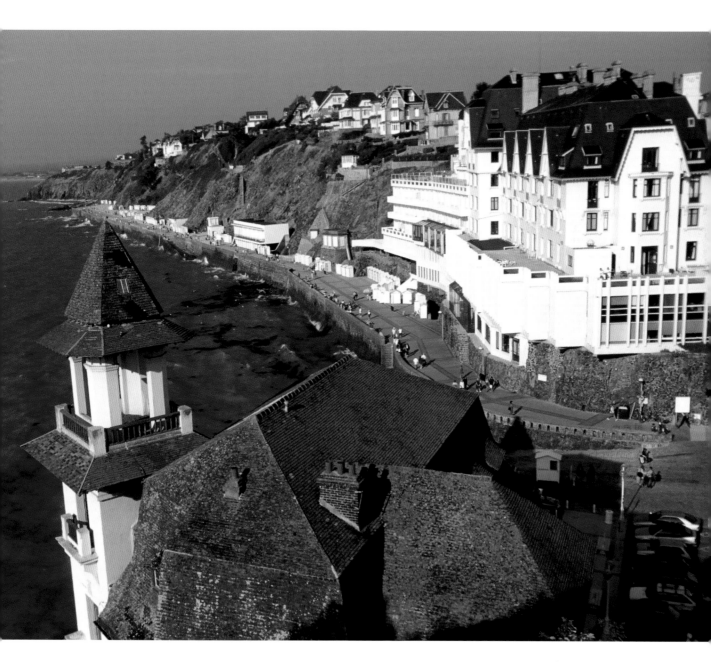

HONFLEUR
IMPRESSIONISM'S SOURCE

ON A GRACEFUL MEANDER IN THE ESTUARY OF THE SEINE at the foot of the Côte de Grâce, Honfleur is the most seductive, fascinating, and authentic little port in Normandy. Its calm and picturesque atmosphere has been inherited from its bucolic past; the countryside is green, and the light is so special that it attracted and created many artists, painters, writers, and musicians in the latter half of the nineteenth century. The writer Alphonse Allais and the musician Erik Satie were both born here. Baudelaire wrote his *Invitation au voyage* here. The artistic school of Honfleur was born here, headed by Eugène Boudin, who was also a native. With the arrival of Claude Monet the school led to the birth of Impressionism. An ideal visit begins with a walk through the old city and around the old dock, built by Louis XIV, with its fleet of boats and delightful quays. On one side are the tall, narrow houses covered with slate, and on the other are the wealthy houses of stone with noble mansard roofs. Serving as a barrier to the ancient dock, one can see the Lieutenence, an ancient sixteenth-century house with towers on two corners. It was the residence of the king's lieutenant, the governor of Honfleur, and gives an idea of the importance of the port in the sixteenth and seventeenth centuries. A nearby plaque marks the expedition of Samuel Champlain, who left from Honfleur in 1608 to found the province of Quebec. The visit continues along the little old streets of the various quarters: Endos, which was once the heart of the city; and rue de la Prison, with the wood-frame *pan de bois* houses and salt warehouses built in the seventeenth century by Colbert to store the salt necessary to equip the cod-fishing fleet. The Sainte-Catherine quarter is beautiful, with its wooden church and detached bell tower. The double nave is shaped like an upturned hull with visible beams and was the work of the local carpenters in the port, who built it after the end of the Hundred Years' War. Rue des Lingots, with its old cobblestones and houses, leads to the heights of Honfleur near the Notre-Dame-de-Grâce chapel, a sailors' shrine. The view from here is stupendous, overlooking the sea, the estuary, and the Tancarville bridge. If one is lucky this will all be graced by the light that made such an impression on Eugène Boudin and his fellow artists. The traditional festival of sailors and fishermen takes place during the weekend of Pentecost. Decorated boats set out in a cortege toward the Baie de Seine to receive the blessing of the sea. Many boats come from ports around the region, and even some foreigners take part in the ceremony. The following day there is a procession of fishermen to Notre-Dame-de-Grâce, where a mass is held in the open-air courtyard. Classic stalls selling sweetmeats line the route to keep one's energy high throughout the celebration.

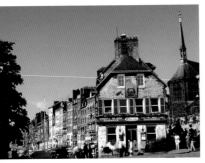

The characteristic quartier Sainte-Catherine, with a church built entirely of wood.

facing page
The inner harbor, locally called the Vieux Bassin, was enlarged in 1681.

From the height of the Côte de Grâce at Honfleur the estuary of the Seine and the beautiful Tancarville bridge are visible. The bridge was inaugurated in 1959 and was the first to be built between Rouen and the sea. Until then, crossing the two banks took place by ferryboat. The name Tancarville comes from the tenth-century castle that dominates the right bank of the Seine. The bridge is supported by two 375-foot-tall cement columns, has a 4,200-foot-long central platform, is suspended 153 feet above the sea, and has two stay cables distribute the weight at the extremities. With the bridge Le Havre is now less than fifty miles from Honfleur and, thanks to the connections to the Normandy highway, only two hours from Paris.

Each autumn during the Fête de la Crevette, Honfleur holds a series of typical regional shows. They take place in the narrow streets around the port and in the splendid setting of the Sainte-Catherine pier. The entertainment includes sailors' songs, the traditional dressing of the sails, shrimp-selling competitions, boat portages *au cabestan*, or by means of a capstan, and the maneuvering of oars. All this is in honor of the gray prawn, the specialty of Honfleur. Visitors can taste mussels, seafood, local cheeses, and the famous *trou normand*, a glass of calvados that is a superior digestif.

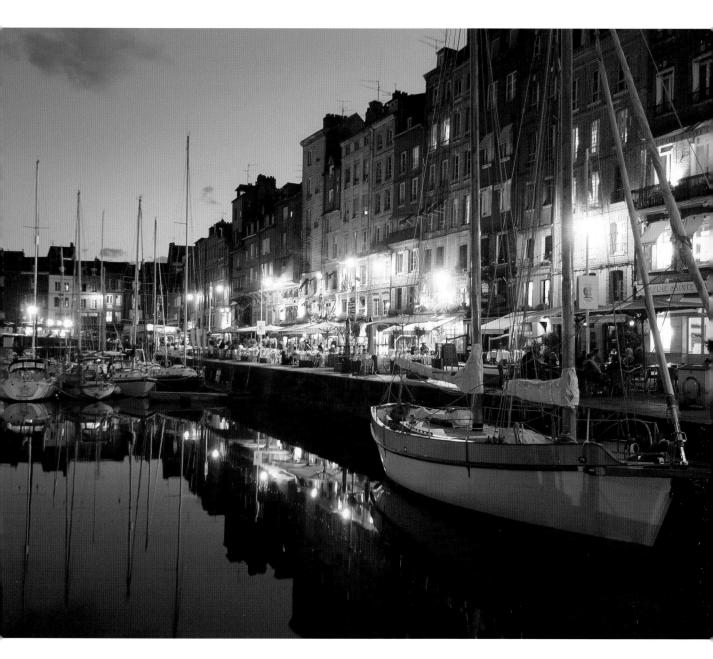

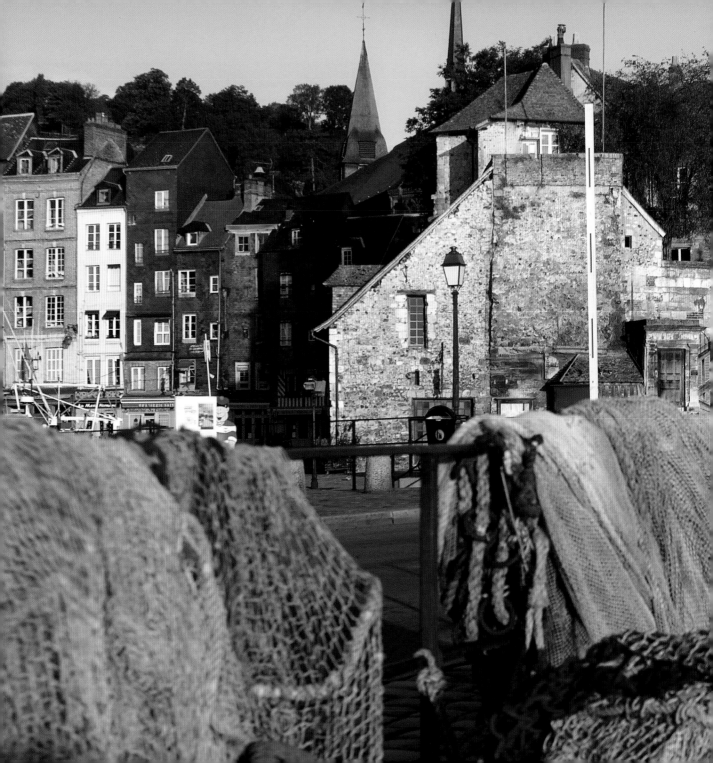

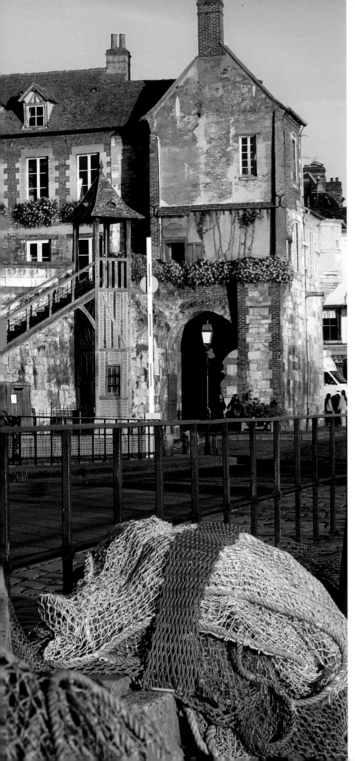

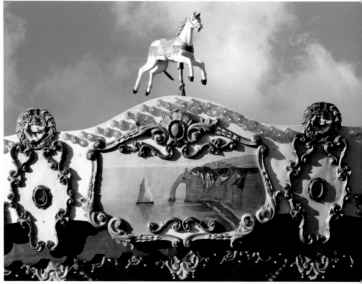

left
The building called the Lieutenence was the home of the king's lieutenant.

above
Detail of an old carousel.

Erik Satie was born on May 17, 1866, at Honfleur and died on July 1, 1925, in Paris. He is thought to be one of the most interesting musicians of the twentieth century, a composer who opened the way to the American repetitive musicians. His style was a sort of naked and somber recitation that was the quintessence of inexpressiveness, which was at the base of a great deal of modern music; John Cage being the foremost pioneer of this style. Satie's name is associated with all the avant-garde movements, and at the same time he was intense and well known. This was different from the other composers and musicians of the same period, and even from the listeners and specialists. Even though Debussy and other greats of the period thought that his music was formidably new and important, Satie was misunderstood by his contemporaries. Was it his need for revolt that was not appreciated by his peers? It is certain that, as time progresses, Satie's legacy continues to take shape.

CAMBRAI
SWEETENED BY SURPRISE

THE ORIGINS OF CAMBRAI DATE BACK TO THE ADVANCE OF THE BARBARIANS, when the Nervi, concerned about the position of Bavay, decided to move their capital to Cambrai. The *castrum*, or Roman garrison, was located at a strategic crossroads and conquered by the Franks in the middle of the fifth century. During the sixth century the town was a bishopric and greatly prospered under the leadership of Bishop Géry, who built a church high above the city on Mont des Bœuf. This church became an abbey and site of pilgrimage, and a little village grew up around it. Another four churches, which subsequently became parishes, marked the birth of Cambrai.

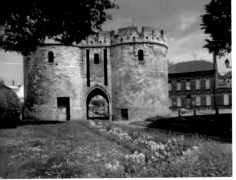

The Porte du Saint-Sépulcre.

The locals became concerned about the successive Barbarian invasions from the north and east, and built fortifications to protect the city. In the eleventh century the prosperity of the city encouraged Bishop Liebert to build another abbey and three parishes protected by additional fortifications. In the thirteenth century, to consolidate his power over a population of merchants and artisans ready to revolt, the bishop built another fortress, the castle of Selles, in the northeastern part of the city. Therefore, during the Hundred Years' War, Cambrai was protected by more than two miles of wall that was more than twenty-four feet high, nine feet thick, and punctuated by about fifty towers and seven gateways. In 1543 Charles V entered Cambrai and built a citadel on Mont des Bœuf protected by ramparts and reinforced walls, creating the last imperial citadel of Europe.

Until it was annexed to the French crown in 1667, Cambrai remained at the heart of many power struggles. Even though there was a stronghold in the second line, the city was subjected to renovations designed by Vauban and his architects. Beginning in 1892 the citizens of Cambrai requested that their city be modernized, and the city underwent a radical change. Today there is a great avenue circling along the traces of the ancient fortifications, and it is decorated by the most beautiful towers and gateways that have been preserved. Cambrai has been marked by history and bears the signs of all the events that have occurred in its past. Culture, tradition, and nature are harmoniously mixed among the town's ancestral stones and green spaces.

Billon is a traditional game in Cambrai. It is played with a piece of wood, the *billon*, a sort of club that weighs roughly six pounds and is about three feet long. The game is normally played in the country on the sidewalks near bars, so that the players and their supporters can quickly quench their thirst between one game and the next. There are two main ways to play: One is *billon* with posts, played with two posts fixed in the ground almost thirty feet apart; holding it by the sharper end, the *billon* is thrown from one post to the other (the target) so that it lands and stays there. The players of each team compete to overlap their *billon* with those of their own team and keep it firm against the post, and if possible they have to knock away the *billon* of the other team. The second version of the game is rake *billon*, whereby the target is a sort of rake with five spikes embedded in the ground, or three holes about five inches apart. The billon is thrown in such a way as to make the pointed end fall into the holes. Nowadays *billon* is only played in some villages, mainly during the holidays of July 14 or in competitions organized in the summer.

facing page
The flowery facade of the Maison Espagnole has a typical slate roof.

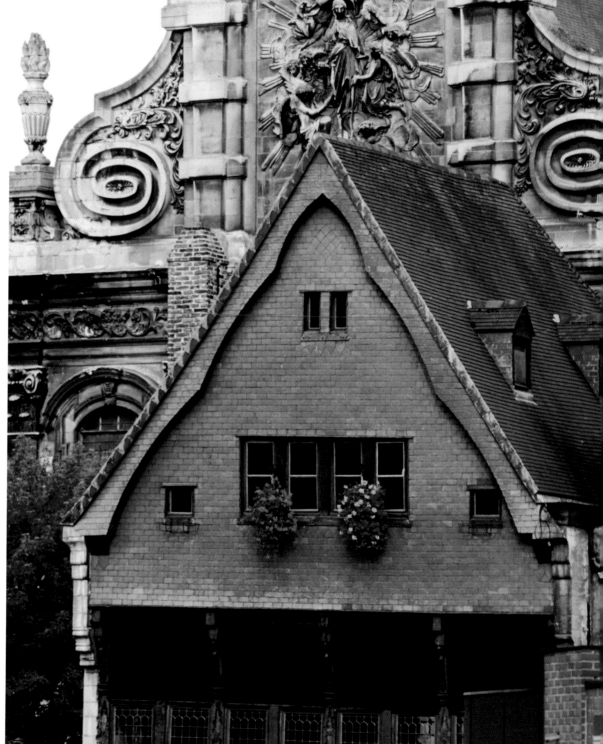

The origin of the famous *bêtises de Cambrai* dates back about two centuries. Émile Afchain was an apprentice confectioner in the family business and had made a mistake with the ingredients while preparing candy, causing his mother to severely scold him. He may have done a stupid thing, but the candy was a success— refreshing and entirely new. From that time on they were called *bêtises* because they were the result of a mistake, and they became a local specialty. Their fame has spread everywhere, and although originally they were characterized by a taste of mint, today they can be found with orange, lemon, raspberry, and green apple flavors. The factory can be visited from Monday to Friday by making an appointment in advance, and the free samples are impossible to resist.

LILLE
TAPESTRIES AND TRADITION

THE FIRST REFERENCE TO LILLE DATES BACK TO THE TENTH CENTURY and records it as the residence of the counts of Flanders, a powerful center where the "money of Lille," or the money of the *Île,* was minted. As the neighboring villages began to grow, so did the city, and this development was due to an unprecedented, dynamic economy. The region's main market was held in Lille, and it later became a center for the textile trade and agricultural products from the surrounding fertile land. The annual fair attracted traders from all over the world, and the traditional textile manufacture was consolidated in the sixteenth century with the development of lighter fabrics.

The city grew and became constricted within the city walls. During the reign of Charles V it was struck by six plague epidemics, but in the seventeenth century some prosperity returned in the form of great artistic activity. Tapestries were ordered from masters including Rubens, Van Dyke, and Jordaens in the neighboring school of Antwerp. Stone and brick houses replaced those made of wood, and there was a flowering of rich decorations with fruit, leaves, cornucopia, and cherubs. Since 1974 Lille has been classified as a city of art, and there are many civil and religious buildings that attest to its rich past. The Citadel, built by Vauban, is one of the most beautiful examples of the

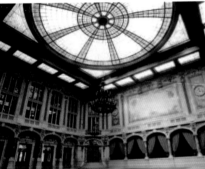

The impressive interior of the Chamber of Commerce.

facing page
The old Bourse and the bell tower.

military architecture of the seventeenth century. The Vieille Bourse, with traces of the Spanish occupation, is an excellent meeting of the Flemish and French cultures. The important Grand Place, the center of the city, proudly flaunts its *Déesse,* the symbol of the resistance against the Austrians in 1792. The Porte de Paris and rue de la Monnaie are where the mint stood. Looking up, visitors can see sculpted cherubs guarding the mansion facades. Sometimes they are made from red bricks and white stone, and shop signs were worked to the taste of the craftsmen of the times. Rihour Palace, the ancient residence of the Dukes of Burgundy, was destroyed in a fire in 1916, but it has been restored and is now the tourist office.

Charles de Gaulle, the general who became president of the Republic, was born in Lille in 1890 at rue Princesse 9. Unforgettable for his appeal for resistance on June 18, 1940, and for having founded the Fifth Republic, de Gaulle always had a special bond with his city. He was an officer during World War I and wrote many books on politics and military strategy. In 1940 he refused the armistice and sent his famous message to the French through the BBC in London. In 1959 he became president of the Republic and inaugurated a foreign policy of prestige and national independence. He resigned in 1969 when his project to reform the Senate and the regions was defeated in a referendum, and he died at Colombey-les-deux-Églises in 1970. Lille has honored him by dedicating a square, memorial, and university to him, and the house in which he was born is now a museum.

Of all Lille's beautiful gardens, the Vauban garden is among the most delightful and covers an area of more than 100,000 square feet between rue Desmazières, avenue Mathias-Delobel, and boulevard Vauban. The harmonious curves of this English-style park offer enchanting walks among the lakes and lawns, with flowering tulips, hyacinths, and forget-me-nots, and more than 500 trees and 400 shrubs line the avenues. There is also a surprising chalet that housed some Tibetan goats in 1879; today it is a marionette theater.

The famous Braderie of Lille takes place on the first weekend of September and is becoming increasingly well known. Collectors and secondhand dealers meet and for forty-eight hours transform the city into a party. The *braderie*'s origin is uncertain, and the tradition might have begun in the Middle Ages, when the servants of Lille's families had permission to sell, from dawn to dusk, used clothes and objects belonging to their masters. This festival has changed over the years, but its spirit of a great autumn party is still the same. For two days and nights people do what they please. Along the town streets apprentice merchants and experienced secondhand dealers exhibit an incredible amount of bric-a-brac that, with considerable negotiation, eventually finds a buyer. It ends on Sunday at midnight, when the street cleaners take the place of the browsers and buyers, who are by now exhausted after scouring the many stalls.

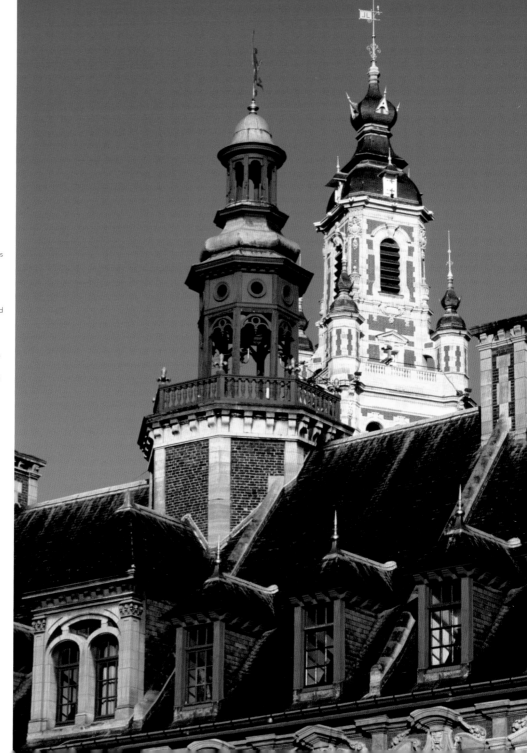

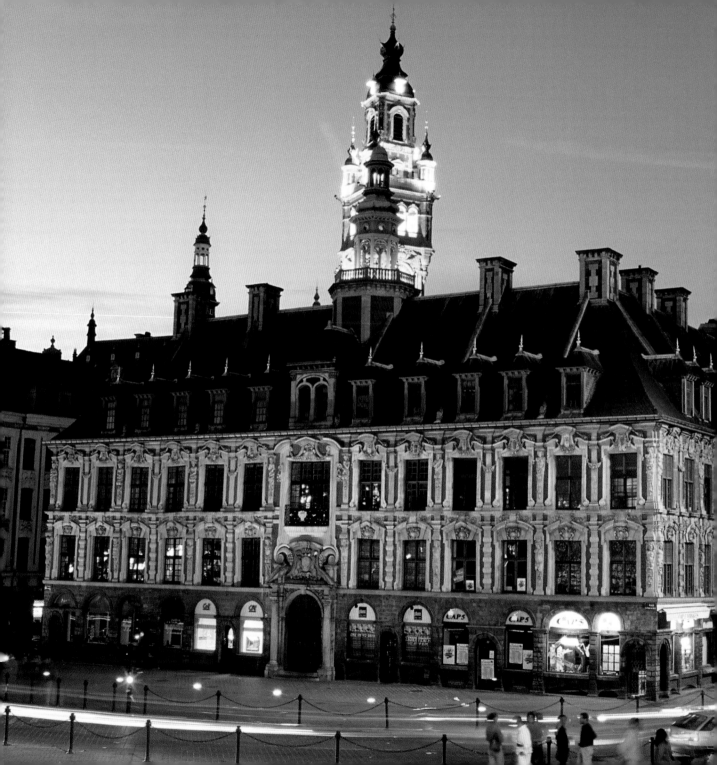

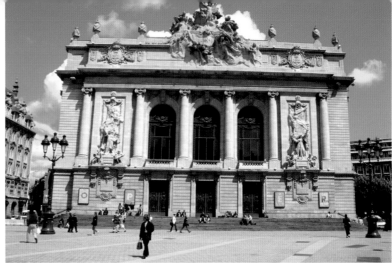

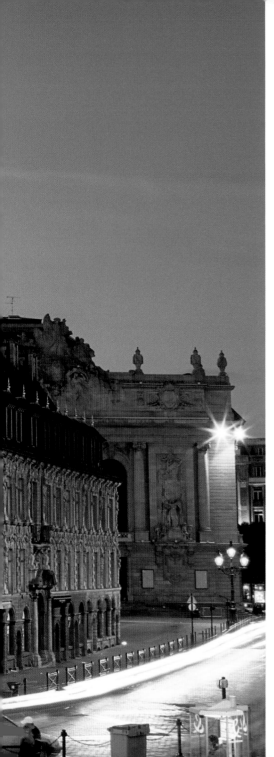

The Palais des Beaux-Artes of Lille is, after Paris, one of the most important museums in France. It is housed in a sumptuous nineteenth-century building that has been completely restored, and displays in its 235,000 square feet the complete panorama of European art from the Middle Ages to the twentieth century. The important part of the collection is Flemish painting, with Rubens and his school, and the nineteenth-century French art of David, Delacroix, Géricalut, Corot, and Courbet. Among the 2,000 paintings in the collection some have changed the history of painting. For example, *Bélisaire* by Jacques-Louis David (1781) was considered the first example of neoclassicism. *Après dîner à Ornana (1849)* by Gustave Courbet is a true manifesto of realism in a romantic mood. *Le Sommeil de Puvis* (1867) by Puvis de Chavannes was the artist's favorite work and an extraordinary symbolic precursor of Picasso's Blue Period. There is also an important design collection that is visited by specialists from all over the world: 4,000 designs—among which are thirty by Raphael—representing about 300 Italian artists of the sixteenth century.

left
The old Bourse on the Grand Place dates back to the Spanish occupation.

above
The facade of the Opéra.

Forms for maroilles cheese can be found at the famous antiques market.

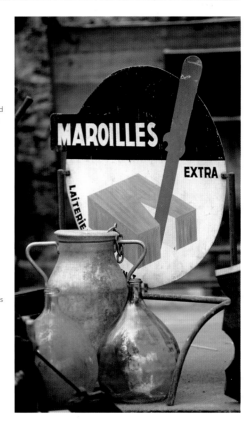

179

GUÉRANDE
SALT FLOWERS OF THE SEA

THE BEAUTIFUL, HISTORIC CITY OF GUÉRANDE OVERLOOKS VAST SALT FLATS and has kept its medieval character intact. Its powerful circle of walls flanked by six towers and four fortified gateways are among its main attractions, and the surrounding landscape is exceptional. This is a strong and generous land of salt and granite, and it occupies an important role in the history of Brittany. A million visitors a year come to admire the collegiate church of Saint-Aubin and its famous walls, which stretch for almost a mile and have inspired writers such as Balzac, Daudet, and Flaubert. After the cathedral at Nantes, Saint-Aubin is the second most visited religious monument in all the towns of the Loire.

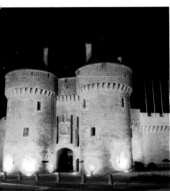

Of the old fortifications, today only the castle remains.

The monumental fifteenth-century gateway of Saint-Michel is the main entrance through the walls and houses the historic governors' residence. It contains a small regional museum where typical objects of the region, such as salt-working tools and the local Croisic ceramic utensils, are displayed on three floors. The austere and modest chapel of Notre-Dame-la-Blanche was the site where, in 1381, the second treaty of Guérande was signed. It put an end to the wars of succession and the disputes between France and Brittany, and enabled the city to enjoy a period of prosperity. The city's wealth developed thanks to vigorous trade in salt and wine, enabling it to maintain an important fleet of ships. From the sixteenth century on, however, the silting of the ports and decreased value of salt in the marketplace led to a loss of its maritime power to other ports, such as Croisic and Pouliguen.

Guérande was also hurt by the disappearance of its vineyards and suppression of its canonical college during the French Revolution, but more recently tourism and other economic activities have reinvigorated the town. Its narrow streets are animated and full of shops, and the collegiate church of Saint-Aubin is in the heart of the city. The Romanesque and Gothic styles of architecture are fused in this building, and its decorations include two altarpieces in stone and marble and a seventeenth-century wood choir. The crypt contains a white granite Merovingian sarcophagus, a vestige of the original sixth-century church. The Musée de la Poupée et des Jouets Anciens is a completely different experience; it contains more than 300 dolls and games collected from around the globe and takes the visitor back to childhood. The nature park of the Brière, the port of Turballe, Piriac, and Le Baule are places of great interest in the area, but the whole of the Guérande peninsula is well worth a visit in order to discover a very special landscape and a wild inland area in balance with the land and the sea.

Guérande, from the Breton Gwen Rann, meaning "white country," owes its name to the proximity of the salt flats, which cover nearly 4,500 acres and have made Guérande world famous. For more than a thousand years the salt workers have continued to model this territory sculpted by the ocean. It is a fragile checkerboard of clay and saltwater, composing a landscape of a thousand surprising facets that reflect a long tradition of expertise. From June to September the salt workers collect the grayish coarse salt and the fine salt, called *fleur de sel* ("flower of salt"), in seemingly countless small basins. The salt appears after the slow evaporation of water by means of sun and wind, leaving no doubt that the salt of Guérande is one of the best in the world. It can be bought directly or at the Maison des Paludiers de Saillé.

Between savory tastes of *crêpes dentelles,* sardines in oil, fish, and seafood, everyone quickly discovers that Brittany is very filling. There is a local sweetmeat made with salted butter and the *fleur de sel* of Guérande, and one can taste salt algae and salt butter for breakfast; while here, one should try it all. The *andouillette maison,* or rustic sausage made of chitterlings, is a curiosity prepared by the sausage maker in the village and best tasted with coffee in the morning. This is a local delicacy to be added in slices to buttered canapés—and salted, of course. If this is too much, then a *quatre-quart* dry biscuit or a nice slice of *brioche vendéenne* will surely satisfy the palate.

facing page
The famous "flowers of salt" bloom on the salt flats.

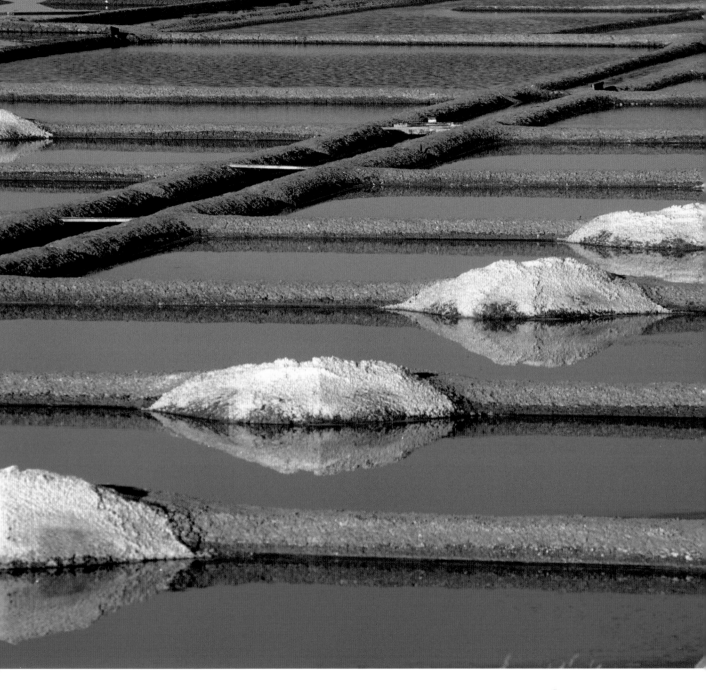

SABLÉ
SUR-SARTHE
MURALS AND MAJOLICA

SABLÉ IS ONE OF MANY ENCHANTING VILLAGES IN THE SARTHE VALLEY, an area fed by three rivers between Maine and Anjou. A walk along its ancient narrow streets and over the medieval bridge that crosses the Erve River is delightful; this river is responsible Sablé's prosperity through the eighteenth century, when the leather trade flourished. The old town offers picturesque medieval buildings, the lockkeeper's house, and a neo-Gothic church with a striking stained-glass window depicting the Crucifixion, a masterpiece made in 1495. Visitors first come to the castle park, which contains the national library's workrooms, then follow the remains of the city walls to reaching the port, which was very active through the nineteenth century and remains the province's most important river port. An excursion or short cruise by boat is a highly recommended luxury. Hidden in the valley one discovers the villages of Saint-Denis-d'Anjou, made in a unique blond stone, and Asnières-sur-Vergé, which is said to be the most beautiful of the Sarthe Valley thanks to its shady banks, fifteenth-century houses, country homes, and picturesque bridges. The impressive murals of the parish church have added to the village's fame.

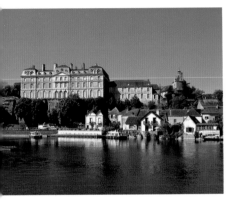

The town overlooks the broad Sarthe River.

facing page
The seventeenth-century moat of the Malicorne castle.

Just a few miles from Sablé is the Benedictine abbey of Saint-Pierre-de-Solesmes, which was founded in 1010 by Geoffroy le Vieiux. It dominates the Sarthe and is one of the most important centers of Gregorian chant. A mass sung in the chapel is an unforgettable and very emotional experience. There are also two groups of marble statues, the *Saints de Solesmes,* which are considered among the most important sculptures of the early sixteenth century. Facing the abbey of Solesmes is a delightful museum full of toys, games, and other curiosities put together by an intelligent and mischievous collector, which will be the highlight of any child's visit. Another jewel is the castle of Plessis Bourré, an elegant fortress reflected, together with the limestone rocks and the piercing blue of Anjou, in its wide moat. Jean Bourré, secretary of finance and treasurer to Louis XI and Charles VIII, built the castle as a defensive complex but inside made it a comfortable Renaissance-style residence with an internal courtyard and richly decorated rooms. At the nearby eighteenth-century castle of Malicorne, Madame de Sévigné stills seems to be in residence —a sign of the area's charm.

The Loire is one of the richest valleys for mural paintings in France. These masterpieces were made between the twelfth and sixteenth centuries and are mainly found in churches. They represent scenes from the life of Christ, the Virgin, and the saints. They all belong to the same school of painting and are distinguished by the similarity of their composition and color, characterized by many ochre and red tones. Many of these paintings have unfortunately been hidden under successive layers of whitewash, but several have been patiently restored. In the Sablé-sur-Sarthe region the most important paintings are in the church of Asnières-sur-Vergé, Saint-Denis-d'Anjou, Miré, Auvers-le-Hamon, Varennes-Boureau, Saint-Martin-de-Vilenglose, and Tassé.

Malicorne has been a famous center of majolica tile production for more than two and a half centuries. Fountains, table objects, and bowls for domestic use made in the local style can be seen during a guided visit to the workshops of the Faïenceries d'Art de Malicorne, which thoroughly describes the ceramics' manufacture following the tradition of the great eighteenth-century masters. From the clay beds to firing and making the fretwork patterns for which Malicorne is famous, the manufacture of majolica will open a door into a rich artistic and historical world. Another place worth visiting is the Malicorne Espace Faïence, a contemporary exhibition center.

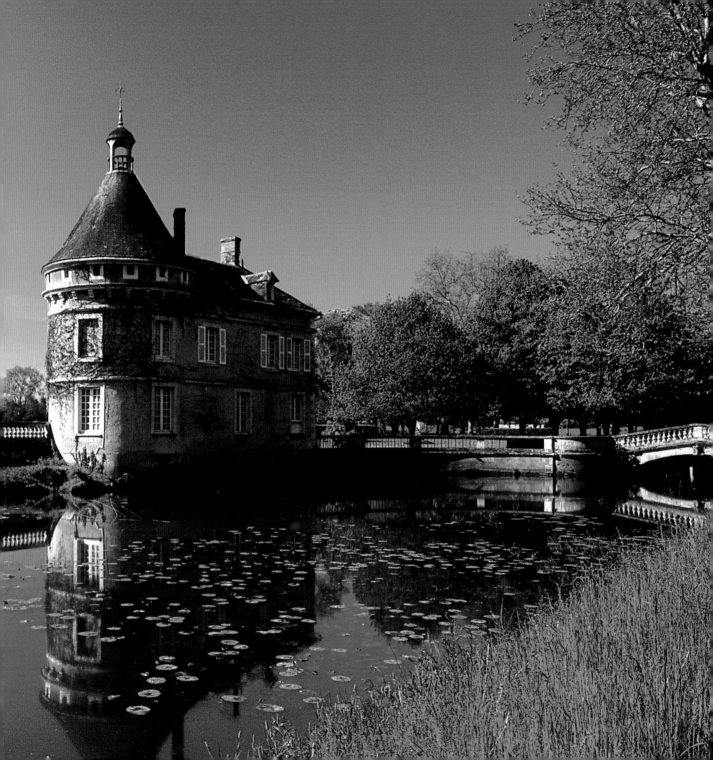

AMIENS

A GOTHIC PANTHEON

GOTHIC FRANCE WAS BORN HERE, IN PICARDY, IN THE THIRTEENTH CENTURY. The cathedrals of Amiens, Beauvais, and Laon have inspired those of Paris and Reims, and the extraordinary stone structure of Amiens is still one of the greatest Gothic buildings ever constructed. The cathedral is one of fifty UNESCO World Heritage buildings, and is notable for its proportions, statues, treasury, fifteenth-century organ, and the 110 exquisitely sculpted wooden choir stalls. Notre-Dame d'Amiens is undeniably one of the world's most beautiful cathedrals, and was even named the "Gothic Pantheon" by John Ruskin. Near the Pantheon we find the *charme fou* of Saint-Leu, a charming medieval quarter whose little houses, with their brightly colored facades, reflect in the waters of the Somme River, which here divides into nine branches, transforming Amiens into a little Venice. The town's historic textile makers, dyers, and leather workers have long since disappeared, and their places have been taken by restaurants, inns, and bars with a pleasant atmosphere frequented by local students. Amiens is a city of water, parks, and gardens, and a little farther downstream the Somme divides again, into innumerable basins and canals. It is fascinating to explore by boat or bridge these 700 acres of floating gardens in the heart of the city, including the *Hortillonnages*, ancient vegetable gardens.

Amiens was extensively rebuilt after World War II and preserves a pleasant nineteenth-century center around the rue de Noyon and rue des Trois-Cailloux. It was the world capital for velvet, was very prosperous indeed, and was granted a tribunal to establish the museum of Picardy, a veritable jewel box decorated by Puvis de Chavannes in the style of Napoleon III, containing collections of sacred art and paintings by Fragonard, Chardin, Van Loo, and many other notable artists. In the nineteenth century a colorful figure dominated Amiens: Jules Verne was town councilor and also in charge of constructing the town circus. The house in which he lived is now a center containing documentation on his works. The nearby Hôtel de Berny also stands in the historic center and was the historic site of the *Trésoriers de France*. It later became a local museum of art and regional history, with fine collections of Louis XV and Louis XVI furniture, and the Galerie du Vitrail displays ancient stained-glass pieces in a magnificent thirteenth-century crypt.

Nearby is the Marquenterre, the largest expanse of dunes in northern France. The Samara archaeological park tells the exceptional story of this valley, whose history goes back more than 600,000 years, supporting many locals' claim that France was indeed born here.

The feeling of freedom here is absolute. The light, with its infinite variety of colors as it bathes the bay of the Somme, has seduced many artists and writers. Rocks, dunes, basins, and estuaries stretch for thirty miles along the Picardy coast. The bay of the Somme is also a paradise for birds, and two-thirds of all European bird species can be viewed here. The Marquenterre ornithological park is undoubtedly a favorite place for migrating birds, and also has a striking seascape. Enthusiasts go to Cap Hornu to contemplate one of the most beautiful and vast panoramas of the bay, and then visit the pleasant port of Le Crotoy, renowned for being the only beach in the north that faces south. Le Crotoy had a period of prosperity at the beginning of the twentieth century when Guerlain, perfumer to the Empress Eugénie, attracted the whole of the Parisian *bel monde* to the beaches here. Jules Verne also lived there for many years. In nearby Rue, the chapel of the Holy Ghost, with its flamboyant fourteenth-century Gothic style, is very interesting, with extraordinarily rich interior and exterior decorations.

facing page
The beautifully colored decorations of Notre-Dame's interior.

A glimpse of the deep arcades of Notre-Dame's portals.

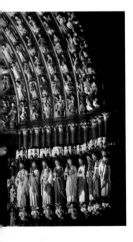

The *ficelle picarde*, *flamiche* with leeks, whipped desserts, and above all the *macarons d'Amiens*—with a hint of almonds, honey, jelly, or apricots—and chocolate "tiles" are the most appreciated local delicacies. Thanks to the long stretch of coast, the Somme bay supplies the markets and the restaurants with sole, shrimp, scallops, and its famous *coques* (cockles). Freshwater and saltwater eels are also a regional specialty that can be eaten smoked or fresh, in a terrine or *en matelote*, with a wine and onion sauce. Parmentier, the man who introduced potatoes to Europe, was born here. Potatoes are still in abundant use in many dishes and can be found in the vegetable soup commonly called *soupe des Hortillons*, and named after the *Hortillonnages* of Amiens.

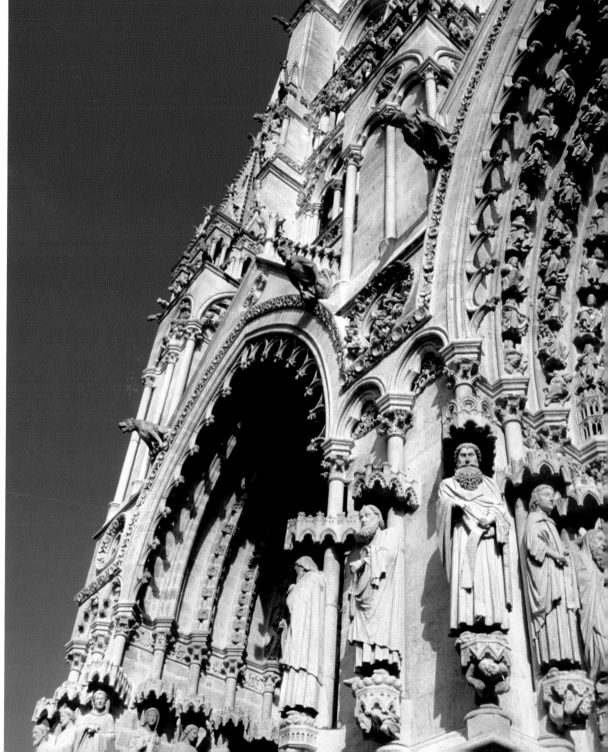

The *Hortillonnages* extend for more than 600 acres in the heart of the urban area of Amiens. These gardens are surrounded by water and date back to the era of Roman Gaul, when marshes were used for vegetable cultivation. Today it is an exceptional trip to take by boat. A guide takes visitors inside this delightful tangle of gardens and water, letting them discover exotic birds among the reeds and water lilies and allowing them to relive the area's rich history. Guides often recount, among other tales, the legend that the cathedral of Amiens was built on a field of artichokes donated by some rich farmers. The omnipresent water will mark the rhythm of the trip, crossing a broad range of different landscapes. The canal branches wind around the gardens and under the bridges, some in wrought iron, some in wood, others that look very old indeed, and some that resemble Eastern bridges. Little gardeners' huts are painted in bright colors that stand out prominently against the luxuriant greenery of plants and the bright blue sky, making an exceptional visit for all.

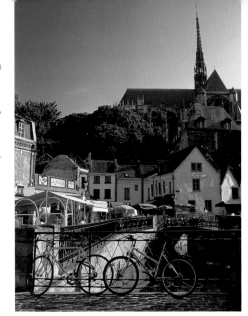

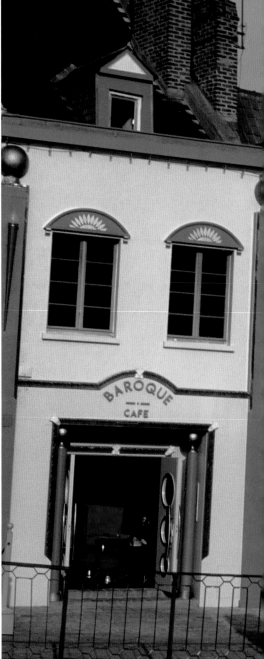

above
A glimpse of the area surrounding the cathedral.

below
The high naves of the cathedral of Notre-Dame.

right
The colorful facades of the houses in quartier Saint-Leu.

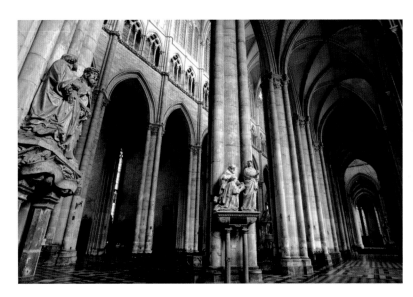

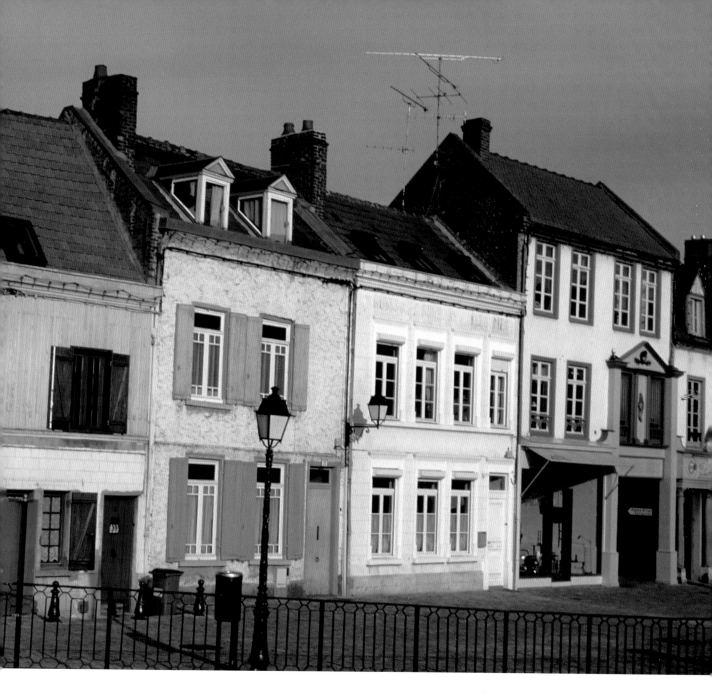

CHANTILLY
CONDÉ'S COLLECTION

JUST UNDER TWENTY MILES FROM PARIS, CHANTILLY COMBINES A LOVE OF ART with a rich equestrian tradition. Porcelain, black lace, and its delicious cream make up part of Chantilly's fame. Four great families turned this town into the marvel that visitors admire today: *Connétable* Anne de Montmorency, the Grand Condé, the Duke of Bourbon, and the Duke of Aumale. The last owner was Henri d'Orléans, Duke of Aumale, fourth son of Louis-Philippe. In 1886 he donated the estate to the Institute of France, ending an 800-year history of illustrious residents. The Chantilly castle, with its magnificently decorated apartments, houses the Musée Condé, which contains the second-largest French collection of ancient painting after the Louvre. It also has a park designed *à la française* by André Le Nôtre in 1663, which is unique for the diversity of gardens and plants on its nearly 20,000 acres, with exceptionally preserved monuments, a hippodrome, and a collection of forests and agricultural land, all of which attest to the taste of the princes who commissioned it. Facing the castle and hippodrome, the Great Stables of Chantilly are certainly among the most beautiful in the world. They were built by Jean Aubert in the eighteenth century and contain an internationally recognized living museum of horses, a private museum created by Yves Bienaimé in 1982. Everything to do with the art of equitation is gathered here: more than 1,000 sculptures, paintings, drawings, commentaries on dressage, and demonstrations on mounting styles and working with horses in the open. Every first Sunday of the month, from February to November, the museum exhibits the horses' beauty and the splendor of the costumes (created by the Opéra de Paris), harnesses, music, and riders' ability. The hippodrome of Chantilly, created in 1834, is reserved for racehorses and—having won the *Prix du Jockey-Club* and *Prix de Diane*—is one of the most prestigious buildings of its kind. The museum of Patrimonie et de la Dentelle relates the history of the city and the products that contributed to its fame: porcelain, fine majolica, and silk lace. Thanks to the latter Chantilly is known throughout the world, and its mythical, creamy lightness matches the other famous product of the city, a deliciously sweet concoction enjoyed everywhere. According to legend, Chantilly cream was born out of an accident in the kitchen. It seems that there was no more *crème frâiche* at an important meal, so the scullery boy had the idea of whipping it up to increase its volume in order to serve all the guests. For best results very dense cream should be used, a little milk should be incorporated, and it should be left in the refrigerator for at least one hour before it is whipped; vanilla sugar is added for the final touch.

A carriage ride.

facing page
The castle reflected in the calm waters of the Oise River.

The French *Art de Vivre* is represented at Chantilly by the Chambres au château, a bed and breakfast at the castle, and the sublime dining rooms in the *relais de chasse*, ancient hunting lodges. The Relais d'Aumale is a fine example in the heart of the Chantilly forest. Visitors still feel the pull of its past and the Duke of Aumale's spirit in the woods. The atmosphere is welcoming and its cuisine is famous. The Château de la Tour at Gouvieux is an elegant twentieth-century building in English-Norman style with traditional, elegant rooms decorated in a fashionable contemporary style.

The Musée Condé contains an important collection of French paintings and drawings, with works by Clouet, Poussin, Mignard, Nattier, Watteau, Ingres, and Delacroix. There are several masterpieces by Italian artists, including Fra Angelico, Raphael, and Carracci, while Flemish art is represented by Van Dyck and Teniers. The Duke of Aumale (1822–1897) loved books and built a large collection of 30,000 rare volumes and about 700 illuminated manuscripts. Among them are the famous *Très Riches Heures* of the Duc de Berry, from the fifteenth century, and the *Forty Miniatures* of Jean Fouquet. Among the art objects is a beautiful collection of Chantilly soft-paste porcelain dated 1725 and directly inspired by designs from the Far East.

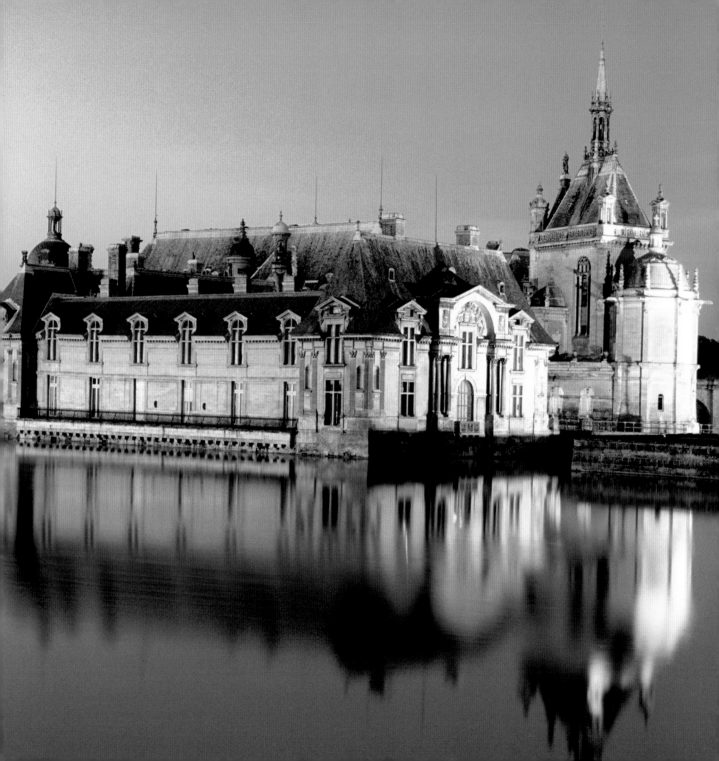

COMPIÈGNE
MEROVINGIANS AND MONARCHS

COMPIÈGNE HAS BEEN A CENTER OF IMPORTANT HISTORICAL EVENTS FOR CENTURIES and is still rightly proud of the remnants of its glorious past. The town's origin is intertwined with that of the French monarchy and dates back to the Merovingian dynasty. It was a "royal and imperial city," and an impressive number of crowned heads, from Clovis to Napoleon, have lived here. Its final location was decided after several moves. King Charles V built a fortress in 1380 that underwent successive improvements and, along with Versailles and Fontainebleau, became one of France's three royal residences. After their coronation at Reims, all the French kings made a traditional stop at Compiègne. It was here that King Louis XIV organized spectacular military maneuvers for the instruction of the Duke of Burgundy. These "Compiègne encampments" became a tradition and served uniquely for the princes' education. They continued until the middle of the nineteenth century and were also famous abroad. The upcoming King Louis XVI and Archduchess Marie-Antoinette of Austria met here for the first time.

The castle was entirely rebuilt by Louis XV, but between 1751 and 1788 architect Ange-Jacques Gabriel, and later his student Le Dreux de la Châtre, made what would become the present castle of Compiègne, one of the most somber monuments of the French neoclassical style. After the French Revolution, Napoleon Bonaparte commissioned the architect Berthault to restore the areas damaged by the revolts in order to welcome his second wife, Archduchess Marie-Louise of Austria. Following the fall of the empire in 1870, the castle became a national museum, and a detailed historical restoration of the castle began in 1945.

There are many intriguing sights to admire in the historical center of town, such as the bell tower in which the oldest city bell in France, dating back to 1303, is preserved. The pride of Compiègne is hidden in three priceless *Piquantins*, three wooden puppets made in 1875 and representing three bitter enemies of the sixteenth century: Langlois the Englishman, Flandrin the Flemish man, and Lansquenet the German. The nearby castle of Pierrefonds is also well worth a visit. It is an old monumental fortress restored by Viollet-le-Duc upon orders from Napoleon III, as is the Alexandre Dumas Museum at Villers-Cotterêts. This museum displays the life and work of the three Dumas writers: General Dumas; his son Alexandre, author of *The Three Musketeers* who was born here in 1802; and his nephew Alexandre, author of *The Lady of the Camellias*.

facing page
Typical half-timbered houses.

The municipality lies in the heart of town.

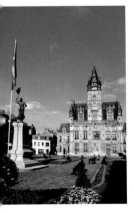

During the Second Empire the castle of Compiègne became a privileged holiday resort for the imperial court. This is when the so-called *Séries de Compiègne* were initiated. When the court decided that within the next three to six weeks it would move to Compiègne, it was accompanied by important figures sent according to a strict ceremony, called *séries*. Each *série* lasted one week, and each consisted of about 100 guests, including princes, ambassadors, ministers, and marshals, as well as writers, artists, and scientists. Among them were Jean-Baptiste Carpeaux, Delacroix, the younger Alexandre Dumas, Gustave Flaubert, Théophlie Gautier, Gounod, Verdi, Claude Bernard, and Pasteur.

Picardy cuisine is most generous, and the inhabitants of the region are fine judges of good food. Among the specialties typical of Compiègne, above all for enthusiasts of desserts and sweetmeats, are the various qualities of chocolate, including *Piquantins* (not to be confused with the eponymous puppets), little delicacies of chocolate and nougat, *Muscadines*, *Impromptus*, and *Orangines*, chocolate orange truffles. The *Gâteau de Compiègne* is the famous dessert of Napoleon Bonaparte, created for the banquet on the occasion of his wedding to Marie-Louise of Austria. It is a puff pastry, cooked and cut into slices, dusted with icing sugar, glazed in the oven, decorated with pineapple and candied fruit, and drizzled with kirsch and maraschino.

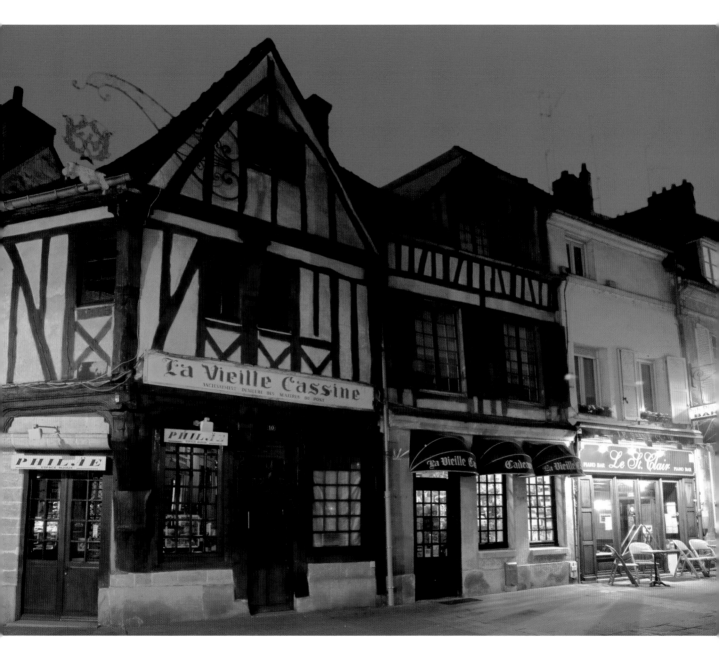

L A O N
A PROUD STANDARD

WHILE LAON'S VINEYARDS HAVE MADE THE TOWN AN OENOLOGICAL center since the twelfth century, they are not its only claim to fame. Its nearly four miles of medieval walls, monumental gateways, and eighty-four monuments are the important architectural traces of the history that makes this town the largest protected territory in France. Rodin declared that, seen from a distance, the towers of Laon "are like standards that symbolize the just pride of man." Resting on a hill overlooking the plains of Champagne, the citadel of Laon has been inhabited since the Gallic era. It was the seat of the Carolingian reign, and between the eighth and tenth centuries was the residence of the French kings, while in the eleventh century the École de Laon flourished here under the auspices of the powerful bishops. In the twelfth century a fire destroyed the first church, which was replaced by the present cathedral. Its construction was begun in 1155, and it became one of the first Gothic cathedrals in France, introducing many architectural innovations. The gallery of little arches inspired the cathedral of Notre-Dame in Paris, its porticoes ornately decorated by triangular Gothic pediments that predate those of Chartres, and the towers

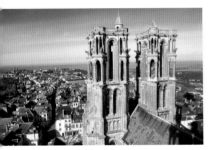

The towers of the cathedral.

facing page
The arcaded gallery of the cathedral of Notre-Dame.

became a model for those at Reims. A sublime collection of windows of the School of Laon-Soissons illuminated the apse, and their beauty dates back to the first quarter of the thirteenth century. In the Middle Ages Laon became a famous religious and intellectual center and later a military stronghold subjected to many sieges. Today the city is a well-known destination at the crossroads between the Île de France, the Champagne region, and Picardy. Walks in the narrow *grimpettes*, the rugged, picturesque paths that cross Laon from top to bottom, are the best way to discover all these treasures. The archaeological museum in the center of the city is located in the old Templar benefice, and displays a beautiful series of pieces from the Bronze Age to the first centuries AD found in the Mediterranean basin. It contains one of the most important collections of Greek vases, figurines, and sculptures outside of the Louvre. Scattered among the Laonnois, an ancient territory of vineyards, are Romanesque churches and houses for the *maîtres de chais,* who would make rounds to check the harvests. There are more than twenty vineyards at Orgeval, Presles-et-Thierry, and Burguignon-sous-Montbavin, where the wine cellars of the Le Main brothers are based. They descend from a seventeenth-century family of artists to whom we owe two paintings, *Famille de Paysans* and *Repas des Paysans*, displayed in the Louvre. The forest of Saint-Gobain is famous for the royal factory founded by Colbert, whose studio produced the mirrors in the eponymous hall at the palace of Versailles.

Erosion has modeled the landscape of the region for more than 40 million years. It has excavated valleys whose colors change with the seasons and chiseled out the limestone plateau that creates such splendid views. South of Laon, the Chemin des Dames was named only because in 1770 it was already paved, which was rare for a secondary road. It was the route used by the daughters of Louis XV to reach the castle of Bove, where they usually spent the summer. This road is also famous as the site of many battles. Julius Caesar fought here in 57 BC, and Napoleon fought here in 1814 against the Russians. During World War I its strategic position on a ten-mile-long ridge made it the site of the continuous massacres between the Allied and Axis armies. Today the Chemin des Dames is scattered with ruins, cemeteries, and memorials and has become a symbol for the absurdity of war.

There is a monthly market of regional produce in Laon attended by farmers, local craftsmen, and lovers of Picardy cuisine. On one Friday each month there is a gathering of vegetable producers, bakers, cheese makers, butchers, bee-keepers, and local musicians. Having enjoyed the atmosphere of tastes, sights, and scents, visitors can take a walk in the afternoon along the market stalls at the cloister of the abbey of Saint-Martin. The best local specialties include asparagus, artichokes, straw-berries, and, more exotically, ginger.

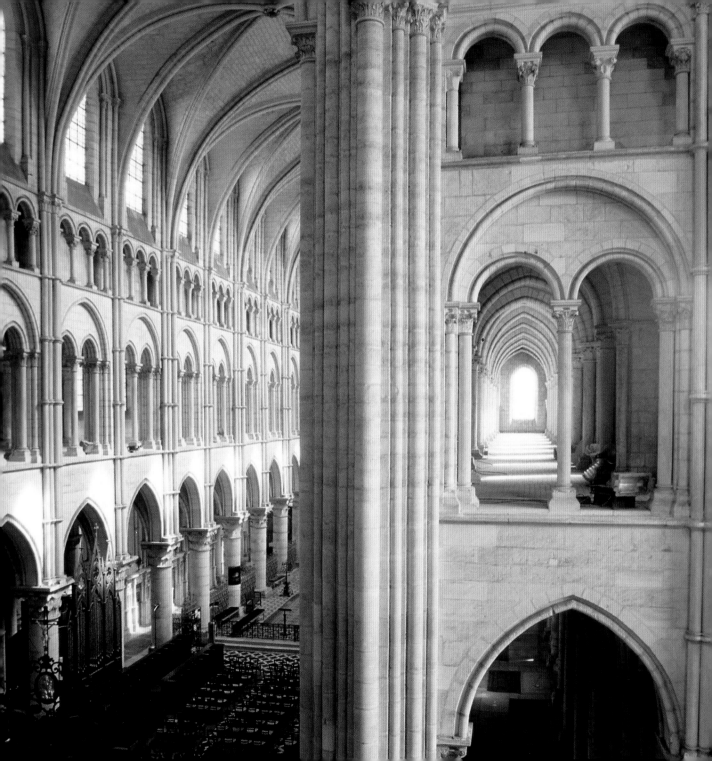

SENLIS
A CINEMATIC CITY

SENLIS IS ONE OF THE SPECIAL CITIES WHOSE INHABITANTS ARE NOT SURPRISED to meet hussars in high uniform, courtesans, or beggars in rags at a café, in a tearoom, or in a tobacco shop. More than 100 films and television programs have been shot in the old town, so such characters seem quotidian. The layout of the city is tortuous, with narrow medieval streets that have been perfectly restored, irregular cobblestones, sloping sidewalks, and little squares. The raised curb protecting the old walls, niches that give refuge to little statues, beautiful carnations in the spring, and Gallo-Roman arenas all make for a perfect setting. Even the picturesque street names have been preserved, such as Chat-Haret, Apport-au-pain, and the street of White Pigeons. Senlis was beautified in the seventeenth and eighteenth centuries by the majestic *hôtels particuliers*, the nobles' residences with stables and courtyards built in the pale stone of the region, sometimes with bricks added. Their imposing gates open onto somber, paved interior courtyards where the facades preserve their look of harmonious nobility, creating a true delight for film directors and visitors. The cathedral, the church of Saint-Pierre, the place du Parvis, the royal castle, and the abbey of Saint Vincent are generally the backdrop of films. It is not rare, however, to see floodlights installed in front of the train station, the hospital, or the buildings in the place Les Halles. Films that have been shot here include Philippe de Broca's *Cartouche*, Luis Buñuel's *The Milky Way*, Andrzej Wajda's *Danton*, Patrice Leconte's *The Hairdresser's Husband*, and many others.

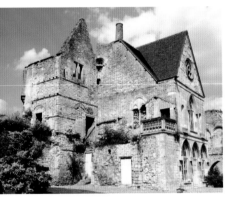

The remains of the royal castle, built in 1130 by King Louis VI.

Because it is near the forests of Chantilly and Halatte, the old hunting ground of the kings, this city on the banks of the Nonette River also offers other attractions. Senlis was deemed a royal city because Hugues Capet was crowned king here in 987. From that moment, thanks to his generosity, this little diocese became important. Churches, chapels, presbyteries, and the cathedral of Notre-Dame were built, and today remain an exceptional heritage. The Vénerie Museum in the old castle must be visited, and beside the bishop's palace is an art museum displaying an important *ex-voto* collection from a Gallic sanctuary in the forest of Halatte. The museum also has a room dedicated to Thomas Couture, a native of Senlis.

Portraiture was a fundamental part of the art of Thomas Couture (1815–1879), whose opus is virtually a gallery of all historical protagonists' faces spanning from the end of the July Monarchy to the beginning of the Second Empire. Because of his large historical and allegorical compositions Couture is considered one of the best representatives of Eclecticism, an art movement in the second half of the nineteenth century. Couture was Edouard Manet's teacher, and by the age of thirty had painted monumental portraits of the artistic, intellectual, and political figures of the ruling classes. These works were done before his triumph at the Paris Salon of 1847 with *Les Romains de la Décadence*, now at the Musée d'Orsay in Paris. At the end of the 1850s he retired to his hometown and later moved to Villiers-le-Bel. His talent invites us to venture into the secrets behind the expressions of his solemn, dreaming, sitters.

facing page
The old church of Saint-Pierre now hosts art exhibitions and concerts.

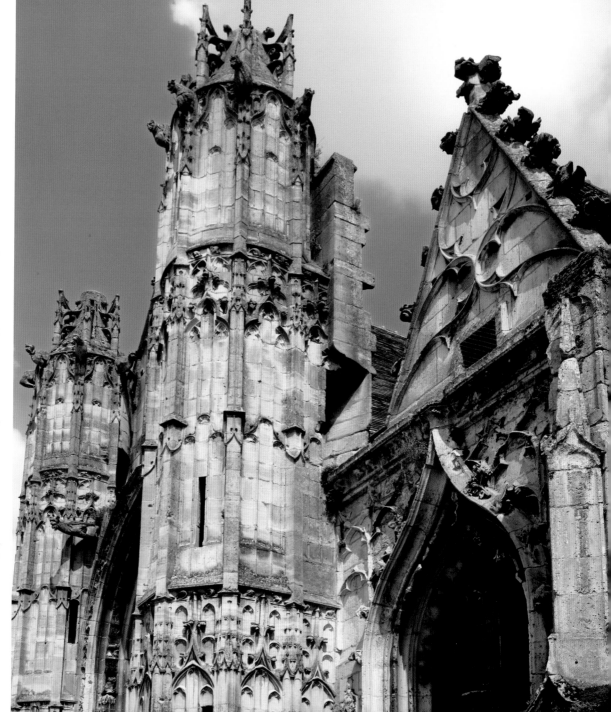

Henri Noiret manages the Scaramouche Restaurant, a beautiful house with a painted wooden facade that looks out onto the cathedral of Notre-Dame. Begin by ordering lobster, refreshed by a bowl of gazpacho, sautéed duck foie gras with Espelette peppers, or a lamb chop grilled with fresh thyme and Provençal chartreuse. Taste the *crêpes soufflés* with Grand Marnier for dessert, unless the unique cold tomato soup with red fruit on ice with vanilla and basil is too tempting. Noiret is creatively inventive, and with the first taste his diners know that his reputation is justly earned.

ARS-EN-RÉ
BICYCLE TO THE BEACH

A LONG STRETCH OF LAND BATHED BY THE SEA, a mild climate, a Riviera-like sunshine, and a unique setting distinguish the Île de Ré from its surroundings. The flat landscape offers a fascinating view of an open space in which nature, the beaches' fine sand, salt flats, woods, and the dunes are all imbued with an Atlantic scent. Following its thirty miles of coastline are a series of harmonious whitewashed houses with blue or green painted shutters and windows that look out onto little streets where roses grow on every wall. This does not, however, give a complete idea of this island's beauty, including local oyster cultivation, agriculture, and tourism. In the north, at Fiers d'Ars, is the nature reserve of Lilleau des Niges, where thousands of migratory birds gather. A few miles away are the national forests of Trousse-Chemisé, Lizay, Combe à l'Eau, and the woods of Henry IV, which descend gently to the dunes, beaches, and exquisite coastline. Farther along are stands of maritime pines and Holm oaks that protect the undergrowth of Atlantic vegetation and plants characteristic of the Mediterranean scrubland.

The architectural heritage of the Charente-Maritime area, with its castles, ancient residences, coastal fortifications, river and sea ports, and Romanesque churches, is perfectly preserved here. Visitors must do as the inhabitants on the island and travel by bicycle from one village to the next, passing by beaches, vineyards, and the forests. The bicycle is an ideal means for discovering the medieval covered markets of La Flotte, a peaceful village whose port used to equip the tuna-fishing boats. From nearby Saint-Martin the ships of the *Royale* departed for the penal colonies of Cayenne and New Caledonia, and here the Vauban Citadel remains as a memory of those times. The ramparts follow the coastline, and the nearby Renaissance galleries of the Hôtel de Clerjotte and a labyrinth of little streets have given the village the nickname of "Saint-Tropez on the Atlantic." On the southern part of the island, Ars-en-Ré is certainly the most charming of the villages, with a mere 1,340 residents and a strange church that unites two twelfth- and fifteenth-century buildings. One part is an extension of the other, and the bell tower still acts as a lighthouse for the ships that come to anchor here. Since 1854, on the western part of the island, the lighthouse of the Whales has offered a beautiful view of Ré and l'Arche de Noé (Noah's Ark), a surprising universe of embalmed animals, corals, and shells. Île de Ré is the jewel of this region and is less than two miles from La Rochelle by car.

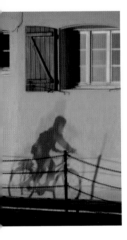

facing page
The sunrise at Trousse-Chemise on the Île-de-Ré.

Discover the beauties of the landscape by bike.

Aix is the third island, between Ré and Oléron, and bears a reminder of Napoleon; it was here on Aix that, after the defeat at Waterloo, he signed the surrender on July 13, 1815. The museum, which is in the house where the emperor stayed, displays some interesting objects. On the mainland, Brouage is a fortified town in the heart of the *marais* salt marshes. One can feel the presence of Samuel Champlain, the founder of Quebec, and visitors can easily imagine the love affair between Marie Mancini and Louis XIV. At Rochefort, in place du Marché, now renamed place Jacques-Demy, one can still hear the footsteps of the *Demoiselles de Rochefort*, the 1966 cult film with Catherine Deneuve and Françoise Dorléac. Here, too, is the astonishing and marvelous house of Pierre Loti, completely furnished and decorated by this writer and traveler. Off the island of Aix, alone amid the open sea, stands the old stone monster of Fort Boyard, a stronghold created by Napoleon to protect the route to the island of Aix and the naval dockyard of Rochefort.

The oyster reigns at Ars and Saint-Martin. The type cultivated here is called the *Marenne d'Oleron*, the most famous in France, together with that found in the basin of Arcachon. Its flesh is gray-green, and it has a strong taste of iodine. Try it *nature* (plain with just a drop of lemon), with a little vinegar and minced scallions, or with a slice of buttered rye bread. Oysters can also be served "cooked." Marenne oysters pair best with a very dry, non-fruity white wine such as Muscadet, Chablis, or Meursault, or with a very light red wine. They are even better with Champagne; in this case, try them *en papillotte* with some foie gras. A visit to an oyster farm on the Île de Ré is highly recommended, as the moment of tasting here is truly magical.

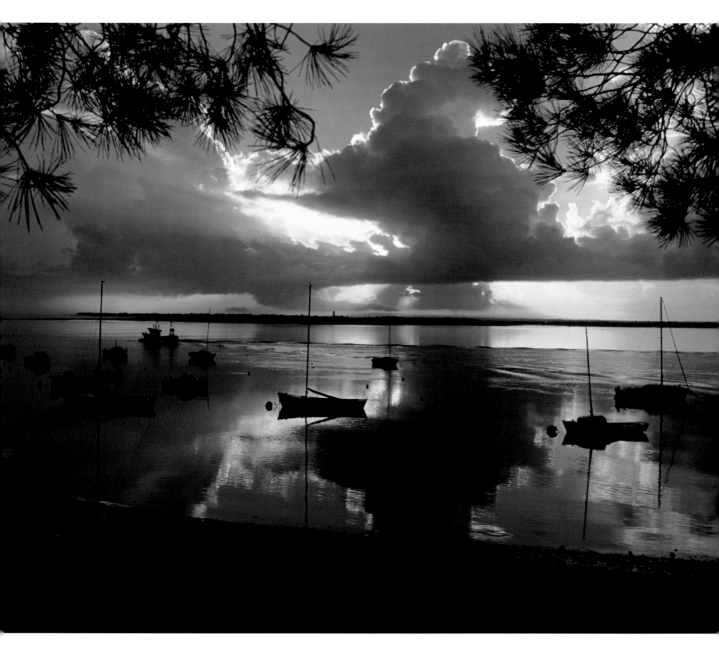

LA ROCHELLE
LOCAL TRADITION, WORLD TRADE

LA ROCHELLE'S OLD PORT, PORTICOES, WOODEN HOUSES, MUNICIPALITY, and eighteenth-century *hôtels particuliers* all face the sea, attesting to the unchanging ties the town has with the ocean. Lined up in front of this architectural procession are the commercial port of La Pallice, the Chef de Baie port reserved for fishermen, and the Les Minimes port, which faces the lighthouse of the Bout du Monde, the second-largest tourist port after Marseilles. In the middle of all this, guarded by two imposing and emblematic fourteenth-century towers, is the old port and the ancient Lanterne lighthouse. They have maintained their charm, just like the multicolored facades of the houses in the fishermen's quarter. Farther inland near the place du Marché, beginning on rue des Merciers, the historic center begins, characterized by gargoyle- and mask-decorated facades, dormer windows, and many sculptures.

Until the fifteenth century La Rochelle was one of the largest ports of the Atlantic coast and was commercially active in the wine and salt trades. During the Renaissance the city embraced reformist ideas and became Protestant. In the eighteenth century its commerce extended all the way to the new world, beginning a prosperous period of trade between France, Africa, and the Antilles. The Museum of the New World is in a magnificent eighteenth-century *hôtel particulier*, and its collection gives a detailed account of the relations between La Rochelle and the Americas from the sixteenth century on. The paintings, prints, furniture, and decorative arts on display all evoke distant lands and the horrific history of slavery. The Natural History Museum also displays many nineteenth-century pieces from the four continents, brought here by travelers, soldiers, and missionaries. The sea, distant voyages, and exoticism all can be felt in a visit to the local aquarium, which is one of the largest in Europe, with approximately 10,000 examples of fish from all over the world, from the microscopic to the great predators, almost all known species are represented here. Before casting off with a boat to visit the beaches or the Île de Ré, two small cultural stops in the town are highly recommended. First is the Musée des Beaux-Arts, on the second floor of the Hôtel de Crussol d'Uzes, with its collection of European painting, which includes works by Camille Corot, Gustave Doré, Eugène Fromentin, Alberto Magnelli, and others. The second is the Musée d'Orbigny-Bernon, famous for its precious collection of French majolica and an exceptional section dedicated to the arts of the Far East, all of which are an invitation to travel to distant lands.

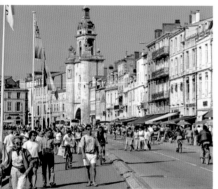

The seafront is a favorite place for a stroll.

facing page
The imposing tower on the old harbor.

The first *Francofolies* of La Rochelle was created in 1985 by the radio announcer and actor Jean-Louis Foulquier. It is a show that presents new talent to the public every summer. It includes French, Belgian, Swiss, Canadian, African, and Caribbean performers, and has been so successful as a Francophone musical showcase that it has been exported around the world. Another important event is the International Film Festival, which began in 1973 and attracts the second-largest number of spectators after Cannes. In September, there is the *Jazz entre deux tours* festival and the *Grand Pavois*, which is a boat show that provides a great opportunity to take a virtual tour around the globe.

When old ships transported wine they had to make sure at all costs that the long voyage would not alter the quality of the wine. This prompted English and Dutch merchants to begin distilling it, a practice initially done on its arrival, and later before it left its port of origin. A few miles from La Rochelle the village of Cognac invented double distillation in the seventeenth century. This process allowed the concentrated and unalterable alcohol to be transported. Its inventors named this brandy after the town, and realized that, when allowed to age, its quality improved—cheers!

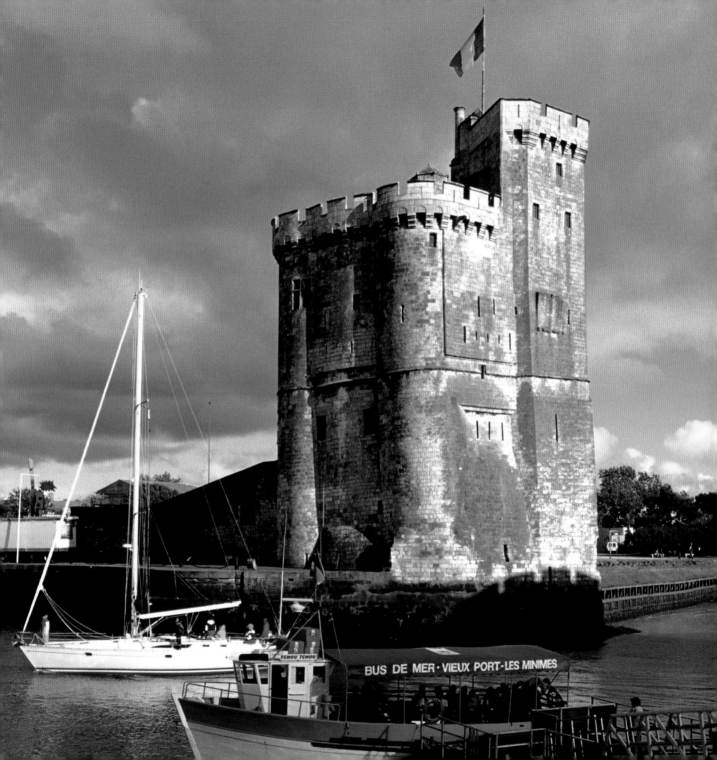

BUS DE MER · VIEUX PORT · LES MINIMES

POITIERS
A FRESCOED CAPITAL

GOTHIC MONUMENTS AND ROMANESQUE CHURCHES, MEDIEVAL STREETS and wooden houses, Haussmann-style boulevards and contemporary architecture—every age imaginable has left its mark here, and what splendid marks! The ancient capital of Poitou was built on a rocky promontory and has a very rich heritage. A great visit begins with the incomparable view from the dunes on Clain Hill, spanning out over the roofs of the old city and surrounding valley. The cathedral of Saint-Pierre stands out among all the other buildings of Poitiers, as it is an immense Gothic-Angevin construction begun at the end of the twelfth century by order of Eleanor of Aquitaine. In the interior visitors can see the imposing collection of about twenty Gothic windows, including one from 1170 depicting a Crucifixion, one of the most valuable in all France. Beside the cathedral stands the baptistery of Saint-Jean, dating back to 350 AD, one of the oldest Christian buildings in Europe. It contains the Merovingian Archaeological Museum. Another treasure, of Romanesque style, is the cycle of frescoes of the twelfth and thirteenth centuries representing the first 200 bishops of Poitiers. They are depicted on the pillars of the seven naves of the church of Saint-Hilaire, a saint who has long been venerated along the pilgrimage route leading to Santiago de Compostela. Among other very interesting monuments is the Palace of Justice, the former residence of the dukes of Aquitaine, with its immense thirteenth-century "hall of the lost footsteps." The building additions were carried out by Jean de Berry, who had jurisdiction over Poitou. The tower of Maubergeon is the ancient keep, from which there is an exceptional view. The Clain River runs through the city, and on its banks stands the ancient collegiate church of Sainte-Radegonde. The portal is splendid and is the final resting place of the saint (who died in 578 AD) who was the bride of Clotaire I Croix. Art enthusiasts can go to the Saint-Croix museum to admire Camille Claudel's bronzes. Among the sculptures are *Bust of a Girl*, *Weeping Venus* by Romaine Brooks, and two small pieces by Boudin and Sisley, plus paintings by Bonnard and Vuillard, Mondrian's *Woods Near Oele* (a work that precedes his interest in abstraction), and works by Max Ernst, Raymond Hains, and Villeglé.

In the area surrounding Poitiers there are many castles, abbeys, and the famous and rather curious Futuroscope. The unique grottoes of Norée are very unusual, and the clever play of light enables us to discover mineral formations, stalactites, and petrified waterfalls along a path that culminates in a secret chamber.

One of the pavilions of the Futuroscope Fair.

facing page
The splendid Romanesque facade of the church of Notre-Dame-la-Grande.

Since opening in 1987 the European Park of Images and Communication, known as the Futuroscope, has become the second most important amusement park in France. Its success was immediate. It occupies an area of more than 110 acres, with more than twenty pavilions, shows, and games for both young and old. It has become a year-round attraction, with a large number of street artists, concerts, exhibitions, and impromptu attractions including, just last year, *La Cité Numerique*, *Les Yeux Grands Fermés*—a sensorial voyage in complete darkness—and *Star du Futur*, a simulation of the making of a film. Every evening at dusk a fantastic tale is projected on the immense water screens, making Futuroscope an interactive, playful, and instructive place full of excitement.

It is said that Pantagruel, the hero of Rabelais' *Gargantua and Pantagruel*, came to Poitiers to study and excelled. *Poitevine* cuisine is best described as heartily healthy and generous. It is true country cooking, and the dishes are hearty. The food is cooked over a low flame for many hours, filling the kitchen with its appetizing scent. Special mention should be made of the local goat cheeses; among them is the famous *Chabichou*, ideally tasted with a glass of Gamay. There are also the melons, chestnuts, walnuts, cabbage, *mojette* beans, and *petits gris* escargots, which are very different from those of Burgundy. Last, but certainly not least, the butter of Poitou is superb enough to have earned the AOC distinction and is often enjoyed each day at breakfast.

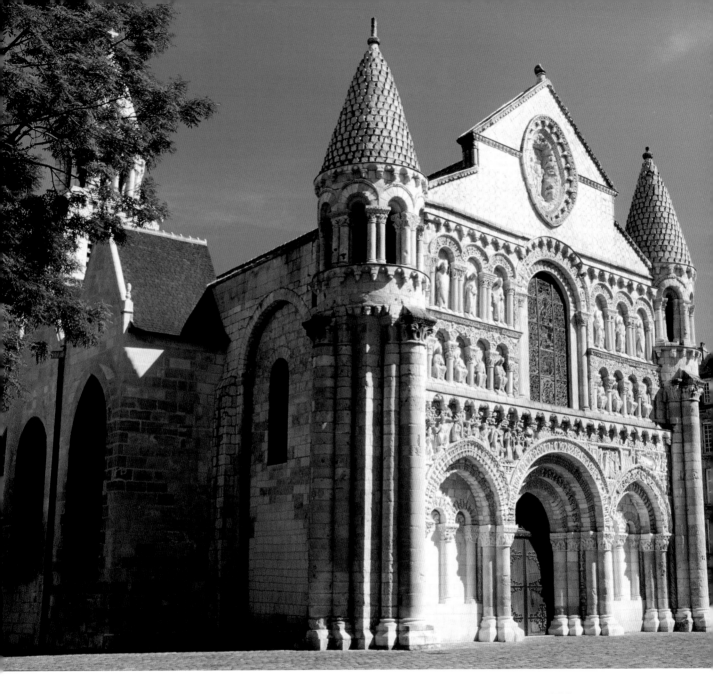

AIX-EN-PROVENCE
THE MOUNTAINS AS MUSE

THE NOBLE MANSIONS OF THIS TOWN MIGHT READILY REMIND VISITORS of an Italian city, but the light and the colors are unmistakably characterized by the sobriety and elegance of nineteenth-century Paris. Aix-en-Provence shows off the beautiful, uniform pink tiles of its roofstops all around the cathedral Saint-Sauveur. This is a city of students, researchers, and artists attracted by the atmosphere of the small historic center. They

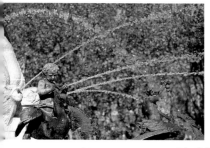

One of the cherubs of the La Rotonde fountain.

facing page
One of two Atlas figures decorating the facade of the Pavillon Vendôme, built in 1665.

stroll around the fountains, laze in the shade of Sycamores, and meet in the town's poetic squares. The enchantment of Aix-en-Provence, sometimes calm and timeless, sometimes lively as a market, lies in the discovery and enjoyment of the shady squares that open onto sculpted fountains, including the *Tanneurs* and *Trois Ormeaux,* masterpieces of water engineering. In 1409 Louis II of Anjou founded the University of Aix-en-Provence, and to this day it marks the rhythms of the town's heartbeat. In the fifteenth century René of Anjou, son of Louis II, proclaimed the city a royal capital. "Good King René," Count of Provence, and for a short time the king of Naples, settled in Aix. The royal palace, Romanesque churches, and cathedral were all enlarged during his reign. Other structures also appeared: new royal buildings, grand officials' mansions, rich residences for the town's merchants, craftsmen, and notaries, and convents and gardens. In the sixteenth century the fortifications were torn down to allow the city to expand beyond the elegant Cours Mirabeau, a cool, shaded gallery with four rows of Sycamores that remains the center of public life and a symbol of Aix's beauty and French *douceur de vivre*. On either side stand shops, cafés, and beautiful mansions, including the Villars residence, Isoard de Vauvenargues mansion (belonging to the Marquis of Entrecasteaux), and above all the Maurel de Pontevès palace, where the Duchess of Montpensier, known as *la grande demoiselle*, lived. The aristocratic atmosphere is still visible in some of the sophisticated and richly decorated Baroque facades. The cathedral is a collection of different architectural styles that parallel the

Paul Cézanne was born into a prosperous family in Aix-en-Provence on January 19, 1839, and went to the Bourbon College, where he befriended Émile Zola. In 1862 he gave up his law studies and left for Paris, where he met Pissarro, Renoir, Monet, and Sisley. He was refused entry to the École des Beaux-Arts because of his "excessive" temperament, and went to Auvers-sur-Oise, where he painted with Pissarro and met Van Gogh. In 1874, during the first exhibition of Impressionists in the studio of the photographer Nadar, his canvases caused a scandal. Three years later Cézanne left the Impressionist movement to search for his own artistic path. By thinking and observing, but above all through endless painting, he achieved a new harmony parallel with nature. Twenty years and hundreds of canvases later he was internationally famous. His last paintings portray such a great variety of compositions—with a powerful synthesis and range of colors laid on with regular brushstrokes—that they were harbingers of the imminent birth of Cubism. Cézanne died of pneumonia on October 22, 1906.

development of the city, with a fifth-century baptistery, Renaissance cupola, and Gothic main door. Inside is the *Triptyque du Buisson Ardent* (*Burning Bush Triptych*) by the painter Nicolas Froment and precious sixteenth-century furniture and tapestries. The Granet Museum contains sculptures and textiles from various European schools, and the nearby Vasarely Foundation is a union of art and architecture. The International Opera Festival is an important annual event, and the studio of Paul Cézanne, in his house, should also be visited.

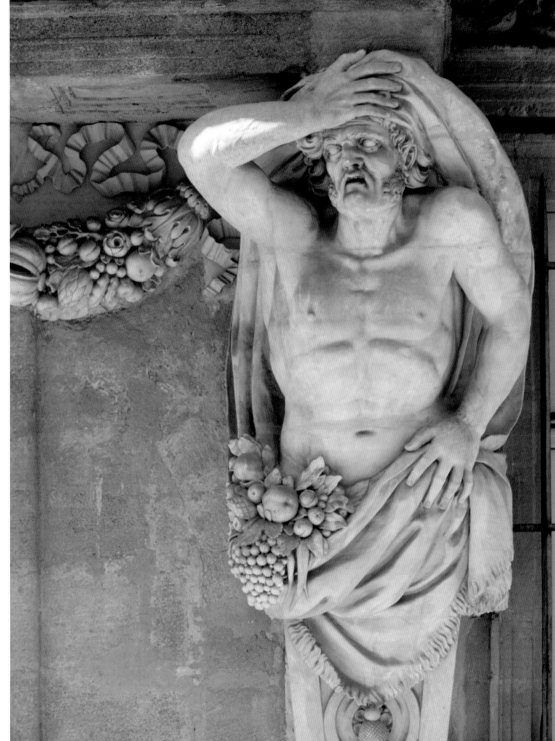

Cézanne was very fond of Aix's ubiquitous potatoes in oil, and, one hopes, of the local *calissons*. These little lozenge-shaped sweetmeats are handmade, and the tradition has been handed down from generation to generation for more than five centuries. The *calisson* of Aix is said to have made its first appearance in 1473 during the wedding banquet for the second marriage of King René. They are still made with the original recipe of crushed almonds, candied melons, and fruit juice wrapped into a wafer and glazed with sugar.

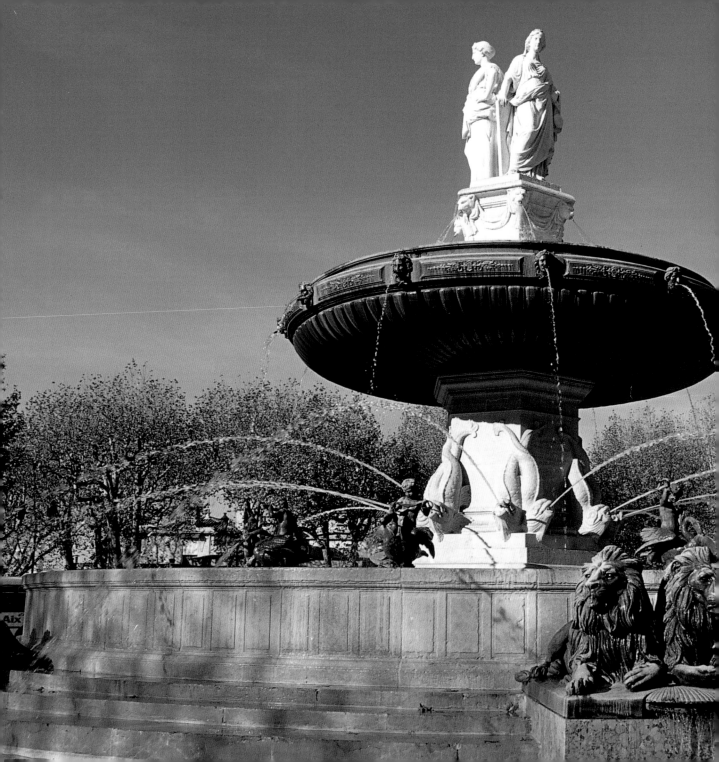

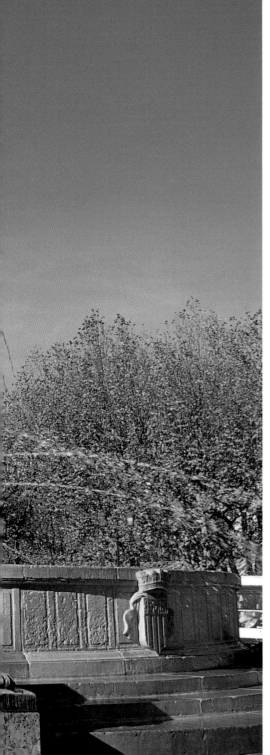

Mont Sainte-Victoire, in the beautiful countryside surrounding Aix, was immortalized in a series of paintings by Cézanne, and is now a symbol of the town. At its summit, Pic des Mouches, it reaches an elevation of more than 3,000 feet. On its south side is a rough wall of limestone that overlooks the basin of Arc, lit by the typical southern light that is so appreciated by painters. A series of plateaus spread gradually to the north toward the Durance River and surrounding plains. The mountain is an emblematic geological oddity that the obsessive eyes of artists like Cézanne have transformed into an artistic event, almost a performance. Sainte-Victoire is also very popular with people who know how to walk in silence, look, admire, climb, and appreciate it. A twelfth-century priory was a site of pilgrimage and can be reached by many footpaths that continue on to Croix de Provence. The view from the dizzying heights stretches over the mountains of Provence as far as the plains and hills of Aix. The beautiful panorama is dotted with villages, cultivated fields, and forests. Nearby is the village of Vaunenargues; in 1958 Picasso bought a beautiful fourteenth-century mansion here, which had been renovated in the seventeenth century, and he rests in eternal peace in the neighboring park.

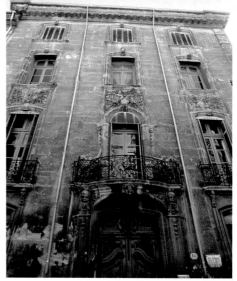

left
The grand La Rotonde fountain, built in 1860, is decorated with lions, swans, dolphins, cherubs, and allegorical statues of justice, agriculture, and the arts.

above
The facade of a house on rue Emeric David.

below
A typical café with sidewalk seating.

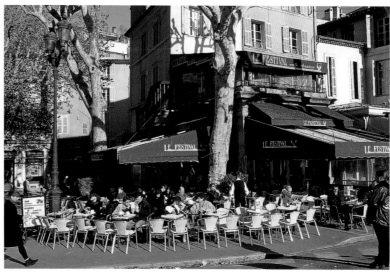

ANTIBES
THE RIVIERA'S POETS

One of the many restaurants that serve fresh local oysters.

facing page
The Fort Carré, or Grimaldi castle, has dominated the town for more than 400 years.

"THE JOJOBA FACTORY, THE OLD STREETS OF ANTIBES, 4,000 INHABITANTS, and, up there, the view, easy steps for asthmatics. The Vauban fortress looks like a ship, the church dates back to the thirteenth century, and the tower seems to be made of wax. Nets are spread under the Sycamores, and the shade spreads over the brows of the children. One could say that the walls and ancient war machinery have been weakened by a climate that is too mild, and the gentlemen officers, and even the simple soldiers, have lost any semblance of warlike behavior—but I am not to know." This is how Max Jacob described Antibes and its beauty in free verse. Antibes is the most Greek of France's cities and was founded by Greek sailors in the fifth or fourth century BC. The settlement was named Antipolis, or "the city facing," but facing what? This reference point was set by Greeks sailing north from Corsica, so Antibes was the city that faced them at the end of their marine approach. Protected from the fashionable world of Cannes and the snobbish wealth of Montecarlo, Antibes is gentle and lazy, lying languidly between the sea and the mountains. It attracts many lovers—either those of the city or couples enamored of one another, as André Breton recounts while in search of the beautiful Suzanne, the heroine of his short story *Nadja*, who fled one day from the circus to run off with Emmanuel Berl. The great poet Gerard de Nerval also came here, but did so to forget his great love, Jenny Colon. Graham Greene, on the other hand, lived in an apartment with a view of the port, wrote a great deal, and gave little thought to love.

In *Madame Parisse* Guy de Maupassant describes the coastline with vivid imagery: "This little city encroaches on the sea, enclosed between the heavy walls built by Vauban, in the middle of the enormous gulf of Nice. The high waves from offshore came to crash at his feet, surrounding him with flowers of foam, and above one could see the houses climbing, one atop of the other, as far as the two towers straining to the sky like the two horns of an ancient helmet . . . . These two towers painted in the whiteness of the milk of the Alps, on the enormous and distant wall of snow that blocked the horizon . . . and the blue sky above the Alps was almost white, as though the snow had faded it, and a silver cloud or two fluttered around the pale mountain tops. Nice, on the other side of the gulf, crouched on the water, lies like a white thread between the sea and the mountain." Only a visit can surpass these two descriptions, each so unique and poetic, to capture the beauty and the nature of Antibes.

The Maeterlinck mansion is not exactly in Antibes but is close enough that it should not be ignored. It is also called Villa Orlamonde, is one of the most magnificent buildings on the Riviera, and has a remarkable history. It is the ancient residence of the count and poet Maurice Maeterlinck, who built it in 1920 and later described it as the "place of no place and out of time." Work was stopped in 1928 for lack of funds, and the building was never finished, but this little corner of paradise facing the sea was, for a time, one of the most fashionable and cultural spots on the Riviera. Martin du Gard, André Gide, and Jules Romain were all guests here, and the legendary Antonin Artaud said, "Maeterlinck has been blessed with a splendid word. His thought cannot be analyzed; its philosophy resides in this gift that it has for revealing obscure sensations with images and in descriptions unknown to ordinary thought."

The Grimaldi castle was built on the town's ancient acropolis, atop the ancient Roman *castrum* (garrison). It was the bishops' residence in the Middle Ages (from 442 to 1385), and in 1385 it was inhabited by the Monaco family who gave it its name. In 1925 the Grimaldi castle was sold for 80,000 francs to the city of Antibes, and it soon became the Grimaldi Museum. In September 1945 Pablo Picasso visited its exhibition of children's drawings, and he was later offered part of the building to use as a studio. He accepted and as a deposit left 232 canvases and forty-four drawings to the city. Among them are the famous *La Joie de vivre*, *Satyre*, *Faune et centaure au trident*, *Le Gobeur d'oursins*, *La Femme aux oursins*, *Nature morte à la chouette et aux trios oursins*, and *La Chèvre*.

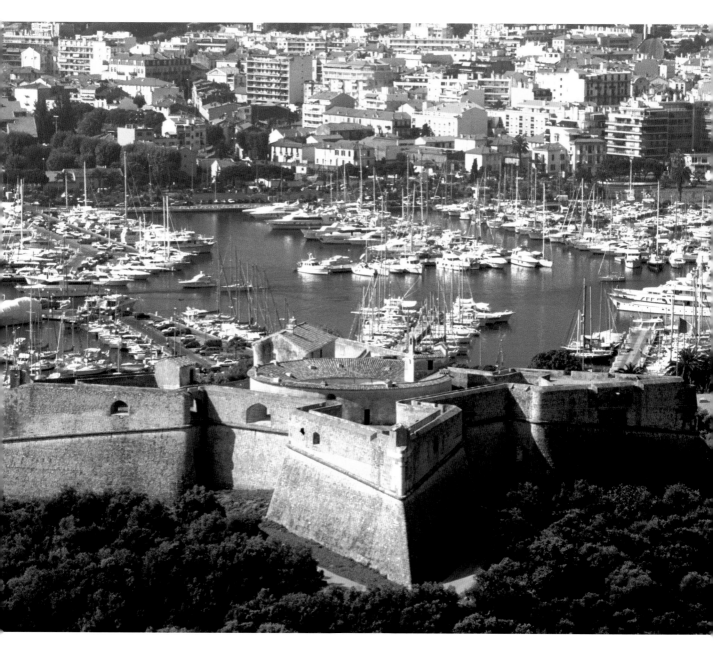

ARLES
GATEWAY TO THE CAMARGUE

The amphitheater in the heart of Arles is one of the most beautiful in Provence and was built as a copy of Rome's Coliseum. Bullfights have been held here for the last 2,000 years, and the ancient rites of the struggle between man and bull continue each season. *Gardian* and *farandole* are the key words connected to the historical passion for bullfighting. Arles is one of the few cities where the Spanish recognize the authenticity of the *corrida*. The feverish excitement in bodegas on the festive evenings contrasts with the peaceful days passed between siestas and long meals on the Boulevard des Lices, on the banks of the Rhône, or in the Forum. Evenings are washed down with cool and deceitfully smooth regional wines, and aficionados have interminable discussions about the *novillada* and the *rejon*. The ancient theater was built during the reign of Augustus, in the first century BC, and the cloister of Saint-Trophime is a symbol of a radiant Christian past; between them an air of grace pervades, tempered with a vein of sweet madness. The church of Saint-Trophime was a cathedral until 1801 and is one of the most charming examples of Romanesque art in Provence. The sobriety of its interiors and the pure austerity of line make it an intensely spiritual space composed with great aesthetic fluidity. This city is richly woven with life and death, and the presence of death is very evident in the necropolis of Alyscamps. Just outside the city gates there is an avenue lined with tombs leading to Saint-Honorat, a sanctuary whose origins date back to the fifth century. The twelfth-century octagonal bell dominates this infinite realm of the deceased, and both pagans and Christians have been buried here for more than fifteen centuries.

Presence and absence exist together here, as one can see in the works of Van Gogh, who managed to capture the luminosity and color of Arles. The arena was the background of the same painting repeated over and over again, each time with a different atmosphere. The hospital where he was taken after his great crisis of December 24, 1889, has recently been restored; it is a moving place, with the air of a convent, and it is not difficult to feel the tormented soul of the man who inhabited its rooms. Curiously, the town does not have a single Van Gogh canvas, but in the painter's honor tours and visits are organized "with the absent artist."

Even in daily life one feels the atmosphere of a special city here. The streets have an almost Italian air, and looking up you can see the splendid attics that look so much like those of Rome. This likeness is not so strange, though, when one realizes that Arles was the metropolis of ancient Roman Gaul.

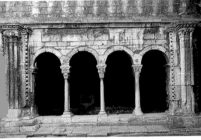

The cloister in the church of Sainte-Trophime.

facing page
The ancient arena of Arles is one of the most beautiful in Provence.

Arles is at the gates of the Camargue, a land of saltwater marshes crossed by ditches and rivers of mud, beached on sands lined with reeds waving in the calm breeze. This regional natural park, in the form of an island embraced by the Rhône River, is fascinating for its wild beauty and its unique fragility. Bulls and Camargue horses of many breeds live in freedom or within the lands of the *Manade*, where *gardians* and animals live together. An ideal example is the Domaine des Méjanes, near the Vaccarès basin. Rare species of migratory birds can be seen in the ornithological park of the Pont de Gau. Birds rest here for long periods of time, spending the mild winters nesting and nurturing their young in peace. The old village of Saintes-Maries-de-la-Mer was built at the mouth of the river. Each year there is a gathering of gypsies from all over Europe to celebrate their traditional pilgrimage.

There is a mythical
hotel right in the
heart of Arles, one
of those places that,
for reasons no one
can explain, the
most creative artists
and the strangest
travelers have always
known how to find,
as though they had
a radar system.
Hemingway,
Cocteau, and
Picasso all lived for a
time at the Hôtel
Pinus. In this curious
atmosphere—which
looks as though it
means to welcome
guests back from a
safari—sunk into the
lounge's armchairs,
they sipped their
cocktails and left
their imprint on
the 1930s.

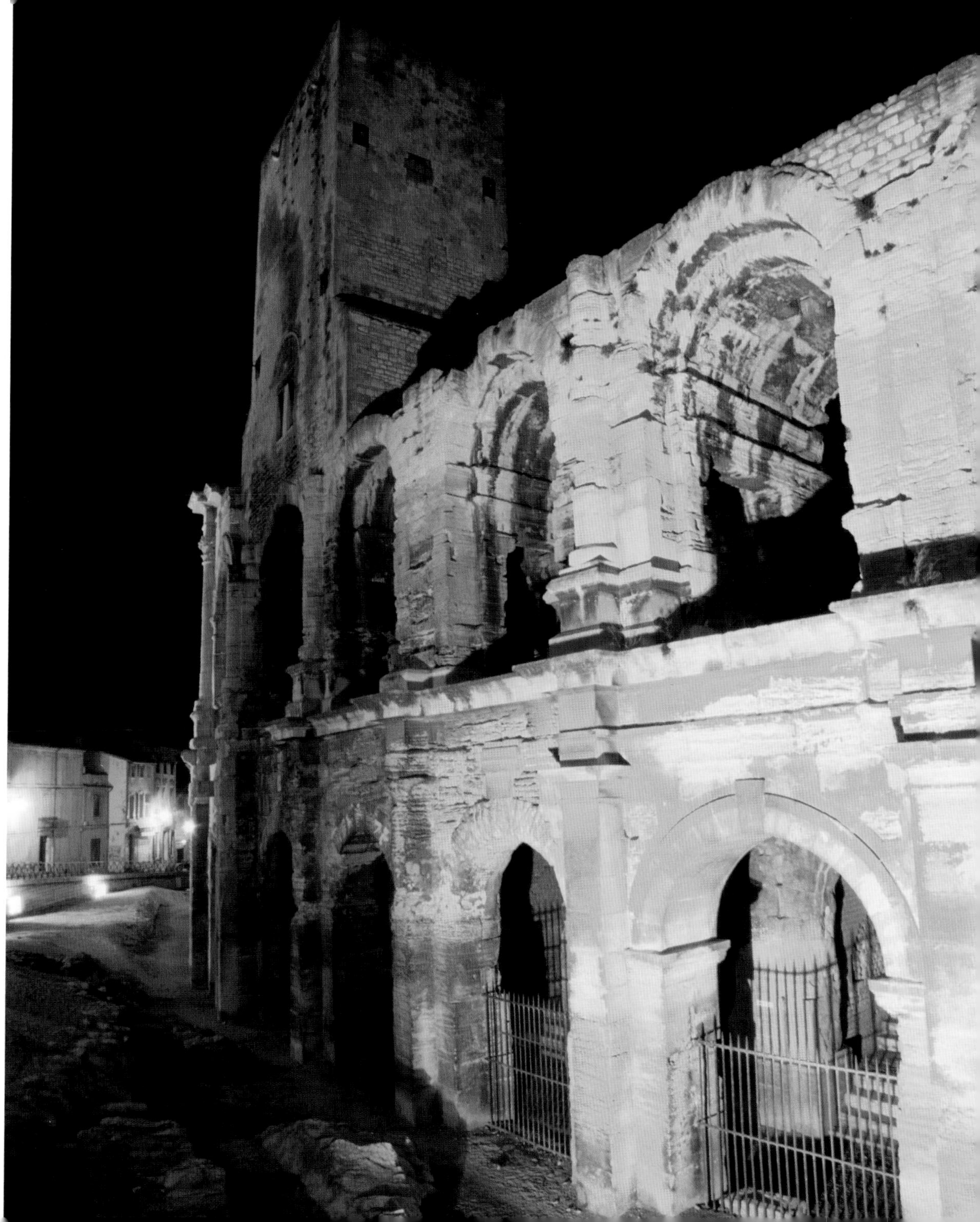

The Rencontres Internationales de la Photographie d'Arles (Arles's International Meeting of Photographers) was created in 1969, and takes place each summer at the beginning of July. It is one of the most important gatherings for photographers, both professional and amateur, as well as enthusiasts of photography. Large and small shows are organized all over the town, with work by photographers, artists, and reporters from around the world. Retrospectives, conferences, meetings, and evening events are held at the Théâtre Antique. It is an opportunity to discover everything about photography in all its aspects, as well as contemporary creative processes and the work of photographic pioneers, as this has become one of the major arts of our era. Prizes and awards are conferred on distinguished work that deals with concerns of the contemporary world. Current affairs become much more comprehensible as these visual thoughts come into focus before our eyes. Many courses are organized for the general public, and the École Nationale Supérieure de la Photographie (National School of Photography) was set up here in 1982. "Photogenic" Arles is reborn every year in the special light of this southern town, illuminated by the most beautiful sights.

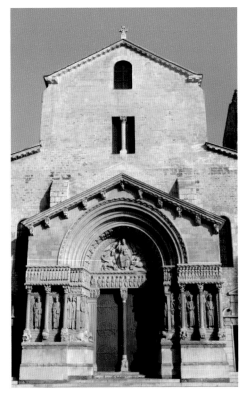

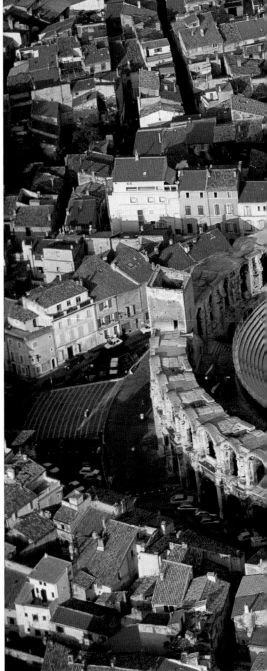

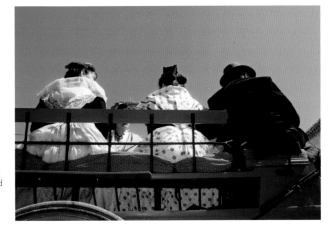

above
The elegant Romanesque facade of the church of Sainte-Trophime.

right
Traditional costumes are worn for the town's festivals.

far right
The Course Camarguaise still takes place in the amphitheater, and the bull is given the highest honors.

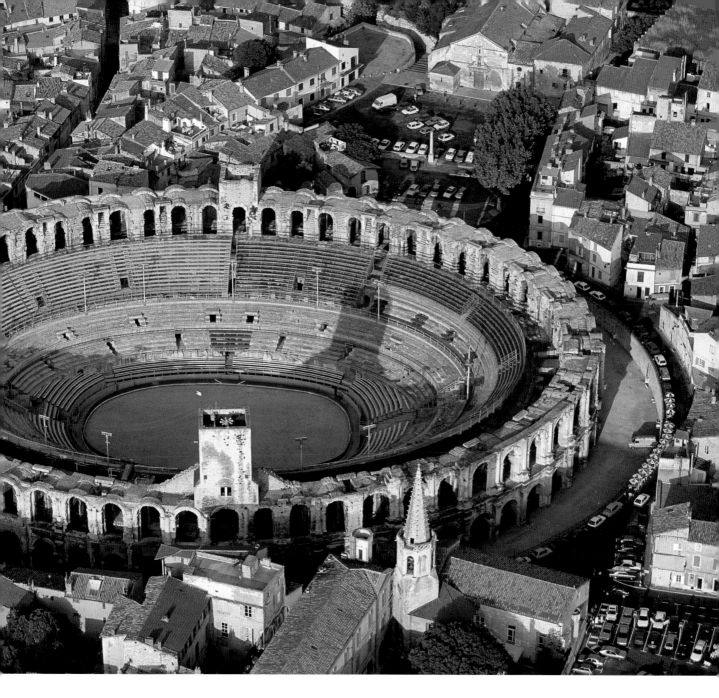

AVIGNON
PAPAL PALACES

Avignon appears unexpectedly between the Rhône and Durance rivers, among deep shadows and over-exposed light. Avignon is synonymous with the Theater Festival during the month of July, but it also stands for the city of popes and intrigue in a monumental palace of straw-colored, soft stone aged by time. The palace of the popes lies at the end of rue de la République, the city's liveliest thoroughfare that begins in front of the train station. Avignon's destiny changed at the beginning of the fourteenth century, during the exile of the papal court to France. Pope Clement VI bought Avignon from Queen Jeanne for 80,000 florins and installed himself and his entourage in unparalleled splendor, transforming it into a court of artists, clergy, merchants, and pilgrims, making it the envy of all Europe. The city was a strange mixture of people with a desire to be saintly but exposed to the corruption of a papacy in evident decadence. Avignon had its period of splendor, which seems to continue today, judging from its beautiful architecture that remains intact after several centuries. The clock tower is the starting point for a walk around the maze of streets where visitors easily—and delightfully—lose themselves wandering the lanes. The cultivation of a supreme leisure seems to be the city's main activity.

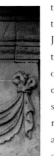

Details of the facade of the Musée Pierre de Luxembourg.

The visitor's first image of Avignon is of its balconies, crenellated towers, and the lozenge-like shape of the city enclosed within a bend of the Rhône. Life seems to pulsate in the streets, the lovely houses are the color of honey, ochre, and saffron, and there is a feeling that everybody takes their time with everything, making the city a true symbol of summer. The swallows dive into the sunset, and the scents of jasmine and sun-warmed streets fill the air. Avignon is calm and sleepy in the morning, and slowly the shopkeepers open their Baroque windows, the cafés fill up, the restaurants update their daily menu, and card players quarrel in archetypal voices. Avignon is the exacerbated fusion of a calm past and a self-assured present; the bars empty only at dawn, and Coca-Cola advertisements alternate with the facades of fifteenth-century buildings. But all one has to do is look up to see the traces of its ancient beauty. The busy sidewalks are full of bright Provençal fabrics, and a little farther on, in the scented gardens, the cicadas' song is enchanting.

The city's thirteen museums allow visitors to discover prehistoric, Egyptian, and Gallo-Roman sculptures, some natural history, some Art Deco, Provençal traditions, contemporary art, the history of the town, the theater, and art of the Italian primitives. There are as many as 28,000 important works of art in the Musée Calvert, providing a satisfying stroll through the history of art in its galleries.

Each July Avignon becomes a huge, temporary theater. The Festival of Avignon was founded in 1947 by Jean Vilar. That first year, during an exhibition of painting and sculpture organized by the collector Christian Zervos and the poet René Char in the chapel of the papal palace, Vilar presented three plays. The first was Shakespeare's *Richard II*, one of the lesser-known works of his in France; the second was *Tobie et Sara* by Paul Claudel; and finally there was Maurice Clavel's *The Midday Terrace*. The festival began humbly, but since then all the stars of the stage have appeared here. There are about twenty venues featuring the best contemporary works, while the fringe festival offers works by young playwrights.

To see the area's best market one must go to Villeneuve-lèz-Avignon, where at the entrance to the town, in the main square, the stalls and umbrellas are set out like a Cartier shop window. The tomatoes are perfumed with the scent of moist earth, the *olivettes* taste like fruit, scents of basil and croissant waft in the air, and one's nose twitches near the cheeses, where rounds of goat cheese look like cakes served in a tender crust that dissolves before the cream makes itself felt. This is the kind of market where one can discover the taste of genuine produce and flavors never before experienced.

facing page
The papal palace contains an endless number of rooms, salons, corridors, chapels, and stairways.

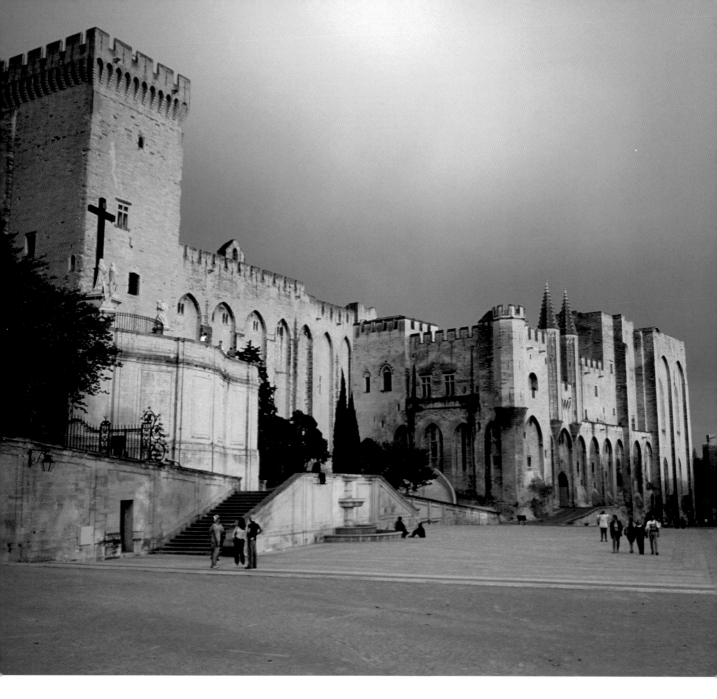

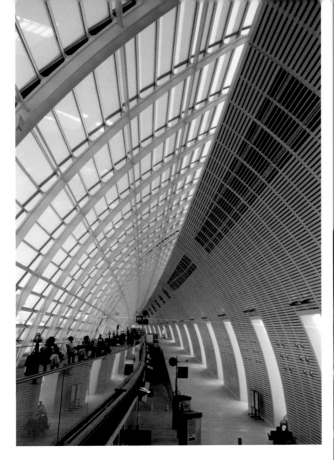

The Festival of Avignon is one of the most important art and theater shows in France. It is now recognized all over the world, and attracts groups from many countries, offering a formidable number of events and repertories, ranging from the great classics to the most extravagant experimental theater, from tragedy to comedy. The two branches, one mainstream and the other experimental, unfold before an enthusiastic and attentive public. Concerts are also performed during the festival, as well as dance and street theater. One can see that founder Jean Vilar wanted theater to be for the people, and wanted it to take place right here. The Palais des Papes and its sublime Cour d'Honneur used to be the venue of the festival; gradually the whole city began to take part, finding places for the shows, and becoming a show in itself. During these days the atmosphere is electric, there is an indescribable frenzy and vitality, and when evening comes the whole city is lit up with fireworks from the ramparts that continue until late into the night. It is an incredible time, and an ideal place to enjoy creative culture. The artistic success of the festival grows from season to season.

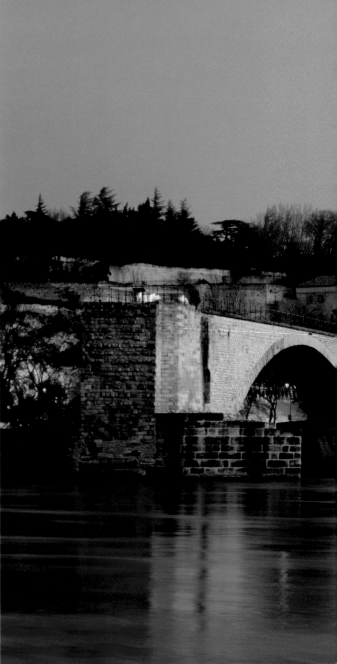

above
The very modern railroad station.

facing page
The Saint-Bénézet bridge once spanned nearly 3,000 feet; part of it collapsed in the fifteenth century.

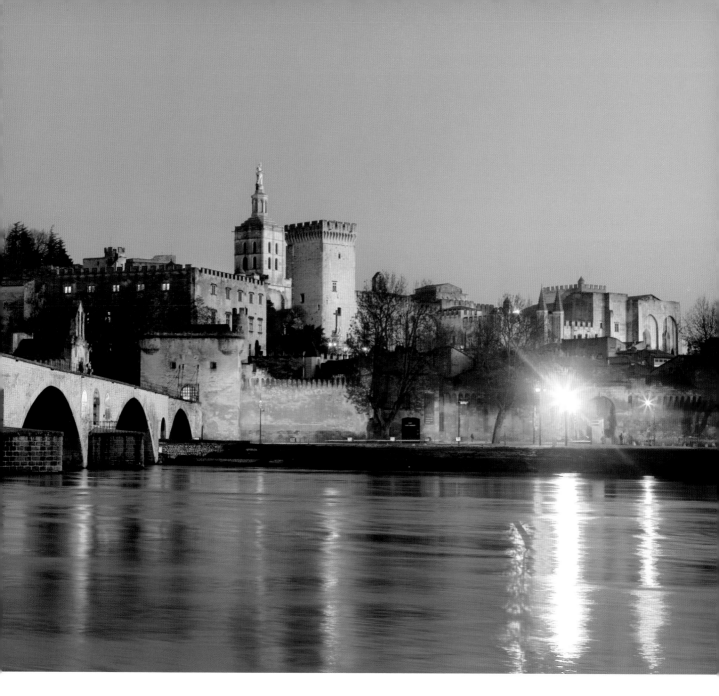

BAUX-DE PROVENCE
ATOP THE HIGHEST PROMONTORY

Baux is perched atop a cliff that overlooks inhospitable marshes and watches over the Alpilles hills. Over the centuries it has been a place of refuge and surveillance and has always been a true eagle's nest—a protected and populated hideaway. There are many ancient traces of human presence here, including remnants of the Fairies' Grotto, the Oppidum des Bringasses (a hilltop fort), a Celtic cemetery on the Vayède hillside, and sculptures of the Tremaïe. In the Middle Ages the village grew under the protection of the fortress built in the tenth century by the lords of Baux. They claimed to be descendants of the Magi, and on their crest they proudly portrayed the star of Venus with sixteen rays and their motto, *au hazard Balthazard*.

This race of warriors conducted the fortune of Baux and its seventy-nine fiefs for almost five centuries. They allied with the greatest European families, challenged their powerful neighbors in Toulouse and Provence, and were progressively encircled by the kingdom of France. A series of seemingly interminable wars destroyed the region, making it a theater of great violence, sackings, and fires. This tormented period gave rise to some emblematic characters, such as Hugues I, founder of the first fortress; Raymond de Turenne, nicknamed the Scourge of Provence; and Alix des Baux, the last of this turbulent stock. Upon Alix's death, in 1426, Baux was incorporated into the house of the Counts of Provence and transformed into a barony thanks to the good offices of King René and his wife, Jeanne de Provence. The village enjoyed great prosperity under their reign, and splendid mansions were built on the cliff, adding to its natural beauty.

In the second half of the fifteenth century Baux was connected to the crown of France, and in 1483 Louis XI had the castle demolished in order to put the fortress under the control of the local captain governors. The most famous of these rulers was Anne de Montmorency, counselor to Francis I, who transformed Baux into a small capital of 3,000 inhabitants and rebuilt the castle.

In 1639 Baux was finally elevated to a marquisate and handed over to the Grimaldi family as a sign of gratitude to the Prince of Monaco for having expelled the Spanish from the city. Once peace was reestablished the cliff lost its defensive character and the town expanded to the foot of the plateau, as far as the marshes that had since been reclaimed. Thus reduced to a simple village of shepherds, Baux was again annexed to France, during the French Revolution in 1791, in exchange for an indemnity.

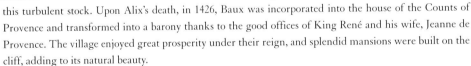

Harvesting olives.

facing page
The castle atop the cliff was a natural place for refuge.

In the Baux Valley olive cultivation has received its *lettre de noblesse*, a prestigious certificate of quality and nobility. The oil produced here is particularly fine and widely sought-after. It has received DOC recognition as the protected olive oil of the Baux-de-Provence Valley. No fewer than five varieties of olives are used to achieve this ideal alchemy: salonenque, verdale, grossan, aglandau, and picholine. The salonenque and aglandau varieties are also served in little pieces in a brine scented with fennel, making a typical winter dish that has also been granted DOC status—*olives cassées* of the Baux-de-Provence Valley.

Bauxite is a mineral made of one or more hydrates of aluminum. It was discovered in various parts of the world during the nineteenth century, but it was with samples from Baux-de-Provence that, in 1858, scientists managed to make a double chloride of aluminum from which the extraction of the metal became easier. This achievement enabled the village of Baux-de-Provence to give it the name bauxite, and until 1939 France was the largest producer of this mineral. Aluminum, the metal extracted from bauxite, has been used industrially since the nineteenth century, and it is the very first of all non-ferrous metals to come into use. It is light, unalterable, a good conductor of electricity and heat, and in certain alloys has an exceptional mechanical resistance.

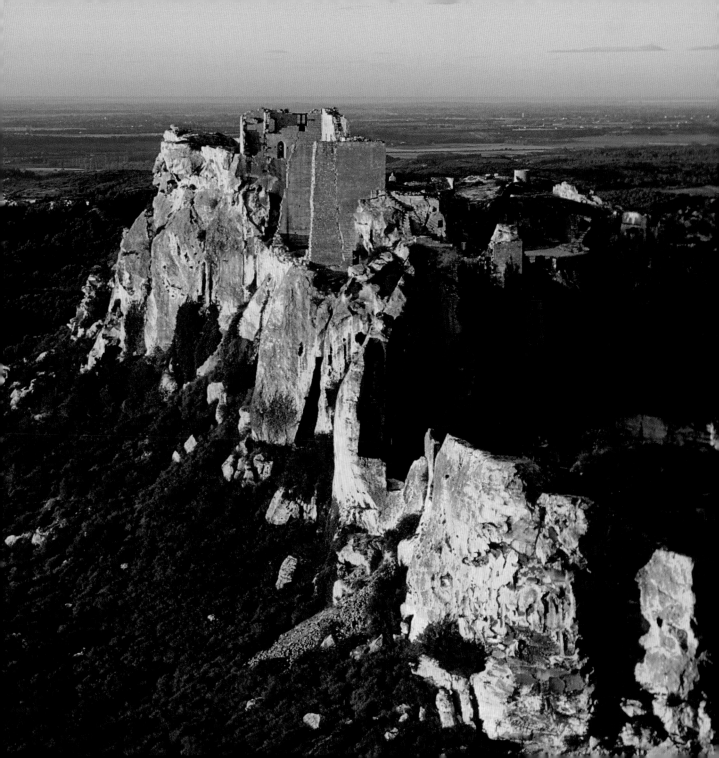

CANNES
A HILLTOP CINEMA

THERE ARE MANY THEORIES ABOUT THE ORIGIN OF THE NAME CANNES. The most likely dates to the Indo-European word *Kan*, a "mountaintop" or "high place." The high part of Cannes, the hill called Mont Cheva-lier, would seem to confirm this, as would Suquet (meaning "summit" in Provençal dialect), the nearby site of the castle built by the monks of Lérins. Cannes belonged to the counts of Provence until the end of the fif-teenth century. Upon the death of their last descendant, King René, brother of Louis XI, in 1480, the region passed into the hands of Charles du Maine, René's nephew. King Louis XI indemnified Charles for having given up the succession and required that he leave the region to him in his will. The very next day, du Maine died at Marseilles from indigestion, and Provence, along with Cannes, became definitively French. In December 1834 Lord Henry Brougham–Vaux, Lord Chancellor of England, traveled to Italy with his daughter Eleonora Louise. The frontier between France and Italy was closed because of a cholera epidemic, so Lord Brougham went to Grasse instead. On the way he spent a night in Maitre Pinchinat's hotel in Cannes, on what is now the rue du Port. Brougham was fascinated by the place and decided to build an elegant villa, naming it Villa Eleonora, which he inaugurated in the pres-ence of London's high society two years later. In just a few years the harbor was transformed, and new dis-tricts replete with villas and châteaux were under construction. In 1837 the English General Taylor built the castle of Saint George. The following year construction began on the first bridge, and the trail that skirted the coastline was broadened. It was originally christened chemin de la petite Croix, and later became the famous promenade de la Croisette. There was little water and very few streams in the surrounding countryside, so Lord Brougham formed a company to supply water to his property, creating the Siagne Canal, which today remains the city's source of water. Over the years Cannes attracted ever more important people from the world of politics and the arts. King Edward VIII and his wife Wallis Simpson became frequent visitors after Edward's abdication in favor of his brother, Albert. Other visitors were Churchill, Maurice Chevalier, painters Jean Gabriel Domergue and Van Dongen, and the writer Tristan Bernard. The Cannes of the cinema and fashion worlds is also not to be forgotten. The streets of this holiday resort are packed with extraordi-nary boutiques for stars and royalty, with haute couture shops, jewelers, and watchmakers. Cannes is character-ized by a contemporary luxury that is always up to date.

The Hotel Carlton, with its sinuous form, overlooks the beach.

facing page
The main entrance of the Carlton, a historic symbol of high society.

Jean Gabriel Domergue was already living for part of the year in Cannes at La Bocca when, in 1926, he bought land below La California and built a villa in the style of the Fiesole villas outside Florence. In 1936 his Villa Fiesole was inaugurated, entirely designed by the artist. The most famous and most beautiful women have posed in his studio, including Gina Lollobrigida, Brigitte Bardot, and Mylène Demongeot. He was active in the organization of important gala events, and in the 1920s he created the grand gala of automobile history, held at the Casino. In 1939 Domergue painted the poster for the first International Cinema Festival, which was due to open on September 1 but was canceled because of the outbreak of war. For the first edition, held in 1946, the artist designed the sumptuous garden decorations, fireworks, and parties. After his death in 1962, and that of his wife eleven years later, Villa Fiesole was donated to the city of Cannes. Today it is called Villa Domergue.

A visit to Île Sainte Marguerite, the charming island just a few minutes away by ferry that faces Cannes from the sea, must not be missed. It is almost two miles long and a half-mile wide and is the largest of the Îles de Lérins. There are no cars, so the only sounds are breezes through the pines and eucalyptus, waves breaking on the white beaches, cicadas' songs, and the sailing boats floating in calm coves. Like a quiet garden, this island is a bona fide Eden, ideal for a picnic or summertime swim. According to legend the island's name comes from one of the sisters of Saint-Honorat, who managed the religious community on the neighboring island. At the time women were not allowed to set foot on the island of these monks, but Saint-Honorat permitted access to his sister, limiting her visits to the period when the almond trees blossomed. By a miracle, after her visits the almonds began to flower more than once a year.

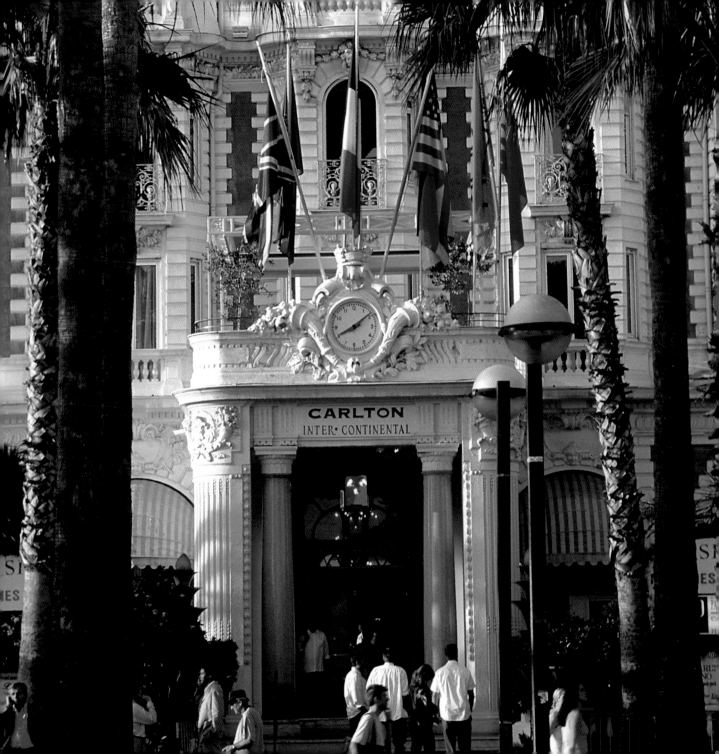

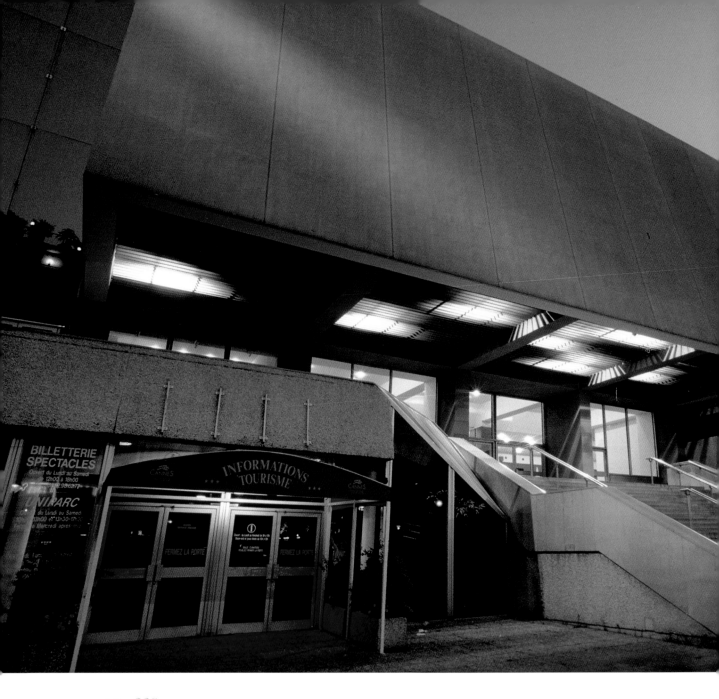

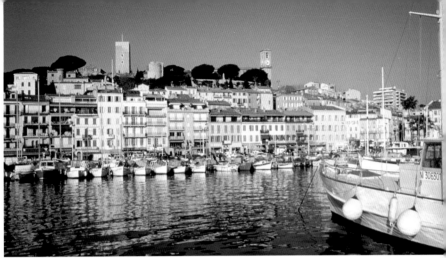

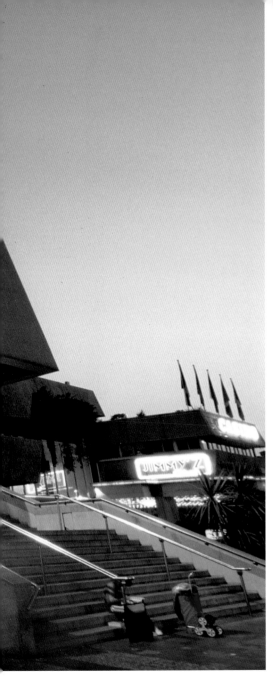

Marianne, played by Anna Karina, famously mentioned Cannes, and why one might visit it, in Jean Luc Godard's 1965 film *Pierrot le Fou*: "You know what you should write in a novel? The story of a man who walks to Paris; he meets Death, so he goes south to avoid it." Scandal, controversy, cult films, and nearly naked starlets have all taken turns appearing at the Cannes festival. In 1951 the director Isidore Isou presented a "film without film," that is, an incomplete film, and a festival official slapped him for having dared to show such disrespect to the organization. Over the decades the Cannes Film Festival has been, and continues to be, one of the greatest events of international cinema, a meeting place of glittering stars and unbridled fans. Every year it manages to renew its arsenal of outrages both true and false, disgraces and sins, cleverly publicized scandals, and equally clever ways to avoid the paparazzi by renting villas protected by sinister watchdogs for mountains of gold, making daily life here a movie in itself.

above
The vibrantly colored old port.

below
A concert during the Nuits du Suquet Festival.

The Palais du Féstival du Cinema.

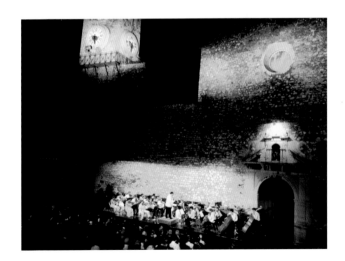

G A P

AN ALPINE EMPIRE

GAP IS A SOUTHEASTERN TOWN NESTLED BETWEEN GRENOBLE and Aix-en-Provence. A stop on the historic itinerary known as the *route Napoleon*, the capital of the Hauts Alpes is also the most important city of the Southern Alps. Lying at the foot of Bayard Hill at an altitude of nearly 2,400 feet, near Lake Serre-Ponçon and the Ecrins nature preserve, Gap is a link between the Dauphinate and Provence, between the alpine passes of Oisans and the gentle hills of Haut Provence. The town's origins date back to 14 BC, when it was founded as a Roman encampment, Vapincum, built on the *Cottia per alpem* road, along the route that connected Turin to the Rhône Valley. In the fifth century the city consisted of circular defensive walls for resisting invasions, was protected by bishopric authority, and became prosperous. In the Middle Ages, thanks to the development of wool and leather manufacturing, it became a vital commercial center, and was most prominent in the fourteenth century, when the papal court resided in Avignon. In the sixteenth century, during the religious wars that were particularly bloody in this region, Gap was destroyed. In 1692 it was set on fire by the army of Savoy, and of 953 houses only 155 remained intact. In 1790 the Dauphinate province was composed of three *départements*—Drome, Isère, and Hauts Alpes—and Gap became the prefecture of the most important *département* in France. Prefect Ladoucette, nominated in 1802, had new roads built across the Col de Cabre and Mongénève, thereby opening up communication with Valence and Italy. He also redefined the city's structure by modifying the medieval roads and razing unnecessary defensive walls. In 1875 the arrival of the railroad gave a push to the timber industry and heralded the modernization of Gap. This development continued over time, particularly from the 1960s onward. The population was not much more than 17,000 in the 1950s, and now it is twice that. The city has become the beating heart of one of the most important tourist *départements* in the region.

The "balcony" of the domaine de Charance leans against the mountain at nearly 3,000 feet in altitude and is well protected from the wind. Since the Middle Ages there has been a fortress here; over the centuries it has been destroyed and rebuilt, and it exists today as the headquarters of the Parc Nationale des Ecrins. The stables house the Conservatoire Botanique National, whose task it is to preserve and evaluate the heritage of Alpine flora. Thanks to its geographical position and the variety of equipment on offer, Gap is very keen on sports and has a variety of activities to satisfy every taste and age.

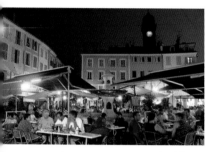

Place Jean Marcelin is the lively heart of town.

facing page Pastel painted facades of the houses on place aux Herbes.

On the hills of Charance there is a medieval fortress, complete with towers and moat, that was given to the viscounts of Gap by the counts of Provence. In 1307 it was bought by the bishop of Gap, and came to be called the bishop's castle. In 1569, during the Reformation, it was sacked, and it was only restored in 1644 by Bishop Arthur of Lionne. In 1692 the Duke of Savoy put the town to sword and fire. The castle was destroyed and once again rebuilt by the bishops. In the eighteenth century Bishop De Concorcet decided to transform Charance into a place of *plaisance*. The castle was embellished, and particular attention was paid to the gardens. Bishop De La Tour Landry lived there permanently until 1784. During the Revolution the castle was sold at auction on February 26, 1791, as a national treasure. It was bought by the town government in 1973 and soon after opened to the public. The terraced gardens were restored and are now on the list of historical monuments.

Saint-Marcellin is a mountain cheese that is used in many recipes, including the *tourton de Champsaur* with apples, and is mentioned in documents dating back to the fifteenth century. King Louis XI, son of Charles VII, governor of the Dauphinate, and his wife, Louise Charlotte of Savoy, enjoyed this delicacy at the castle of Bouqueron. According to legend the future Louis XI discovered Saint-Marcellin after a hunting accident in the forest of Lente, near the Vercors and Diois massifs. Two woodsmen welcomed him to rest and heal in a wooden hut and offered him bread and the local cheese; the prince appreciated it so much that he introduced it to his court when he became king.

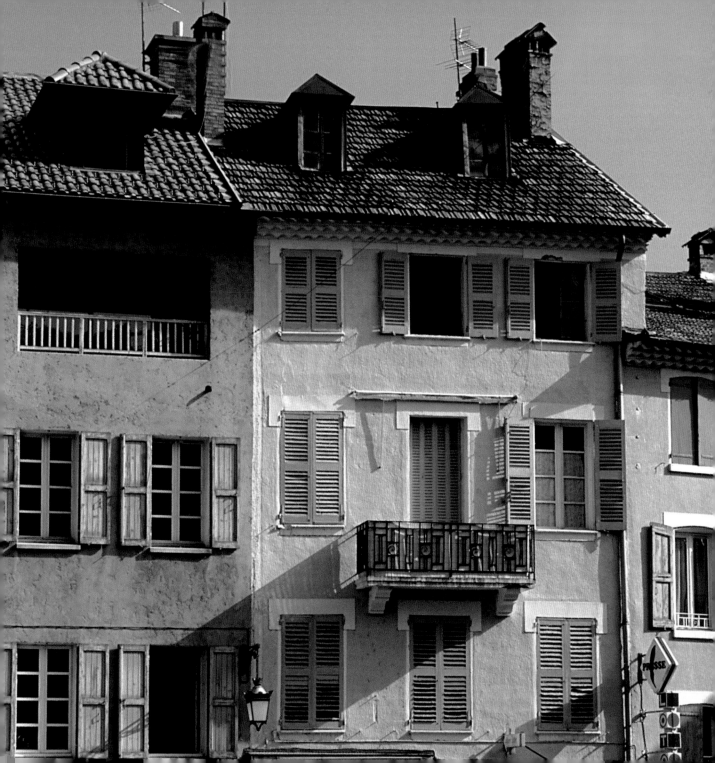

GORDES

CISTERCIAN CONTOURS

FROM A STEEP PROMONTORY NEARLY 900 FEET HIGH GORDES overlooks the Coulon Valley and offers a dreamlike view over the Lubéron Massif. Olive and almond trees seem to overtake this village, which is among the most beautiful of France. The houses are built into the rocks and made of the stone taken from the great cliff walls. The narrow, gently sloping streets snake along, clinging to the hillside and recounting

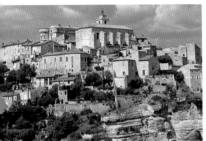

Typical stone houses overlook the valley.

facing page
Fields of lavender surround the abbey of Sénanque.

thirty centuries of history and legends. The light on the roads and the typical shades of red and yellow ochre have seduced many artists, including André Lhote, Marc Chagall, and Victor Vasarely in particular—credit for the castle's restoration goes to Vasarely, and one of his works is displayed at the entrance to the village. The Flemish artist Pol Mara came here for inspiration, and the beautiful Renaissance salons of the castle are dedicated to his surrealistic work.

Gordes still attracts writers, politicians, and artists, causing many to call it a summertime Latin Quarter. The les Terrasses Theater is partially excavated in the cliff, and in the summer, during the Soirées d'été festival, it welcomes actors, singers, and social gatherings. Many contemporary-art exhibitions take place in the thirteenth-century chapel of Saint-Jacques, which was an old stopping place for pilgrims from Piedmont on their way to Compostela di Santiago. Gordes lovingly protects its heritage, and its recent success as a fashionable village has been no deterrent. The village has a tangle of narrow streets, and traces of the twelfth-century ramparts can still be seen, including the Vieux and Savoy gates, and the beautiful external staircase, the remnant of an earlier fifteenth-century construction, against the bell tower of the eighteenth-century church of Saint-Firmin. There are other treasures to be seen in the area, including the village of des Bories, with its curious constructions of rounded stones that in many ways resemble Apulian *trulli*. A few miles away, in the heart of a green valley, lies the abbey of Sénanque, an exceptional example of twelfth-century Cistercian architecture. It is a rare gem, and is still inhabited by a community of monks. The

The unique *bories* area is characterized by a harmonious series of horizontal and vertical massifs, patches of vegetation and rock, and a mixture of light slipping over shadow. Chicken coops, ovens, cellars, narrow paths, enclosures, and encircling walls create an unusual village built of stone that inspires strange sensations for most travelers. The origin of the *bories* dates back to the Bronze Age, and they were abandoned after the eighteenth century, when the most recent constructions were left. They were soon overgrown with weeds, but the village was rediscovered, restored, and classified as a historical monument in 1977. This is the most important group of this type of dwelling, which is characteristic of the area. A museum of rural habitations displays traditional objects and tools of the region, with documentation on mortar-free stone architecture in France and in the rest of the world. It is a place that is ideally visited calmly in the first light of morning.

ancient des Bouillons olive mill has an impressive press that weighs seven tons and has been in use for nearly five centuries. The prehistoric caves, the buildings' cisterns, and the underground stairways of Saint-Firmin are all very interesting. Among the reflections of ochre light visitors will rediscover a shimmering of warm light, from dawn to dusk, that makes this special town particularly enchanted, as though the sun had broken into a thousand pieces and mixed with the earth tones of the Grand Canyon.

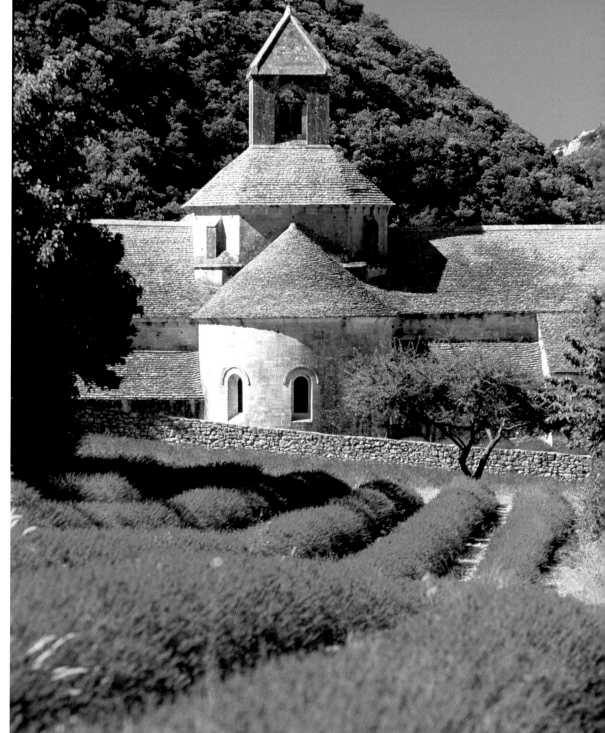

In Gordes and the surrounding villages one never refuses a plate of asparagus, cherries, or the succulently sweet melon of Cavaillon when in season. These are the best of the local produce. The Côtes de Ventoux is the regional DOC wine, and both a red and rosé variety can be sampled. It is fruity, light, pleasant, and best savored when young.

HYÈRES
THE PALMS OF PROVENCE

IN THE FOURTH CENTURY BC GREEK SAILORS FROM MARSEILLES founded a fortified commercial center called Olbia, which was derived from the Greek word for "happy." This was on the coast in a place known as Almanarre. Excavations at Olbia and the shrine of Aristaeus have uncovered evidence of a Greek presence extending to the Giens peninsula, which may well have been an island then; toward the second century BC the Romans created a labor camp near Olbia. The first document to refer to Hyères dates back to 963, but as a royal city it disappeared into obscurity until the reign of Francis I. In 1254 Saint Louis, king of France, landed at Hyères on his return from a crusade. Because the city was plagued by war and Barbary pirate attacks, the people asked the king for special protection so that they could defend themselves from future assaults. From then on the city enjoyed a relative calm that continued until the eighteenth century.

Hyères has long been appreciated for its *douceur de vivre*, its market gardens, and the nurseries devoted to tropical trees and rare and exotic plant species. In the nineteenth century the city underwent a total change and acquired an aristocratic air. With its mild, healthy climate, brilliance, and hospitality, Hyères began to attract illustrious figures who built luxurious houses; among them were Queen Victoria, Lamartine, Tolstoy, Michelet, Stevenson, Godillot, and many others. The Grand Hotel and the Moorish villas attest to its taste for the romantic Near East. The Anglican church, castle of Sainte Claire, avenues of palm trees, and prestigious villas all document this elegant and sumptuous past. Hyères was declared a health resort and mineral spa in 1913 and was soon also deemed a seaside resort thanks to its beautiful beaches. Intellectuals and the middle class contributed to an animated cultural life. The Grand Hotel and Casino were very popular, as was the famous Villa Noailles. Conceived and designed by the extravagant and astonishing architect Robert Mallet Stevens, this villa was the dream of the Noailles family. Work began on it in 1924 and lasted about ten years. Although it was never really finished, it was nevertheless a setting for experimentation and creativity.

After World War II, thanks to the construction of the seaport and airport, the city continued to develop, and new districts were added. After the 1980s the city once again became an important center in the Var region because of its trade, cultural life, and tourism.

A fishing boat moored in the harbor.

facing page
The Sainte-Agathe fort is hidden by palms on the island of Porquerolles.

Palm trees are an integral part of the local landscape and gave the city its full name of Hyères les Palmiers. It seems that the palm tree appeared here about 400 years ago, and controlled cultivation began in 1867. Very soon the city became the European center for palms; by 1909 there were more than 100 cultivated acres, and about 362,000 plants (the equivalent of 135 truckloads) were exported to Belgium, Germany, and the rest of Europe. Between 1920 and 1925 the annual production of cultivated palms reached 100,000 plants. The Gros Pins nurseries applied advanced technology for their cultivation, and were the first to cultivate palms *in vitro*. Today ten species carry the name of Hyères palms.

Provençal wines have a venerable history of more than twenty-six centuries. Grapevines first appeared here in 700 BC after being brought by the Etruscans. A curious, little-known fact is that the first wine in history was a rosé; the remains of the oldest barrel in the world were found in Fréjus in 1976.

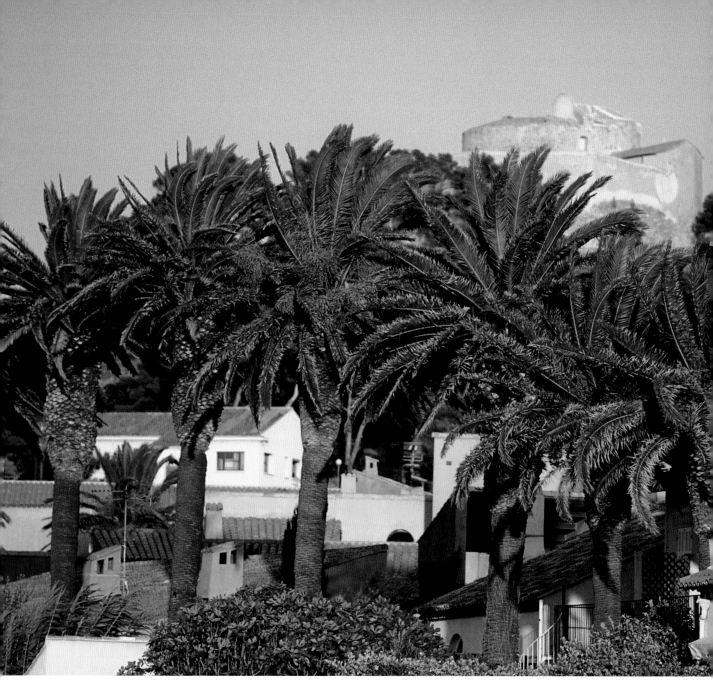

MANOSQUE
MILLENNIAL MAGIC

"AND HERE IN FRONT OF ME," WRITES JEAN GIONO IN *Noé*, "IS THE MONT D'OR HILL, that of Toutes-Aures, of Espel, the Savels quarter, Champs Clos, the Soubeyran . . . the reality that is in my blood. Besides, starting with this, everything begins again, in imaginary towns. But the *micheline* has ended, and we are at Manosque." Giono, the city's most famous son, was correct in his observation that this is a "city of convents, hidden gardens, interior courtyards, wells, and splendid fountains."

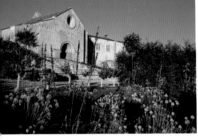

The medieval garden in the priory of Salagon.

facing page
The city shines in golden light.

Manosque is still an important center in the Alps of Haute Provence, with approximately 20,000 inhabitants in town and another 20,000 in the surrounding areas. Demographically Manosque is the largest city in the region, even though it is not geographically large. The city's development has been relatively recent, essentially due to the proximity of several large urban centers, since Manosque is huddled in the rich Durance Valley at the crossroads of the axis connecting Marseilles, the Alps, and Italy with the road from Lubéron to the Verdon gorges and the high plateau of Valensole. It is a truly delightful town, at an altitude of nearly 1,100 feet, with beautiful hills nearby, scents of the Mediterranean, and woods surrounded by untamed nature. Its lively little roads and typically Provençal squares, old sycamores, and houses with colored balconies add to its charm. Strolling in the old pear-shaped part of the city one comes to the twelfth-century church of Saint-Sauveur, the church of Notre-Dame de Romiguer, and the beautiful chapel of Saint Pancrace-de-Toutes-Aures. Remnants of the ancient city walls, the fourteenth-century Suavene gate, the thirteenth-century Soubeyan gate, and the lovely des Observantins and de la Présentation convents are all well worth visiting. In order to have a better view of the city a climb up the Mont d'Or is in order—a pleasant round-trip walk of just under two miles. From here one can admire the magnificent view over the Lubéron, the Sainte Baume, and the upper Var, with Mont d'Aiguines, as far as the first ridges of the Alps. *Tout est dans les mains de Dieu* (Everything is in God's hands) is the motto of this country town. From a

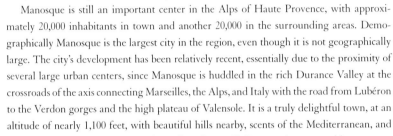

The old Prieuré de Salagon is composed of a twelfth-century church, the fifteenth-century prior's house, and adjoining farm buildings from the sixteenth and seventeenth centuries. It was built on a site steeped in over two millennia of history. During the Gallo-Roman period Salagon was a farm and was converted to Christianity very early, when a Christian cemetery and a basilica were added. The settlement was completely restored between the fifth and seventh centuries, and today there is an exquisite fourteenth-century fresco in the church. From a completely different—and perhaps more poetic—viewpoint, the area is now also a conservatory for the vegetation of Haute Provence. The plants used for daily medicinal needs were grown in medieval gardens long before more modern scientific discoveries. They are divided into checkerboard beds in keeping with the monastic spirit of the time. Other gardens are being planned, including an ecological garden, a willow collection, an ancient vegetable garden, and a garden based on old documents pertaining to magic and sorcery.

cultural viewpoint the city is not static; the famous jazz festival, Musiks à Manosque, is one of many notable musical events. Coming to Manosque across the countryside scented with lavender fields and scattered with olive trees, one should take a respite at Prieuré de Salagon, an ancient Benedictine convent of warm, pale stone that beautifully fits into the gentle surroundings.

Jean Giono is still a greatly admired and appreciated author. The writer-craftsman was born here, and his father was a cobbler whose work he always admired. "In order to be free, it would be enough to have a trade that you love and that you are good at. Work should be a pleasure: Thus you can aim to create masterpieces. The greatest artistic objects are simply works by craftsmen who are in love with their trade." Giono worked regularly (and stubbornly) at the Parais, his home in Manosque. His most lyrical passages were written slowly, at a pace of no more than eight pages per day, but he knew, as a craftsman, how to study and diversify his techniques and had an unparalleled understanding of how to scrupulously select the right rhythms, colors, style, and words.

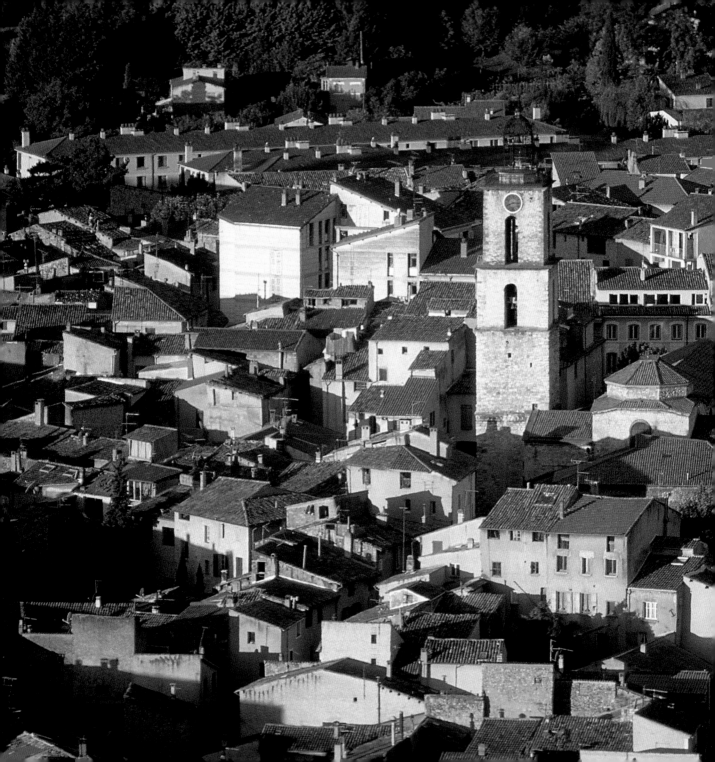

MENTON
THE SUN'S SEASIDE PROMENADE

A PLEASANT CLIMATE AMONG THE MILDEST OF EUROPE, an exceptional geographical setting, and an admirable *douceur de vivre* make Menton one of the most attractive cities on the French Riviera. The vegetation is stunning, with fruit-laden lemon and orange trees and palm trees decorating the promenade, while the inland hills are dotted with olive trees. Menton's charms lie in the faded walls that turn blue in the sun, the jasmine climbing up the yellow and gold houses, the iron balconies weathered by the salty marine air, and the unusual paths along which one can almost hear the footsteps of the last century's youth, who came here looking to regain lost health.

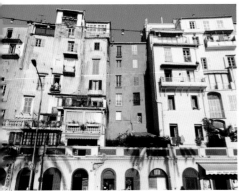

The yellow facades of the buildings soak up the sun's warmth.

facing page
The town's charm is evident even in the smallest of streets.

English visitors commonly go to see the old cemetery clinging to the hilltop above the city that in the nineteenth century was called the Castle of the Dead. Looking at the stones one must ask why so many young people are buried here, and in which battle they perished. With a knowing look the guides invariably confirm that they died in the battle with tuberculosis. Maupassant, in *Sur l'eau: de Saint Tropez à Monte-Carlo*, writes that there was "never a coffin in the streets, no one dressed in mourning, never a funeral bell. The thin man of yesteryear no longer passes under your windows, that's all." Katherine Mansfield and Nietzsche both came here in search of peace, or another burst of inspiration, on this clement seashore. They moved on, and Menton became a mere pause in their tormented lives. The city has remained as it was, always peaceful and timeless, with Italy only a breeze away, just around the corner.

The gardens of Menton are among the Riviera's most poetic. Take the opportunity to cross the border into Italy and savor the delicate splendor of the garden of Mortola, and then take in the seafront—rightly called the *promenade du soleil*—and sunbathe on les Sablettes beach beneath the old city. A walk as far as the old port and the Palais d'Europe (the old Casino) is highly recommended, as is a visit to the Palais Carnolés, the Russian church, the church of Saint-Michel, the museum and the wedding rooms decorated by Jean Cocteau, and the new Casino.

Hans-Georg Tersling, who was born in 1857 in Denmark and died in 1920 in Menton, is the architect of the Riviera. He designed the Palais Carnolés and the Palais d'Europe here, Cap Martin and Villa Masséna in Nice, the Bristol in Beaulieu, and many other buildings. It is difficult to imagine that all of these buildings were made by the same architect, a Dane who settled in Menton and brought with him a unique vision of the Riviera. The great building sites of the early nineteenth century, many mansions, and several elegant villas are his work, making him an architect to be discovered during a visit here.

At the end of February and beginning of each March the enchanting lemon festival and brightly colored orchid show take place. Both are a perfect chance to visit this small town, where there is also an excellent cuisine as a result of the culinary creativity developed over the centuries by a rural and modest population, and, naturally, favored by the surroundings.

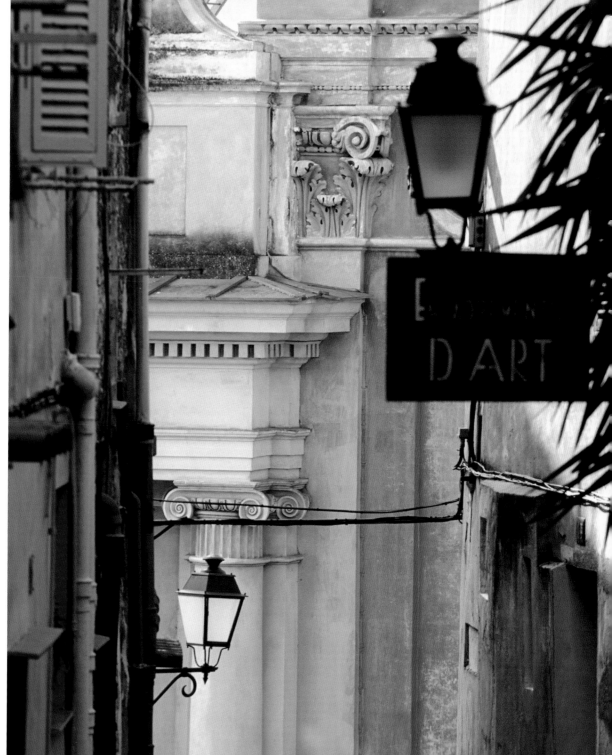

Menton has a number of gastronomic specialties in common with the surrounding area and nearby Italy. Above all are the simple and very tasty dishes: *socca* (oven-baked chickpea flour mixed with oil), *panisses* (chickpea flour fritters), and *pan bagna* (a small sliced loaf of bread filled with tomatoes, anchovies, salad, peppers, and black olives drizzled with olive oil). Then there are the stuffed legumes, ravioli, the *omelettes de poutine* (with alevin fished in the spring), pesto soup, *brousse* (highly scented mountain cheese soaked in brandy that is best drizzled with extra virgin olive oil on lightly toasted bread), and the famous *bagna cauda* (an assortment of raw vegetables served with a hot anchovy sauce).

MOUSTIERS
SAINTE-MARIE
LOFTY MONASTERIES

MOUSTIERS-SAINTE-MARIE IS MORE LIKE A LARGE VILLAGE THAN A CITY, and is one of the most beautiful in France. It is shaped like an amphitheater wedged between hills more than 1,800 feet high and enjoys the ideal Mediterranean climate so characteristic of Provence. The surrounding countryside is also extraordinary, nestled in the heart of the Verdon national park, between mountains, fields of lavender, and the lake of Sainte-Croix. The name derives from the Latin *monasterium*, referring to the several area monasteries. The first inhabitants were indeed monks, who came from the Lérins Islands to evangelize. Local farmers helped them work the land and created the village nucleus where the first sanctuaries began. Later on the community was regularly sacked by the Franks, Visigoths, and Vikings, and in the ninth century even the Saracens.

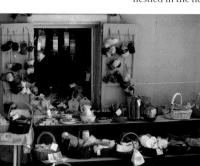

Embroidery, straw baskets, and the famous majolica decorate local shops.

The paths of Moustiers are intricate and lead through narrow trails from which unimaginable little squares appear, hidden behind the facades of houses with red tiled roofs. By following the shaded alleyways scattered with stone fountains, one comes to the heart of the city, where the church of Notre-Dame rises to great heights. It was originally the chapel of an important monastery. The singular Lombard bell tower was built in 1447 and is one of only four mobile bell towers in Europe; they are special because they move in time with the sound of the ringing bells. For many years it was thought that this was a defect in the construction of the tower, so the walls were reinforced to stop the movement. Another curious characteristic of this church is the fourth-century white marble sarcophagus that now stands in the choir, in place of the old altar. During the twelfth century the city was densely populated; it stretched out from the Riou gateway and continued west of the Sainte-Anne gateway. There were two distinct quarters separated by a stream. One was the faubourg de Paillerois, which was destroyed in 1382 by Charles de Duras; the other was the city, known as the Baumettes, which was burned in 1383 by the supporters of Louis d'Anjou. However, once Moustiers was rebuilt, it was prey mostly to bad weather and natural calamities. In 1685 a flood swept away the sustaining walls of the stream and the entire cemetery. In 1692 another flood destroyed the bridge and main square. Today the church of Notre-Dame de Beauvoir is an important center of pilgrimage. It stands in an inlet of the Riou River, carved into tufa caves, where the first monks settled. Looking up toward the church, one can see an unusual golden star suspended nearly 750 feet over the void. It dangles from a chain between two spurs of rock that overhang the torrent. According to local legend it was left by a knight of Blacas, in the twelfth century, in gratitude for having returned alive from the crusades.

The origin of the star suspended between two rocky spurs that overlooks the town is a mystery. The most widely known legend connects the star to the story of a knight of the crusades, Blacas d'Aulps. While he was a prisoner in the Holy Land he made a promise to the Virgin to hang the chain when he returned home a free man. Some say that it is the representation of the crest of a local lord. Others say that it comes from Pius King Robert, founder of the Order of Knights of the Star, and was left during a pilgrimage to the sanctuary. Yet another theory is that two antagonistic local lords forbade their children to marry one another, and that the desperate lovers threw themselves into the void. United in pain, the fathers decided to unite their fiefs with a chain as a symbol of their friendship.

Moustiers is famous all over the world for its seventeenth- and eighteenth-century ceramics, whose beauty was greatly admired by kings and potentates. The best artisans of this splendid local craft were Clérissy, Viry, Olérys, Laugier, Fouque, Pelloquin, the Ferrat brothers, Féraud, and Berbégier. The kilns slowly began to stop burning in the 1840s, and the last one was extinguished in 1874, when English porcelain and fine majolica became the fashion. In 1927 a craftsman by the name of Marcel Provence reopened one of the kilns to revive this art, and today there are nineteen active kilns in Moustiers.

facing page
A town from a fairy-tale world, Moustiers is nestled in the mountains.

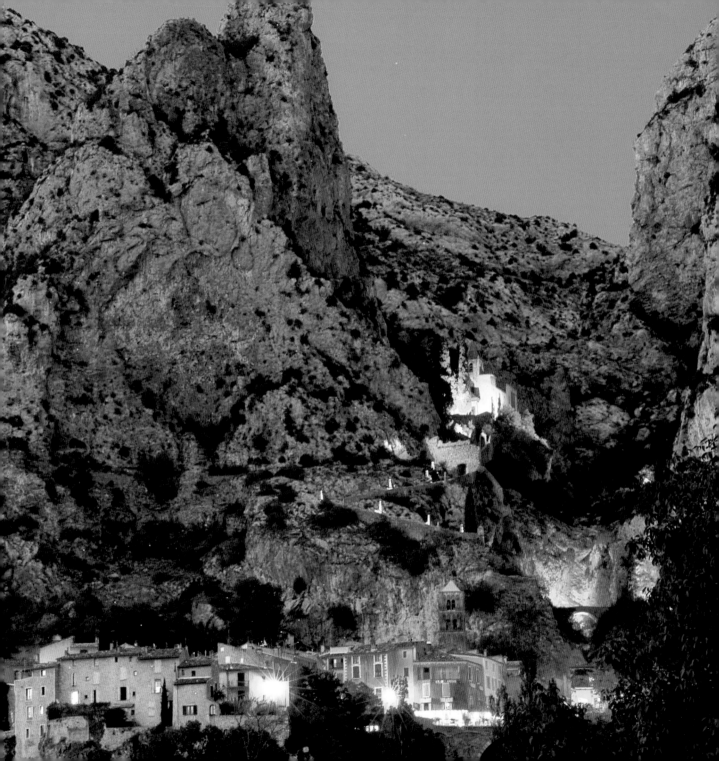

SAINT-PAUL DE-VENCE
ETERNALLY ARTISTIC SUMMER

"SAINT-PAUL-DE-VENCE IS AN OLD LADY WHO STILL CHARMS. She is made of bricks, pebbles, and cement, and forgotten by everyone except the sun. White and new, she was created for the violent sweetness of an Othello, and her features have something Moorish about them. Her present color is purely olive. She is still statuesque and haughty on her pedestal atop the hill amid a land of vineyards. One could say that the inebriation of the wine has brought her up there in one leap, as though a wave of stone had come to rest on that hill. She is enclosed in a corset of fortified walls. The faded rooftops are bathed by the sun and soak up the light like a sponge. The aligned facades of the red and blue houses form a frieze illustrated with greenery. Her age is summed up between the narrow walls of the little streets, on the cobblestones scored by the rare footsteps of passersby."
—Franz Hellens, *Notes from a Garret*, 1925.

It is not surprising that many artists, writers, poets, and celebrated painters have chosen this special town as their home. King Francis I had Saint-Paul-de-Vence built on a rocky outcrop and surrounded by an encircling wall, and it is undoubtedly one of the most beautiful villages in Provence. There is a splendid view from the walls overlooking the hills, the Riviera, and the sea, creating an unparalleled panorama of majestic landscapes. A walk along the picturesque little streets of the village, from Porte Royale to Port Sud via the pedestrian area of rue Grande, reveals the magnificent stone facades of palaces built between the sixteenth and eighteenth centuries. Visitors pleasantly lose themselves in the mysterious alleys, and the exuberant gardens, picturesque little squares, ancient fountains, porticoes, and finely decorated windows are a delight for photographers. One can also make the most of the promenade, visit local craft workshops, art galleries, museums, and also do a little shopping in the Provençal boutiques. Saint-Paul-de-Vence is truly at the height of its reputation, and has perhaps a few too many people during the high season, but one need only choose another time of the year, and all its Moorish charms remain crystal clear. The Collegiate church and its treasury, the chapel of Saint Matthieu, the Maeght Foundation, and the museum of local history are well worth a visit.

The uniquely artistic quality of light here has attracted creative souls for many years. Since the 1920s this region has seduced some of the greatest names in art—Picasso and Gillot, Renoir, Matisse, Léger, and Chagall all came to work and play here. Upon entering the surrounding sun-drenched valley, visitors quickly discover why this idyllic town was such an artistic center, and both modern art lovers and connoisseurs of continental style will be equally charmed.

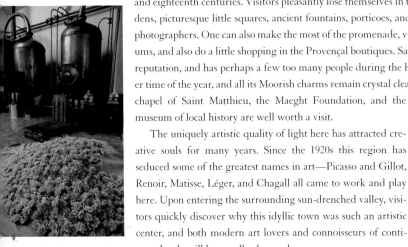

facing page
Little alleyways and narrow streets lead from town to the gardens and market.

Marvelous perfumes are produced at Gallimard, in nearby Grasse.

The Marguerite and Aimé Maeght Foundation is a private European art foundation. Painters and sculptors worked closely with the architect Josep-Lluis Sert to create a monumental work that is perfectly integrated with the building and its surroundings. Here one can admire Giacometti's *Cour*, Miró's labyrinth, filled with fine sculptures and painted ceramics, the mosaics of Chagall and Tal-Coat, Braque's vases and stained glass, and Bury's fountain. The problems of lighting the spaces were brilliantly solved by Sert—he used natural noonday light, which dramatically bathes all the exhibition rooms. The Maeght Foundation possesses one of the most important collections of painting, sculpture, drawings, and graphic art of the twentieth century in Europe, and includes some of the greatest artists of this period. Works by Bonnard, Braque, Calder, Chagall, Giacometti, Léger, and Miró are all represented.

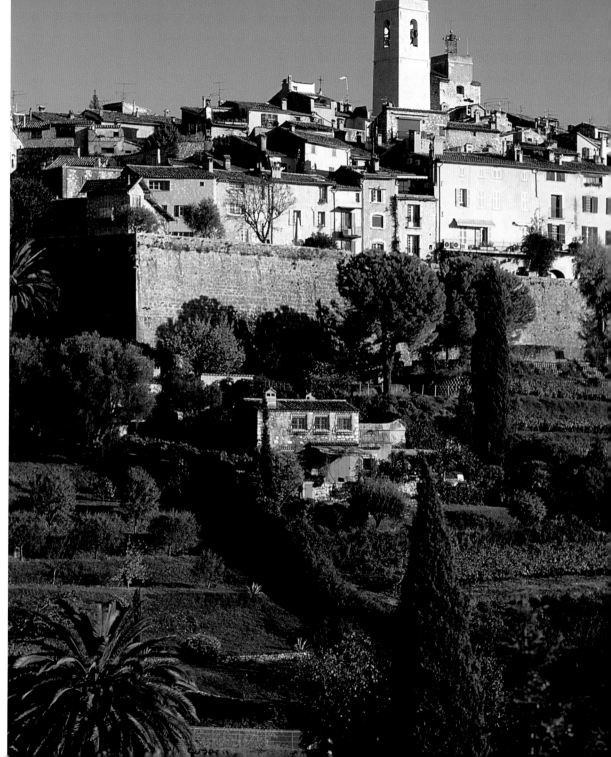

Artists of every era have stayed at least one night at the Hôtel Colombe d'Or. This fine hotel's fame continues to grow, and even today it is easy to imagine Arcimboldo at the Colombe d'Or, painting his portraits of green almonds, olive branches, lemons, and red figs in the bright sun, as Braque and Léger watch over his work and give their opinions. Let us not forget Villon seated in a corner, along with many other great artists.

The hotel lies at the entrance to the village and has sixteen rooms and ten apartments. It has always been a favorite with artists, where they could meet other artists and also find themselves far away from the trendy, fashionable world. Modigliani, Soutine, Picasso, Chagall, and Dubuffet particularly loved this beautiful place.

SAINT-TROPEZ
SANDALS AND STARLETS

LET US SHED A TEAR FOR THE SAINT-TROPEZ OF BRIGITTE BARDOT, COLETTE, Anaïs Nin, Jean Cocteau, Paul Barclay (the mythical music producer), and Paul Poiret; weep for the Saint-Tropez of the first topless bathing-suit scandals, beautiful girls in leather sandals, and the marvelous wooden yachts. Gone are the 1960s, the improvised parties on the beach, and the days when Jean-Paul Sartre sat on the terrace of the Sénéquier.

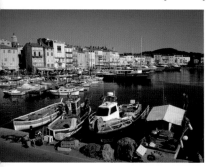

Fishing and recreational boats are side-by-side in the harbor.

facing page
A wonderful view from the hill.

We must also forget the "brave and salty village" attested to by Maupassant, when the writer discovered Saint-Tropez from the deck of the *Bel Ami*, which kept port off the still very isolated small town. No longer do travelers go to Saint-Tropez to live from one pleasurable experience to another, from one secret date to another, from sunbathing on one deserted beach to a private beach with crystal-clear water. No more dances with sailors, no sneaking from one room to another, and from lunch with her to dinner with clandestine company, no hopping from one club to another until dawn. Françoise Sagan summed it up well: "No more living like happy hunters or willing prey."

Times have changed, and Saint-Tropez is not what it was. At most it is a meeting place for the rich, a setting for sponsored weddings, a town for television starlets looking for promotion. Despite all this, everybody comes here and everybody returns. It is a coveted place for the rich with their first Porsches, and the port is most lively in the summer, when the paparazzi are everywhere. The curious stop enthusiastically to look at the white yachts, entertainment stars excite onlookers' attention, and luxury shops somehow still enchant with their sky-high prices. The memory of Saint-Tropez is there, floating like a Proustian madeleine, distilling the dream of an exotic life of clear water that is no more, with living sculptures of beauty exiting miniature boutiques, narrow ochre alleys that get lost at the crossroads, little curtains at the windows, and bicycle rides through the pines. Inexplicably, however, the sweetness remains even amid the clamor. As long as it's seen in any month but August, this town still resembles those of one's dreams, especially in May and September. In these calmer periods one can better see the charming pastel houses that look out over the coast, the flirtatiousness of the port that has never gone out of fashion, the clicking sound of a yacht's

Les Voiles de Saint-Tropez is the great event that takes place at the beginning of October, when there is a gathering of about 3,000 owners, teams, and true sea enthusiasts. This is a unique engagement because there is no other place in the world where one can see 250 of the most incredible sailing boats all at one time. There are modern ones, prototypes of racing boats with the latest technological innovations, and boats built more than a century ago that have written the history of yachting and proudly display their ketches. To the joy of the spectators and participants, some of whom have taken part in the America's Cup, this is a show of the most beautiful fleet of modern and classic sailing boats, including the famous *Niolargue*.

rigging, and the immaculate cupola of the church immortalized by Signac, Picabia, and Bonnard, now in the Annonciade Museum. In the off-season the beaches are divine, and the shade of the maritime pines provides shelter from the mistral's gusts. Like Errol Flynn or Jean Marais, one can still enjoy the homemade nougat and the café glace of the Sénéquier.

Alain Rondini's shop, just a few steps from the port, has been making sandals for three generations, and they produce about 5,000 pairs of leather sandals a year. Among them are the famous *tropéziennes* worn by the film stars—a flat, robust, flexible, and simple sandal made of strips of leather, copied from the model of ancient Greco-Roman statues. Every day dozens of tourists crowd around in front of the shop to give themselves a gift of a pair of these Spartan shoes. To have a handmade pair designed to one's measurements there is only a few days' wait. These masterpieces of beautiful economy have been made since 1927 and remain identical to this day.

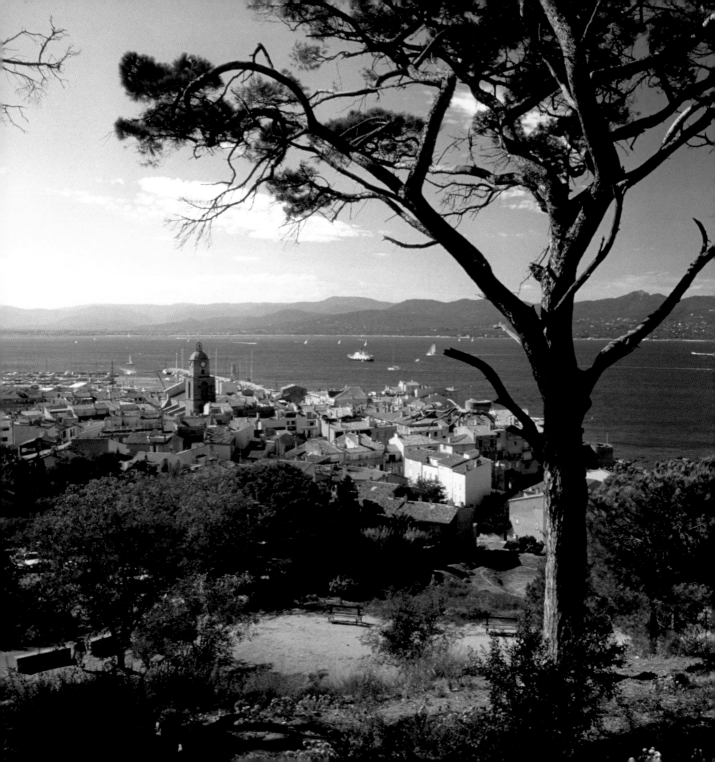

right
A room in the Café des Arts on the place des Lices.

facing page
The bright bell tower at Saint-Tropez silhouetted against the deep blue sea.

below
Beautiful sandals are locally crafted by hand from the finest leather.

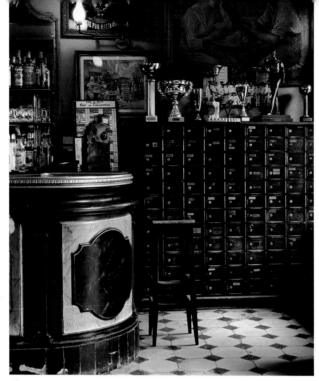

Ever since the great writer Colette taught us—now more than a century ago—about the other Saint-Tropez by taking us to the abbeys of de la Verne and Thoronet, or toward the chaste nudity of the Maures Peaks, the reasons to flee Saint-Tropez have become too many. Yet its beautiful blue sea, pink houses, sky, and little port at dawn still call, prompting wise travelers to come in the winter. Reading what the writers had to say never hurts. In 1887, when passing on his *Bel Ami*, Maupassant hailed this "brave and salty village" that was connected to the outside world only by one steam train and an old stagecoach. The town's isolation began to end in the 1920s, when the legend of Saint-Tropez began. Françoise Sagan, one of the town's most representative residents, noted evocatively that "like a Greek tragedy, wherein a boulevard Euripides was inspired by a Feydeau sociologist, no 'love' exists unless it is commented upon, no beach exists unless the chairs are expensive, no desire exists unless it can be bought or sold . . . ."

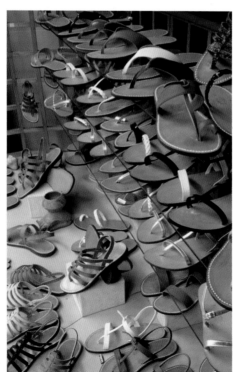

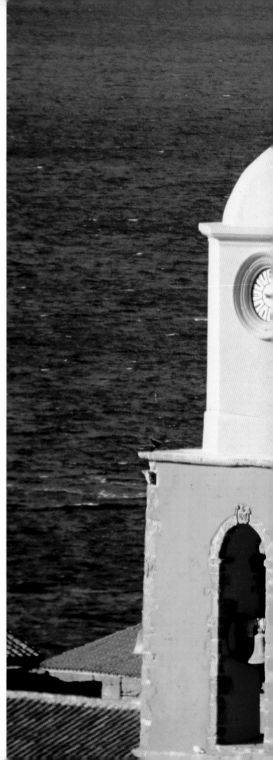

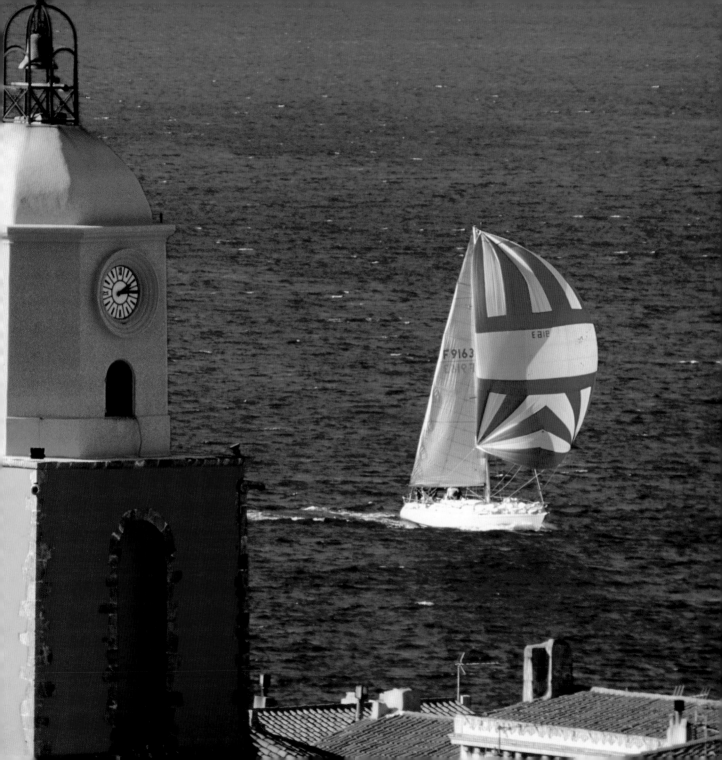

VAISON
CELTIC CHORISTERS

Situated in a strategic position linking the Baronnies Mountains, the Montmirail Dentelles Massif, and the plains of Comtat, the aptly named city of Vaison-la-Romaine still possesses much evidence of the splendor of its past, when it was a federated city allied with Rome. Called Vasio Vocontiorum in antiquity, after it was conquered by the Romans in the second century BC, the Celtic capital of Voconces was beautified

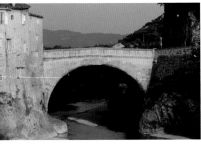

An ancient Greco-Roman bridge joins the village center to the medieval town.

facing page
The ancient first-century Roman amphitheater held up to 6,000 spectators.

with monuments, patrician houses, thermal baths, gardens, and a theater. Unlike Arles and Orange, whose buildings followed an urban-planning design, Vaison had no regulated development. Ancient Roman Vaison was completely destroyed in the sixth century, and after the fall of the Roman Empire the city came under bishopric rule. The bishops left two important buildings, both of which are masterpieces of Provençal Romanesque art. One is the chapel of Saint-Quentin, dedicated to the sixth-century bishop of the city. The fragment of a holy *vasio* (vase) on the portico gave the city its name of Vaison-la-Romaine. The other is the cathedral of Notre-Dame-de-Nazareth, which was modified in the eleventh and thirteenth centuries to incorporate some Roman parts on the bell tower and in the apse. In its interior the stone throne of Saint Quentin, behind the altar, has miraculously survived to the present day. To one side, the eleventh-century cloister is the epitome of Romanesque art's supreme grace. Sarcophagi and pre-Christian remains can be found in the galleries; the ancient ruins of Vaison are scattered over the sites of Puymin and Villasse, and were only catalogued at the beginning of the twentieth century. The area of Puymin resembles a miniature Pompeii. The house of the Messii is paved with colored marble, the Pavone villa contains splendid mosaics, and the theater was built circa 20 BC. The archeological museum displays the best excavated pieces, including imperial statues in white marble and the silver bust of a patrician. In the area of Villasse we can see the ruins of the most elegant houses. The House of the Silver Bust is, with an area of more than 15,000 square feet, the largest in the Roman world. Shops, thermal baths, runoff channels, and sidewalks are all still visible, making for a vast, tranquil, and breath-taking universe. The city was built on a rocky promontory that basks in the Provençal sunshine. A stroll along the *calades*, the ancient narrow streets paved with packed rubble, makes for a pleasant walk to the feudal castle. Although the last flood, in the fall of 1992, took thirty-seven victims and destroyed 150 houses, Vaison remains to this day a beautiful and ancient city, solid and fragile at the same time.

All around Vaison there are paths leading to beautiful wine-growing villages, and it's no rarity to see people emerging from the cellars with a glass in their hands. Each fall the Soupes des Villages festival, a very popular and most unusual celebration, is held here. Whether hot or cold, with pumpkin or mushrooms, these soup recipes are handed down to the girls of each new generation. For fourteen evenings, in fourteen villages, soups are prepared by the local women, then tasted and voted on every evening at the confraternity of the *Louchiers Voconces.*

In 1906 Joseph Sautel (1880–1955), a young priest and professor of history and geography at Avignon, became impassioned by the history of Vaison, and undertook some excavations for a thesis at the University of Aix-en-Provence. The results confirmed his hypothesis, and in 1912 the ancient theater was found. He continued excavating and uncovered almost the whole site of present Vaison-la-Romaine. The work, begun modestly, soon found a patron in Maurizio Burrus, a deputy from Haut-Rhine. Vaison became an official archaeological dig, and sometimes even the locals would excavate and find other marvels hidden in Puymin and Villasse. In 1924 Vaison was called "La Romaine." Since 1953, every three years during the month of August the ancient theater becomes the venue for the concerts of the Choralies, hosting more than 4,000 musicians and choristers. Other concerts are improvised on the terraces of nearby cafés.

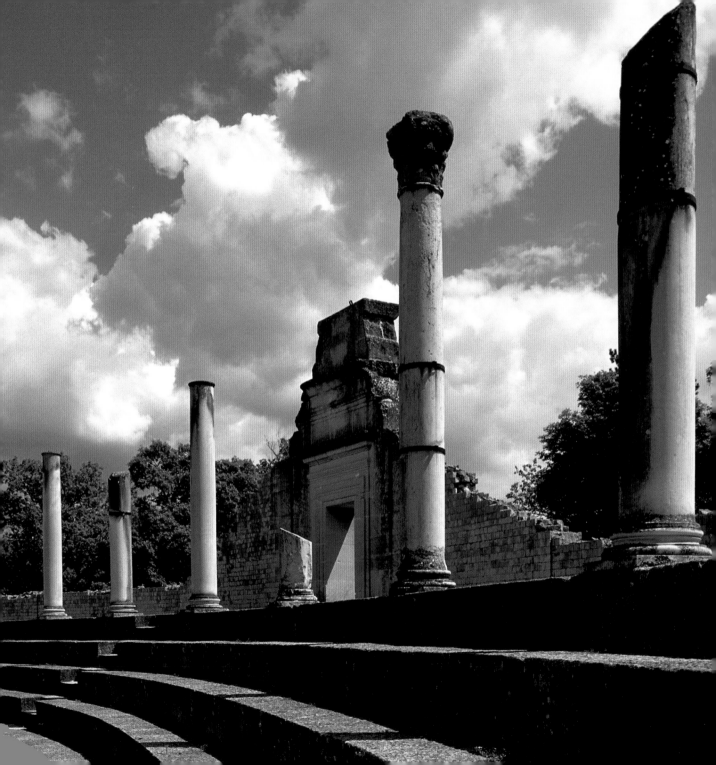

ANNECY
CRYSTALLINE POOLS

ANNECY IS IN THE NORTHERN ALPS AND IS PROBABLY THE CITY that has best known how to preserve its oldest human traces. The story begins in the Gallo-Roman period, circa 50 BC, when a *vicus*, or encampment, of about 2,000 souls quickly grew in the Fins Valley. This settlement was named Boutae, and traces remain so well intact that it is possible to make out the forum, basilica, baths (visible in avenue des Romains, at number thirty-six), and the theater, which has not yet been restored.

The Boutaeans were dispersed in the sixth century, and a new phase began in the twelfth century, until evidence of progressive settlements on the banks of the river at the confluence of Lake Thiou. This is a strategically important location, an obligatory passage along the north-south axis to cross the river at the height of the isle, the former seat of the local lord.

After this the medieval town of Annecy centered on the two banks of the Thiou River, protected by fortifications that later became a castle, and the new town flourished. Unexpected growth occurred when the Count of Geneva transferred his court here, having been expelled from his capital and defeated by the bishops. The castle became a princely residence until the family died out in 1394, and in 1401, with the annexation of the county of Geneva to Savoy rule, Annecy became part of Savoy territory under the authoritative Amedeo VIII, first Duke of Savoy.

The ancient capital of the counts was later stripped of its title and passed through a difficult period. A succession of devastating fires destroyed a large part of it in 1412 and again in 1448. Amedeo VIII helped Annecy rise from the ruins by building the castle and city. Annecy became a bishopric after the sudden departure of Geneva's bishop on the eve of the Protestant Reformation in 1535. Many other prelates soon arrived, reinforcing the religious character of Annecy. The city has preserved some beautiful monuments from this period, including the Logis de Nemours, the cathedral of Saint-Pierre, Maison Lambert, and the bell tower of the church of Notre-Dame de Liesse. Today Annecy is one of the most charming of French towns, with a lovely lake framed by the mountains, whose banks are green and pleasant, and streams that cross the old city and create a special atmosphere. It is perfectly restored, with cobblestone streets, massive city walls, and windows and doors that give visitors a desire to peek below the surface, proving that one can spend a truly lovely weekend in Annecy.

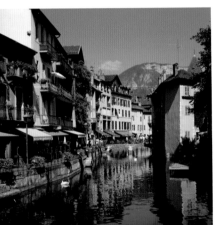

The placid waters of the old town.

facing page
The Palais de l'Isle has the unique triangular shape of a ship's prow.

The church of Notre-Dame de Liesse was built between 1846 and 1851 on the site of a thirteenth-century sanctuary dedicated to the Virgin Mary. The construction was entrusted to François Justin, an engineer who was very familiar with the rules of neoclassical style. Despite the period's rigid rules he was asked to preserve the sixteenth-century bell tower, part of the south wall, and an interesting fifteenth-century Gothic window as a precious reminder of the early sanctuary—all of which he did quite successfully.

Among the gastronomic specialties of the Savoy region are its cheeses. They are the protagonists of many recipes, including *raclette* and *tartiflette*, and should not be missed. The most famous is reblochon, a DOC cheese of raw cow's milk. It is a small cheese, typically uncooked, made with the milk of Alpine cows of the Tarine, Montéliarde, and Adondance types. It is easily recognizable by its saffron yellow crust covered with a fine white skin that indicates ideal ageing, and the cheese itself is ivory in color, velvety, and very tasty.
In the thirteenth century small producers had to pay an *ocière* (a tax) in proportion to the amount of milk they produced, so on collecting day they would not milk all the cows. Milking was completed after the visit of the owner, and this was the milk used to make the reblochon, named for *reblochi*, the local dialect's word for "second milking."

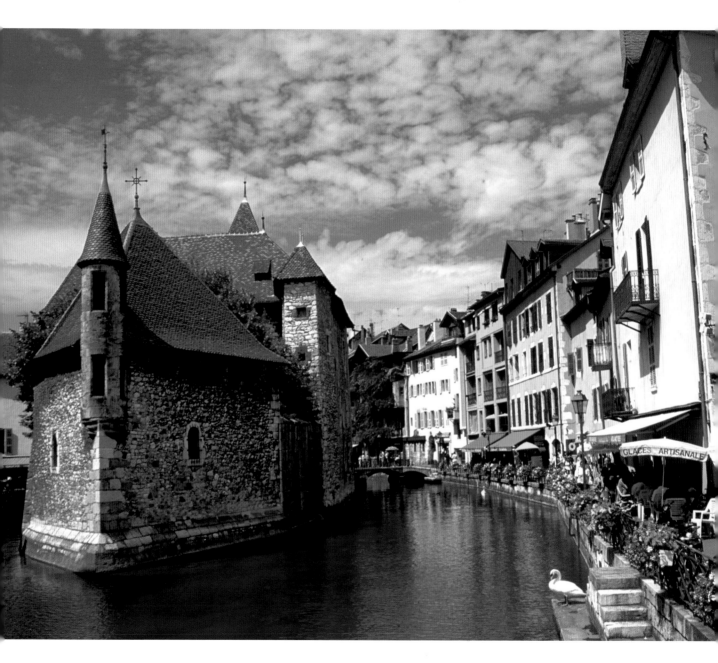

Jean-Jacques Rousseau (1712–1778) was born in Geneva and lived in Annecy for a long time. The city preserves many memories of this author and philosopher, whose ideas are still central in discussions regarding the core values of society.

In *Reveries of a Solitary Walker*, IV, he wrote, "General abstract truth is the most precious of all things. Without it man is blind. It is the eye of reason. It is through this that man learns to behave, to be that which he must be, to do what he must do, to tend toward his principal objective." The character and work of Rousseau are still pertinent today. His ideas on liberty and equality, his thoughts on the French Revolution, and the great themes of literature and the liberal arts form the essence of his reflections. Stendhal said, in praise of Rousseau, that he detested withered souls. Rousseau is buried in the Panthéon in Paris, facing his bitterest enemy, Voltaire. The Balustre d'Or at Annecy is a monument to his meeting with Madame de Warens.

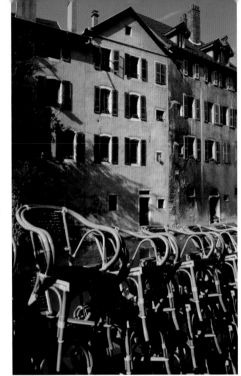

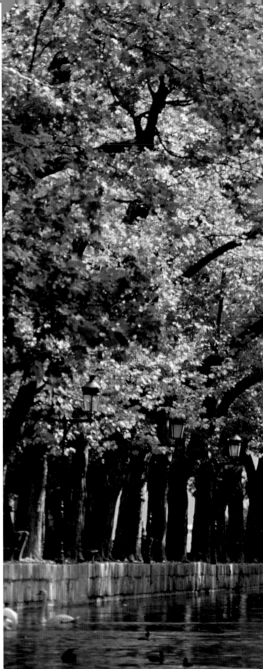

above
Wicker chairs at an open-air café.

right
Houses on the banks of the Thiou River.

facing page
The Pont des Amours joins the tree-lined banks of the canal.

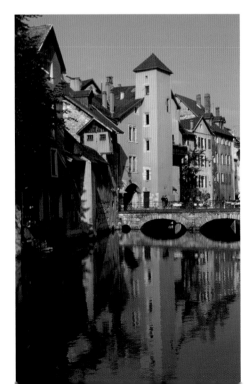

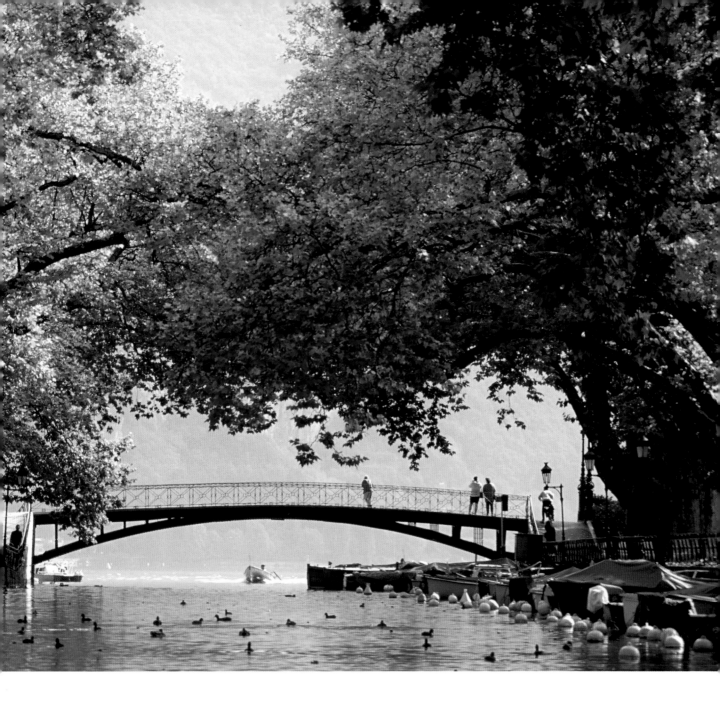

E V I A N
THE FOUNTAIN OF YOUTH

THE NAME OF EVIAN-LES-BAINS FIRST APPEARED IN 1864, WHEN SAVOY was annexed to France. Previously it had been called Aquianum (in 1150), Aquiano (in 1219), and Ayviens (in 1420). The town's expansion began with the construction of the castle by Count Pierre in the middle of the thirteenth century. For 200 years it was a favored town of the Savoy family, and it was protected by a ring of walls more than 100 feet high on each side and four round towers. The castle, reached by a drawbridge that crossed the Nant de Bennevy River, included a chapel, two greenhouses, a garden, and an orchard. It was partially destroyed by fire in 1390, and the medieval fortress was transformed into a noble residence by Aymonet Croviaux, architect to Duke Amedeo VIII.

As early as the thirteenth century the city was protected by a ring of fortified walls formed by circular towers starting at the fortress. In the fourteenth century the walls enclosed the city too tightly and prevented its expansion, so in order for Evian to breathe and grow the Touvière quarter was built to the east outside of the walls. The city soon became a commercial center concentrated around the market square where many craftsmen set up their workshops. The river port had an important part to play, as the northern bank of Lake Léman was an important meeting place for the merchants who traveled along the lake to get to the Rhône and on to the large markets of Geneva and Lyon. The boatmen, who had a monopoly on lake transportation, unloaded their goods on the gravel riverbed below the square. People traded in local and exotic goods, including fabrics, mirrors, and luxury goods imported by Lombard merchants.

It is said that in 1790 Count Laizer, a gentleman from Auvergne, refreshed himself during a walk by drinking the water from the Sainte-Catherine fountain and discovered that it stood on the property of a man named Cachat. He enjoyed the water and decided to drink it regularly, regardless of its ownership. Laizer, who had problems with his kidneys and liver, noticed an improvement in his health, and began praising what he deemed the water's miraculous properties; soon even local doctors began to prescribe it as a cure. Success was so rapid that Cachat closed down access to the fountain and began to sell the water. The first Evian thermal center was opened in 1824, and two years later the king of Sardinia authorized bottling of the water. The first Société des Eaux Minerales was founded in 1829, when the thermal baths were enlarged and other thermal centers were built, along with luxury hotels, a theater, a casino, and a funicular.

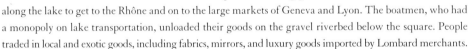

A spring of the famous local mineral water.

facing page
The Hotel de Ville, formerly the Villa Lumière.

The garden of Pré-Curieux was created in 2001 by the landscape architect Laurent Daune. An eight-acre park thus became a themed garden with two separate areas, a structured one with a water garden and one with a more natural area. The first, created around an exhibition building, displays ornamental plants and shrubs such as thyme, lavender, hydrangeas, rhododendrons, and azaleas. The plant beds are tended by gardeners, and water is channeled in artificial basins both to irrigate the plants and to provide ornamentation, as it also contains some beautiful fish. In the second garden different natural aquatic ecosystems have been created by restoring the water and the natural flora and fauna of the Léman riverbanks. Daune has also taken advantage of a little stream to simulate the life of a torrent from the spring to the outlet. Visitors can clearly see the interdependence between the flora and the current's speed, among other natural forces.

The Église quarter comes alive each Tuesday and Friday morning with the colorful market that offers all the flavors of Haut Savoie. One can find local cheeses, salted fish and meat, and fresh fish from the lake. No visitor should leave Evian without drinking the water; the Cachat spring, at the old Sainte-Catherine fountain, is the most famous. Built in 1903, its water flows year round, and is there for everyone to drink. A few feet away is the well-known des Cordeliers spring. The Société des Eaux Minèrales of Evian, situated in the pedestrian area of rue Nationale at number 19, offers an exhibition every year from May to September of Evian products, videos, educational games, and information about the water's properties.

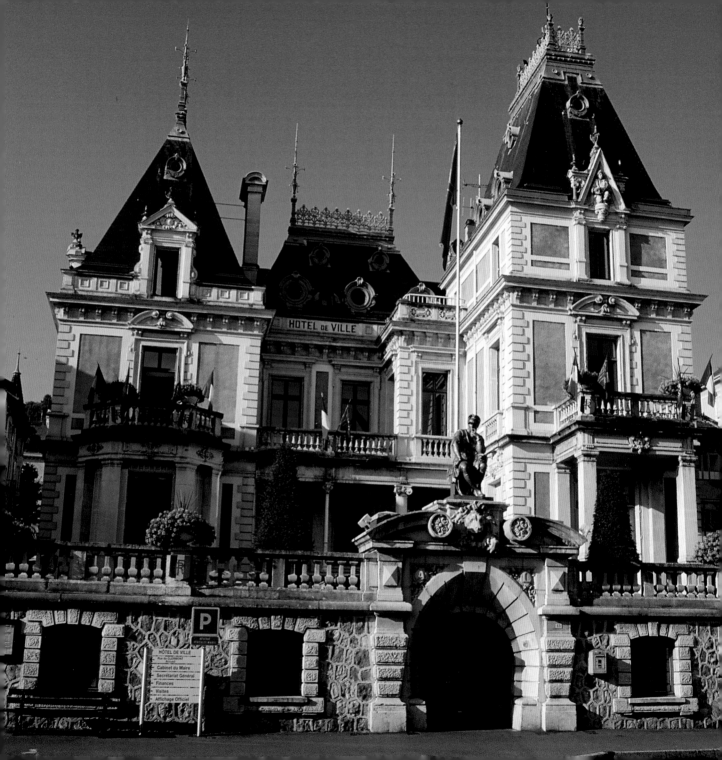

MONTÉLIMAR
A LAND OF LAVENDER

MONTÉLIMAR IS BORDERED BY THE BEAUTIFUL VINEYARDS where the *grands crus* famous throughout the world are made. The entire town is scented with the great encircling fields of lavender, and the climate and its natural beauty combine to create an unparalleled *douceur de vivre*.

The first village appeared about 6,000 years ago in the region of Gournier, which later became a Roman province. In the first century BC Agrippa built a road between Arles and Lyon, and a staging post was constructed at Acunum (present-day Aygu). In 1032 the village was part of the kingdoms of Burgundy and Provence, and fell under the Holy Roman Empire's sphere of influence. The local Adhémar de Monte family was very powerful and built the great palace for which the town is named. The inhabitants were granted a Charter of Freedom, and in 1440 Montélimar was annexed to the Dauphinate by the future King Louis XI. The reconstruction and transformation of the collegiate church of Sainte-Croix was carried out in this period. Because the city was besieged almost incessantly during the religious wars, it was quickly reinforced by a citadel. The bridge across the Roubion River, which had been destroyed at the end of the fourteenth century, was only reconstructed in 1806. In the twentieth century the old rue de Combat became the Nationale 7 highway, the famous road that vacationers have been taking to the sea since 1936, as this was the first year of government-instituted paid holidays. In the nineteenth century Montélimar grew and modernized; the walls were razed, and a long footpath was created in the place of the exterior ramparts. A public garden was designed, the municipality and court buildings were built, and in 1854 the railroad arrived. Emile Loubet, mayor of Montélimar, was elected president of the Republic in 1899. In those years the famous nougat industry developed, and to this day it remains the pride of the city. During World War II Montélimar was occupied by the Germans, and it was liberated in August 1944 by the Allies. A new era began with the construction of the highway, the lateral canal of the Rhône, and the arrival of the high-speed railway, electricity, and nuclear power plants.

Regardless of such modern amenities, Montélimar is full of art treasures immersed in the green of its gardens, and they are well worth a visit. The walk from the Saint-Martin gateway, built in 1762, to the neoclassical Municipal Theater, passing through the market square, is a delight. The ancient square is now known as the place aux Herbes.

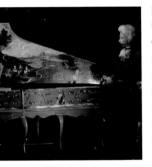

A scene depicting Wolfgang and Leopold Mozart in the Museum of Miniatures.

facing page
The Adhémar château.

The castle of Montélimar is a rare example of a Romanesque residential palace. It was built on a hill at the end of the twelfth century by the Adhémar family and gave its name to the city, as the name Monteil Adhémar became Montélimar. It was restructured by the popes in 1383 and was transformed into a fortified citadel at the end of the sixteenth century. It later fell into decline and was used as a prison between 1791 and 1926. In the nineteenth century it was bought and restored by the General Counsel, and it has been a historical monument since 1889. Since 1995 it has housed a center for contemporary art, offering many prestigious exhibitions of Mirò, Braque, Chagall, Masson, and others, following an ambitious program of five exhibitions every year. The summer exhibition has acquired international fame, with a cycle of conferences on contemporary art, ateliers, and entertainment to draw a younger public.

Montélimar nougat has been famous since the end of the seventeenth century, when Olivier de Serre planted the first almond trees in the region. These almonds, combined with Provençal honey, constitute the *nux gatum o mougo*, which is a sweetmeat that was imported by the Greeks to Marseilles and has been known for a long time in the towns of the Languedoc. Sugar, honey, egg whites, almonds, and pistachios are the traditional ingredients of nougat. Honey and sugar are melted and mixed in a kneading machine, to which beaten egg whites are added. The sugar that has previously been brought to a very high temperature is then mixed in, and when it is all cooked it turns into a thick paste, typical of the nougat of Montélimar. After a second kneading, the paste is poured into a mold lined with unleavened bread in paper-thin wafers. Needless to say, this scrumptious treat is on sale everywhere in the city and the surrounding areas.

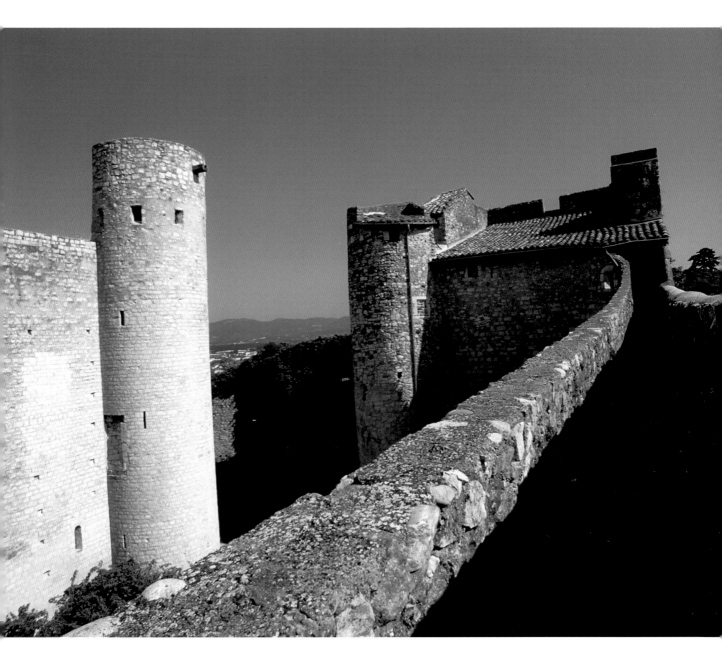

PÉROUGES
A WALK THROUGH THE MIDDLE AGES

PÉROUGES WAS BUILT ON A HILL AND IS THE PROTOTYPICAL MEDIEVAL CITY. It was a town of craftsmen, where no noble ever ruled, and whose principal resources were agriculture and above all textile making, activities for which the inhabitants enjoyed special benefits from the local authorities beginning in 1236.

Traversing Pérouges today means starting at the Porte d'En Haut and crossing history-filled streets and squares to arrive at Porte d'En Bas. The city has kept its medieval walls, which were built together with the castle in the twelfth century. The so-called church fortress rises above the castle, with arches bearing the crest of the Savoy and a sentry path with numerous embrasures. The winds of the Revolution blew here too, as can be seen from the great lime tree that shades the place des Halls—this "tree of freedom" was planted in October 1792. Turning one's gaze, the Middle Ages and Renaissance take over thanks to the thirteenth-century dovecote houses, a Gothic gallery, and a sundial. Rue des Rondes, whose central runoff canal was used to collect waste water, reminds us of the times when the French expression *tenir le haut du pavé* (to stay above road level) had a practical sense. A Roman

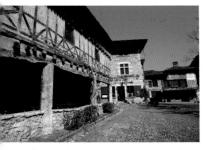

The traditional *pan de bois* facade of a local Ostellerie.

facing page
An ancient cobblestone road leads to the Ostellerie du Vieux Pérouges.

tower rose on the place where the city was built, and according to legend Pérouges was founded by a colony of Gauls upon their return from the Italian city of Perugia, from which it takes its name. Pérouges was most prosperous between the thirteenth and seventeenth centuries because of the thriving hemp tapestry manufacturing, and was contested between the sovereigns of Dauphiné and Savoy. It withstood many sieges, including the siege of 1468, which is remembered by an inscription on the Porte d'En Bas. At that time all the fortresses in that region had succumbed to the Dauphinois, who were allied with Louis XI. Pérouges resisted and, in recognition of his good subjects, the Duke of Savoy granted them freedom from tax payments for twenty years. Pérouges's wealth slowly declined until 1910–20, when the population fell from 1,500 to a low of ninety and ran the risk of disappearing. In 1911 the Committee for the Defense and Conservation of Vieux-Pérouges was created, and since then restoration has been carried out with great success thanks to public and private contributions. The village is proud to have welcomed many important figures of the world of pol-

At the entrance to rue des Princes stands the Ostellerie, a splendid thirteenth-century building in front of which is a museum containing a collection of tapestries, parchments, antique furniture, ceramics, and statues. On rue des Bontreforts, the third house on the right holds the city's "treadmill" olive press. A few miles from Pérouges in the direction of Amberieu-en-Bugey, one can get delightfully lost in a splendid natural labyrinth open from June to September—a maze of maize that changes each year.

itics, art, and literature, including Saint-Exupéry, René Clerc of the Académie Française, Albert Lebrun, the painter Utrillo, and more recently the former president of the United States, Bill Clinton. Pérouges is an enchanting village, a true gem of art treasures, refined architecture, and an old-fashioned way of life. The medieval ambiance is favored by many filmmakers, and the town is often transformed into a set for theatrical and television films. In person, more than onscreen, it is a delightful place to discover.

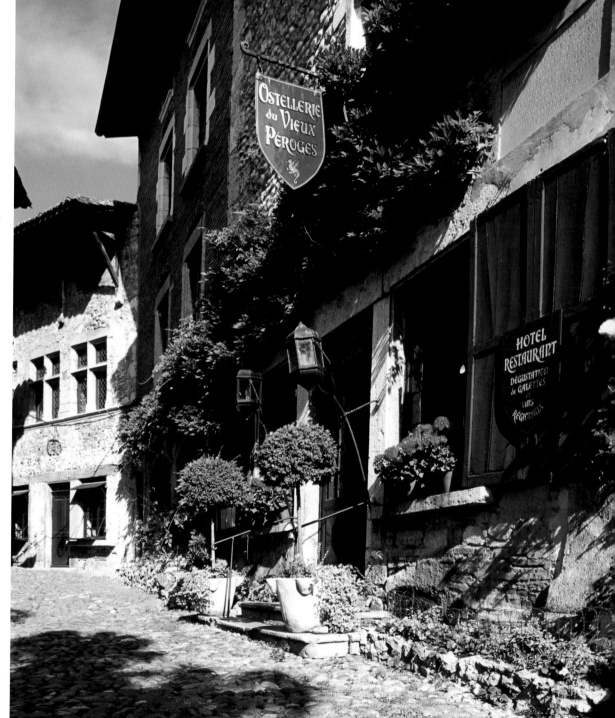

The *galette au sucre* is the simple and tasty dessert of Pérouges, prepared with a flour base, eggs, butter, sugar, and a dash of yeast. According to local traditional lore the recipe was invented at the beginning of the twentieth century, but the confectioners and bakers of the town relate that its origin comes from the leftovers of dough after the preparation of bread, which was made in large quantities once or twice a month, back in the not-so-distant times when nothing was thrown away. Two great places where one can fill a shopping basket with these delicious *galettes* are Chez Françoise and Chez P. Vernay.

ADDRESSES

20000 Ajaccio
phone +33 04 95214254

L'Escarbouche (Leather)
16, rue du Roi-de-Rome
20000 Ajaccio
phone+33 04 95256606

U Ghjuvan Chris (Souvenirs)
4, via Bonaparte
20000 Ajaccio
phone +33 04 95211074

A Grotta (Ceramics)
16, via del Roi-de-Rome
20000 Ajaccio
phone +33 04 95211001

albi (midi-pyrénées)

Office de tourisme
Palais de la Berbie
Place Sainte-Cécile
81000 Albi
phone +33 05 63494880
www.albi-tourisme.fr

Hostellerie Saint-Antoine
17, rue Saint-Antoine
81000 Albi
phone +33 05 63540404
fax +33 05 63471047

Hostellerie Du Vigan
16, place du Vigan
81000 Albi
phone +33 05 63433131
www.hotel-vigan.com
hotelduvigan@wanadoo.fr

Hôtel Chiffre
50, rue Séré de Rivières
81000 Albi
phone +33 05 63485848
fax +33 05 63472061
www.hotelchiffre.com
hotel.chiffre@wanadoo.fr

Hôtel Cantepau (Logis De France)
9, rue Cantepau
81000 Albi
phone +33 05 63607580
fax +33 05 63600161
hotel.cantepau@tiscali.fr

Hôtel Cardiff
41, avenue du Maréchal Foch
81000 Albi
phone +33 05 63470171
fax +33 05 63477364
ondesque@aol.com

Hôtel Des Pasteliers
3, rue Honoré de Balzac
81000 Albi
phone +33 05 63542651
fax +33 05 63470440

Hôtel Laperouse
19-21 place Lapérouse
81000 Albi
phone +33 05 63546922
fax +33 05 63380369

Restaurant Le Clos Sainte-Cécile
3, rue du Castelviel
81000 Albi
phone / fax +33 05 63381974

Restaurant L'Epicurien
42, place Jean Jaurès
81000 Albi
phone +33 05 63531070
fax +33 05 63431690

Restaurant L'Esprit du Vin
11, quai Choiseul
81000 Albi
phone +33 05 63546044
fax +33 05 63545479

Restaurant Le Goulu
Place Stalingrad
81000 Albi
phone +33 05 63541656
fax +33 05 63541656

Restaurant Le Lautrec
13-15, rue Toulouse-Lautrec
81000 Albi
phone / fax +33 05 63548655

Restaurant Le Parvis
27, place Sainte-Cécile
81000 Albi
phone +33 05 63462710
fax +33 05 63385529
elajmi.noueddine@wanadoo.fr

L'Artisan Pastellier
5, rue Puech Bérenguier
81000 Albi
phone +33 05 63385918

L'Antiquaire - A côté
12, rue Saint Julien
81000 Albi
phone +33 05 63431590

Michel Belin (Chocolat)
4, rue du Docteur Camboulives
81000 Albi
phone +33 05 63541846

amboise (centre)

Office de Tourisme Val d'Amboise
Quai du Général-de-Gaulle
37402 Amboise
phone +33 02 47570928
www.amboise-valdeloire.com

Hotel Le Manoir Les Minimes
34, quai Charles-Guinot
37400 Amboise
phone +33 02 47304040
fax +33 02 47304077
www.manoirlesminimes.com

Hôtel Domaine de le l'Arbrelle
Route des Ormeaux
37000 Amboise
phone +33 02 47575717
www.arbrelle.com

Pâtisserie Bigot
Place Michel-Debré
37000 Amboise
phone +33 02 47570446

Office du tourisme
6 bis, rue Dusevel
80000 Amiens
phone +33 03 22716051
www.amiens.fr/tourisme
www.somme-tourisme.com

Hôtel Alsace Lorraine
18, rue de la Morlière
80000 Amiens
phone +33 03 22913571
fax +33 03 22804390
www.alsace-lorraine.fr.st/

Hôtel-restaurant Les Tourelles
2-4, rue Pierre-Guerlain
80550 Le Crotoy
phone +33 03 22271633
fax +33 22271145
www.lestourelles.com

Restaurant Les Marissons
Pont de la Dodane
80000 Amiens
phone +33 03 22929666

Restaurant Au relais des orfèvres
14, rue des Orfèvres
80000 Amiens
phone +33 03 22923601

Restaurant La Couronne
64, rue Saint-Leu
80000 Amiens
phone +33 03 22918857

annecy (rhône-alpes)

Office de Tourisme d'Annecy
1, rue Jean-Jaurès
74000 Annecy
phone +33 04 50450033

Hotel Savoyard
41, avenue de Cran
74000 Annecy
phone +33 04 50570808

Hotel Le Pré carré
27, rue Sommeiller
74000 Annecy
phone +33 04 50521414

Hotel L'Impérial Palace
Allée de l'Impérial
74000 Annecy
phone +33 04 50093000

Hotel Allobroges
11, rue Sommeiller
74000 Annecy
phone +33 04 50450311

Hotel Belvédère
7, chemin du Belvédère
74000 Annecy
phone +33 04 50450490

Best Western Hotel International
19, avenue du Rhône
74000 Annecy
phone +33 04 50523535

Best Western-Carlton
5 rue des Glières
74000 Annecy
phone +33 04 50100909

Hotel Bonlieu
5, rue de Bonlieu
74000 Annecy
phone +33 04 50451716

Hotel Faisan doré
34, avenue d'Albugny
74000 Annecy
phone +33 04 50230246

Restaurant Auberge de savoie
1, place Saint-François
74000 Annecy
phone +33 04 50450305

Restaurant Aux Délices d'Enzo
17, rue Pâquier
74000 Annecy
phone +33 04 50453536

Brasserie de l'Hôtel-de-Ville
Place de l'Hôtel-de-Ville
74000 Annecy
phone +33 04 50450081

Brasserie des Europeens
23, rue Sommeiler
74000 Annecy
phone +33 04 50513070

Restaurant L'Etage
13, rue Pâquier
74000 Annecy
phone +33 04 50510328

Brasserie Saint-Maurice
7 et 9, rue du Collège
74000 Annecy
phone +33 04 50512449

Restaurant Cordon bleu
12, rue Perrière
74000 Annecy
phone +33 04 50455176

Les Jolies Choses
7, rue Sommeiller
74000 Annecy
phone +33 04 50450651
fax +33 04 50451670

Les Etains du Lac—Atelier
2443, route d'Albertville
74320 Sevrier
phone +33 04 50524891

Bateaux du Lac d'Annecy
2, place aux Bois
74000 Annecy
phone +33 04 50510840
fax +33 04 50518094

Delta Plane, Team Delta Evasion
Col de la Forciaz
74000 Annecy
phone +33 06 08324959

antibes (paca)

Office de Tourisme d'Antibes
11, place du Général de Gaulle—BP 37
06601 Antibes
phone +33 04 92905300
fax +33 04 92905301

Office de Tourisme de Juan-les-Pins
55, boulevard Charles Guillaumont
06160 Juan-les-Pins
phone +33 04 92905305
fax +33 04 93615513

Hôtel Impérial Garoupe
770, chemin de la Garoupe
06600 Le Cap d'Antibes
phone +33 04 92933161
fax +33 04 92933162
www.imperail-garoupe.com

Hôtel Don César
46, boulevard de la Garoupe
06160 Le Cap d'Antibes
phone +33 04 93671530
fax +33 04 93671825
www.hotel-donsesar.com

Hôtel Du Cap Eden-Rroc
Boulevard Kennedy—BP 29
06601 Le Cap d'Antibes
phone +33 04 93613901
fax +33 04 93677604
www.edenroc-hotel.fr

Hôtel La Baie Dorée
579, boulevard de la Garoupe
06160 Le Cap d'Antibes
phone +33 04 93673067
fax +33 04 92937639

Hôtel Beau Site
141, boulevard Kennedy
06160 Le Cap d'Antibes
phone +33 04 93615343
fax +33 04 93677816
www.hotelbeausite.net

Hôtel Chrys
50, chemin de la Parouquine—RN7
06600 Antibes
phone +33 04 92917020
fax +33 04 92917021
www.chrys-hotel.com

Hôtel Ambassadeur Concorde
50-52, chemin des Sables—BP 49
06161 Juan-les-Pins
phone +33 04 92937410
fax +33 04 93677985
www.hotel-ambassadeur.com

Hôtel Belles Rives
33, boulevard Edouard Baudoin
06160 Juan-les-Pins
phone +33 04 93610279
fax +33 04 93674351
www.bellerives.com

Hôtel Le Méridien Garden Beach
15-17, boulevard Baudouin
06160 Juan-les-Pins
phone +33 04 92935757
fax +33 04 92935756
www.juanlespins.lemeridien.com

Astoria Best Western
15, avenue Maréchal Joffre
06600 Juan-les-Pins
phone +33 04 93612365
phone +33 04 93671040
www.hollastoria.com

Restaurant Albert 1er
46, boulevard Albert 1er
06600 Antibes
phone +33 04 93343354

Restaurant Don Juan
17, rue Thuret
06600 Antibes
phone +33 04 93345863

Restaurant Da Cito
23, cours Masséna
06600 Antibes
phone +33 04 93347004

Restaurant La famiglia
34, avenue Thiers
06600 Antibes
phone +33 04 93346082

Restaurant La storia
1, boulevard Dugommier
06600 Antibes
phone +33 04 93743311

Restaurant La Terasse de la Baie Thalazur
770, chemin des Moyennes Bréguières
06600 Antibes
phone +33 04 92918200

arles (paca)

Office de Tourisme d'Arles
BP 121, 13633 Arles Cedex
Esplanade Charles de Gaulle
13200 Arles
phone +33 04 90184120
www.toursiem.ville-arles.fr

Hôtel Atrium
1, rue Emile Fassin
13200 Arles
phone +33 04 90499292
fax +33 04 90933859
www.hotelatrium.com

Hôtel Cheval Blanc
35, boulevard Georges-Clemenceau
13200 Arles
phone +33 04 90183410
fax +33 04 90962954
www.hotellechevalblanc.fr

Hôtel Constantin
59, boulevard de Craponne
13200 Arles
phone +33 04 90960405
fax +33 04 90968407

New Hôtel Arles Camargue
45, avenue Sadi Carnot
13200 Arles
phone +33 04 90994040
fax +33 04 90933250
www.new-hotel.com

Hôtel Mercure
1, avenue 1ère division française libre

13200 Arles
phone +33 04 90939880
fax +33 04 90499276

Hôtel Mireille
2, place Saint Pierre
13200 Arles
phone +33 04 90937074
fax +33 04 90938728

Hôtel-restaurant Jules César
9, boulevard des Lices
BP 116, 13631 Arles
phone +33 04 90525252
fax +33 04 90525253
www.hotel-julescesar.fr

Restaurant Dune
8, rue Réattu
13200 Arles
phone +33 04 90496667

Restaurant Amandier
34, rue Porte de Laure
13200 Arles
phone +33 04 90961675
fax +33 04 90961675

Bistrot de la Mule Blanche
9, rue du président Wilson
13200 Arles
phone +33 04 90939854
fax +33 04 90960930

Restaurant Bohème
6, rue Balze
13200 Arles
phone +33 04 90185892
fax +33 04 90185892

Restaurant Caravelle
1, place Constantin
13200 Arles
phone +33 04 90963904
fax +33 04 90433220

Restaurant Escalou
39, rue des Arènes
13200 Arles
phone/fax +33 04 90969669

Camargue Hôtel
58, boulevard de la Camargue
Salin de Giraud - Camargue
13129 Arles
phone +33 04 42868852
fax +33 04 42868395

Camargue Découverte
Mas Saint Bertrand
Route du Vaccarès, D36 C
Salin de Giraud - Camargue
13129 Arles
phone +33 04 42488069

Camarguaise Mas Montredon
Route de Gageron—Camargue
13200 Arles
phone +33 04 90961826

Relais Le Paty de la Trinité
Albaron - Camargue
13123 Arles
phone +33 04 90971240
fax +33 04 90971240

Le Domaine de la Palissade
www.conservatoire-du-littoral.fr

Les Marais du Vigueirat
13104 Mas-Thibert
phone +33 04 90987940
fax +33 04 90987254
marais-vigueirat@espaces-naturels.fr
www.marais-vigueirat.reserves-naturelles.org

**La Capelière—Centre d'Information de la
Réserve Nationale de Camargue**
13200 Arles
phone +33 04 90970097
fax +33 04 90970144
infos@reserve-camargue.org
www.reserve-camargue.org

Le Parc Ornithologique de Pont de Gau
Route d'Arles
13460 Saintes Maries de la Mer
phone +33 04 90978262
fax +33 04 90977477
contact@parcornithologique.com
www.parcornithologique.com

ars-en-ré (poitou-charentes)

Office du tourisme
Place Carnot
17590 Ars-en-Ré
phone +33 05 46294609
www.iledere.fr

Hôtel Le Sénéchal
6, rue Gambetta
17590 Ars-en-Ré
phone +33 05 46294042
fax +33 05 46292125
www.hotel-le-senechal.com

Hôtel Le Vieux Gréement
13, place Carnot
17670 La Couarde-sur-Mer
phone +33 05 46298218
fax +33 05 46295079
www.levieuxgreement.com

Hôtel-restaurant Le Richelieu
44, avenue de la Plage
17630 La Flotte
phone +33 05 46096070
fax +33 05 46095059
www.hotel-le-richelieu.com

Hôtel-restaurant Le Chat Botté
17590 Saint-Clément-des-Baleines
phone +33 05 46292193
fax +33 05 46292997
www.hotelchatbotte.com

Hôtel la Maison Douce
25, rue Mérindot
17410 Saint-Martin
phone +33 05 46092020
fax +33 05 46090990
www.lamaisondouce.com

Le Bistrot de Bernard
1, quai de la Criée
17590 Ars-en-Ré
phone +33 05 46294026

Restaurant L'Ecailler
3, quai de Sénac

17630 La Flotte
phone +33 05 46095640

Auberge de la Rivière
La Rivière
17880 Les Portes
phone +33 05 46295455

auch (midi-pyrénées)

Office de Tourisme d'Auch
1, rue Dessoles—BP 174
32003 Auch
phone +33 05 62052289
fax +33 05 62059204
www.auch-tourisme.com

Hôtel de France - Restaurant Le Jardin des Saveurs
2, place de la Libération
32000 Auch
phone +33 05 62617171
fax +33 05 62617181
www.hoteldefrance-auch.com
roland.garreau@wanadoo.fr

Hôtel de Paris
38, avenue de la Marne
32000 Auch
phone +33 05 62632622
fax +33 05 6600427

Hôtel Robinson
Route de Tarbes
32000 Auch
phone +33 05 62050283
fax +33 05 62059454
www.hotelrobinson.net

Hotel Campanile
Route de Toulouse
32000 Auch
phone +33 05 62636305
fax +33 05 62600292
www.envergure.fr
auch@campanile.fr

Etap'hôtel - Restaurant Courtepaille
Endoumingue av. J. Jaurès
32000 Auch
phone +33 08 92680903
www.etaphotel.com

Le Bartok
1, rue Gambetta
32000 Auch
phone +33 05 62058782

Bistrot Des Gourmandises
8, avenue de la Marne
32000 Auch
phone +33 05 62051079

Au Bivouac
6, rue de Dijon
32000 Auch
phone +33 05 62633657

La Bodega
7, rue Dessoles
32000 Auch
phone +33 05 62056917

La Casa Bonita
Rue Marceau—rue Kléber

32000 Auch
phone +33 05 62051230

Chez Wen
14, rue d'Etigny
32000 Auch
phone +33 05 62059655

Trou Gascon
19 bis, rue Marceau
32000 Auch
phone +33 05 62052933

Table d'ostes
7, rue Lamartine
32000 Auch
phone +33 05 62055562

La Cave d'Artagnan
3, rue de la République
32000 Auch
phone +33 06 78850574

The Comedie
12, rue Louis-Aucoin
32000 Auch
phone +33 05 62612623

Maison de Gascogne
Place Jean David
32000 Auch
phone +33 05 62051208

Le Panache Gascon
Route de Lussan
32550 Montegut-Auch
phone +33 05 62656515
fax +33 05 62656260
www.panache-gascon.com

La Ferme de Bordeneuve
32 320 Monesquiou
phone +33 05 62709420
www.fermedebordeneuve.com

Armagnac Marcel Trepout
Les Armagnacs du Château Notre-Dame
14, rue du Pont Notre-Dame
32190 Vic-Fezensac
phone +33 05 62063383
fax +33 05 62644095

Armagnac Dauriac
Domaine de Gaston
32190 Lannepax
phone +33 05 62063740
fax +33)5 62644400

Armagnac Delord
32190 Lannepax
phone +33 05 62063607
fax +33 05 62644198
www.armagnacdelord.com

Les Vignerons de la Ténarèze
Cave coopérative de Vic-Fezensac
route de Mouchan
32190 Vic-Fezensac
phone +33 05 62580525
fax +33 05 62063421

Pâtisserie, Salon de thé Fauché
Spécialités gersoises
8, rue de la République
32190 Vic-Fezensac
phone +33 05 62064533

Art Gascogne Atelier
4, rue Victor Hugo
32190 Vic-Fezensac
phone +33 05 62580967

auray (brittany)

Office du tourisme d'Auray
Chapelle de la Congrégation
20, rue du Lait
56400 Auray
phone +33 02 97240975
www.auray-tourisme.com

Hôtel-restaurant Abbatiale
Manoir de Kerdréan
56400 Le Bono
phone +33 02 97578400
fax +33 02 97578300
www.abbatiales.com

Hôtel-restaurant du Loch
2, rue Guhur, La Forêt
56400 Auray
phone +33 02 97564833
fax +33 02 97566355
www.hotel-du-loch.com

Restaurant La Closerie de Kerdrain
20, rue Louis-Billet
56400 Auray
phone +33 02 97566127

Restaurant La Chebaudière
6, rue de l'Abbé-Joseph-Martin
56400 Auray
phone +33 02 97240984

Salmonerie du Loch
ZA de Toul-Garros
56400 Auray
phone +33 02 97507880

La Trinitaine
Kerlois
56470 Saint-Philibert
phone +33 02 97550204

Ker-Jeanne
Kergou
56550 Belz
phone +33 02 97553897

Sidre du Pays d'Auray
Kervihern
56550 Locoal-Mendon
phone +33 02 97246745

Saumonerie du Loch
ZA de Toul Garros
56400 Auray
phone +33 02 97507880
fax +33 02 97507881

Pâtisserie Ker-Jeanne Kergou
56550 Belz
phone +33 02 97553897
fax +33 02 97552088

Cidre fermier du Pays d'Auray
Kervihern
56550 Locoal-Mendon
phone +33 02 97246745
fax +33 02 97246745

Boutiques cadeaux Armort et Argoat
52, rue du Château
56400 Auray
phone +33 02 97508456
fax +33 02 97508456

Porcel'Anne
34 rue du Belzic
56400 Auray
phone +33 02 97508452
www.porcelanne.com

aurillac (auvergne)

Office de Tourisme d'Aurillac et de son Pays
Place du Square
15000 Aurillac
phone +33 04 71484658
www.iaurillac.com

Hôtel-Restaurant Hôtel du Palais
4, rue Beauclair
15000 Aurillac
phone +33 04 71482486
fax +33 04 71649792
www.hotel-aurillac.com

Hôtel-Restaurant Grand Hôtel de Bordeaux
2, avenue de la République
15000 Aurillac
phone +33 04 71480184
fax +33 04 71484993
www.hotel-de-bordeaux.fr

Hôtel-Restaurant Hôtel la Thomasse
28, rue du Docteur-Mallet
15000 Aurillac
phone +33 04 71482647
fax +33 04 71488366
www.hotel-la-thomasse.com

Restaurant La Reine Margot
19, rue Guy-de-Veyre
15000 Aurillac
phone +33 04 71482646

Restaurant Le Bouchon fromager
Place des Docks
15000 Aurillac
phone +33 04 71480780

Parapluies Piganiol
28, rue des Forgerons
15000 Aurillac
phone +33 04 71430551

Coutellerie Destannes
7, rue des Frères
15000 Aurillac
phone +33 04 71483287

Les Etains d'Auvergne
Route de Toulouse
15000 Aurillac
phone +33 04 71636680

Distillerie Louis-Couderc
14, rue Victor-Hugo
15000 Aurillac
phone +33 04 71480150

Office du tourisme
41, cours Jean-Jaurès
84000 Avignon
phone +33 04 32743270
www.ot-avignon.fr

Hôtel-restaurant La Mirande
4, place de la Mirande
84000 Avignon
phone +33 04 90142020
fax +33 04 90862685
www.la-mirande.fr

Hôtel-restaurant Le Prieuré
7, place du Chapitre
30400 Villeneuve-lèz-Avignon
phone +33 04 90159015
fax +33 04 90254539
www.leprieure.fr

Hôtel de l'Atelier
5, rue de la Foire
30400 Villeneuve-lèz-Avignon
phone +33 04 90250184
fax +33 04 90258006
www.hoteldelatelier.com

Restaurant Le Jardin des Frênes
645, avenue des Vertes-Rives
84140 Montfavet
phone +33 04 90311793

Restaurant Aubertin
1, rue de l'Hôpital
30400 Villeneuve-lèz-Avignon
phone +33 04 90259484

Restaurant L'Epicerie
10, place Saint-Pierre
84000 Avignon
phone +33 04 90827422

Restaurant Le Woolloomooloo
16 bis, rue des Teinturiers
84000 Avignon
phone +33 04 90852844

Pâtisserie La Tropézienne
22, rue Saint-Agricol
84000 Avignon
phone/fax +33 04 90862472
www.latropezienne.net

Antiquités Yannerick Serignan
Chapelle de l'Abbaye de Senanque
9, rue de la Petite Fusterie
84000 Avignon
phone +33 04 90853604
fax +33 04 90279674

Les Grands Bateaux de Provence
Berges du Rhône, allée de l'Oulle
phone +33 04 90856225
www.avignon-et-provence.com/mireio

Office de tourisme
55, Grande Rue
77630 Barbizon
phone +33 01 60664187
www.barbizon-france.com

Hôtel-restaurant Hôtellerie du Bas-Bréau
22, Grande Rue
77630 Barbizon
phone +33 01 60664005
fax +33 01 60692289
www.bas-breau.com

Hôtel-restaurant Auberge Les Alouettes
4, rue Antoine-Barye
77630 Barbizon
phone +33 01 60664198
fax +33 01 60662069
www.barbizon.net

Restaurant L'Angélus
31, Grande Rue
77630 Barbizon
phone +33 01 60664030

Restaurant Le Relais de Barbizon
2, avenue Charles-de-Gaulle
77630 Barbizon
phone +33 01 60664028

Musée Départemental de l'Ecole de Barbizon
92, Grande Rue
77630 Barbizon
phone +33 01 60662227
fax +33 01 60662296

Les Impressionnistes
71, Grande Rue
77630 Barbizon
phone +33 01 60662302

La Forêt des Arts - Galerie d'Art, Salon de thé -Librairie
52, Grande Rue
77630 Barbizon
phone +33 01 60692463

La Verrerie de Barbizon
82 bis, Grande Rue
77630 Barbizon
phone +33 01 64149051

Pimentine
59, Grande Rue
77630 Barbizon
phone +33 01 60662970

Villa Cyrano
54, Grande Rue
77630 Barbizon
phone +33 01 64813094

Galerie 53 - E. Amigues & C. Lefloch
53, Grande Rue
77630 Barbizon
phone +33 01 60664121

Mignonne, allons Voir Si La Rose
56 bis, Grande Rue
77630 Barbizon
phone +33 01 60660291

Office du tourisme
Îlot Post Tenebras Lux, maison du Roy
13520 Les Baux-de-Provence
phone +33 04 90543439

Hôtels Le Cabro d'Or
Carita, route d'Arles
13520 Les Baux-de-Provence
phone +33 04 90543321

Carmen Dumas
Vallon Fontaine
13520 Les Baux-de-Provence
phone +33 90543413

Fabian des Baux
Quartier Mas de la Dame
Route départementale 5
13520 Les Baux-de-Provence
phone +33 04 90543787

Hostellerie de la Reine Jeanne
Grand rue
13520 Les Baux-de-Provence
phone +33 04 90543206

Hôtel Mas de l'Oulivié
Chemin départemental 78F
13520 Les Baux-de-Provence
phone +33 04 90543578

Hôtel-restaurant Bautezar
Grand rue
13520 Les Baux-de-Provence
phone +33 04 90543209

La Riboto de Taven
D27, Val d'Enfer
13520 Les Baux-de-Provence
phone +33 04 90543423

Mas d'Aigret
Chemin départemental 27A
13520 Les Baux-de-Provence
phone +33 04 90542000

Oustau de Baumanière
Chemin départemental 27
13520 Les Baux-de-Provence
phone +33 04 90543307

Le Benvengudo
Chemin départemental 78F
13520 Les Baux-de-Provence
phone +33 04 90543254

Restaurant Léon Philippe
rue Trencat
13520 Les Baux-de-Provence
phone +33 04 90545048

Restaurant Le Jardin des délices
Rue Trencat
13520 Les Baux-de-Provence
phone +33 04 90544838

La Boutique du Château
Culture Espace
phone +33 04 90543602

Le Marché provençal
Grand Rue Frédéric Mistral
13520 Les Baux-de-France
phone +33 04 90544031

La Maison de Provence
Rue Neuve et rue du Château
13520 Les Baux-de-France
phone +33 04 90543829 / 90898163

La Lanvandine
Rue de la Calade
13520 Les Baux-de-France
phone +33 04 90544095

Mas de la Dame - Vins A.O.C. Les Baux de Provence
Route de Saint-Rémy
13520 Les Baux-de-France
phone +33 04 90543224
www.masdeladame.com

Mas Sainet-Berthe - Vins A.O.C. Les Baux de Provence
Route de Saint-Rémy
13520 Les Baux-de-France
phone +33 04 90543901

Caves de Sarragan Vins A.O.C. Coteaux d'Aix en Provence
Route de Maillane
13520 Les Baux-de-France
phone +33 04 90543358

Producteur d'Huile d'olive Castellas
Mas de l'Olivier
13520 Les Baux-de-France
phone +33 04 90545086

Huiles d'olive de la vallée des Baux Moulin Jean-Marie Cornille
Rue Charloun Rieu
13520 Maussane-les-Alpilles
phone +33 04 90543237 / 90543812

Atelier de la Céramique
Rue Trencat
13520 Les Baux-de-France
phone +33 04 90543436

Mosaïques et Vitraux d'art
Quartier Fréchier
13520 Les Baux-de-France
phone +33 04 90543342

Le Santonnier
Rue de l'Orme
13520 Les Baux-de-France
phone +33 04 90544178

Office du Tourisme de Beaucaire Terre d'Argence
24, cours Gambetta—BP 61
30301 Beaucaire
phone +33 04 66592657

Service des affaires taurines
BP 134
30302 Beaucaire
phone +33 04 66597134

Hotel L'Oliveraie
Route de Nîmes
30300 Beaucaire
phone +33 04 66591687

Hotel La Luna
3, boulevard du Maréchal-Foch
30300 Beaucaire
phone +33 04 66590542

Hotel Les Doctrinaires
Quai du Général-de-Gaulle
30300 Beaucaire
phone +33 04 66592370

Hotel Les Vignes blanches
67, avenue de Farciennes
30300 Beaucaire
phone +33 04 66591312

Hotel Robinson
Route de Remoulins
30300 Beaucaire
phone +33 04 66592132

Auberge L'Amandin
Quartier Saint-Joseph
30300 Beaucaire
phone +33 04 66595507

Restaurant L'Ail... heure
Place Raimond-VII
30300 Beaucaire
phone +33 04 66596775

Restaurant La Table de Marguerite
Mas de la Cassole
Route de Fourques
30300 Beaucaire
phone +33 04 66591700

Restaurant Le Soleil
30, quai du Général-de-Gaulle
30300 Beaucaire
phone +33 04 66592852

Restaurant Le Napoléon
4, place Frédéric-Mistral
30300 Beaucaire
phone +33 04 66590517

Navarro Sabatier - Chaises provençales
2, rue Persil
30300 Beaucaire
phone +33 04 66591200

Melia France
20, rue des Bijoutiers
30300 Beaucaire
phone +33 06 24759036

Céramiques Françoise Rebord
Rue Roquecourbe—place Vieille
30300 Beaucaire
phone +33 04 66682832 / 78648716

Château Mourgues du Grès
Vins AOC costières de Nîmes
Route Bellegarde
30300 Beaucaire
phone +33 04 66594610

Domaine des Consuls
Mas Consul
30300 Beaucaire
phone +33 04 66744916

Domaine de Tavernel
Route Fourques
30300 Beaucaire
phone +33 04 66585701
fax +33 04 66593830

Domaine de la Tour
Route Saint-Gilles
30300 Beaucaire
phone +33 04 66016186

Huilerie Coopérative de Beaucaire
42, rue Redoute
30300 Beaucaire
phone/fax +33 04 66592800

Domaine du Petit Milord
Route de Fourques
30300 Beaucaire
phone +33 04 66595532
fax +33 04 66595533

beaune (bourgogne)

Office du Tourisme
6, boulevard Perpreuil, BP 87
21203 Beaune

Domaine Albert Ponnelle
Clos Saint-Nicolas
21200 Beaune
phone +33 03 80220005

Alésia Hôtel
4, avenue des Sablières
21200 Beaune
phone +33 03 80226327

Château de Challange
Rue des Templiers
21200 Beaune
phone +33 03 80263262

Hôtel de la Cloche
40-42, rue du Faubourg-Madeleine
21200 Beaune
phone +33 03 80246633

Hôtel de la Poste
3-5, boulevard Clemenceau
21200 Beaune
phone +33 03 80220811

Hotel Le Home
138, route de Dijon
21200 Beaune
phone +33 03 80221643

Restaurant Aux Vignes rouges
45, rue Maufous
21200 Beaune
phone +33 03 80247128

Restaurant Dame Tartine
3, rue Nicolas-Rolin
21200 Beaune
phone +33 03 80226420

Restaurant La Calèche
Avenue Charles-de-Gaulle
21200 Beaune
phone +33 03 80222200

Restaurant Le Jardin des remparts
10, rue de l'Hôtel-Dieu
21200 Beaune
phone +33 03 802479

Musée du vin de Bourgogne
Hotel des Ducs, rue de l'Enfer
21100 Beaune
phone +33 03 80220819
fax +33 03 80245620

Musée des Beaux-Arts
6, boulevard Perpreuil

21200 Beaune
phone +33 03 80245692

Musée E.J. Marey
Hôtel de ville
21200 Beaune
phone +33 03 80245692 / 80 24 56 92

Cavistes La Reine Pédauque
Porte Saint-Nicolas
21200 Beaune
phone +33 03 80222311
fax +33 03 80227020

Caves Daniel Duvernois
38, boulevard Foch
21200 Beaune
phone +33 03 80224374

belfort (franche-comté)

Maison du Territoire de Belfort
2 bis, rue Clémenceau
90000 Belfort
phone +33 03 84559090
fax +33 03 84559070
www.ot-belfort.fr

Hotel-restaurant Le Tonneau d'or
1, rue Reiset
90000 Belfort
phone +33 03 84585756

Hotel-restaurant Molière
6, via de l'Etuve
90000 Belfort
phone +33 03 84218638

Epicerie du Lion
4, via Porte-de-France
90000 Belfort
phone +33 03 84280433

biarritz (aquitaine)

Office du tourisme
1, square Ixelles
64200 Biarritz
phone +33 05 59223710
www.ville-biarritz.fr

Hôtel-restaurant du Palais
1, avenue de l'Impératrice
64200 Biarritz
phone +33 05 59416400
fax +33 05 59416799
www.hotel-du-palais.com

Hôtel-restaurant Sofitel Miramar
13, rue Louison-Bobet
64200 Biarritz
phone +33 05 59413000
fax +33 05 59247720
www.thalassa.com

Hôtel-restaurant Le château du Clair de Lune
8, avenue Alan-Seeger
Route d'Arbonne
64200 Biarritz
phone +33 05 59415320
fax +33 05 59415329
www.chateauduclairdelune.com

Hôtel Maison Garnier
29, rue Gambetta
64200 Biarritz
phone +33 05 59016070
fax +33 05 59016080
www.hotel-biarritz.com

Restaurant Les Platanes
32, avenue Beausoleil
64200 Biarritz
phone +33 05 59231368

Café de Paris
5, place Bellevue
64200 Biarritz
phone +33 05 59241953

Restaurant La Goulue
3, rue Etienne-Ardoin
64200 Biarritz
phone +33 05 59249090

Restaurant Le Clos Basque
12, rue Louis-Barthou
64200 Biarritz
phone +33 05 59242496

Restaurant Campagne et Gourmandise
52, avenue Alan-Seeger
Route d'Arbonne
64200 Biarritz
phone +33 05 59411011

Pâtisserie-Salon de thé Dodin
7, rue Gambetta
64200 Biarritz
phone +33 05 59241637

bonifacio (corsica)

Office du tourisme
2, rue Fred-Scamaroni
20169 Bonifacio
phone +33 04 95731188
www.bonifacio.fr

Hôtel Genovese
Quartier de la Citadelle
20169 Bonifacio
phone +33 04 95731234
fax +33 04 95730903
www.hotel-genovese.com

Hôtel-restaurant Marina di Cavu
Route de Calalonga
20169 Bonifacio,
phone +33 04 95731413
fax +33 04 95730482
www.marinadicavu.com

Hôtel-restaurant A Cheda
Cavallo Morto
20169 Bonifacio
phone +33 04 95730283
fax +33 04 95731772
www.acheda-hotel.com

Hôtel-restaurant Caravelle
35-37, quai Comparetti
20169 Bonifacio
phone +33 04 95730003
fax +33 04 95730041
www.hotel-caravelle-corse.com

Hôtel-restaurant A Trama
Cartarana, route de Santa Manza
20169 Bonifacio
phone +33 04 95731717
fax +33 04 95731779
www.a-trama.com

Restaurant Stella d'Oro
7, rue Doria
20169 Bonifacio
phone +33 04 95730363

Restaurant Chez Marco
Plage de la Tonnara
20169 Bonifacio
phone +33 04 95730224

Casa Corsa
Rue Saint-Dominique
20169 Bonifacio
phone +33 04 95735354
fax +33 04 95735354

La Boutique du Corailleur
3, place Montepagano
20169 Bonifacio
phone +33 06 07313955 / 06 08274142
info@corailrouge.com

La Taillerie du Corail
15, montée Rastello
20169 Bonifacio
phone +33 04 95231783 / 95702121
fax +33 04 95709276

Galerie d'art Méditerranée
3, rue Fred Scamaroni
20169 Bonifacio
phone +33 04 95735909
fax +33 04 95735909

Aquarium de Bonifacio
71, quai Comparetti
20169 Bonifacio
phone +33 04 95730369
fax +33 04 95730369

Casadoria - Arts de vivre Méditerranée
8, rue Doria
20169 Bonifacio
phone +33 04 95730840

Pâtisserie Sorba
3, rue Saint-Erasme
20169 Bonifacio
phone +33 04 95730364
fax +33 04 95730446

bourges (centre)

Office du tourisme
21 rue Victor Hugo
18000 Bourges
phone +33 02 48230260
www.bourges-tourisme.com

Hôtel de Bourbon
Boulevard de la République
18000 Bourges
phone +33 02 48707000
www.alpha-hotellerie.com

Hôtel Les Bonnets Rouges
3, rue de la Thaumassière
18000 Bourges

phone +33 02 48657992
www.bonnets-rouges.bourges.net/

Restaurant D'Antan Sancerrois
50, rue Bourbonnoux
18000 Bourges
phone +33 02 48659626

Restaurant Le Jardin Gourmand
15 bis, avenue Ernest Renan
18000 Bourges
phone +33 02 48213591

Restaurant L'Abbaye Saint-Ambroix
60-62 avenue Jean-Jaurès
18000 Bourges
phone +33 02 48708000

Maison des Forestines
3, place Cujas
18000 Bourges
phone +33 02 48240024

Pâtisserie Rossignon
18 bis, rue Moyenne
18000 Bourges
phone +33 02 48240264

cahors (midi-pyrénées)

Maison du Tourisme
Place François Mitterrand
46000 Cahors
phone +33 05 65532065
fax +33 05 65532074
cahors@wanadoo.fr

Hotel Le terminus
Le Balandre
5, avenue Charles-de-Freycinet
46000 Cahors
phone +33 05 65533200
fax +33 05 65533226

Hotel La chartreuse
Quartier Saint-Georges
46000 Cahors
phone +33 05 65351737
fax +33 05 65223003

Hotel Le melchior
Avenue Jean-Jaurès
46000 Cahors
phone +33 05 65350338
fax +33 05 65239275

Restaurant Le balandre
5 avenue C. de Freycinet
46000 Cahors
phone +33 05 65533200
fax +33 05 65533226

Restaurant Le Rendez-Vous
49, rue Clément Marot
46000 Cahors
phone +33 05 65226510
fax +33 05 65351105

Restaurant La Garenne
Saint Henri—RN 20
46000 Cahors
phone +33 05 65354067
fax +33 05 65354067

Au fil des douceurs
(Péniche à quai)
90, quai de la Verrerie
46000 Cahors
phone +33 05 65221304
fax +33 05 65356109

L'o a la bouche
134, rue Sainte-Urcisse
46000 Cahors
phone +33 05 65356569

Tour du Pape Jean XXII
3, boulevard Léon Gambetta
46000 Cahors
phone +33 05 65353952

Maison du Vin
Avenue Jean-Jaurès—BP199
46004 Cahors
phone +33 05 65232224
fax +33 05 65232227

Syndicat des Vins des Coteaux du Quercy
42, avenue du Général Leclerc
82300 Caussade
phone +33 05 63650201
fax +33 05 63939239

Mémé du Quercy
Halles de Cahors
46000 Cahors
phone +33 05 65222880

Cahors Saveur
Pech d'Angély Sud
46000 Cahors
phone +33 05 65202080

Chai des Halles
Halles 46000 Cahors
phone +33 05 65222883

Alain Dominique Perrin
546, allée Soupirs
46000 Cahors
phone +33 05 65350612

Sudreau Foies Gras
91, boulevard Gambetta
46000 Cahors
phone +33 05 65352606

Foies Gras Ph. Martegoute
2, place Sainte-Urcisse
46000 Cahors
phone +33 05 65222989

Foies Gras Paul et Marie Decaysac
Quai Lagrive
46000 Cahors
phone +33 05 65539844
fax +33 05 65539881

cambrai (nord-pas-de-calais)

Office du tourisme
48, rue de Noyon
59400 Cambrai
phone +33 03 27783615

Hôtels Beatus
718, avenue de Paris
59400 Cambrai
phone +33 03 27814570

Hôtel de France
37, rue de Lille
59400 Cambrai
phone +33 03 27813880

Hôtel Le Cluny
20, place Aristide-Briand
59400 Cambrai
phone +33 03 27813308

Hôtel Le Taximan
21, rue du Maréchal-Juin
59400 Cambrai
phone +33 03 27813266

Hôtel Le Cristal
2, place de la Gare
59400 Cambrai
phone +33 03 27813826

Restaurant L'Escargot
Rue du Général-de-Gaulle
59400 Cambrai
phone +33 03 27812454

Restaurant La Flambée
Rue Alsace-Loraine
59400 Cambrai
phone +33 03 27813673

Restaurant La Marolette
7, place Saint-Sépulcre
59400 Cambrai
phone +33 03 27707080

Restaurant La Taverne de Lutèce
Avenue de la Victoire
59400 Cambrai
phone +33 03 27785434

Restaurant Le Buffet de la gare
Place de la Gare
59400 Cambrai
phone +33 03 27810359

Restaurant Le Milord
Rue Louis-Blériot
59400 Cambrai
phone +33 03 27814166

Restaurant Le Petit chef
Rue des Docks
59400 Cambrai
phone +33 03 27814746

Restaurant Le Relais Saint-Géry
Grand-rue Vander-Burch
59400 Cambrai
phone +33 03 27812755

Restaurant Le Resto du Beffroi
Rue du 11 Novembre
59400 Cambrai
phone +33 03 27815010

Chocolaterie du Cambrésis
189, avenue Georges Nuttin
59400 Cambrai
phone +33 03 27707500

Chocolats Diot
15, rue Gén. de Gaulle
59400 Cambrai
phone +33 03 27832448
fax +33 03 27831010

Confiserie Afchain
Rue du Champ de Tir
59400 Cambrai
phone +33 03 27812549

Bêtises de Cambrai - Afchain
Z.I. de Cantimpré
59400 Cambrai
phone +33 03 27812549
fax +33 03 27812040
www.betises-de-cambrai.com

Tome de Cambrai
72 Grand Rue
Seranvillers
phone +33 03 27786625
fax +33 03 27787290

Bière – Brasserie La Chouette
16, rue des écoles Hordain
phone +33 03 27357244
fax +33 03 27359929
www.lachoulette.com

Ruiz Glacier
9 bis, rue Quartier de Gavalier
59400 Cambrai
phone +33 03 27813349

Tropic'ice Glacier
17, rue Pré d'Espagne
59400 Cambrai
phone +33 03 27376153

cancale (brittany)

Office du tourisme
44, rue du Port
35260 Cancale
phone +33 02 99896372

Hôtel-restaurant Les Maisons de Bricourt
1, rue Duguesclin
35260 Cancale
phone +33 02 99896476
fax +33 02 99898847
www.maisons-de-bricourt.com

Hôtel-restaurant Le Querrien
7, quai Duguay-Trouin
35260 Cancale
phone +33 02 99896456
fax +33 02 99897935
www.le-querrien.com

Hôtel-restaurant Le Continental
6, quai Administrateur-Chef-Thomas
35260 Cancale
phone +33 02 99896016
fax +33 02 99896958
www.hotel-cancale.com

Hôtel Pointe du Grouin
Auberge de la Motte Jean
Pointe du Grouin
35260 Cancale
phone +33 02 99894199
fax +33 02 99899222
www.hotelpointedugrouin.com

Restaurant Le Saint-Cast
Route de la Corniche
35260 Cancale
phone +33 02 99896608

Restaurant Le Cancalais
12, quai Gambetta
35260 Cancale
phone +33 02 99896193

Restaurant Le Surcouf
Port de la Houle
7, quai Gambetta
35260 Cancale
phone +33 02 99896175

**Huîtres, coquillages, crustacés
Daniel Tony**
37, quai J. Kennedy
35260 Cancale
phone +33 02 99896266

Désirée
7, place de la Chapelle
35260 Cancale
phone +33 02 99896413

Les viviers de Cancale
4, rue de l'Huîtrier
35260 Cancale
phone +33 02 23151700
fax +33 02 23151701
www.viviers-de-cancale.com

Aux Delices de Cancale
11, rue Vauhariot
35260 Cancale
phone +33 02 99896934

Audic Roland
13, rue Vauhariot
35260 Cancale
phone +33 02 99899554

Boutiques souvenirs Au Cancaven
8, quai Gambetta
35260 Cancale
phone +33 02 99899456

L'Effet Mer
7, place du Calvaire
35260 Cancale
phone +33 02 99897657

L'Epicier Breton
3, quai Administrateur Chef Thomas
35260 Cancale
phone +33 02 23151915

cannes (paca)

Office du tourisme
Esplanade Georges-Pompidou—BP 272
06403 Cannes Cedex
phone +33 04 92998422

Hôtel Alan Robert's Hôtel
16, rue Jean-Jaurès
6400 Cannes
phone +33 04 93380507

Hôtel Albert 1er
68, avenue de Grasse
06400 Cannes
phone +33 04 93392404

Hôtel Amirauté
17, rue Maréchal-Foch
06400 Cannes
phone +33 04 93391053

Hôtel Mimont
39, rue de Mimont
06400 Cannes
phone +33 04 93395164

Hôtel Chanteclair
12, rue Forville
06400 Cannes
phone +33 04 93396888

Hôtel Atlantis
30, rue du 24-Août
06400 Cannes
phone +33 04 93391872

Hôtel Cannes Gallia
36, boulevard Montfleury
06400 Cannes
phone +33 04 97062828

Restaurant Le Relais des semailles
9-11, rue Saint-Antoine
06400 Cannes
phone +33 04 93392232

Restaurant Félix
63, boulevard de la Croisette
06400 Cannes
phone +33 04 93940061

Restaurant La Villa des Lys
10, boulevard de la Croisette
BP 163, 06407 Cannes
phone +33 04 92987741

Restaurant Le Mesclun
16, rue Saint-Antoine
06400 Cannes
phone +33 04 93994519

Restaurant Mantel
22, rue Saint-Antoiene
06400 Cannes
phone +33 04 93391310

Cartier
57, boulevard de la Croisette
06400 Cannes
phone +33 04 92592820

Inès de la Fressange
3, rue Commandant André
06400 Cannes
phone +33 04 93682990

Kenzo
65, rue d'Antibes
06400 Cannes
phone +33 04 93995454

Yves Saint Laurent
44, boulevard de la Croisette
06400 Cannes
phone +33 04 93383915

Le Jardin de Laura
79, rue Felix Faure
06400 Cannes
phone +33 04 92989192

Palazzo
19, rue Jean de Rioufle
06400 Cannes
phone +33 04 92990358

Office de Tourisme
28, rue de Verdun
11890 Carcassonne Cédex 9
phone +33 04 68102430
fax +33 04 68102438
accueil@carcassonne-tourisme.com

Hôtel de la Cité (Orient Express Hôtels)
Place Auguste Pierre Pont—La Cité
11000 Carcassonne
phone +33 04 68719871
fax +33 04 68715015

Hôtel Aragon
15, montée Combéléran
11000 Carcassonne
phone +33 04 68471631
fax +33 04 68473353

**Hôtel Le Donjon – Les remparts
(Best Western)**
2, rue du Comte Roger—La Cité
11000 Carcassonne
phone +33 04 68112300
fax +33 04 68250660

Hôtel Montségur
27, allée d'Iéna
11000 Carcassonne
phone +33 04 68253141
fax +33 04 68471322

Restaurant Comte Roger
14, rue Saint-Louis
La Cité
11000 Carcassonne
phone +33 04 68119340
fax +33 04 68119341

Restaurant Languedoc
32, allée d'Iéna
11000 Carcassonne
phone +33 04 68252217
fax +33 04 68250414

Restaurant Au Bon Pasteur
29, rue Armagnac
11000 Carcassonne
phone +33 04 68254963

Restaurant Chez Fred
31, boulevard Omer Sarraut
11000 Carcassonne
phone +33 04 68720223
fax +33 04 68715264

Restaurant L'oeil
32, rue de Lorraine
11000 Carcassonne
phone +33 04 68256481

Restaurant L'Opéra Bouffe
7, place Davilla
11000 Carcassonne
phone +33 04 13023417

Restaurant Domaine d'Auriac
Route de Saint-Hilaire—BP 554
11009 Carcassonne
phone +33 04 68257222
fax +33 04 68473554

Le Païcherou, Café-restaurant Guinguette
Quai du Païcherou

11000 Carcassonne
phone +33 04 68251205
fax +33 04 68258634

La Cure Gourmande
5 et 7, rue Cros-Mayrevielle
11000 Carcassonne
phone +33 04 68716482

chantilly (picardy)

Office de tourisme
60, avenue du Maréchal-Joffre
60500 Chantilly
phone +33 03 44673737
www.chantilly-tourisme.com

Hôtel-restaurant Dolce Chantilly
Route d'Apremont
Vineuil-Saint-Firmin
60500 Chantilly
phone +33 03 44584777
fax +33 03 44585011
www.chantilly.dolce.com

Hôtel-restaurant Le Relais d'Aumale
37, place Fêtes-Delaunay-Montgrésin
60560 Orry-la-Ville
phone +33 03 44546131
fax +33 03 44546915
www.relais-aumale.fr

Hôtel-restaurant Le château de la Tour
Chemin de la Chaussée
60270 Chantilly-Gouvieux
phone +33 03 44623838
fax +33 03 445731 97
www.lechateaudelatour.fr

Hôtel-restaurant Le Pavillon Saint-Hubert
Avenue de Toutevoie
60270 Gouvieux
phone +33 03 44570704
fax +33 03 44577542
www.pavillon-saint-hubert.com

Hôtel et auberge La Grange aux Loups
8, rue du 11-Novembre
60300 Apremont
phone +33 03 44253379
fax +33 03 44242222
www.lagrangeauxloups.com

Restaurant La Tour d'Apremont
Golf Club
60300 Apremont
phone +33 03 44256111

Restaurant Le Verbois
Route nationale 16
60740 Saint-Maximin
phone +33 03 44257663

Château de Chantilly – Musée Condé
BP 70243; 60631 Chantilly
phone +33 03 44626262
fax +33 03 44626268

Grandes Ecuries et Musée vivant duCheval
7, rue Connétable Grande Ecuries—BP60242
60631 Chantilly Cedex
phone +33 03 44574040
fax +33 03 44572992

Musée de la Dentelle Chantilly
34, rue d'Aumale,
60500 Chantilly
phone +33 03 44582844

Maison de la Porcelaine
1, route de Creil
60500 Chantilly
phone +33 03 44575419
www.maisonporcelaine.com

Les porcelaines de Chantilly
2, place Omer Vallon
60500 Chantilly
phone +33 03 44581797
fax +33 03 44581032
www.maisonporcelaine.com

Société Pierre Lang
(Jewelry)
56, Deuxième Avenue
60260 Lamorlaye
phone +33 03 44215916 / 20 58 60 31
www.pierre-lang.com

chartres (centre)

Office du tourisme
Place de la Cathédrale
28000 Chartres
phone +33 02 37182626
www.chartres-tourisme.com

Hotel-restaurant Le Grand Monarque
22, place des Epars
28000 Chartres
phone +33 02 37181515
fax +33 02 37363418
www.legrandmonarque.com

Hotel Châtelet
6-8, avenue Jehan-de-Beauce
28000 Chartres
phone +33 02 37217800
fax +33 02 37362301
www.hotelchatelet.com

Restaurant La Vieille Maison
5, rue au Lait
28000 Chartres
phone +33 02 37341067

Restaurant Le Moulin de Ponceau
21, rue de la Tannerie
28000 Chartres
phone +33 02 37353005

Restaurant Saint-Hilaire
11, rue du Pont-Saint-Hilaire
28000 Chartres
phone +33 02 37309757

Restaurant L'Estocade
1, rue de la Porte-Guillaume
28000 Chartres
phone +33 02 37342717

Artisanat d'art Ariane
39, rue des Changes
28000 Chartres
phone +33 02 37212068

Galerie Le Parnasse
17, cloître Notre-Dame
28000 Chartres
phone +33 02 37361003

Au Plaisir d'Offrir
28, place Jean Moulin
28000 Chartres
phone +33 02 37213196

La Crypte
18, cloître Notre-Dame
28000 Chartres
phone +33 02 37215633

Magasin Tuvache et Fils
34, rue des Changes
28000 Chartres
phone +33 02 37216043

Galerie Saint-Fulbert
6, cloître Notre-Dame
28000 Chartres
phone +33 02 37364504

La Galerie du Vitrail
17, cloître Notre Dame
28000 Chartres
phone +33 02 37361003

Ateliers Lorin Hermet Juteau
(Master glassblower)
46, rue de la Tannerie
28000 Chartres
phone +33 02 37 34 00 42

Ateliers Picol
(Master glassblower)
1 bis, rue du chapeau rouge
28000 Chartres
phone +33 02 37284081

chinon (centre)

Office du tourisme
Place d'Hofheim
37000 Chinon
phone +33 02 47931785
www.chinon.com

Hôtel-Restaurant Château de Marçay
37500 Marçay
phone +33 02 47930347
fax +33 02 47934533
www.chateaudemarcay.com

Hôtel Château de Danzay
37420 Beaumont-en-Véron
phone +33 02 47584686
fax +33 02 47580594
www.chateaudedanzay.com

Hôtel-restaurant Manoir de la Giraudière
37420 Beaumont-en-Véron
phone +33 02 47584036
fax +33 02 47584606
www.hotels-france.com/giraudiere

Hôtel de France
47, place du Général-de-Gaulle
37500 Chinon
phone +33 02 47933391
fax +33 02 47983703

Hôtel Agnès Sorel
4, quai Pasteur
37500 Chinon
phone +33 02 47930437
fax +33 02 47930637
www.agnes-sorel.com

Restaurant Au plaisir Gourmand
2, rue Parmentier
37500 Chinon
phone +33 02 47932048

Restaurant La Boule d'Or
21, rue Rabelais
37500 Chinon
phone +33 02 47984088

Musée Jeanne d'Arc
Tour de l'Horloge du Château de Chinon
phone +33 02 47932257

Musée Rabelais
Maison de La Devinière
37500 Seuilly
phone +33 02 47959118
fax +33 02 47958937
www.cg37.fr

Musée Honoré de Balzac
Château de Saché
37190 Saché
phone +33 02 47268650
fax +33 02 47268028
www.cg37.fr

Demeure de Pierre Ronsard
Prieuré de Saint-Cosme
37520 La Riche
phone +33 02 47373270
fax +33 02 47372520
www.cg37.fr

Musée du Vin et de la Tonnellerie
12, rue Voltaire
37500 Chinon
phone +33 02 47932563
fax +33 02 47930134

Cave de Monplaisir
Quai Pasteur
37500 Chinon
phone +33 02 47932075

Caves des Vins de Rabelais
Saint-Louans
37500 Chinon
phone +33 02 47934270

Domaine de Beauséjour
(wines)
Marie Claude Chauveau
37220 Panzoult
phone +33 02 47586464

Elsie's Garden
1-5, Route de Huismes
37500 Chinon
phone +33 02 47980758
www.elsiederaedt.com

collioure (languedoc-roussillon)

Office de tourisme de Collioure
Place du 18-Juin—BP 2
66190 Collioure
phone +33 04 68821547

Hotel Les Princes de Catalogne
Rue des Palmiers
66190 Collioure
phone +33 04 68983000

Relais des 3 Mas
Route de Port-Vendres
66190 Collioure
phone +33 04 68820507

Hotel Triton
1, rue Jean-Bart
66190 Collioure
phone +33 04 68983939

Hostellerie des Templiers
Quai Amirauté
66190 Collioure
phone +33 04 68983110

Hotel - restaurant Les Caranques
Route de Port-Vendres
66190 Collioure
phone +33 04 68820668

Hotel La Frégate
Quai Amirauté
66190 Collioure
phone +33 04 68820605

Hôtel Le Mas des citronniers
66190 Collioure
phone +33 04 68820482

Restaurant San Vicens et Vieux Remparts
Avenue Boramar
66190 Collioure
phone +33 04 68820512

Restaurant La Bonne Table
24, avenue Camille-Pelletan
66190 Collioure
phone +33 04 68980908

Restaurant La Balette
Route de Port-Vendres
66190 Collioure
phone +33 04 68820507

Restaurant Le Copacabana
6, boulevard Boramar
66190 Collioure
phone +33 04 68820674

Etablissements Roque
17, route d'Argeles-sur-Mer
66190 Collioure
phone +33 04 68820499

Etablissements Desclaux
3, route d'Argeles-sur-Mer
66190 Collioure
phone +33 04 68820525

colmar (alsace)

Office du tourisme
4, rue des Unterlinden
68000 Colmar
phone +33 03 89206892
www.ot-colmar.fr

Hôtel-Restaurant La Maison des Têtes
19, rue des Têtes
68000 Colmar
phone +33 03 89244343
fax +33 03 89245834
www.la-maison-des-tetes.com

Hôtel-Restaurant Le Maréchal
4, place Six-Montagnes-Noires
68000 Colmar
phone +33 03 89416032
fax +33 03 89245940
www.hotel-le-marechal.com

Hôtel Colombier
7, rue de Turenne
68000 Colmar
phone +33 03 89239600
fax +33 03 89239727
www.hotel-le-colombier.fr

Restaurant Au Fer Rouge
52, Grande Rue
68000 Colmar
phone +33 03 89413724

Restaurant Rendez-vous de Chasse Grand-Hôtel Bristol
7, place de la Gare
68000 Colmar
phone +33 03 89411010
www.grand-hotel-bristol.com

Restaurant Aux Trois Poissons
15, quai de la Poissonnerie
68000 Colmar
phone +33 03 89412521

Restaurant Chez Hansi
23, rue des Marchands
68000 Colmar
phone +33 03 89413784

Les Fameuses Bretzels de Colmar
6, rue des Boulangers
68000 Colmar
phone +33 03 89243243
fax +33 03 89413621

L'Epicerie d'Alsace
54, rue des Marchands
68000 Colmar
phone +33 03 89249622

Better Marie-Elisabeth
Fine foods
9, rue Franklin Roosevelt
68000 Colmar
phone +33 03 89230117
fax +33 03 89418103

Domaine viticole de la Ville de Colmar
2, rue Stauffen
68000 Colmar
phone +33 03 89791187
fax +33 03 89803866

Maison des Vins d'Alsace
12, avenue Foire aux Vins
68012 Colmar
phone +33 03 89201620
fax +33 03 89201630

Maison Pfister
11, rue Marchands
68000 Colmar
phone +33 03 89413361
fax +33 03 89414461

Terroir et Cépages d'Alsace
15, rue des Marchands
68000 Colmar
phone/fax +33 03 89415950

Cave Wolfberger
Chemin Fecht
68000 Colmar
phone +33 03 89304070
fax +33 03 89797825

compiègne (picardy)

Office du tourisme
Place de l'Hôtel-de-Ville
60200 Compiègne
phone +33 03 44400100
www.compiegne.fr

Hôtel Domaine du Bois d'Aucourt
60350 Pierrefonds
phone +33 03 44428034
fax +33 03 44428036
www.boisdaucourt.com

Hôtel Les Beaux-Arts
33, cours Guynemer
60200 Compiègne
phone +33 03 44922626
fax +33 03 44922600
www.bw-lesbeauxarts.com

Restaurant La Part des Anges
18, rue de Bouvines
60200 Compiègne
phone +33 03 44860000

Restaurant Rive Gauche
13, cours Guynemer
60200 Compiègne
phone +33 03 44402999

Restaurant Le Bistrot des Arts
33, cours Guynemer
60200 Compiègne
phone +33 03 44201010

Restaurant Le Palais Gourmand
8, rue du Dahomey
60200 Compiègne
phone +33 03 44401313

Château de Compiègne
60200 Compiègne
phone : +3 3 03 44384702
fax +33 03 44384701

Musée de la figurine historique
28, place de l'Hôtel de Ville
60200 Compiègne
phone : +33 03 44407255
fax +33 03 44202309

Musée Antoine Vivenel
2, rue d'Austerlitz
60200 Compiègne
phone : +33 03 44202604
fax +33 03 44202309

Château de Pierrefonds
Rue Viollet Le Duc
60350 Pierrefonds
phone : +33 03 44427272
fax +33 03 44423659

concarneau (brittany)

Office du tourisme
Quai d'Aiguillon

29100 Concarneau
phone +33 02 98970144
www.tourismeconcarneau.fr

Hôtel-restaurant Les Grandes Roches
Rue des Grandes-Roches
29910 Trégunc
phone +33 02 98976297
fax +33 02 98502919
www.hotel-lesgrandesroches.com

Hôtel-restaurant des Halles
Place de l'Hôtel-de-Ville
Rue Charles-Linement
29900 Concarneau
phone +33 02 98971141
fax +33 02 98505854
www.hoteldeshalles.com

Restaurant Chez Armande
15, avenue du Docteur-Nicolas
29900 Concarneau
phone +33 02 98970076

Restaurant La Coquille
Quai du Moros
29900 Concarneau
phone +33 02 98970852

Restaurant Le Buccin
1, rue Duguay-Trouin
29900 Concarneau
phone +33 02 98505422

Biscuiterie de Concarneau
3, place Saint-Guénolé
29900 Concarneau
phone +33 02 98970767

Conserverie Courtin
3, quai du Moros
5, place Saint-Guénolé
29900 Concarneau
phone +33 02 98970180

Confiserie des Remparts
21, rue Vauban
29900 Concarneau
phone +33 02 98507091

Sidro François Séhédic
Ty Glas
29940 La Forêt-Fouesnant
phone +33 02 98568518

conques (midi-pyrénées)

Office de Tourisme
12320 Conques
phone +33 05 820820803
fax +33 05 65728703
tourisme@conques.fr

Hôtel Le Sainte-Foy
Rue Gonzague Florens
12320 Conques
phone +33 05 65698403
fax +33 05 65728104
www.hotelsaintefoy.fr
hotelsaintefoy@hotelsaintefoy.fr

Hôtel Le Moulin de Cambelong
12320 Conques
phone +33 05 65 72 84 77
fax +33 05 65 72 83 91

www.moulindecambelong.com
domaine-de-cambelong@wanadoo.fr

Auberge Saint-Jacques
Rue Gonzague Florens
12320 Conques
phone +33 05 65728636
fax +33 05 65728247
www.aubergestjacques.fr
info@aubergestjacques.fr

Auberge du Pont Romain
Conques Faubourg
12320 Conques
phone +33 05 65698407
fax +33 05 65698912

Café Restaurant le Charlemagne
M. Alain Garcenot
12320 Conques
phone +33 05 65698150

Grill bar le Conquérant
La Rivière
12320 Conques
phone +33 05 65729050

Bar Brasserie Au Parvis
Place de l'abbatiale
12320 Conques
phone +33 05 65728281

La Boutique du Musée
Produits du Trésor
12320 Conques
phone +33 0 820820803

Atelier de gravure en taille douce
rue Gonzague Florens
12320 Conques
phone +33 05 65698385

Artisan coutelier-dinandier
Rue Emile Roudié
12320 Conques
phone +33 05 65728766

Sculpture et taille de pierre
Atelier Cairn
Rue Gonzague Florens
12320 Conques
phone +33 05 65729135
fax +33 05 65698161

Tapisserie contemporaine de basse lice
La Vaysse
12320 Conques
phone +33 05 65728560

Sculpteur sur bois
La Vaysse
12320 Conques
phone +33 05 65728560

Au tympan de Conques
(Souvenirs, regional crafts)
12320 Conques
phone +33 05 65698616

Aux armes de Conques
(Souvenirs, crafts, books)
12320 Conques
phone +33 05 65728044

La dentellière
Place de l'Eglise

12320 Conques
phone +33 05 65728093

La boutique du Potier
Rue des Ecoles
12320 Conques
phone +33 05 65729201

cordes-sur-ciel (midi-pyrénées)

Office du Tourisme de Cordes-sur-Ciel
Maison Fonpeyrouse
81170 Cordes sur Ciel
phone +33 05 63560052
Fax +33 05 63561952
officedutourisme.cordes@wanadoo.fr

Hotel Château de Laborde
81170 Cordes-Sur-Ciel
phone +33 05 63563563
fax +33 05 63560881
contact@chateaudelaborde.com
www.chateaudelaborde.com

Hotel-Restaurant Le Grand Ecuyer
79, Grand-Rue Raymond VII
81170 Cordes-Sur-Ciel
phone +33 05 63537950
fax +33 05 63537951
grand.ecuyer@thuries.fr
www.thuries.fr

Hostellerie du Vieux Cordes
21, rue Saint-Michel
81170 Cordes-Sur-Ciel
phone +33 05 63537920
fax +33 05 63560247
vieux.cordes@thuries.fr

Hôtel de la Cité
19, Grand-Rue Raimond VII
81170 Cordes-sur-Ciel
phone +33 05 63560353
fax +33 05 63560247
cite@thuries.fr
www.thuries.fr

Hostellerie du Parc
81170 Les Cabannes
phone +33 05 63560259
fax +33 05 63561803
izardclaude2@wanadoo.fr
www.hostellerie-du-parc.com

Restaurant Chez Babar
Le Bourg
81170 Les Cabannes
phone +33 05 63560251
fax +33 05 63560251

Restaurant Les Ormeaux
3, rue Saint Michel—BP 1
81170 Cordes-sur-Ciel
phone +33 05 63561950
fax +33 05 63561950
les-ormeaux@wanadoo.fr
www.lesormeaux.com

Restaurant Etape Occitane
1, place de la Bride
81170 Cordes-sur-Ciel
phone +33 05 63563887
fax +33 05 63563887

Restaurant Chez G & G
12, place de la Bouteillerie
81170 Cordes-sur-Ciel
phone +33 05 63560009
fax +33 05 63560009

Impression à la planche
Maybourn Rowena
4, Gd Rue de la Barbacane
81170 Cordes-sur-Ciel
phone/fax +33 05 63560376
www.rowenamaybourn.com

Céramique Mozaïque
Dugois Gérald
Le Village
81170 Mouzieys-Panens
phone +33 05 63534171 /
06 32410850

Céramique raku et grès
Dupuy Joly Christiane et Thierry
2, rue du Fourmiguier
81170 Cordes-sur-Ciel
phone/fax +33 05 63560074
www.ceramique-dupuyjoly.com

Malaussena-Perret Yvan
55, Grand Rue Raymond VII
81170 Cordes-Sur-Ciel
phone/fax +33 05 63561419

Broderie Jacobs Bernard
La Gaudane
4, rue de la Gaudane
81170 Cordes-sur-Ciel
phone +33 05 63530982
fax +33 05 63531281

Artisan en Broderie
Quenesson Josiane et Robert
81170 Cordes-sur-Ciel
phone +33 05 63539576 /
05 63339825

Sculpteur mosaïste
Kristic Stanko
Jardin de la Mairie
81170 Cordes-sur-Ciel
phone +33 05 63561363
www.catimi.free.fr/stankoktristic.htm

corte (corsica)

Office du tourisme
Citadelle
Caserne Campana
20250 Corte
phone +33 04 9546270
www.corte-tourisme.com

Hôtel Dominique Colonna
Vallée de la Restonica
phone +33 04 95460913
fax +33 04 95462238
www.dominique-colonna.fr

Hôtel Les Jardins de la Glacière
Gorges de la Restonica
20250 Corte
phone +33 04 95452700
fax +33 04 95452701
www.lesjardinsdelaglaciere.com

Hôtel-restaurant Le Refuge
Vallée de la Restonica
20250 Corte
phone +33 04 95460913
fax +33 04 95462238
www.lerefuge.fr.fm

Auberge de la Restonica
Route de Restonica
20250 Corte
phone +33 04 95460958

Auberge Casa Balduina
Le Couvent
20224 Calacuccia
phone +33 04 95480857

Ferme-auberge Osteria di l'Orta
Pont de l'Orta
Casa Guelfucci
20250 Corte
phone +33 04 95610641

Pâtisserie Casanova
6, cours Paoli
20250 Corte
phone +33 04 95460079

Casa di u Legnu
(Wooden toys)
1, place Gaffory
20250 Corte
phone +33 06 8318328

U Salgetu
(Wool)
20218 Ponte-Leccia
phone +33 04 95484379

dinan (brittany)

Office du tourisme de Dinan et du Pays de Rance
9, rue du Château
22100 Dinan
phone +33 02 96876976
www.dinan-tourisme.com

Hôtel L'Ecrin—Restaurant Jean-Pierre Crouzil
22130 Plancoët
phone +33 02 96841024
fax +33 02 96840193
www.crouzil.com

Hôtel-restaurant Manoir du Vaumadeuc
22130 Pleven
phone +33 02 96844617
fax +33 02 96844016
www.vaumadeuc.com

Hôtel-restaurant Château de La Motte
Beaumanoir
35720 Pleugueneuc-Plesder
phone +33 02 23220500
fax +33 02 23220108
www.lamottebeaumanoir.com

Hôtel-restaurant Le Jerzual
26, quai des Talards
Le Port de Dinan
22100 Lanvallay
phone +33 02 96870202
fax +33 02 96870203
www.dinan-hotel-jerzual.com

Hôtel-restaurant Le Challonge
29, place Duguesclin
22100 Dinan
phone +33 02 96871630
fax +33 02 96871631
www.hotel-dinan.fr

Restaurant Chez ma mère Pourcel
3, place des Merciers
22100 Dinan
phone +33 02 96390380

L'Auberge du Pélican
3, rue Haute-Voie
22100 Dinan
phone +33 02 96394705

Restaurant Le Cantorbery
6, rue Sainte-Claire
22100 Dinan
phone +33 02 96390252

Restaurant La Caravelle
14, place Duclos
22100 Dinan
phone +33 02 96390011

Brocantes Galerie de l'Occasion
14, boulevard de Préval
22100 Quevert
phone +33 02 96851922
fax +33 02 96851922

Biscuiterie du Graal
5, Place des Merciers
22100 Dinan
phone +33 02 96392220
fax +33 02 96399320

Biscuiterie Loc Maria
Boutique centre ville : 9, rue du Château
Boutique usine : Route de Dinard
22100 Dinan/Taden
phone +33 02 96870648
www.locmaria.fr

Cadeaaux souvenirs Le Triskell
21, rue de l'Horloge
22100 Dinan
phone +33 02 96394056
fax +33 02 96394056

Cave des Jacobins
3, rue Sainte-Claire
22100 Dinan
phone +33 02 96390382
fax +33 02 96851657
www.cavejacobins.com

Cadeaux Déco Esprit de Campagne
21 bis, rue de la Mittrie
22100 Dinan
phone +33 02 96874657

Cadeaux La Crémaillère
3, rue de l'Apport
22100 Dinan
phone +33 02 96390526

dinard (brittany)

Office du tourisme
2, boulevard Féart
22100 Dinan
phone +33 02 99469412
www.ot-dinard.com

Hôtel-restaurant Grand Hôtel Barrière
46, avenue George-V
35800 Dinard
phone +33 02 99882626
fax +33 02 99882627
www.lucienbarriere.com

Hôtel-restaurant Novotel Thalassa
1, avenue du Château-Hébert
35800 Dinard
phone +33 02 99167810
fax +33 02 99167829
www.accorthalassa.com

Hôtel Villa Reine Hortense
19, rue de la Malouine
35800 Dinard
phone +33 02 99465431
fax +33 02 99881588
www.villa-reine-hortense.com

Hôtel-restaurant des Tilleuls
36, rue de la Gare
35800 Dinard
phone +33 02 99827700
fax +33 02 99827755
www.hotel-des-tilleuls.com

Restaurant Didier Méril
6, rue Yves-Verney
35800 Dinard
phone +33 02 99469574

Restaurant Le Prieuré
1, place du Général-de-Gaulle
35800 Dinard
phone +33 02 99461374

Restaurant La Salle à Manger
25, boulevard Féart
35800 Dinard
phone +33 02 99160795

L'Atelier Manoli. Musée et jardin de sculpture
9, rue du Suet
35780 La Richardais
phone +33 02 99885553
www.manoli.org

dol-de-bretagne (brittany)

Office du tourisme
3, Grande Rue des Stuarts
35120 Dol-de-Bretagne
phone +33 02 99481537
www.pays-de-dol.com

Hôtel-restaurant de Bretagne
17, place Chateaubriand
35120 Dol-de-Bretagne
phone +33 02 99480203
fax +33 02 99482575

Hôtel-restaurant Le Château de Bonaban
35350 La Gouesnière
phone +33 02 99582450
fax +33 02 99582841
www.hotel-chateau-bonaban.com

Restaurant La Bresche Arthur
36, boulevard Deminiac
35120 Dol-de-Bretagne
phone +33 02 99481632
fax +33 02 99480144

Restaurant La Grabotais
4, rue Ceinte
35120 Dol-de-Bretagne
phone +33 02 99481989

Cathédraloscope
Place de la Cathédrale
35120 Dol-de-Bretagne
phone +33 02 99483530
fax +33 02 99481353

Antiquités J. Laick
27, Grand Rue des Stuarts
35120 Dol-de-Bretagne
phone +33 02 99483346

Ty-Breiz
26, rue Lejamptel
35120 Dol-de-Bretagne
phone+33 02 99480623

Ka'Dol Boutic
40, Grande Rue des Stuarts
35120 Dol-de-Bretagne
phone +33 02 99807831

Hodbert Marie-Thérèse
15, avenue Aristide Briand
35120 Dol-de-Bretagne
phone +33 02 99809756

Cultimer France Producteurs Associés
Les Rolandières
35120 Dol-de-Bretagne
phone +33 02 99806060
fax +33 02 99806070

Hesry Stéphane
17 ter, rue Ponts
35120 Dol-de-Bretagne
phone +33 02 99484559

dole (franche-comté)

Office du tourisme du Jura dolois
6, place Jules-Grévy
39100 Dole
phone +33 03 84721122
www.dole.org

Hôtel-restaurant La Balance
47, rue de Courcelles
39600 Arbois
phone +33 03 84374500

Hôtel-restaurant Le Relais Castan
6, square Castan
25000 Besançon
phone +33 03 81650200
www.hotelcastan.fr

Musée Pasteur
Maison natale de Pasteur
43, rue Pasteur
39100 Dole
phone +33 03 84722061
fax +33 03 84721463

Le Chat Noir
28, rue Arènes
39100 Dole
phone+33 03 84720741

Chou Rose
48, rue Arènes

39100 Dole
phone +33 03 84826931

douarnenez (brittany)

Office de tourisme du Pays de Douarnenez
2, rue du Docteur-Mével
29100 Douarnenez
phone +33 02 98921335
www.douarnenez-tourisme.com

Hôtel-restaurant Le Clos de Vallombreuse
7, rue d'Estienne-d'Orves
29100 Douarnenez
phone +33 02 98926364
fax +33 02 98928498
www.closvallombreuse.com

Hôtel-restaurant de la Plage
Sainte-Anne-la-Palud
29550 Plonevez-Porzay
phone +33 02 98925012
fax +33 02 98925654
www.plage.com

Hôtel-auberge de Kerveoch
42, route de Kerveoch
29100 Douarnenez
phone +33 02 98920758
fax +33 02 98920358
www.auberge-kerveoch.com

Au Goûter breton, Crêperie Tudal
36, rue Jean-Jaurès
29100 Douardenez
phone +33 02 98920274

Pâtisserie Chez Lucas
20, rue de Plormach
29100 Douarnenez
phone +33 02 98923724

Sardines Penn Sardin
7, rue Le Breton
29100 Douarnenez
phone +33 02 98927083

evian (rhône-alpes)

Office du tourisme d'Evian
place d'Allinges—B.P. 18
74501 Evian
phone +33 04 50750426

Hotel Oasis
11, boulevard du Bennevy
74500 Evian
phone +33 04 50751338

Hotel Savoy
17, quai Besson
74500 Evian
phone +33 04 50831500

Hotel Continental
65, rue Nationale
74500 Evian
phone +33 04 50753754

Hotel Les Cygnes
8, avenue de Grande-Rive
74500 Evian
phone +33 04 50750101

Hôtel du Palais
69, rue Nationale
74500 Evian
phone +33 04 50750046

Hotel Panorama
Grande Rive
74500 Evian
phone +33 04 50751450

Hotel Terminus
32, avenue de la Gare
74500 Evian
phone +33 04 50751507

Restaurant La Bernolande
1, place du Port
74500 Evian
phone +33 04 50707260

Restaurant Le Campagnard
1 ter, avenue Anna-de-Noailles
74500 Evian
phone +33 04 50749040

Restaurant Le Bourgogne
73, rue Nationale
74500 Evian
phone +33 04 50750105

Restaurant Le Franco-Suisse
Place Jean-Bernex
74500 Evian
phone +33 04 50751474

Restaurant Histoire de goût
1, avenue du Général-Dupas
74500 Evian
phone +33 04 50700998

Restaurant Le Grand Café
5, place du Port
74500 Evian
phone +33 04 50754673

Restaurant La Rotonde
1, place Charles-Cottet
74500 Evian
phone +33 04 50752997

Danou-Traditions
Rue Nationale
74500 Evian-les-Bains
phone+33 04 50756601

Sabatier-Monnin
11, avenue d'Abondance
74500 Evian-les-Bains
phone +33 04 50750428

Le Goarant Lardo
8, rue Monnaie
74500 Evian-les-Bains
phone +33 04 50751661

Atelier de l'Immédiat
(Painter and wood sculptor)
8, rue Pierre Girod
74500 Evian-les-Bains
phone/fax +33 04 50756694

Camaleon Phenix
7, avenue d'Abondance
74500 Evian-les-Bains
phone +33 04 50755478

Kubilai Kahn
(Jewelry)
40, rue Nationale
74500 Evian-les-Bains
phone +33 04 50754860

fécamp (normandy)

Maison du Tourisme de Fécamp
113, rue Alexandre Le Grand—BP 112
76403 Fécamp
phone +33 02 35285101
fax +33 02 35270777
www.fecamptourisme.com

Ferme de la Chapelle
Cote de la Vierge
76400 Fécamp
phone +33 02 35101212
fermedelachapelle@fermedelachapelle.fr

Hôtel d'Angleterre
93, rue de la Plage
76400 Fécamp
phone +33 02 35280160
fax +33 02 35286295
hotel-d-angleterre@wanadoo.fr
www.hotelangleterre.com

Hôtel Normandy
2 bis, avenue Gambetta
76400 Fécamp
phone +33 02 35295511
www.normandy-fecamp.com

L'Escalier
101, quai Brétigny
76400 Fécamp
phone +33 02 35282679
fax +33 02 35100457

Restaurant La Marine
23, quai Vicomté
76400 Fécamp
phone +33 02 35281594

Restaurant Le Maritime
5, place Nicolas Selle
76400 Fécamp
phone +33 02 35282171

Restaurant Le Maupassant
2 bis, avenue Gambetta
76400 Fécamp
phone +33 02 35295511

Casino de Fécamp
Boulevard Albert 1er
76400 Fécamp
phone +33 02 35280166

Le Marché aux Poissons
2, rue du Commandant Riondel
Grand Quai
76403 Fécamp
phone +33 02 35281357
fax +33 02 35288656

Artisan crêpier, Glacier
Place de l'éclipse
76403 Fécamp
phone +33 06 13148710

Bol E Shop
48, rue Maurice Renault

76403 Fécamp
phone +33 02 35 10 78 69

Aux ducs de Fécamp
2, rue des Forts
76403 Fécamp
phone/fax +33 02 35281399

La Fermette
64, route d'Auberville
76400 Ereville
phone +33 02 0235297257

La Maison du Terre-Neuvas
69, rue Emmanuel Foy
76111 Yport

foix (midi-pyrénées)

Office de Tourisme du Pays de Foix
2ç, rue Delcassé—BP 20
09001 Foix
phone +33 05 61651212
fax +33 05 61656463
www.ot-foix.fr
foix.tourisme@wanadoo.fr

Hotel Lons
6, place Duthil
09000 Foix
phone +33 05 34092800
fax +33 05 61026818
hotel-lons-foix@wanadoo.fr

Hotel Pyrene
Le Vignoble
09000 Foix
phone +33 05 61654866
fax +33 05 61654669
hotel.pyrene@wanadoo.fr

Hotel La barbacane
1, av de Lérida
09000 Foix
phone +33 05 61655044
fax +33 05 61027433

Hôtel Du Lac
Lieu dit Couloumié
09000 Foix
phone +33 05 61028888
fax +33 05 61652949

L'echauguette
Rue Paul Laffont
09000 Foix
phone +33 05 61028888
fax +33 05 61652949

Le Sainte-Marthe
21, rue Peyrevidal
09000 Foix
phone +33 05 61028787
fax +33 05 61051900
restaurant@le-saintemarthe.fr

Le Jeu de l'Oie
17, rue Lafaurie
09000 Foix
phone +33 05 61026939

Restaurant Le Mediéval
42, rue des Chapeliers
09000 Foix
phone +33 05 34090172

fax +33 05 34090173
restaurant-le-medieval@wanadoo.fr

Le Phoebus
3, cours Irénée Cros
09000 Foix
phone +33 05 61651042
www.ariege.com/le-phoebus

Au Grilladou
7, rue Lafaurie
09000 Foix
phone +33 05 61640074
fax +33 05 61641950

Croustades sucrées et salées
Martine Crespo
21, rue des Marchands
09000 Foix
phone +33 05 34 09 34 27

Au fil du Temps
3, place Georhes Duthil
09000 Foix
phone +33 05 61651834

La Cloche d'Or
12, rue Lafaurie
09000 Foix
phone +33 05 61653955

Bijoux anciens
Franck Ferme
2, place Lazema
09000 Foix
phone +33 05 61016671

Lou Grani
11, rue Labistour
09000 Foix
phone +33 05 61014437

Cave Fuxéenne
6, rue Peyrevidal
09000 Foix
phone +33 05 61656572

Grande Halles Saint-Volusien
Rue du 19 Mars
09000 Foix
phone +33 05 34098523

fontainebleau (ile-de-france)

Office de Tourisme du Pays de Fontainebleau
4, rue Royale
77300 Fontainebleau
phone +33 01 60749999
www.fontainebleau.fr
www.musee-chateau-fontainebleau.fr

Grand Hôtel de l'Aigle Noir
27, place Napoléon
77300 Fontainebleau
phone/fax +33 01 60746000
www.hotelaiglenoir.fr

Hôtel Napoléon
9, rue Grande
77300 Fontainebleau
phone +33 01 60395050
fax +33 01 64222087

Restaurant Croquembouche

43, rue de France
77300 Fontainebleau
phone +33 01 64220157

Chocolatier Cassel
71, rue Grande
77300 Fontainebleau
phone +33 01 64222959

Epicerie Fine Hédiard
2, rue de France
77300 Fontainebleau
phone +33 01 64224781

Les Terroirs de France
41, rue des Sablons
77300 Fontainebleau
phone +33 01 64225080

fougères (brittany)

Office du tourisme
2, rue Nationale
35300 Fougères
phone +33 02 99941220
www.ot-fougeres.fr

Parc floral de Haute Bretagne
Château de la Foltière
Chambres d'hôtel
35133 Le Châtellier
phone +33 02 99954832
fax +33 02 99954774
www.parcfloralbretagne.com

Hôtel-restaurant Balzac
15, rue Nationale
35300 Fougères
phone +33 02 99994246
fax +33 02 99996543
www.balzachotel.com

Hôtel-restaurant Les Voyageurs
10, place Gambetta
35300 Fougères
phone +33 02 99990820 - 99991417
fax +33 02 99999904

Restaurant Le Haute Sève
37, boulevard Jean-Jaurès
35300 Fougères
phone +33 02 99942339

Restaurant Au Cellier
29, rue Victor-Hugo
35133 Landéan
phone +33 02 99972050

Magasin d'usine JB Martin
47, boulevard Edmond-Roussin
35300 Fougères
phone +33 02 99946060
fax +33 02 99941220

gap (paca)

Office de tourisme de Gap
2A, cours Frédéric-Mistral—BP 41
05000 Gap
phone +33 04 92525656

Hotel L'Ange Roubaud
55, avenue Commandant-Dumont
05000 Gap

phone +33 04 92511070

Hotel Le Carina
Chabanas, route de Veynes
05000 Gap
phone +33 04 92520273

Hotel Le Fons Regina
13, avenue de Fontreyne
05000 Gap
phone +33 04 92539899

Hotel Le Michelet
Place de la Gare
05000 Gap
phone +33 04 92512786

Hotel Le Verdun
20, boulevard de la Libération
05000 Gap
phone +33 04 92258850

Hotel Gapotel
18, avenue Emile-Didier
05000 Gap
phone +33 04 92523737

Restaurant Le Biberon
6, rue des Cordiers
05000 Gap
phone +33 04 92521325

Restaurant Le Tourton des Alpes
1, rue des Cordiers/6, rue Jean-Eymar
05000 Gap
phone +33 04 92539091

Restaurant Les Olivades
Route de Veynes, quartier de Malcombe
05000 Gap
phone +33 04 92526680

Le Jardin du coeur
1, place de la République
05000 Gap
phone +33 04 92515923

Le Tourton des Alpes
1, rue des Cordiers
05000 Gap
phone +33 04 92539091

Le Pressoir
10, place de la République
05000 Gap
phone +33 04 92493871

Les Vignerons du Mont Ventoux
5, rue Cheminots
05000 Gap
phone +33 04 92523075

gien (centre)

Office du tourisme
Place Jean-Jaurès
45500 Gien
phone +33 02 38672528

Chambre d'hôtel
Domaine de Sainte-Barbe
Route de Lorris
45500 Gien
phone +33 02 38675953
fax +33 02 38672896

Restaurant Le Régency
6, quai Lenoir
45500 Gien
phone +33 02 38670496

S.N. des Faïenceries de Gien
Place de la Victoire
45500 Gien
phone +33 02 38670005
fax +33 02 38 674492

La Boutique d'usine
Et le Musée de la Faïencerie
78, place de la Victoire
45500 Gien
phone +33 02 38678999
fax +33 02 38674492

giverny (normandy)

Syndicat d'Initiative des Andelys et Région
Rue Philippe Augutse
27700 Les Andelys
phone +33 02 32544193

Auberge Musardière
123, rue Claude Monet
27620 Giverny
phone +33 02 32210318
fax +33 02 32216000

Hôtel Les 3 Trois Saint-Pierre
& Auberge Les Canisses
Le Goulet
27600 Saint-Pierre la Garenne
phone +33 02 32525061
fax +33 02 32525074
www.lescanisses.com

Hôtel Moderne
Place de la Gare
27140 Gisors
phone +33 02 32552351
fax +33 02 32550875
hotel-moderne@free.fr
www.hotel-moderne-gisors.fr

Hôtel Normandy
1, avenue Pierre Mendès-France
27200 Vernon
phone +33 02 32519797
fax +33 02 32210166
www.le-normandy.net

Auberge du Vieux Moulin
21, rue de Falaise
27620 Giverny
phone +33 02 32514615

Restaurant Les Jardins de Giverny
1, rue Milieu
27620 Giverny
phone +33 02 32216080

Restaurant Les Nymphéas
109, rue Claude Monet
27620 Giverny
phone +33 02 32212031

Restaurant Terra Café
99, rue Claude Monet
27620 Giverny
phone +33 02 32519461

Restaurant La Bonne Etable

9, rue Falaise
27620 Giverny
phone +33 02 32516632

Restaurant La Terrasse
87, rue Claude Monet
27620 Giverny
phone +33 02 32513609

Restaurant Baudy Giverny
81, rue Claude Monet
27620 Giverny
phone +33 02 32211003

Fondation Claude Monet
Et La Boutique
84, rue Claude Monet
27620 Giverny
phone +33 02 32512821
fax +33 02 32515418

Le Verger de Giverny
1, rue Ste Geneviève
La Chapelle Saint Ouen
27620 Bois-Jérôme
phone +33 02 32512936
fax +33 02 32511744

gordes (paca)

Office du tourisme
Le château
84220 Gordes
phone +33 04 90720275

Hôtel-restaurant La Bastide
Le village
84220 Gordes
phone +33 04 90721212
fax +33 04 90720520
www.bastide-de-gordes.com

Hôtel-restaurant Les Bories
Route de l'abbaye de Sénanque
84220 Gordes
phone +33 04 90720051
fax +33 04 90720122
www.hotellesbories.com

Hôtel Le Gordos
Route de Cavaillon
84220 Gordes
phone +33 04 90720075
fax +33 04 90720700
www.hotel-le-gordos.com

Restaurant L'Estellan
Quartier La Nouï, Les Imberts
84220 Gordes
phone +33 04 90720490

Apel Michèle
Rue de l'Eglise
84220 Gordes
phone +33 04 90720039

Co.To.Rel
6, place Château
84220 Gordes
phone +33 04 90720151

Imagine
Place Château
84220 Gordes
phone +33 04 90720494

Acanthe
Rue Murs
84220 Gordes
phone +33 04 90721572

Office du tourisme
4, cours Jonville
50406 Granville
phone +33 02 33913003
www.ville-granville.fr

Hôtel Le Grand Large
5, rue de la Falaise
50406 Granville
phone +33 02 33911919
www.hotel-le-grand-large.com

Hôtel La Beaumonderie
20, route de Coutances
50290 Bréville-sur-Mer
phone +33 02 33503636
www.la-beaumonderie.com

Hôtel du Fort et des îles
Chausey
phone +33 02 33502502

Hôtel L'Inconnu
20, rue Paul Poirier
Chausey
phone +33 02 33613021
fax +33 02 33613021

Restaurant La Citadelle
34, rue du Port
50400 Granville
phone +33 02 33503410

Restaurant Le Cabestan
70, rue du Port
50400 Granville
phone +33 02 33616158

Restaurant Pierrot L'Hippocampe
16, rue Clément Desmaisons
50400 Granville
phone +33 02 33 50 09 29

Restaurant du Port
19, rue du Port
50400 Granville
phone +33 02 33500055
fax +33 02 33504010

Restaurant Le Phare
11, rue du Port
50400 Granville
phone +33 02 33501294

Restaurant de la Poste
8, rue de l'Abreuvoir
50400 Granville
phone +33 02 33500225

Crêperie L'Echaugette
24, rue Saint-Jean
La Haute Ville
50400 Granville
phone +33 02 33505187

Restaurant Chez François
2 rue Jérémie
50530 Genêts

Musée et Jardin Christian Dior
Villa Les Rhumbs
50400 Granville
phone +33 02 33614821
fax +33 02 33619915

Théze et Théo
71, rue Couraye
50400 Granville
phone +33 02 33618706

Marie Famille
100, rue Couraye
50400 Granville
phone +33 02 33518263

La Caverne d'Alain
2, rue Générale Patton
50400 Granville
phone +33 02 33502215

La P'tite Boutique
3, rue St. Sauveur
50400 Granville
phone +33 02 33695093

Office du tourisme
1, place du Marché-au-Bois
44350 Guérande
phone +33 02 40249671
www.ot-guerande.fr

Hôtel-restaurant Le Fort de l'Océan
La pointe du Croisic
44490 Le Croisic
phone +33 02 40157777
fax +33 02 40157780
www.fort-ocean.com

Hôtel-restaurant La Bretesche
44780 Missillac
phone +33 02 51768696
fax +33 02 40669947
www.bretesche.com

Hôtel-restaurant Les Voyageurs
Place du 8-Mai
44350 Guérande
phone +33 02 40249013

Restaurant Les Remparts
14, boulevard du Nord
44350 Guérande
phone +33 02 40249069

Restaurant Le Vieux Logis
1, place de la Psalette
44350 Guérande
phone +33 02 40620973

Crêperie La Salorge
12, rue de la Croix-Serot
Saillé
44350 Guérande
phone +33 02 40151419

La Maison des Paludiers
18 rue des Prés-Garnier Saillé
44350 Guérande
phone +33 02 40622196

Musée des Marais Salants
29 bis, rue Pasteur
44740 Batz-sur-Mer
phone +33 02 40238279

Office de Tourisme de Honfleur
Quai Lepaulmier
14600 Honfleur
phone +33 02 31892330
fax +33 02 31893182
www.ot-honfleur.fr

Hôtel des Loges
18, rue Brûlée
14600 Honfleur
phone +33 02 31893826
fax +33 02 31894279
hoteldesloges@wandoo.fr
www.hoteldesloges.com

Castel Albertine
19, cours Albert-Manuel
14600 Honfleur
phone +33 02 31988556
fax +33 02 31988318
info@honfleurhotel.com
www.honfleur-hotels.com

La Maison de Lucie
44, rue des Capucins
14600 Honfleur
phone +33 02 31144040
fax +33 02 31144041
www.lamaisondelucie.com
info@lamaisondelucie.com

Hôtel Le Cheval Blanc
2, quai des Passagers
14600 Honfleur
phone +33 02 31816500
fax +33 02 31895280
lechevalblanc@wanadoo.fr
www.hotel-honfleur.com

L'Absinthe Hôtel
1, rue de la Ville
14600 Honfleur
phone +33 02 31892323
fax +33 02 31895360
www.absinthe.fr

Hôtel Antares
Rue Saint-Clair
14600 La Rivière Saint Sauveur
phone +33 02 31891010
fax +33 02 31895857
info@antares-honfleur.com
www.antares-honfleur.com

Les Deux Ponts
20, quai Quarantaine
14600 Honfleur
phone +33 02 31890437
www.Lesdeuxponts.fr

Restaurant Au Vieux Honfleur
13, rue Saint-Etienne
14600 Honfleur
phone +33 02 31891531

Restaurant Entre Terre et Mer
12, place Hamelin
14600 Honfleur

phone +33 02 31897060
www.restaurants-honfleur.com
L'Absinthe
10, quai Quarantaine
14600 Honfleur
phone +33 02 31893900
www.absinthe.fr

Au Gars Normand
8, quai des Passagers
14600 Honfleur
phone +33 02 31890528

La Bisquine
54, quai Sainet-Catherine
14600 Honfleur
phone +33 02 31893715

La Grenouille
16, quai Quarantaine
14600 Honfleur
phone +33 02 31890424

Vit Marie
18, place Hamelin
14600 Honfleur
phone +33 02 31894265

La Belle Frégate
26, rue Montpensier
4600 Honfleur
phone +33 02 31892215

Ca Me Dit Dimanches et Fêtes
32, place Hamelin
14600 Honfleur
phone +33 02 31988150

Evasion Voyages
6, rue Haute
14600 Honfleur
phone +33 02 31148998

Office du tourisme
3, avenue Ambroise-Thomas
83400 Hyères
phone +33 04 94018450

Hotel Casino des Palmiers, 1
avenue Ambroise-Thomas
83400 Hyères
phone +33 04 94128080

Etap Hôtel
14, avenue de la 1ère-Division-Brosset
83400 Hyères
phone +33 08 92680796

Hôtel du Parc
7, boulevard Pasteur
83400 Hyères
phone +33 04 94650665

Hotel Ibis Centre
Avenue Jean-Moulin
83400 Hyères
phone +33 04 94005050

Hotel Le Lion d'or
2, rue de la République
83400 Hyères
phone +33 04 94652555

Hotel Le Portalet
4, rue de Limans
83400 Hyères
phone +33 04 94653940

Hotel Les Orangers
64, avenue des Îles-d'Or
83400 Hyères
phone +33 04 94005511

Hotel Les Printanières
20, impasse Saint-Joseph
83400 Hyères
phone +33 04 94005252

Restaurant Cannelle Boutique
22, rue de Limans
83400 Hyères
phone +33 04 94653113

Restaurant Guillaume Tell
9, avenue Gambetta
83400 Hyères
phone +33 04 94650272

Restaurant La Fontaine d'Aristée
20, impasse Saint-Joseph
83400 Hyères
phone +33 04 94005252

Restaurant La Taverne royale
28, rue de Limans
83400 Hyères
phone +33 04 94652188

Restaurant L'Atrium
Avenue Jean-Moulin
83400 Hyères
phone +33 04 94386124

Restaurant Le Bistrot de Marius
1, place Massillon
83400 Hyères
phone +33 04 94358838

Restaurant Le Café italien
5, avenue des Îles-d'Or
83400 Hyères
phone +33 04 94003805

Restaurant Le Chaudron magique
8, place Massillon
83400 Hyères
phone +33 04 94353845

Au Jardin des Roses
3, rue Porches
83400 Hyères
phone +33 04 94652341

Baladins Cadeaux
4, place Massillon
83400 Hyères
phone/fax +33 04 94357337

Chriss Provence
28, rue Massillon
83400 Hyères
phone +33 04 94654268

Design Shop
32, avenue Édith Cawell
83400 Hyères
phone +33 04 94484280

La Nature en Provence
4, rue Portalet
83400 Hyères
phone +33 04 94356652

laon (picardy)

Office du tourisme
Place du Parvis-Gauthier-de-Mortagne
02000 Laon
phone +33 03 23202862
www.laonnois.com
www.tourisme-paysdelaon.com

Hôtel-restaurant Domaine du Château de Barive
02350 Sainte-Preuve
phone +33 03 23221515
fax +33 03 23220839
www.chateau-de-barive.com

Hôtel-restaurant La Bannière de France
11, rue Franklin-Roosevelt
02000 Laon
phone +33 03 23232144
fax +33 03 23233156
www.hoteldelabannieredefrance.com

Hôtel-restaurant La Tour du Roy
02140 Vervins
phone +33 03 23980011
fax +33 03 23980072
www.latourduroy.com

Hostellerie Saint-Vincent
111, avenue Charles-de-Gaulle
02000 Laon
phone +33 03 23234243
fax +33 03 23792255
www.stvincent-laon.com

Restaurant La Petite Auberge
45, boulevard Brossolette
02000 Laon
phone +33 3 23230238

Le Relais Charlemagne
4, rue de Laon
028400 Samoussy
phone +33 03 23222150

La Toison d'Art (SARL)
54, rue Eugène Leduc
02000 Laon
phone +33 03 23232303
fax +33 03 23234682

Les Merlettes
5, place Marché
02000 Laon
phone +33 03 23201239

Prélude
32, rue Eugène Leduc
02000 Laon
phone +33 03 23794833

la rochelle (poitou-charentes)

Office de tourisme
Place de la Petite-Sirène
17000 La Rochelle
phone +33 05 46411468
www.larochelle-tourisme.com

Hôtel de la Monnaie
3, rue de la Monnaie
17000 La Rochelle
phone +33 05 46506565
fax +33 05 46506319
www.hotel-monnaie.com

Hotel France Angleterre & Champlain
20, rue Rambaud
17000 La Rochelle
phone +33 05 46412399
fax +33 05 46411519
www.bw-fa-champlain.com

Restaurant Richard Coutanceau
Plage de la Concurrence
17000 La Rochelle
phone +33 05 46414819

Restaurant Le Comptoir du Sud
4, rue de la Chaîne
17000 La Rochelle
phone +33 05 46410608

Restaurant Le Comptoir des Voyages
22, rue Saint-Jean-du-Pérot
17000 La Rochelle
phone +33 05 46506260

Bistrot La Guilbrette
16, rue de la Chaîne
17000 La Rochelle
phone +33 05 46415705

Cognac et pineau Bossuet
21, rue Gargoulleau
17000 La Rochelle
phone +33 05 46413192

lille (nord-pas-de-calais)

Office du tourisme de Lille
Palais Rihour, place Rihour—BP 205
59002 Lille
phone +33 0891 562004 (from France),
+33 0359 579400 (from abroad)
www.lilletourisme.com

Hôtel des Tours
27, rue des Tours
59000 Lille
phone +33 03 59574700

Hôtel de la Treille
7-9, place Louise-de-Bettignies
59000 Lille
phone +33 03 20554546

Agora Hôtel
14, rue du Molinel
59000 Lille
phone +33 03 20552511

Hôtel Le Coq hardi
34, place de la Gare
59000 Lille
phone +33 03 20060589

Hôtel Mister Bed
57, rue de Béthune
59000 Lille
phone +33 03 20129696

Hôtel Continental
11, place de la Gare
59000 Lille
phone +33 03 20062224

Restaurant La Chicorée
15, place Rihour
59000 Lille
phone +33 03 20548152

Restaurant Les 3 Brasseurs
18-22, place de la Gare
59000 Lille
phone +33 03 20064625

Restaurant Aux Moules
34, rue de Béthune
59000 Lille
phone +33 03 20571246

Restaurant La Terrasse des remparts
Logis de la Porte-de-Gand
59000 Lille
phone +33 03 20067474

Restaurant La Petite Table
59, rue de la Monnaie
59000 Lille
phone +33 03 20556047

Restaurant Le Lion bossu
1, rue Saint-Jacques
59000 Lille
phone +33 03 20060688

Restaurant Le Flam's
8, rue de Pas
59000 Lille
phone +33 03 20541838

Alice délice
Tout pour la cuisine
5, rue Esquermoise
59800 Lille

Artop
(Contemporary art)
83, rue de la Monnaie
59000 Lille
phone +33 03 20 42 12 12

Bernardaud art
(Interior design)
44, rue de la Grande Chaussée
59800 Lille
phone +33 03 28 38 17 07

Claude Le Mevel
Antiquités Brocante
12, rue Basse
59000 Lille

loches (centre)

Office du tourisme
Place de la Marne
37600 Loches
phone +33 02 47918282
www.loches-tourainecotesud.com

Hotel-restaurant Chateau d'Artigny
37250 Montbazon
phone +33 02 47343030
fax +33 02 47343039
www.slh.com

Hotel-restaurant Château Belmont
57, rue Groison
37100 Tours
phone +33 02 47414111
fax +33 02 47516872
www.relaischateaux.com/bardet

Hotel-restaurant Georges Sand
39, rue Quinefol
37600 Loches
phone +33 02 47593974
fax +33 02 47915575
www.hotelrestaurant-georgesand.com

Hotel de France
6, via Picois
37600 Loches
phone +33 02 47590032
fax +33 02 47592866
www.hoteldefranceloches.com

Culture Thé
6, Grande Rue
37600 Loches
phone +33 02 47593935

Maison Galland
Produits locaux
Les Bournaichères
37600 Betz-le-Château
phone +33 02 47923085
fax +33 02 47923128
www.les-bournaicheres.fr

Côté Déco
21, Grande Rue
37600 Loches
phone +33 02 47590102

Graine de Malice
10, rue Agnès Sorel
37600 Loches
phone +33 02 47940249

Jeanne-Marie de Jadis
8, place Hôtel de Ville
37600 Loches
phone +33 02 47595979

Le P'tit Kado
33, Grande Rue
37600 Loches
phone +33 02 47594118

manosque (paca)

Office de tourisme de Manosque
Place du docteur Joubert
04100 Manosque
phone +33 04 92721600
fax +33 04 92725898
www.manosque-tourisme.com

Hôtel Le pré Saint-Michel
Montée de la Mort d'Imbert
Route de Dauphin
04100 Manosque
phone +33 04 92721427
fax +33 04 92725304
www.presaintmichel.com

Hôtel Le mas de Quintrands
RN 96—Route de Sisteron
04100 Manosque
phone +33 04 92723103

fax +33 04 92874807
www.lemasdesquintrands.com

Hôtel François 1er
18, rue Guilhempierre
04100 Manosque
phone +33 04 92 72 07 99
fax +33 04 92875485

Hostellerie de la Fuste
Route d'Oraison, lieu-dit la Fuste
04210 Valensole
phone +33 04 92720595
fax +33 04 92729293
www.lafuste.com

Bel'Alp Hôtel
Avenue de Lattre de Tassigny
04100 Manosque
phone +33 04 92726682
fax +33 04 92720894
www.hotel-belalp.com

Hôtel du Terreau
21, Place du Terreau
04100 Manosque
phone +33 04 92721550
fax +33 04 92728042

Restaurant Campanile
RN 96—Carrefour de Sisteron
04100 Manosque
phone +33 04 92717350
fax +33 04 92717389
www.campanile.fr

Restaurant Mercure
Boulevard du Général de Gaulle
04100 Manosque
phone +33 04 92877858
fax +33 04 92726660
www.mercure.com

menton (paca)

Office du Tourisme de Menton
8, avenue Boyer—BP 239
06506 Menton
phone +33 04 92417676
fax +33 04 92417696
tourisme@menton.fr

Résidence de Vacances El Paradiso
71, porte de France
06500 Menton
phone +33 04 93357402
fax +33 04 92109676
www.univac.net

Résidence Maeva
17, rue Partouneaux
06500 Menton
phone +33 04 39575102
fax +33 04 93286780

Hôtel des Ambassdeurs
3, rue Partouneaux
06500 Menton
phone +33 04 93287575
fax +33 04 93356232
www.ambassadeurs-menton.com

Hôtel Royal Westminster
1510, promenade du Soleil
06500 Menton

phone +33 04 93286969
fax +33 04 92101230

Hôtel Riva
600, Promenade du Soleil
06500 Menton
phone +33 04 92109210
fax +33 04 93288787
www.rivahotel.com

Hôtel Princess & Richmond
617, Promenade du Soleil
06500 Menton France
phone +33 04 93358020
fax +33 04 930574020
www.princess-richmond.com

Best Western Hôtel Prince de Galles
4, Av. du Général de Gaulle
06500 Menton
phone +33 04 93282121
fax +33 04 93359291
www.princedegalles.com

Hôtel Paris Rome
79, porte de France
phone +33 04 93357345
fax +33 04 93352930
www.paris-rom.com

Restaurant Don Ciccio
11, Rue saint michel
06500 Menton
phone +33 04 93579292

Restaurant Le Versailles
15, avenue Verdun
06500 Menton
phone +33 04 92410612

Restaurant Le Bruit Qui Court
31 quai Bonaparte
06500 Menton
phone +33 04 93359464

Restaurant Plage Napoléon
13, Promenade de la Mer
06500 Menton
phone +33 04 92109260

Restaurant Balico
3, Place aux Herbes
06500 Menton
phone +33 04 93416699

Restaurant Au Pistou
9, quai Gordon Bennett
06500 Menton
phone +33 04 93574589

La Pescaccia Chez Tiziana
7, Promenade de la Mer
06500 Menton
phone +33 04 93352833

Le Café du Vieux Port
9, quai Bonaparte
06500 Menton
phone/fax +33 04 92410568

Maison du patrimoine
5, rue Ciapetta
06500 Menton
phone +33 04 92103366
fax +33 04 93284685
Hôtel d'Adhémar de Lantagnac

24, rue Saint-Michel
06500 Menton
phone +33 04 22109710
fax +33 04 93284685

Saveurs d'Eléonor
Place du marché
06500 Menton
phone +33 04 93576001

Les Huileries du Soleil
5, rue Bréa
06500 Menton
phone +33 04 92073255
fax +33 04 92073256

Le Marché Gourmand
13, quai Bonaparte
06500 Menton
phone +33 04 93578542

Comtesse du Barry
36, rue Partouneaux
06500 Menton
phone +33 04 93353505
fax +33 04 93354200

metz (lorraine)

Office de Tourisme
Place d'Armes—BP 80367
57007 Metz Cedex 1
phone +33 0387 555376
tourisme@ot.mairie-metz.fr

Hôtel La Citadelle
5, avenue Ney
57000 Metz
phone +33 03 87171717
fax +33 03 87171718

Hôtel de la Cathedrale
25, place de chambre
57000 Metz
phone +33 03 87750002
fax +33 03 87754075

Hôtel Novotel
Centre Saint-Jacques
57000 Metz
phone +33 03 87373839
fax +33 03 87361000

Hôtel du Theatre
Port Saint-Marcel
3, rue du Pont Saint-Marcel
57000 Metz
phone +33 03 87311010
fax +33 03 87300466

Hôtel Mercure
29, place Saint-Thiébault
57000 Metz
phone +33 03 87385050
fax +33 03 87754818

Hôtel Le Royal
23, avenue Foch
57000 Metz
phone +33 03 87668111
fax +33 03 87561316

Holiday Inn
1, rue Félix Savart / Technopôle
57070 Metz

phone +33 03 87399450
fax +33 03 87399455

Auberge du Mini Golf
Île du Saulcy
57000 Metz
phone +33 03 87307402
fax +33 03 87307402

Au gourmet alsacien
22, rue du Coëtlosquet
57000 Metz
phone +33 03 87360062
fax +33 03 87365864

Restaurant L'antre deux
3, rue des Parmentiers
57000 Metz
phone +33 03 87373149

Restaurant El Theatris
2, place de la Comédie
57000 Metz
phone +33 03 87560202
fax +33 03 87566548

Restaurant L'ntrée des artistes
16, place de Chambre
57000 Metz
phone +33 03 87752408
fax +33 03 87751713

Restaurant L'Epicurien
33, rue Vigne Saint Avold
57000 Metz
phone +33 03 87366911
fax +33 03 87366911

C'est Comme Ça
Design
9, rue Dupont des Loges
57000 Metz
phone +33 03 87210018

Création en carton
Tine Krumhorn
1 bis, rue Maurice Barrès
57000 Metz
phone +33 03 87769620

millau (midi-pyrénées)

Office de Tourisme
1, place du Beffroi—BP 331
12103 Millau
phone +33 05 65600242
fax +33 05 65609508
office.tourisme.millau@wanadoo.fr

Cévenol Hôtel
115, rue du Rajol
12100 Millau
phone +33 05 6560744
fax +33 05 65608599
cevenol@wanadoo.fr
www.cevenol-hotel.fr

Deltour Hôtel
Chemin de sallèles, cap du Crès
12100 Millau
phone +33 05 65608525
fax +33 05 65608589
www.detourhotel.com

Hericelea Hôtel Sport

Rue Louis Balsan
12100 Millau
phone +33 05 65611554
info@millau-larzac.com

Hôtel des Causses (Logis de France)
56, avenue Jean Jaurès
12100 Millau
phone +33 05 65600319
fax +33 05 65608690
contact@hotel-des-causses.com
www.hotel-des-causses.com

Hôtel Emma Calvé
28, avenue Jean Jaurès
12100 Millau
phone +33 05 65601349
fax +33 05 65609375
hotel.emmacalve@wanadoo.fr
www.ifrance.com

Hôtel La Capelle
7, place de la Fraternité
12100 Millau
phone +33 05 65601472
fax +33 05 65602269
contact@hotel-millau-capelle.com
www.hotel-millau-capelle.com

Hôtel La Musardière
34, avenue de la République
12100 Millau
phone +33 05 65602063
fax +33 05 65597813

Restaurant Au Bec Fin
22, rue de la Capelle
12100 Millau
phone +33 05 65606304

Restaurant Au Jeu de Paume
2, rue Saint-Antoine
12100 Millau
phone +33 05 65602512

Aubgerde de la Borie Blanque
La Borie blanche
12100 Millau
phone +33 05 65608588

Crêperie Le Chien à la fenêtre
10, rue Peyrollière
12100 Millau
phone +33 05 65604922

Golf Café
Avenue de Millau Plage
12100 Millau
phone +33 05 65613557

Le Jardin Bleu
7, rue Peyrollière
12100 Millau
phone +33 05 65616239

Le Pot d'Etain
115, rue du Rajol
12100 Millau
phone +33 05 65607444

Les Deux Vallées
87, avenue Jean-Jaurès
12100 Millau
phone +33 05 65613473

Musée de Millau

Hôtel de Pégayrolles
Place Foch
12100 Millau
phone +33 05 65590108

Maison de la peau et du gant à Millau
1, rue Saint-Antoine
12100 Millau
phone +33 05 65612593
fax 05 65 613587
www.cuir-gant-millau.com

Maison Fabre
(Boutique)
2, boulevard Gambetta
12100 Millau
phone +33 05 65605824

minerve (languedoc-roussillon)

Syndicat d'Initiative de Minerve
Hôtel de Ville
2 rue des Martyrs
34210 Minerve
phone +33 04 68918143
www.ot-herault.com

Relais-restaurant Chantovent
17, Grand Rue
34210 Minerve
phone +33 04 68911418
fax +33 04 68918199

Contact Hôtel
115, avenue Aube Rouge
34170 Castelnau-le-Lez
phone +33 04 67795060

Contact Hôtel
10, avenue Alizées
34300 Le Cap d'Agde
phone +33 04 67267780

Hôtel Restaurant Pont de Lunel
RN 113—Chemin du Pont de Lunel
34400 Lunel
phone +33 04 67710162

Maynadier Alain Resto Grill
1, rue du Porche
34210 Minerve
phone +33 04 68912761

Senteurs et Couleurs du Sud
(Souvenirs, gifts)
1, rue de la Tour
34210 Minerve

montélimar (rhône-alpes)

Office du tourisme
Les Allées provençales
Avenue Rochemaure
26200 Montélimar
phone +33 04 75010020

Hotel Auberge La Pignata
106, avenue Jean-Jaurès
26200 Montélimar
phone +33 04 75018700

Hotel Blue Gin Café
3, place Saint-Martin
26200 Montélimar

phone +33 04 75013946

Hostellerie des Pins
148, route de Marseille
26200 Montélimar
phone +33 04 75011588

Hôtel Beau Soleil
14 bis, boulevard du Pêcher
26200 Montélimar
phone +33 04 75011980

Hôtel Dauphiné Provence
41, avenue Général-de-Gaulle
26200 Montélimar
phone +33 04 75924040

Hôtel du Printemps
Chemin de la Manche
26200 Montélimar
phone +33 04 75010680

Hôtel Pierre
7, place des Clercs
26200 Montélimar
phone +33 04 75013316

Sphinx Hôtel
19, boulevard Marre-Desmarais
26200 Montélimar
phone +33 04 75018664

Restaurant Aire Campagne
Avenue de Villeneuve
26200 Montélimar
phone +33 04 75511814

Restaurant Au Bonheur du jour
14, place du Temple
26200 Montélimar
phone +33 04 75532420

Restaurant Aux Gourmands
8, place du Marché
26200 Montélimar
phone +33 04 75011621

Restaurant L'Amandier
5, rue du Lion-d'Or
26200 Montélimar
phone +33 04 75537229

Restaurant La Petite France
34, impasse Raymond-Daujat
26200 Montélimar
phone +33 04 75460794

Restaurant Le Colonel Moutarde
6, rue Chemin-Neuf
26200 Montélimar
phone +33 04 75518631

Le Chaudron d'Or
7, avenue du 52e RI—BP 171
26204 Montélimar Cedex
phone +33 04 75010395
fax +33 04 75530875

Lor Nougat
Parc d'activités Fortuneau
26202 Montélimar
phone +33 04 75015555
fax +33 04 75520805

Nougat Chabert et Guillot
9, rue Charles Chabert
26200 Montélimar
phone +33 04 75922020
fax +33 04 75922030

Magasin d'usine
Place de la gare
9, rue Charles Chabert
26200 Montélimar
phone +33 04 75008213

Nougat Diane de Poytiers
99, avenue Jean Jaurès
26200 Montélimar
phone +33 04 75016702
diane-de-poytiers@wanadoo.fr

Nougats Delavant
40, rue Pierre Julien
26200 Montélimar
phone +33 04 75017688

moustiers-sainte-marie (paca)

Office de tourisme
Place de l'Eglise
04360 Moustiers-Sainte-Marie
phone +33 04 92746784

Hotel Le Baldaquin
Place Clérissy
04360 Moustiers-Sainte-Marie
phone +33 04 92746392

Hotel Le Belvédère
Rue Orville
04360 Moustiers-Sainte-Marie
phone +33 04 92746604

Hotel La Bonne Auberge
Route de Castellane
04360 Moustiers-Sainte-Marie
phone +33 04 92746618

Hotel Le Relais
Place du Couvent
04360 Moustiers-Sainte-Marie
phone +33 04 92746610

Restaurant La Bastide de Moustiers
Chemin de Quinson
04360 Moustiers-Sainte-Marie
phone +33 04 92704747
fax +33 04 92704748
contact@bastide-moustiers.com
www.bastide-moustiers.com/

Restaurant Le Bellevue
Le Village
04360 Moustiers-Sainte-Marie
phone +33 04 92746606

Restaurant Le Blacas
Chemin de Quinson
04360 Moustiers-Sainte-Marie
phone +33 04 92746559
fax +33 04 92746352
leblacas@wanadoo.fr

Restaurant Les Comtes
Rue Bourgade
04360 Moustiers-Sainte-Marie
phone +33 04 92746388

Restaurant Côté Jardin
Chemin Maladrerie
04360 Moustiers-Sainte-Marie
phone +33 04 92746891

Restaurant L'Etoile de Mer
04360 Moustiers-Sainte-Marie
phone +33 04 92746224

Restaurant Ferme Sainte Cécile
Quartier Saint-Michel
04360 Moustiers-Sainte-Marie
phone +33 04 92746418

Restaurant Les Santons
Place de l'Eglise
04360 Moustiers-Sainte-Marie
phone +33 04 92746648

Restaurant La Treille Muscate
Place de l'Eglise
04360 Moustiers-Sainte-Marie
phone +33 04 92746431
fax +33 04 92 74 63 75
la.treille.muscate@wanadoo.fr

nancy (lorraine)

Office du tourisme
Place Stanislas
54000 Nancy
phone +33 03 85352241
www.ot-nancy.fr

Hôtel Le Grand Hotel de la Reine
2, place Stanislas
54000 Nancy
phone +33 03 83350301
fax +33 03 83328604
www.hoteldelareine.com

Hotel Crystal
5, rue Chanzy
54000 Nancy
phone +33 03 83175400
fax +33 03 83175430
www.bestwestern.fr/hotelcrystal

Restaurant Cap Marine
60, rue Stanislas
54000 Nancy
phone +33 03 83 37 05 03

Restaurant La Toque Blanche
1, rue Monseigneur-Trouillet
54000 Nancy
phone +33 03 83301720

Restaurant La Mignardise
28, rue Stanislas
54000 Nancy
phone +33 03 83322022

Restaurant Les Agaves
2, rue des Carmes
54000 Nancy
phone +33 03 83321414

Restaurant Aux Bouchons Lyonnais
15, rue des Maréchaux
54000 Nancy
phone +33 03 83375577

Restaurant Les Nouveaux Abattoirs
4, boulevard d'Austrasie

54000 Nancy
phone +33 03 83354625
Restaurant Les Pissenlits
25 bis, rue des Ponts
54000 Nancy
phone +33 03 83374397

Brasserie L'Excelsior
50, rue Henri-Poincaré
54000 Nancy
phone +33 03 83352457

Epicerie fine Chez Jean-Marie
Marché couvert
Place Henri-Mengin
54000 Nancy
phone +33 06 80424528

Confrérie gourmande du macaron
5, rue Saint-Nicolas
54000 Nancy
phone +33 03 83352774

Epicerie fine Gaulard
1, rue Saint-Nicolas
54000 Nancy
phone +33 03 83323210

Daum—Art verrier
14, place Stanislas
54000 Nancy
phone +33 03 83322165

Baccarat
2, rue des Dominicains
54000 Nancy
phone +33 03 83305511

Design
4, rue Saint-Nicolas
54000 Nancy
phone +33 03 83328557

Horizons
35 ter, rue Saint-Nicolas
54000 Nancy
phone +33 03 83325280

Adéquat
Tissus
1, rue du Général Hoche
54000 Nancy
phone +33 03 83402747

narbonne (languedoc-roussillon)

Office de tourisme de Narbonne
Place Salengro
11100 Narbonne
phone +33 04 68651560

Hôtel du Languedoc
22, boulevard Gambetta
11100 Narbonne
phone +33 04 68651474

La Résidence
6, rue du 1er–Mai
11100 Narbonne
phone +33 04 68321941

Hôtel de France
6, rue Rossini
11104 Narbonne
phone +33 04 68320975

Hôtel du Midi
4, avenue de Toulouse
11104 Narbonne
phone +33 04 68410462

Le Méditerranée
265, rue Félix-Aldi
11104 Narbonne
phone +33 04 68322142

Hôtel d'Occitanie
Avenue de la Mer
11104 Narbonne
phone +33 04 68654760

Restaurant L'Estagnol
5 bis, cours Mirabeau
11104 Narbonne
phone +33 04 68650927

Restaurant Au Fin Gourmet
14, rue Péclet
11104 Narbonne
phone +33 04 68321669

Restaurant Auberge des Jacobins
8, place des Jacobins
11104 Narbonne
phone +33 04 683243

Restaurant La Petite Cour
22, boulevard Gambetta
11104 Narbonne
phone +33 04 68904803

Restaurant Le Jardin de Narbonne
72, rue Droite
11104 Narbonne
phone +33 04 68653550

Restaurant Le Petit Comptoir
4, boulevard du Maréchal-Joffre
11104 Narbonne
phone +33 04 68423035

Laine de Miel
Domaine Hospitalet
Rue Narbonne Plage
11100 Narbonne
phone +33 04 68272993

Accent d'Oc
54, rue Droite
11100 Narbonne
phone +33 04 68322413

Brûlerie Narbonnaise
38, rue Ancien Courrier
11100 Narbonne
phone +33 04 68652460
fax +33 04 68492331

La Cave du Palais
Le Palais du Vin
Domaine Saint-Crescent
11100 Narbonne
phone +33 04 68414967
fax +33 04 68410109

nîmes (languedoc-roussillon)

Office de Tourisme
6, rue Auguste
30000 Nîmes
phone +33 04 66583800

fax +33 04 66583801
www.ot-nimes.fr

Hôtel Imperator Concorde
15, rue Gaston Boissier
30000 Nîmes
phone +33 04 66219030
fax +33 04 66677025

Acanthe du Temple Hôtel
1, rue Charles Babut
30000 Nîmes
phone +33 04 66675461
fax +33 04 66360436

Cat Hôtel
22, boulevard Am. Courbet
30000 Nîmes
phone +33 04 66672285
fax +33 04 66215751

Côté Patio
31, rue Beaucaire
30000 Nîmes
phone +33 04 66676017
fax +33 04 66678802

Hôtel La Maison de Sophie
31, avenue Carnot
3000 Nîmes
phone +33 04 66709610

Hôtel-Restaurant l'Orangerie
75, rue Tour l'Evêque
30000 Nîmes
phone +33 04 66845057
fax +33 04 66294455

Hôtel-Restaurant Le Pré Galoffre
Route du général Leclerc
30900 Nîmes
phone +33 04 66296541
fax +33 04 66382349

Brasserie des Arènes
4, boulevard des Arènes
30000 Nîmes
phone +33 04 66672305
fax +33 04 66677693

Restaurant Chez Moi
15, rue Fresque
30000 Nîmes
phone +33 04 66216459

Restaurant La Source d'Assas
2, rue Voltaire
30000 Nîmes
phone +33 04 66389959

Restaurant Le Bouchon de l'assiette
5 bis, rue Sauve
30900 Nîmes
phone +33 04 66620293
fax +33 04 66620357

Restaurant l'Ancien Thêatre
4, rue Racine
30900 Nîmes
phone +33 04 66213075

Restaurant Le Chapon Fin
3, rue Château Fadaise
30900 Nîmes
phone +33 04 66673473

Piano Bar Le Carré d'Art
2, rue Gaston Boissier
30900 Nîmes
phone +33 04 66675240

Intemporel
(Museum shop)
2, place de l'Horloge
30000 Nîmes
phone +33 04 66218118

La Boutique des Arènes
Boulevard des Arènes
30000 Nîmes

Céramique Provençales
(Ceramics)
4, rue du Grand Couvent
30000 Nîmes
phone +33 04 66672161

Cuisines et dépendances cabinet de curiosités
3, Place du marché
30000 Nîmes
phone +33 04 66212823

Atelier Sud
(Ceramics)
21, rue Emile Jamais
30000 Nîmes
phone +33 04 66670044

noyers-sur-serein (bourgogne)

Syndicat d'initiative du canton de Noyers
22, place de l'Hôtel-de-Ville
89310 Noyers-sur-Serein
phone +33 03 86826606

Auberge du Serein
24, place du Grenier-à Sel
89310 Noyers-sur-Serein
phone +33 03 86828053

Restaurant L'Etape nucérienne
27, place de la Petite-Etape-aux-Vins
89310 Noyers-sur-Serein
phone +33 03 86826092

Restaurant Le Bistrot
1, place du Marché-au-Blé
89310 Noyers-sur-Serein
phone +33 03 86828165

Musée d'Art naïf
Rue de l'Eglise
89310 Noyers-sur-Serein
phone +33 03 86828909

obernai (alsace)

Office du tourisme
Place du Beffroi
67120 Obernai
phone +33 03 88956413
www.obernai.fr

Hôtel-restaurant Le Parc
169, route d'Ottrott
67210 Obernai
phone +33 03 88955008
fax +33 03 88953729
www.hotel-du-parc.com

Hôtel-restaurant A la cour d'Alsace
3, rue de Gail
67210 Obernai
phone +33 03 88950700
fax +33 03 88951921
www.cour-alsace.com

Hostellerie des Châteaux
11, rue des Châteaux
67530 Ottrott
phone +33 03 88481414
fax +33 03 88481418
www.hostellerie-chateaux.fr

Hôtel-restaurant L'Ami Fritz
8, rue des Châteaux
67530 Ottrott
phone +33 03 88958081
fax +33 03 88958485
www.amifritz.com

Restaurant Chatelain
41, rue Monseigneur-Medard-Barth
67530 Boersch
phone +33 03 88958333

Maison Gross
66, rue du Général Gouraud
67210 Obernai
phone +33 03 88955113
fax +33 03 88952323

Distillerie Lehmann
Chemin des Peupliers
67210 Obernai
phone +33 03 88504129

Vins d'Alsace Seilly
18, rue du Général Gouraud
67210 Obernai
phone +33 03 88955580

Viticulteur Lang
3, rue des Soeurs
67210 Obernai
phone +33 03 88499445

Viticulteur Domaine Strohm
5, rue des Pèlerins
67210 Obernai
phone +33 03 88955402

ornans (franche-comté)

Office du tourisme
7, rue Pierre Vernier
25290 Ornans
phone +33 03 81622150
fax +33 03 81620263
www.pays-ornans.com

Hôtel-restaurant Domaine de la Vallée Heureuse
Route de Genève
39800 Poligny
phone +33 03 84371213
fax +33 03 84370875
www.hotelvalleeheureuse.com

Hotel-restaurant Chateau de Germigney
Rue Edgar-Faure
39600 Port-Lesney
phone +33 03 84738585
fax +33 03 84738888
www.chateaudegermigney.com

Musée Gustave Courbet
Place Robert Fernier
25290 Ornans
phone +33 03 81622330
fax +33 03 81624958
www.museecourbet.org

Au Marché Comtois Epicerie Régionale
9 bis, rue Pierre Vernier
phone +33 03 81571751
25290 Ornans

La Sauccisse Ornanaise Pernet Jacky
21, rue Pierre Vernier
25290 Ornans
phone +33 03 81622032
fax +33 03 81621734

Atelier de Cécile Peinture décorative sur meubles et objets
63, rue Pierre Vernier
25290 Ornans
phone/fax +33 03 81620617

pau (aquitaine)

Office du tourisme
Hôtel de ville
Place Royale
64000 Pau
phone +33 05 59272708
www.pau.fr

Hôtel Roncevaux
25, rue Louis-Barthou
64000 Pau
phone +33 05 59270844
fax +33 05 59270801
www.hotel-roncevaux.com

Hôtel Gramont
3, place Gramont
64000 Pau
phone +33 05 59278404
fax +33 05 59276223
www.hotelgramont.com

Restaurant Au Fin Gourmet
24, avenue Gaston-Lacoste
64000 Pau
phone +33 05 59274771

Restaurant Chez Pierre
16, rue Louis-Barthou
64000 Pau
phone +33 05 59277686

Restaurant La Michodière
34, rue Pasteur
64000 Pau
phone +33 05 59275385

Restaurant Le Fer à Cheval
1, avenue Martyrs-du-Pont-Long
64000 Pau
phone +33 05 59321740

Restaurant La Planche de Bœuf
30, rue Pasteur
64000 Pau
phone +33 05 59276260

Chez Ruffet
3, avenue Charles-Touzet
64110 Jurançon
phone +33 05 59062513

Chocolaterie Blasco
17, rue Pasteur
64320 Bizanos
phone +33 05 59270061

pérouges (rhône-alpes)

Syndicat d'Initiative
01800 Pérouges
phone +33 04 74467084
fax +33 04 74610114
www.perouges.org

Ostellerie du Vieux Pérouges
Place du Tilleul
01800 Pérouges
phone +33 04 74610088
www.ostellerie.com

Hôtel La Bérangère
01800 Pérouges
phone +33 04.74.34.77.77
www.hotel-la-berengere.com

Hôtel Le Petit Casset
RN 84, La Boisse
phone +33 04 78062133
www.lepetitcasset.com

Auberge Chez Ginette
Bourg Saint-Christophe
01800 Pérouges
phone +33 04 74610149
www.auberge-chez-ginette.com

Auberge du Cocq
Rue des Rondes
01800 Pérouges
phone +33 04 74610547
www.membres.lycos.fr/aubergeducoq

Le Relais de la Tour
Place du Tilleuls
01800 Pérouges
phone +33 04 74610103

Restaurant Le Veneur Noir
Entrée de la Cité
01800 Pérouges
phone +33 04 74610706

Restaurant Les Terrasses de Pérouges
Rue des Rondes
01800 Pérouges
phone +33 04 74613868
www.Lesterrasses.fr

Chocolaterie de Pérouges
(Chocolatier)
Route de Meximieux
01800 Pérouges
phone +33 04 74613078

Caveau Saint-Vincent
(Wine tasting and selling)
Rue des Rondes
01800 Pérouges
phone +33 04 74611939
fax +33 04 74611939

Le Péage de Bernadette et Rolland Tanzilli
(Antiques)
Route de Meximieux
01800 Pérouges
phone +33 04 74610711
fax +33 04 74612910

Au Vieux Saint-Georges
(Antiques)
Rue des Rondes
01800 Pérouges
phone +33 04 74610630

Le logis du Cadran Solaire
(Gifts and Souvenirs)
Place de la halle
01800 Pérouges
phone +33 04 74614940

Verrerie de Pérouges
(Glassworks)
Entrée de la Cité
01800 Pérouges
phone +33 04 74614596
www.stefatelier.com

Chez Françoise
(Galettes de Pérouges)
Rue des Rondes
01800 Pérouges
phone +33 04 74610359

Chez P. Vernay
(Galettes de Pérouges)
Entrée de la Cité
01800 Pérouges
phone/fax +33 04 74612276

poitiers (poitou-charentes)

Office de Tourisme de Poitiers
45, place Charles De Gaulle
86009 poitiers
phone +33 05 49412124
www.ot-poitiers.fr

Le Grand Hôtel
28, rue Carnot
86000 Poitiers
phone +33 05 49609060
fax +33 05 49628189
www.grandhotelpoitiers.fr

Hôtel-restaurant Château du Clos de la Ribaudière
86360 Chasseneuil-du-Poitou
phone +33 05 49528666
fax +33 05 49528632
www.ribaudiere.com

Restaurant Les Trois Piliers
37, rue Carnot
86000 Poitiers
phone +33 05 49550703

Restaurant Le Saint-Hilaire
65, rue Théophraste-Renaudot
86000 Poitiers
phone +33 05 49411545

Restaurant Le Chalet de Venise
6, rue du Square
86280 Saint-Benoît
phone +33 05 49884507

La Maison de Poupée
151, Grand Rue
86000 Poitiers
phone +33 05 49881708
fax +33 05 49602724

Au Flambeau d'Argent
Ciergerie Guédon
113, Grand Rue
86000 Poitiers
phone +33 05 49410743
fax +33 05 49529688

Biscuiterie Chocolatier
Rannou-Métivier
13 bis, rue des Cordeliers
86000 Poitiers
phone +33 05 49303010

Lutherie Laurent Gayraud
7, place de La Liberté
86000 Poitiers
phone +33 05 49609796
fax +33 05 49428360

Fromagerie, Cave Pain Jean-Marie
26, place de Provence
86000 Poitiers
phone +33 05 49475178
fax +33 05 49428526

pont-aven (brittany)

Office de Tourisme
5, place de l'Hôtel-de-Ville
29930 Pont-Aven
phone +33 02 98060470
www.pontaven.com

Hôtel-restaurant Le Domaine de Kerstinec-Kerland
Route de Moëlan-sur-Mer
29340 Riec-sur-Belon
phone +33 02 98064298
fax +33 02 98064538
www.hotelbelon.online.fr

Hôtel-restaurant du Port
30, rue de l'Aven
Port-Manech
29920 Nevez
phone +33 02 98068217
fax +33 02 98066270
www.Hotelduport.com

Hôtel-restaurant Le Manoir du Ménec
Saint-Jacques
29380 Bannalec
phone +33 02 98394747
fax +33 02 98394617
www.manoirdumenec.com

Hôtel-restaurant Les Ajoncs d'or
1, place de l'Hôtel-de-Ville
29930 Pont-Aven
phone +33 02 98060206
fax +33 02 98061891
www.ajoncsdor-pontaven.com

Restaurant Le Moulin de Rosmadec
Venelle de Rosmadec
29930 Pont-Aven
phone +33 02 98060022

Restaurant La Taupinière
Croissant Saint-André
29930 Pont-Aven
phone +33 02 98060312

Biscuiterie Penven
1, quai Théodore Botrel
29930 Pont-Aven
phone +33 02 98060587

Traou Mad, les galettes de Pont-Aven
10, place Paul Gauguin
29930 Pont-Aven
phone +33 02 98060194
www.traoumad.com

La Boutique de Pont Aven
9, place Hôtel de Ville
29930 Pont-Aven
phone +33 02 98060765

Biscuiterie de Pont Aven
3, rue Emile Bernard
29930 Pont-Aven
phone +33 02 98091584

provins (ile-de-france)

Office de tourisme
Chemin de Villecran
77482 Provins
phone +33 01 64602626
www.provins.net

Hôtel-Restaurant Aux Vieux Remparts
3, rue Couverte
77160 Provins
phone +33 01 64089400
fax +33 01 60677722
www.auxvieuxremparts.com

Hôtel du Sauvage
27, rue de Paris
77320 La Ferté-Gaucher
phone +33 01 64040019
fax +33 01 64040250
www.hotel-du-sauvage.com

Pâtissier-Chocolatier Maison Gaufillier
5, place du Maréchal-Leclerc
77160 Provins
phone +33 01 64000371

Le Carreau de Provins
16, boulevard Carnot
77160 Provins
phone +33 01 60676454

puy-en-velay (auvergne)

Office du tourisme
Place du Clauzel
43000 Puy-en-Velay
phone +33 04 71093841
www.ot-lepuyenvelay.fr
www.roideloiseau.com

Hotel du Parc Restaurant François Gagnaire
4, avenue Clément-Charbonnier
43000 Puy-en-Velay
phone +33 04 71024040
fax +33 04 71021872
www.hotel-du-parc-le-puy.com

Hotel-restaurant Le Régina
34, boulevard du Maréchal Fayolle
43000 Puy-en-Velay
phone +33 04 71091471
fax +33 04 71091857
www.hotelrestregina.com

Restaurant Lapierre
6, rue des Capucins
43000 Puy-en-Velay
phone +33 04 71090844

Restaurant Tournayre
12, rue Chênebouterie
43000 Puy-en-Velay
phone +33 04 71095894

Distillerie de la Verveine du Velay
Avenue René Descartes
43700 Saint-Germain-Laprade
phone +33 04 71030411

quimper (brittany)

Office du tourisme
7, rue de la Déesse
29100 Quimper
phone +33 02 98530405

Hôtel-restaurant Villa Tri Men
16, rue du Phare, Sainte-Marine
29120 Combrit
phone +33 02 98519494
fax +33 02 98519550
www.trimen.fr

Hôtel-restaurant Sainte-Marine
19, rue du Bac, Sainte-Marine
29120 Combrit
phone +33 02 98563479
fax +33 02 98519409
www.hotelsaintemarine.com

Hôtel Gradlon
30, rue de Brest
29000 Quimper
phone +33 02 98950439
fax +33 02 98956125
www.hotel-gradlon.com

Restaurant L'Ambroisie
49, rue Elie-Fréron
29000 Quimper
02 98 95 00 02

Restaurant Les Acacias
88, boulevard Creach-Gwen
29000 Quimper
phone +33 02 98521520

Restaurant La Fleur de sel
1, quai Neuf
29000 Quimper
phone +33 02 98550471

Café de l'Epée
14, rue du Parc
29000 Quimper
phone +33 02 98952897

Faïencerie HB Henriot
Rue Haute
29100 Quimper
phone +33 02 98900936

Cidre au Manoir de Kinkiz
75, chemin du Quinquis
29000 Quimper
phone +33 02 98902057

Vêtements Armor-Lux
60 bis, rue Guy-Autret
ZI de L'Hippodrome
29000 Quimper
phone +33 02 98900529

rambouillet (ile-de-france)

Office du tourisme
Hôtel de ville
Place de la Libération
78514 Rambouillet
phone +33 01 34832121
www.ot-rambouillet.fr
www.parc-naturel-chevreuse.org
www.onf.fr/espaceramb

Hôtel Relays du Château
Place de la Libération
78120 Rambouillet
phone +33 01 30838401

Hôtel Saint-Charles
15, rue de Groussay
78120 Rambouillet
phone +33 01 34830634
fax +33 01 30462684
www.hotelstcharles.fr.st/

Restaurant Le Cheval Rouge
78, rue du Général-de-Gaulle
78120 Rambouillet
phone +33 01 30888061

Restaurant La Poste
101, rue du Général-de-Gaulle
78120 Rambouillet
phone +33 01 34830301

Auberge du Louvetier
19, rue de l'Etang-de-la-Tour
78120 Rambouillet
phone +33 01 34856100

**Antiquités
La Bourse de l'occasion**
35, rue Chasles
78120 Rambouillet
phone +33 01 34839484

La Caverne des Particuliers
32, rue Général de Gaulle
78120 Rambouillet
phone +33 01 34831316

P-y Dionisi
19, rue Georges Clemenceau
78120 Rambouillet
phone +33 01 30888798

reims (champagne-ardenne)

Office du tourisme
2, rue Guillaume-de-Machault
51100 Reims
phone +33 03 26774500
www.reims.fr

Hôtel-Restaurant Les Crayères
64, boulevard Henry-Vasnier
51100 Reims
phone +33 03 26828080
fax +33 03 26826552
www.gerardboyer.com

Hôtel Le Clos Raymi
3, rue Joseph-de-Venoge
51200 Epernay
phone +33 03 26510058
fax +33 03 26511898
www.closraymi-hotel.com

Grand Hotel de l'Univers
41, boulevard Foch
51100 Reims
phone +33 03 26886808
fax +33 03 26409561
www.hotel-univers-reims.com

Restaurant Le Foch
37, boulevard Foch
51100 Reims
phone +33 03 26474822

Restaurant L'Apostrophe
59, place Drouet-d'Erlon
51100 Reims
phone +33 03 26791989

Restaurant Au Petit Comptoir
17, rue de Mars
51100 Reims
phone +33 03 26405858

Café du Palais
14, place Myron-Herrick
51100 Reims
phone +33 03 26475254

Bar de la Comédie
3, chaussée Bocquaine
51100 Reims
phone +33 03 26484900

Maître-verrier Bruno Pigeon
92, rue Ponsardin
51100 Reims
phone +33 03 26853623

Chocolatier Deleans
20, rue Cérès
51100 Reims
phone +33 03 26475635

Biscuits Fossier
11, rue Périn
51100 Reims
phone +33 03 26798383

Champagne Ruinart
4, rue des Crayères
51100 Reims
phone +33 03 26775151

Veuve Clicquot Ponsardin
12, rue Temple
51100 Reims
phone +33 03 26895440 / 26895441
fax +33 03 26406017

Champagne Pommery
5, place du Général Gouraud
51100 Reims
phone +33 03 26616256

Champagne Taittinger
9, place Saint-Nicaise
51100 Reims
phone +33 03 26858433
fax +33 03 26858405

Piper-Heidsieck
51, boulevard Henry Vasnier
51100 Reims
phone +33 03 26844344
fax +33 03 26844384

Champagne Martel
17, rue des Créneaux
51100 Reims
phone +33 03 26827067
fax +33 03 26821912

Champagne Lanson
66, rue de Courlancy
51100 Reims
phone +33 03 26785050

riquewihr (alsace)

**Office de Tourisme du Pays de Ribeauvillé
et de Riquewihr**
2, rue de la Première-Armée
68340 Riquewihr
phone +33 03 89478080
www.ribeauville-riquewihr.com

Hôtel-restaurant Le Schoenenbourg
Rue du Schoenenbourg
68340 Riquewihr
phone +33 03 89490111
fax +33 03 89479588
www.hotel-schoenenbourg.fr

Hôtel L'Oriel
3, rue des Ecuries-Seigneuriales
68340 Riquewihr
phone +33 03 89490313
fax +33 03 89479287
www.hotel-oriel.com

Restaurant Le Relais de Riquewihr
6, rue du Général-de-Gaulle
68340 Riquewihr
phone +33 03 89478988

La Table du Gourmet
5, rue de la Première-Armée
68340 Riquewihr
phone +33 03 89490909

Restaurant Le Sarment d'Or
4, rue du Cerf
68340 Riquewihr
phone +33 03 89860286

Brasserie artisanale Gilbert Holl
8, avenue Jacques-Preiss
68340 Riquewihr
phone +33 03 89490672

Musée Hansi
16, rue Général de Gaulle
68340 Riquewihr
phone +33 03 89479700

Souvenirs La Légende des Sorcières
30, rue Général de Gaulle
68340 Riquewihr
phone +33 03 89860522

Aux Beaux Cadeaux
2, rue des Ecuries
68340 Riquewihr
phone +33 03 89490457

Souvenirs Au Four Banal
9, rue Général de Gaulle
68340 Riquewihr
phone +33 03 89479305

rocamadour (midi-pyrénées)

Office de Tourisme de Rocamadour
Maison du Tourisme
46500 Rocamadour
phone +33 05 65332200
fax +33 05 65332201
rocamadour@wanadoo.fr
www.rocamadour.com

Hôtel Beau Site—Restaurant Jehan de Valon
Le Bourg
46500 Rocamadour
phone +33 05 65336308
fax +33 05 65336523
info@bestwestern-beausite.com
bestwestern-beausite.com

Hôtel du Château
Le château
46500 Rocamadour
phone +33 05 65336222
fax +33 05 65336900
hotelduchateau@gofornet.com
hotelduchateau.com

Hôtel du Domaine de la Rhue
Domaine de la Rhue
46500 Rocamadour
phone +33 05 65337150
fax +33 05 65337248
domainedelarhue@wanadoo.fr
domainedelarhue.com

Hôtel Le Troubadour
Belveyre
46500 Rocamadour
phone +33 05 65337027
fax +33 05 65337199
troubadour@rocamadour.com
hotel-troubadour.com

Hôtel Les Esclargies
Route du Château
46500 Rocamadour
phone +33 05 65387323
infos@esclargies.com
esclargies.com

Restaurant Jardins de la Louve
Place Hugon
46500 Rocamadour
phone +33 05 65336293

Restaurant Chez Anne-Marie
Le Bourg
46500 Rocamadour
phone +33 05 65336581

Restaurant Au Panorama
L'Hospitalet
46500 Rocamadour
phone +33 05 65336213

Restaurant Le Château de la Carreta
Place Carreta
46500 Rocamadour
phone +33 05 65336223

Restaurant La Scala
Place Europe
46500 Rocamadour
phone +33 05 65109885

Restaurant Le Roc du Berer
Route de Padirac—Belvédère
46500 Rocamadour
phone +33 0565331999
fax +33 05 65337246

Le Terminus des Pèlerins
Cité Médiévale
46500 Rocamadour
phone +33 05 65336214
contact@terminus-des-peerins.com

Restaurant du château
Le Château
46500 Rocamadour
phone +33 05 65336222
contact@hotelchateaurocamadour.com

Auberge de la Garenne
Route de La Cave Souillac—D 247
46500 Rocamadour
phone +33 05 65336588

A la Truffe du Périgord
Rue de la Couronnerie
46500 Rocamadour
phone +33 05 65337125

Boutique Valette
L'Hospitalet
46500 Rocamadour
phone +33 05 65388154

La Maison de la Noix
46500 Rocamadour
phone +33 05 65336790

Le Potier et le Sellier
46500 Rocamadour
phone +33 05 65337316

Boutique du Point de Vue
46500 Rocamadour
phone +33 05 65336172

Coutellerie Lapeyre
46500 Rocamadour
phone +33 05 65106286

sablé-sur-sarthe (pays de la loire)

Office de tourisme du Pays de Sablé
Place Raphaël-Elizé
72300 Sablé-sur-Sarthe
phone +33 02 43950060
www.sable-sur-sarthe.com
www.vallee-de-la-sarthe.com

Restaurant et Grand-Hôtel de Solesmes
16, place Dom-Gueranger
72300 Solesmes
phone +33 02 43954510
fax +33 02 43952226
www.grandhotelsolesmes.com

Hôtel-restaurant Haras de la Potardière
Route de Bazouges
72200 Crosmières
phone +33 02 43458347
fax +33 02 43458106
www.potardiere.com

Restaurant Hostellerie Saint-Martin
3, rue Haute-Saint-Martin
72300 Sablé-sur-Sarthe
phone +33 02 43950003

Restaurant Le Martin Pêcheur
Route de Pincé
72300 Sablé-sur-Sarthe
phone +33 02 43959755

Amusant Musée
Le Port
72300 Juigné-sur-Sarthe
phone +33 02 43924462

Malicorne, Espace Faïence
Rue Victor-Hugo
72270 Malicorne-sur-Sarthe
phone +33 02 43480717

Faïenceries d'Art de Malicorne
18, rue Bernard-Palissy
72270 Malicorne-sur-Sarthe
phone +33 02 43948118

saint-jean-de-luz (aquitaine)

Office du tourisme
1, place du Maréchal-Foch
64500 Saint-Jean-de-Luz
phone +33 05 59260316
www.saint-jean-de-luz.com

Hôtel Le Parc Victoria
5, rue Cepé
64500 Saint-Jean-de-Luz
phone +33 05 59267878
fax +33 05 59267808
www.parcvictoria.esds.com

Hôtel La Marisa
16, rue Sopite
64500 Saint-Jean-de-Luz
phone +33 05 59269546
fax +33 05 59511706
www.la-marisa.com

Hôtel La Devinière
5, rue Loquin
64500 Saint-Jean-de-Luz
phone +33 05 59260551
fax +33 05 59512638
www.hotel-la-deviniere.com

La Taverne Basque
5, rue de la République
64500 Saint-Jean-de-Luz
phone +33 05 59260126

Petit Grill Basque
2, rue Saint-Jacques
64500 Saint-Jean-de-Luz
phone +33 05 59268076

Restaurant Chez Dominique
15, quai Maurice-Ravel
64500 Ciboure
phone +33 05 59472916

Espadrilles Nicole Pariès
52, rue Gambetta
64500 Saint-Jean-de-Luz
phone +33 05 59261594

Linge de la Maison Larre
Place Louis-XIV
64500 Saint-Jean-de-Luz
phone +33 05 59260213

saint-malo (brittany)

Office de Tourisme
Esplanade Saint-Vincent
35400 Saint-Malo
phone +33 02 99566448
www.saint-malo-tourisme.com

Hôtel Quic en Groigne
8, rue d'Estrées, Intra-muros
35400 Saint-Malo
phone +33 02 99202220
fax +33 02 99202230
www.quic-en-groigne.com

Hôtel-restaurant de l'Univers
Place Chateaubriand, Intra-muros
35400 Saint-Malo
phone +33 02 99408952
fax +33 02 99400727
www.hotel-univers-saintmalo.com

Grand hôtel des Thermes
Restaurant Le Cap Horn
Les Thermes Marins de Saint-Malo
Grande plage du Sillon
phone +33 02 99407575
fax +33 02 99407600
www.thalassosaintmalo.com

Restaurant Chalut
8, rue de la Corne-de-Cerf, Intra-muros
35400 Saint-Malo
phone +33 02 99567158

Restaurant Gilles
2, rue de la Pie-Qui-Boit, Intra-muros
35400 Saint-Malo
phone +33 02 99409725

Restaurant La Fleur de sel
93, boulevard de Rochebonne
35400 Saint-Malo
phone +33 02 99400993

La Vague
2, Grand Rue
35400 Saint-Malo
phone +33 02 99564913

Le Comptoir de Bretagne
3, rue Broussais
35400 Saint-Malo
phone +33 02 99408969

Skipper Gallery
8, Grande Rue
35400 Saint-Malo
phone +33 02 99404282

Au souvenir Malouin
17, rue de Dinan
35400 Saint-Malo
phone +33 02 99409943

Fumage artisanal amalouin
64, boulevard Rochebonne
35400 Saint-Malo
phone +33 02 99400383

saint-paul-de-vence (paca)

Office de Tourisme
Maison de la Tour
2, rue Grande
06570 Saint-Paul-de-Vence
phone +33 04 93328695
fax +33 04 93326027
www.saint-pauldevence.com

Hôtel La Grande Bastide
1350, route de la Colle
06570 Saint-Paul-de-Vence
phone +33 04 93325030
fax +33 04 93325059
www.la-grande-bastide.com

Hôtel Le Hameau
528, route de la Colle
06570 Saint-Paul-de-Vence
phone +33 04 93328024
fax +33 04 93325575
www.le-hameau.com

Hôtel Les Bastides de Saint-Paul
880, chemin des Blaquières
06570 Saint-Paul-de-Vence
phone +33 04 92020807
fax +33 04 93205041
www.bastides.fr.fm

Hôtel Les Messuges
Domaine des Gardettes
Impasse des Messugues
06570 Saint-Paul-de-Vence
phone +33 04 93325332
fax +33 04 93329415
www.stpaulweb.com/messugues

Hôtel Les Vergers de Saint-Paul
940, route de la Colle
06570 Saint-Paul-de-Vence
phone +33 04 93329424
fax +33 04 93329107
www.stpaulweb.com/vergers

Hôtel-restaurant La Colombe d'Or
Place Général de Gaulle
06570 Saint-Paul-de-Vence
phone +33 04 93328002
fax +33 04 93327778
www.la-colombe-dor.com

Hôtel-restaurant Le Mas de Pierre
Route des Serres
06570 Saint-Paul-de-Vence
phone +33 04 93590010
fax +33 04 93590059
www.lemasdepierre.com

Hôtel-restaurant Le Saint-Paul
86 rue Grande
06570 Saint-Paul-de-Vence
phone +33 04 93326225
fax +33 04 93325294
stpaul@relaischateaux.com
www.lesaintpaul.com

Hostellerie Les Remparts
72, rue Grande

06570 Saint-Paul-de-Vence
phone +33 04 93320988
fax +33 04 93320691
www.hotel-les-remparts.net

Café de la Place
Place De Gaulle
06570 Saint-Paul-de-Vence
phone +33 04 9328003
fax +33 04 93328999

Hostellerie de la Fontaine
10, montée de la Castre
06570 Saint-Paul-de-Vence
phone +33 04 93327412
fax +33 04 93328029

Restaurant La Cocarde
23, rue Grande
06570 Saint-Paul-de-Vence
phone +33 04 93328617
fax +33 04 93325650

Restaurant La Petite Chapelle
Place De Gaulle
06570 Saint-Paul-de-Vence
phone +33 04 93327732

Restaurant Le Sainte-Claire
Espace Sainte-Claire
06570 Saint-Paul-de-Vence
phone +33 04 93320202
fax +33 04 933320132

Restaurant Le Vieux Moulin
Rond Point Sainte-Claire
06570 Saint-Paul-de-Vence
phone +33 04 93321045
fax +33 04 93326916

Restaurant Les Oliviers
838, route de la Colle
06570 Saint-Paul-de-Vence
phone +33 04 93326482
fax +33 04 93326479

Gault
41, rue Grande
06570 Saint-Paul-de-Vence
phone +33 04 93325054
fax +33 04 93327579

Galerie Universalis
12, rue Grande
06570 Saint-Paul-de-Vence
phone +33 04 93325659

Les Trois Etoiles de Saint-Paul
7, place de la Mairie
06570 Saint-Paul-de-Vence
phone +33 04 93327968

A Casta—Les Délices de Saint-Paul
57, rue Grande
06570 Saint-Paul-de-Vence
phone +33 04 93326588

L'Herbier en Provence
7, descente de la Castre
06570 Saint-Paul-de-Vence
phone +33 04 93329151

Olives—Les Huiles du Monde
68, rue Grande
06570 Saint-Paul-de-Vence
phone +33 04 93325835

La Petite Cave de Saint-Paul
7, rue de l'Étoile
06570 Saint-Paul-de-Vence
phone +33 04 93325954

saint-tropez (paca)

Office du tourisme
Quai Jean-Jaurès
83990 Saint-Tropez
phone +33 04 94974521
www.ot-saint-tropez.com

Hôtel Lou Cagnard
18, avenue Paul-Roussel
83990 Saint-Tropez
phone +33 04 94970424
fax +33 04 94970944
www.hotel-lou-cagnard.com

Hôtel-restaurant Byblos
Avenue Paul-Signac
83990 Saint-Tropez
phone +33 04 94566800
fax +33 04 94566801
www.byblos.com

Hôtel-restaurant La Ponche
3, rue des Remparts
83990 Saint-Tropez
phone +33 04 94970253
fax +33 04 94977861
www.laponche.com

La Table du Marché
38, rue Georges-Clemenceau
83990 Saint-Tropez
phone +33 04 94978520

Restaurant Le Girelier
Quai Jean-Jaurès
83990 Saint-Tropez
phone +33 04 94970387

Restaurant Leï Mouscardins
Tour du Portalet
83990 Saint-Tropez
phone +33 04 94972900

Restaurant Le Petit Charron
6, rue des Charrons
83990 Saint-Tropez
phone +33 04 94977378

Salon de thé pâtisserie Le Sénéquier
Quai Jean-Jaurès
83990 Saint-Tropez
phone +33 04 94970090

Brasserie Le Gorille
1, quai de Suffen
83990 Saint-Tropez
phone +33 04 94970393

Atelier Rondini
16, rue Georges-Clemenceau
83990 Saint-Tropez
phone +33 04 94971955

sarlat (aquitaine)

Office du tourisme de Sarlat et du Périgord noir
Rue Tourny

24200 Sarlat
phone +33 05 53314545
www.otspn.com

Hôtel La Hoirie
Rue Marcel-Cerdan
24200 Sarlat
phone +33 05 53590562
fax +33 05 53311390
www.lahoirie.com

Hôtel La Madeleine
1, place de la Petite-Rigaudie
24200 Sarlat
phone +33 05 53591041
fax +33 05 53310362
www.hoteldelamadeleine-sarlat.com

Restaurant Le Quatre Saisons
2, côte de Toulouse
24200 Sarlat
phone +33 05 53294859

Restaurant Le Présidial
Rue Landry
24200 Sarlat
phone +33 05 53289247

Restaurant Le Rossignol
15, rue Fénelon
24200 Sarlat
phone +33 05 53310230

Traditions du Perigord
8, rue de la Liberté
24200 Sarlat
phone +33 05 53313360
fax +33 05 53310941

A l'Olivier
3, place Liberté
24200 Sarlat
phone +33 05 53303787
fax +33 05 53284388

Savonnerie du Peyrou
10, rue Liberté
24200 Sarlat
phone +33 05 53285957

Au Vieux Sarlat
6, rue Victor Hugo
24200 Sarlat
phone +33 05 53592876

Boutique du Dinandier
6, rue Fénelon
24200 Sarlat
phone +33 05 53298979

senlis (picardy)

Office de tourisme
Place du Parvis-Notre-Dame
60300 Senlis
phone +33 03 44530640
www.ville-senlis.fr

Hôtel L'Orangerie
6, rue Nicolas-de-Lancy
60810 Raray
phone +33 03 44541313
fax +33 03 44547506
www.orangerie-raray.fr

Hôtel-restaurant Le Château d'Ermenonville
La Table du Poète
60950 Ermenonville
phone +33 03 44540026
fax +33 03 44540100
www.chateau-ermenonville.com

Hôtel-Restaurant Hostellerie de la Porte Bellon
51, rue Bellon
60300 Senlis
phone +33 03 44530305
fax +33 03 44532994
www.portebellon.com

Restaurant Le Bourgeois Gentilhomme
3, place de la Halle
60300 Senlis
phone +33 03 44531322

Restaurant Le Scaramouche
4, place Notre-Dame
60300 Senlis
phone +33 03 44530126

Visite de Senlis en calèche
Place de la Cathédrale
60300 Senlis
phone +33 03 44531026
compiegne.daniel@wanadoo.fr

Senlis en calèche
32, rue du Haut de Villevert
60300 Senlis
phone +33 03 44531026
fax +33 03 44530306

Guizelin Cadeaux
2, place Halle
60300 Senlis
phone +33 03 44530403
fax +33 03 44537984

Office du tourisme
60, Grand rue
34200 Sète
phone +33 04 67747171

Grand Hôtel
17, quai Mar. de Lattre de Tassigny
34200 Sète
phone +33 04 67747177

Hotel Port Marine
Môle Saint Louis
34200 Sète
phone +33 04 67749234
hotelportmarine@wanadoo.fr

Restaurant Rotonde
17, quai Mar. de Lattre de Tassigny
34200 Sète
phone +33 04 67748614

Restaurant Palangrotte
1, rampe Paul Valéry
Quai de la Marine
34200 Sète
phone +33 04 67748035
fax +33 04 67749720

Petit Bazar de Sète
22, quai Alger
34200 Sète
phone +33 04 67745502

Coup de Soleil
15, promenade Jean Baptiste Marty
34200 Sète
phone +33 04 67749933

Inspiration Marine
7, rue Honoré Euzet
34200 Sète
phone +33 04 67749625

Le Môle
Promenade Jean-Baptiste Marty
34200 Sète
phone +33 04 67741740

Office de tourisme
Château du Pirou
63300 Thiers
phone +33 04 73806565
www.ville-thiers.fr

Hôtel-restaurant Château de Codignat
Lezoux
63190 Bort-l'Etang
phone +33 04 73684303
fax +33 04 73689354
www.relaischateaux.com/codignat
www.codignat.com

Hôtel-restaurant Le Parc de Geoffroy
49, avenue du Général-de-Gaulle
63300 Thiers
phone +33 04 73808700
fax +33 04 73808701
www.parc-de-geoffroy.com

Restaurant La Ferme des trois canards
Route de Maringues, Biton
63920 Peschadoires
phone +33 04 73510670

Restaurant L'Aigle d'or
8, rue de Lyon
63300 Thiers
phone +33 04 73800050

Restaurant Le Moulin Bleu
Courty
63300 Thiers
phone +33 04 73800622

Boutique du Musée de la Coutellerie
23 & 58, rue de la Coutellerie
63300 Thiers
phone +33 04 73805886
fax +33 04 73802939

Decorev
8, rue Terrasse
63300 Thiers
phone +33 04 73804286

Le Coin Gourmand
53, avenue Voltaire
63300 Thiers
phone +33 04 73803005
fax +33 04 73513364

Office de Tourisme de Troyes et sa région
Rue Mignard
10000 Troyes
phone +33 03 25733688
www.tourisme-troyes.com

Hôtel Le Champ des Oiseaux
20, rue Linard-Gonthier
10000 Troyes
phone +33 03 25805850
fax +33 03 25809834
www.champdesoiseaux.com

Hôtel-restaurant Le Royal Hôtel
22, boulevard Carnot
10000 Troyes
phone +33 03 25731999
fax +33 03 25734785
www.royal-hotel-troyes.com

Café de la Paix, La Table du Marché
52, rue du Général-de-Gaulle
10000 Troyes
phone +33 03 25731526

Restaurant Le Bourgogne
40, rue Général-de-Gaulle
10000 Troyes
phone +33 03 25730267

Restaurant Le Vivien
7, place Saint-Rémy
10000 Troyes
phone +33 03 25737070

Restaurant Le Bistroquet
10, rue Louis-Ulbach
10000 Troyes
phone +33 03 25736565

Auberge de Sainte-Maure
99, route de Méry
10150 Sainte-Maure
phone +33 03 25769041

Au Bec Fin
13, rue du Général de Gaulle
10000 Troyes
phone +33 0325731653

Eco-Ferme de la Forêt d'Orient
9, rue Breslay
10000 Troyes
phone +33 0325412653

Délicieusement Vôtre
63, rue Turenne
10000 Troyes
phone +33 03 25736262

Office du tourisme
Place Albert 1er—BP 129
30703 Uzès
phone +33 04 66226888
www.uzes-tourisme.com

Musée du Bonbon
Pont des Charrettes
30700 Uzès
phone +33 04 66227439

Rêves d'un Ane
4, rue Grande-Bourgade
30700 Uzès
phone +33 04 66207789

On Dirait Le Sud
6, place Dammartin
30700 Uzès
phone +33 04 66574070
fax +33 04 66575374

Maison Uzège Pays Terre Truffe
32, place des Herbes
30700 Uzès
phone/fax +33 04 66638645

L'Atelier de Pascaline
18, rue Jacques d'Uzès
30700 Uzès
phone +33 04 66036296

Office du tourisme
Avenue du Chanoine-Sautel
84110 Vaison-la-Romaine
phone +33 04 90360211
www.vaison-la-romaine.com

Hôtel-restaurant Le Beffroi
Rue de l'Evêché
84110 Vaison-la-Romaine
phone +33 04 90360471
fax +33 04 90362478
www.le-beffroi.com

Hotel Le Burrhus
2, place Montfort
84110 Vaison-la-Romaine
phone +33 04 90360011
fax +33 04 90363905
www.burrhus.com

Auberge La Bartavelle
12, place Sus-Auze
84110 Vaison-la-Romaine
phone +33 04 90360216

Restaurant Le Brin d'Olivier
4, rue du Ventoux
84110 Vaison-la-Romaine
phone +33 04 90287479

Restaurant Le Moulin à Huile
1, quai du Maréchal-Foch
84110 Vaison-la-Romaine
phone +33 04 90362067

Vins et Gourmandises
13, avenue Victor Hugo
84110 Vaison-la-Romaine
phone +33 04 90288517

Vacances Romaines
23, place Montfort
84110 Vaison-la-Romaine
phone +33 04 90362860

L'Atelier de Provence
34, Grand Rue
84110 Vaison-la-Romaine
phone +33 04 90360217

Mirabilys artisanat
26, avenue Jules Ferry

84110 Vaison-la-Romaine
phone +33 06 30843380

vendôme (centre)

Office du tourisme
Hôtel du Saillant
Parc Ronsard
41100 Vendôme
phone +33 02 54770507

Hôtel-restaurant Le Capricorne
8, boulevard de Trémault
41100 Vendôme
phone +33 02 54802700
fax +33 02 54773063
www.hotelcapricorne.com

Chambres d'hôtel Ferme de Crislaine
41100 Azé
phone +33 02 54721409
fax +33 02 54721803

**Restaurant Les Caves du Bois
aux Moines**
14, rue du Maréchal-Rochambeau
41100 Vendôme
phone +33 02 54890909

Restaurant Le Petit Bilboquet
Ancienne route de Tours, Villerable
41100 Vendôme
phone +33 02 54771660

Restaurant La Gourmandine
36, route de Vendôme
41100 Pezou
phone +33 02 54234369

Gérard Torcheux
27, rue Les Côteaux
72340 Poncé-sur-le-Loir
phone +33 02 43790569

verdun (lorraine)

**Office de Tourisme de Verdun
et sa région**
Maison du Tourisme
Place de la Nation
55106 Verdun
phone +33 03 29861418
www.verdun-tourisme.com

Hôtel-Restaurant Le Coq hardi
Avenue de la Victoire
55100 Verdun
phone +33 03 29863636
fax +33 03 29860921
www.coq-hardi.com

Hostellerie du Château des Monthairons
55320 Les Monthairons
phone +33 03 29877855
fax +33 03 29877349
www.chateaudesmonthairons.fr

Dragées de Verdun—Maison Braquier
50, rue Fort de Vaux
55100 Verdun
phone +33 03 29843000
fax +33 03 29839051

Boutique
3, rue Pasteur
55100 Verdun
phone +33 03 29860502

versailles (ile-de-france)

Office du tourisme
2 bis, avenue de Paris
78000 Versailles
phone +33 01 39248888
www.versailles-tourisme.com

Hotel le Versailles
7, rue Saint Anne
78000 Versailles
phone +33 01 39506465
fax +33 01 39023785
www.hotel-le-versailles.fr

Hotel la Résidence du Berry
14, rue d'Anjou
78000 Versailles
phone +33 01 39490707
fax +33 01 39505940
www.hotel-berry.com

Hotel Sofitel
2 bis, avenue de Paris
78000 Versailles
phone +33 01 39074646
fax +33 01 39074647

Restaurant Valmont
20, rue au pain
78000 Versailles
phone +33 01 39513900

Restaurant Les trois marches
Hotel Trianon Palace
1, boulevard de la reine
78000 Versailles
phone +33 01 39501321

Le Potager du Roi
10, rue du Maréchal-Joffre
78000 Versailles
phone +33 01 39246262
www.potager-du-roi.fr

Osmothèque
36, rue du Parc de Clagny
78100 Versailles
phone +33 01 39554699
www.osmotheque.fr

vézelay (bourgogne)

Office de tourisme de Vézelay
Rue Saint-Etienne
89450 Vézelay
phone +33 03 86332369

Hôtel Le Cheval blanc
Place du Champ-de-Foire
89450 Vézelay
phone +33 03 86332212

Hôtel Le Lion d'or
Place du Champ-de-Foire
89450 Vézelay
phone +33 03 86332123

Hôtel Le Relais du Morvan
Place du Champ-de-Foire
89450 Vézelay
phone +33 03 86332533

Hôtel La Terrasse
Place de la Basilique
89450 Vézelay
phone +33 03 86332550

Hôtel Le Compostelle
Place du Champ-de-Foire
89450 Vézelay
phone +33 03 86332863

Restaurant Auberge de la Coquille
81, rue Saint-Pierre
89450 Vézelay
phone +33 03 86333557

Restaurant Le Bougainville
28, rue Saint-Etienne
89450 Vézelay
phone +33 03 86332757

Restaurant A la Fortune du pot
Place du Champ-de-Foire
89450 Vézelay
phone +33 03 86333256

Restaurant Le Saint-Etienne
Rue Saint-Etienne
89450 Vézelay
phone +33 03 86332734

Caves du Pèlerin (Winery)
32, rue Saint-Etienne
89450 Vézelay
phone +33 03 86333084

Domaine Camu Frères
Le Clos, route de Saint-Père
89450 Vézelay
phone +33 03 86823566

Clos du Couvent
Rue des Ecoles
89450 Vézelay
phone +33 03 86333501

vichy (auvergne)

Office du tourisme
19, rue du Parc
03200 Vichy
phone +33 04 70987194
www.vichy-tourisme.com

**Aletti Palace Hôtel
Restaurant La Véranda**
3, place Joseph-Aletti
03200 Vichy
phone +33 04 70302020
fax +33 04 70981382
www.aletti.fr

Hôtel-restaurant Le Pavillon d'Enghien
32, rue Callou
03200 Vichy
phone +33 04 70983330
fax +33 04 70316782
www.pavillondenghien.com

Restaurant Jacques Decoret
7, avenue de Gramont

03200 Vichy
phone +33 04 70976506

Brasserie du Casino
4, rue du Casino
03200 Vichy
phone +33 04 70982306

La Table d'Antoine
8, rue Burnol
03200 Vichy
phone +33 04 70989971

Le Grand Café
7, rue du Casino
03200 Vichy
phone +33 04 70971645

Pastillerie de Vichy
94, allée des Ailes
03200 Vichy
phone +33 04 70309470

Confiseur-chocolatier Vichy Prunelle
36, rue Montaret
03200 Vichy
phone +33 04 70982002

SUGGESTED READING

ART AND ARCHITECTURE

Blunt, F. Anthony. *Art and Architecture in France, 1500–1700*. New Haven: Yale University Press, 1999.
Greenhalgh, Paul. *Art Nouveau: 1890–1914*. New York: Harry N. Abrams, 2000.
Murat, Laure. *The Splendor of France: Châteaux, Mansions, and Country Houses*. New York: Rizzoli, 1991.
Philippe, Daniel, and Claire Julliard. *France from the Air*. London: Thames and Hudson, 1997.
Silver, Kenneth E. *Making Paradise: Art, Modernity, and the Myth of the French Riviera*. Cambridge: MIT Press, 2001.

CULTURE

Caro, Ina. *The Road from the Past: Traveling through History in France*. New York: Harvest Books, 1996.
de Borchgrave, Isabelle, and Jean-André Charial. *The Flavors of Provence*. New York: Rizzoli, 2004.
Horne, Alistair. *La Belle France: A Short History*. New York: Knopf, 2005.
Tuchman, Barbara W. *A Distant Mirror: The Calamitous 14th Century*. New York: Knopf, 1978.

LITERATURE

Colette. *The Complete Claudine*. New York: Farrar, Straus and Giroux, 1976.
Dumas, Alexandre. *The Three Musketeers*. New York: Oxford University Press, 1991.
Fitzgerald, F. Scott. *Tender is the Night*. rep. ed. New York: Scribner, 1995.
Flaubert, Gustave. *Madame Bovary*. rev. ed. New York: Penguin Classics, 2002.

TRAVEL

James, Henry. *A Little Tour in France*. Montana: Kessinger Publishing, 2004.
Mayle, Peter. *A Year in Provence*. New York: Knopf, 1991.
Palmer, Hugh, and James Bentley. *The Most Beautiful Villages of the Loire*. London: Thames and Hudson, 2001.

PHOTO CREDITS

First published in the United States of America in 2016
by Rizzoli International Publications, Inc.
300 Park Avenue South
New York, NY 10010
www.rizzoliusa.com

© 2006 Rizzoli International Publications, Inc.

Production: Colophon srl, Venice, Italy

Editorial Direction: Andrea Grandese

Editor-in-Chief: Rosanna Alberti

Editor: Daniela Rossi

Layout: Colophon, Venice

Design Concept: Stephen Fay

English Translation: Judith Goodman

2016 2017 2018 2019 / 10 9 8 7 6 5 4 3 2 1

ISBN: 978-0-8478-4682-5

Library of Congress Control Number: 2015955303